The Agrarian Seeds of Empire

Studies in Critical Social Sciences Book Series

Haymarket Books is proud to be working with Brill Academic Publishers (www.brill.nl) to republish the *Studies in Critical Social Sciences* book series in paperback editions. This peer-reviewed book series offers insights into our current reality by exploring the content and consequences of power relationships under capitalism, and by considering the spaces of opposition and resistance to these changes that have been defining our new age. Our full catalog of *SCSS* volumes can be viewed at https://www.haymarketbooks.org/series_collections/4-studies-in-critical-social-sciences.

Series Editor
David Fasenfest, Wayne State University

Editorial Board
Eduardo Bonilla-Silva (Duke University)
Chris Chase-Dunn (University of California–Riverside)
William Carroll (University of Victoria)
Raewyn Connell (University of Sydney)
Kimberlé W. Crenshaw (University of California–LA, and Columbia University)
Heidi Gottfried (Wayne State University)
Karin Gottschall (University of Bremen)
Mary Romero (Arizona State University)
Alfredo Saad Filho (University of London)
Chizuko Ueno (University of Tokyo)
Sylvia Walby (Lancaster University)

The Agrarian Seeds of Empire

The Political Economy of Agriculture
in US State Building

Brad Bauerly

Haymarket
Books
Chicago, IL

First published in 2016 by Brill Academic Publishers, The Netherlands.
© 2017 Koninklijke Brill NV, Leiden, The Netherlands

Published in paperback in 2018 by
Haymarket Books
P.O. Box 180165
Chicago, IL 60618
773-583-7884
www.haymarketbooks.org

ISBN: 978-1-60846-843-0

Trade distribution:
In the U.S. through Consortium Book Sales, www.cbsd.com
In the UK, Turnaround Publisher Services, www.turnaround-uk.com
In Canada, Publishers Group Canada, www.pgcbooks.ca
All other countries, Ingram Publisher Services International, ips_intlsales@ingramcontent.com

Cover design by Jamie Kerry of Belle Étoile Studios and Ragina Johnson.

This book was published with the generous support of Lannan Foundation and the Wallace Action Fund.

10 9 8 7 6 5 4 3 2 1

Library of Congress Cataloging-in-Publication Data is available.

This book is dedicated to my supportive wife Kim and my two wonderful daughters Addison and Lauren.

∴

Contents

Acknowledgements IX
List of Figures and Tables X
Commonly Used Acronyms XI

1 Introduction 1
    The Agro-Industrial Complex 3
    Transcending State-Market Dichotomies 15
    Overview of the Chapters 28

2 The Agro-Industrial Roots of the US Capitalist Transition through State Capacity Building: 1830–1870 32
    US Land Policy in the North 33
    Early Farmer Resistance to Market Expansion 39
    Land, Debt and Speculation 46
    Canal and Railroad Policy 48
    Early State Involvement in Agriculture 51
    Agro-Industrial Development 56
    Conclusion 70

3 The End of Slavery and Southern Agricultural Class Structure 73
    Slavery, the Civil War and the Transition 74
    The Civil War and State Institutional Expansion 81
    Postbellum Southern Agriculture 83
    Uneven Development across the South 95
    Tenancy and the Class Politics of Reconstruction 99
    Conclusion 102

4 Agrarian Populism: The Rise and Fall of Populism 105
    Farmers and Farming in the Late 19th Century USA 105
    Late 19th Century Agrarian Political Economy 109
    The Rise of Populism 111
    Populist Politics 118
    Populist Fractures 123
    The Decline of Populism 126
    The American Farm Bureau Federation 134
    Conclusion 137

5 State Institutional Capacity Building of the USDA-Research Complex   140
    Institutional Response to Agrarian Movements   142
    The Agro-Industrial Project in Research   147
    State Capacity Building in Trade and Banking   155
    Agro-Industrialization through Farmer Education   158
    State Responses to the Agricultural Crisis of the 1920s   168
    Conclusion   172

6 The New Deal and Agricultural State Institutional Capacity Building   174
    The Politics of the Agricultural Adjustment Act   175
    Southern Tenants and the AAA   184
    Theories of the New Deal Era State   187
    Class Influences on Institutional Development   193
    The Specific Case of California Agriculture   197
    The Consistency of Trade Promotion   203
    Agriculture, the New Deal, and World War II   208
    Conclusion   212

7 Sowing the Seeds of Globalization: Post-War Food Aid, Trade and the Agricultural Roots of US Hegemony   215
    Food Aid as Globalization's Groundwork   217
    Food Aid as Agro-Industrial Development Project   221
    The Institutional Dimensions of Internationalization   225
    The Crisis of the 1970s   231
    Harvesting Free Trade   246
    The Food Regimes Approach   251
    Conclusion   262

8 Conclusion   266

    Appendix A   273
    Appendix B   278
    Bibliography   280
    Index   303

Acknowledgements

I'd like to give a heartfelt, special thanks to my supervisor and mentor, Leo Panitch. He has been motivating, encouraging, and enlightening. His patience, flexibility, genuine caring and concern, and relaxed demeanor have been appreciated. I am very grateful to Jamey Essex and Charles Post for their helpful insightful comments and constructive criticism regarding both theoretical and methodological issues surrounding my research. They all stuck with me through this long journey.

This book is dedicated to my wife Kim and our two wonderful daughters. I must acknowledge with tremendous and deep thanks the love, support and belief in me that Kim gave me, without which I wouldn't have been able to complete this study. I also acknowledge the inspiration of my daughters Addison and Lauren. It is toward their future that the motivation to make the world a better place through the knowledge of this investigation stems.

List of Figures and Tables

Figures

1   Public land sales per year and acres sold   58
2   Capital invested in food manufacturing 1860 and 1900   58
3   Land value per acre adjusted for inflation: 1850–1940   131
4   Average farm size: 1900–1970   202
5   Number of farms in the US: 1900–1970   203
6   Agricultural trade and trade balance: 1930–2010   231
7   P.L. 480 Program exports, FY 1955–1984   241

Tables

1   US Land sales and federal dollars   37
2   Major 18th and 19th Century Agrarian Movements/Revolts   41
3   Agro-Industrial revolution in the 1850s   67
4   Midwestern Agro-Industrial development: Early 1850s to Early 1860s   69
5   Selected southern black codes   90
6   Shifts between 1880 and 1930 in number of employed on farms   132
7   Overview of food for peace program (PL 480)   223

Commonly Used Acronyms

AAA	Agricultural Adjustment Act
AFBF	American Farm Bureau Federation
AFL	American Federation of Labor
BLS	Bureau of Labor Statistics
CAP	Common Agricultural Program (EU)
CBM	Chicago Board of Mercantile
CCC	Commodity Credit Corporation
CEA	Council of Economic Advisors
CFTC	Commodities Futures Trading Commission
EC/EU	European Commission/European Union
FA	Farmers Alliance
FAS	Foreign Agricultural Service
FDI	Foreign Direct Investment
FU	Farmers Union
GATT	General Agreement on Tariffs and Trade
GAO	General Accounting Office
LDC('s)	Least Developed Country
M-H	McNary-Haugen Bill and program for farm recovery
MNC	Multi-national Corporation
OECD	Organization of Economic Co-operation and Development
OFAR	Office of Foreign Agricultural Relations
OMB	Office of Management and Budget
PL 480	Public Law 480 also known as Food for Peace
STFU	Southern Tenant Farmers Union
STR	Special Representative for Trade
USAID	United States Agency for International Development
USAS	United States Agricultural Society
USDA	United States Department of Agriculture
USTR	United States Trade Representative
WTO	World Trade Organization

CHAPTER 1

Introduction

For decades, scholars have been analyzed and debated in multiple disciplines the historic roots of the rise of the United States to a position of global political and economic leadership. Although much of this literature is rich with detail and full of insights, little of it links the historic role of agriculture in that process. One group of literature that has corrected this deficiency is the food regimes approach (Friedmann, 1982, 1989, 1990, 1993, 2000, 2004, 2005, 2009; Friedmann and McMichael, 1989; McMichael, 1992, 2004, 2005, 2007, 2009). This approach locates political economic development of capitalism as emerging out of social relations of food and connects the rise of great powers with various policies of food production or food regimes.

Most often when agriculture is brought in it is most often seen as informing domestic developments that are mostly understood as separate from the US's international role. Missing is the link between the domestic importance of agriculture and the state institutions that enabled the rise of the US internationally. Overcoming this absence is one of the key motivating factors of this study. America's long and unique relationship with agriculture makes it a useful in historical analysis of the process of state institution building and the role this played in propelling the rise of the United States.[1] As will be shown, US state institutions developed the ability to assuage the demands of farmers while simultaneously reconstituting social relations in a manner more market dependent. In the process, farmers we responsible for state building and this in turn directed farmers into commodification, while building up state institutions that would aid the US state in dealing with other interest groups and social movements and help project its power around the globe.

An important part of uncovering the influence of agriculture lies in the specific details of the transition of US farmers to capitalist production. Our ability to comprehend the process of US development is impaired, however, if approached from a preconceived notion of how the process of capitalist development always occurs and simply apply a transhistoric theory of capitalist transition to the US case. We also lose the historically determined specific paths that institutional development, social resistance, and capitalist

---

1   The term state will be used to describe governments in both generic and particular forms. When discussing individual US states they will be referenced by name when possible (i.e.: Alabama, Alaska…).

market penetration took if we apply general theories of capitalist development. Instead, we must seek to historicize the specificity of the US case by highlighting both its differences and similarities with other cases and most importantly, the impact these differences had on social development.

Outlining the process of the development of petty commodity production is the first step towards an understanding of the importance of agriculture in America's rise. What emerged was a form of state development that sought the means to appease social movements while simultaneously pushing agricultural modernization. To advance efforts to throw off the British overlords, the Revolutionary provocateurs used the pressures and fears of farmers by claiming it was the British colonial tax burden, and control of land and commerce behind agrarian problems.[2] Land ownership pressures thus created patriots out of many small to middling farmers (Countryman, 1974, 41). In fact, the numerous mid-century land riots were one expression of this pressure – in New Jersey, the Hudson Valley, and Northeastern Vermont especially (Countryman, 1974, 40). In New Jersey the link between large land holders and the Royal Crown allowed the pressures of emerging petty commodity agriculture to fuel anti-British sentiment (Countryman, 1974, p. 40). In New York it was the presence of the "vestiges of medieval tenant subservience, without the owners offering the physical protection that once had presumably justified such subservience" that fueled colonial era unrest and resentments to "add to the atmosphere of general crisis, the sense of many colonists that something was wrong with the standing order" (Countryman, 1974, p. 41, 61). In Northeastern New York, in what became Vermont, the Green Mountain Boys connected their struggles for land and self-representation antagonistically with the system seen as connected to royal forms of power; as Ethan Allen put it "God Damn your Governor, Laws, King, Council and Assembly" (quoted in Countryman, 1974, 47). Likewise, the Regulator movement of 1766–1771 in the backcountry North Carolina, positioning poor and middling farmers directed against the upper classes, added to the sense of social malfunction used to rile up small farmers against the crown (Young, 1974, 450). "Both radicalism and nostalgia showed themselves in the land riots...In all three affairs (NJ, NY, and Vermont)...a conjuncture of the themes of private property and individualistic acquisition with those of community and fraternity" was present (Countryman, 1974, 53).

In the American case under investigation, this process was aided by the formation of an ideology of an 'independent nation formed of independent farmers' that had traction, in part, due to the opposition to the British crown.

---

2 This quite possibly represents the first American populist movement that in effect was foundational to the nation.

As Agllietta (1979) stressed, it is the "political origins of the American nation which united petty producers with the commercial and financial bourgeoisie in a common struggle against English colonial rule...[and] left a permanent mark on the ideological representations of American social relations and created political institutions governed by those general principles that are legal formalization of relations of commodity exchange" (p. 73). Out of this original genesis in the battle against England, the influence of settler agriculture grew through ideological necessity and out of the form of political system that developed.

The role of market and credit relations, specifically early on in land ownership, reveals the external constraints on farmers which began to transition them through capitalist social relations. Land policy, banking and credit became the motor force of this process of market creation and the embedding of society in the market that followed. A full understanding of this transition requires a detailed description and close analysis of exactly how this transition occurred through concrete historical examination. A historical sociology of US power investigates how this increasing market embeddedness led to alterations in the means of reproduction for farmers, how this altered the social relations and balance of class forces and lead to increased production and declining prices. This is turn, fuelled farmer discontent. Analyzing how this discontent was dealt with through state institutional capacity building that assuaged farmer demands while moving agriculture even further into market mediated social forms reveals the various ways these transformations facilitated both a modernizing industrial capitalism and the rise of the US internationally.

By historically outlining the interaction of state institutions and class actors that created and reproduced the hegemony of the capitalist class, while focusing on specific eras of state-market interaction in the process of state capacity building and market construction used to incorporate and overcome resistance to market expansion in agriculture, this study will provide both a theoretical and empirical account of US dynamism and growth. It will do this by highlighting the much overlooked and underappreciated role of agriculture in US economic development and state formation, uniquely situating the US and setting up the rise of the US and the construction of a global empire.

The Agro-Industrial Complex

A group of scholarship in history, sociology, agricultural economics and geography has sought to highlight the basis of US capitalist development in what has been labeled the *agro-industrial complex* – the progressive integration of agriculture and industry via enhanced market imperatives (Walsh, 1982; Headlee, 1991; Page and Walker, 1991; Kulikoff, 1992).[3] The most sustained and substantial contribution has been made by Charles Post (1983, 1995, 2011). Post builds on Robert Brenner's explanation of the initial transition to capitalism in England as not arising out of the expansion and building up of merchant capital, but instead occurring through the changes in class relations in local agriculture, "driven by the capitalist imperative to augment the forces of production in search of surplus value" (Brenner, 1977, pp. 25–92).

In the US case, Post has identified a pre-civil war transformation of agriculture, what he calls an 'agricultural revolution', which initiated a process of agro-industrial development: "class- struggles…effectively transformed rural household-production, unleashing the agricultural and industrial revolutions" (Post, 2011, p. 4). Through this process farmers were pushed towards heightened specialization in marketable cash crops, decreased self-sufficiency and increased reliance on the purchasing of the elements of subsistence and production. This combined with the imbrication of agricultural production with global circuits of capital, at the time mostly coming from or flowing through London. It was through farmer's mortgages and other loans, Post contends, that US agriculture effectively became connected to the expanding capitalist market and was subsumed under the capitalist law of value (1995, pp. 428–29). Other parts of this transition, in other times and regions, came from the increasing use of farm inputs and machines that ushered in productivity increases, drive down farm commodity prices and push farmers toward expansion (Headlee, 1991; Page and Walker, 1991).

Petty commodity production as a form of social property relations refers to those producers who own the means of production yet must rely on the market to maintain this ownership (O'Conner, 1975; Friedmann, 1978). The market imperatives are enforced through this market dependency which in most cases rests on the need to service debt in the form of mortgages or other loans. Some of this debt comes in the form of farm mortgages, emerging due to land policy (Gates, 1973; Post, 2011).

Importantly this transition from simple production to petty commodity production took different forms at different times and in different regions. In

---

3 "Agroindustrialization" comprises three related sets of changes: (a) growth of commercial, off-farm agroprocessing, distribution and input provision activities, (b) institutional and organizational change in the relations between farms and firms both upstream and downstream, such as increased vertical integration and contract-based procurement, and (c) related changes in product composition, technologies, and sectoral and market structure (Reardon and Barrett, 2000).

the earlier northeastern US the transition emerges out of different social and economic pressures, takes on different political forms and produces different forms of farmer resistance than what occurred later with the Midwestern transition. Along the way, and learning from the eastern process and being informed by the resistant it encountered in the Midwest, the state increasingly developed new tools to deal with, incorporate, and negated agrarian resistance to the encroaching market forces.

As some areas of the Eastern United States started to run out of land acquired through disposition of the native populations, an increasing number of farmers began specializing in crops to sell to local markets in an effort to maintain or expand their land ownership in the face of increasing land prices and taxes. Because of the depression of 1837–42, in which farmers were hard hit, there was an increase in and an accelerated process of, this increasing market dependence. The depression left farmers with crushing debt, while it also increased state-taxation pressure, thus, "Farmers were compelled to specialize in output, introduce new and labour-saving tools and methods and accumulate landholdings" (Post, 2011, p. 232). This process first occurred in the east and spread westward, over the course of the first half of the 19th Century, as petty commodity production replaced subsistence agriculture or independent household production (Post, 2011; Clark, 1990). Post stated that "the subordination of free farming to the law of value unleashed a process of increasing labour-productivity, technological innovation and social differentiation in the 1840s and 1850s" (Post, 2011, p. 24). This occurred, he claimed, through "the activities of merchant-capital" (especially in land speculation) and "merchant-sponsored state-policies" (the conversion of the frontier into farming land through settler colonialism and land policies favorable to speculative capital) (Post, 2011, p. 24).

The development of petty commodity production in rural New England in the late 18th and early 19th Century was based on production for local markets due to the need to raise cash to maintain ownership, and possibly expand ownership, of the land required to reproduce (Clark, 1990). It is well documented that most of this involvement in local markets was done in an effort to preserve some independence from the dictates of international markets or as an attempt to return to an era of greater independence and often simple commodity production (Gates, 1973; Clark, 1990; Headlee, 1991; Henretta, 1991; Post, 1995). The goal of maintaining some aspects of independent household production undermined many of the early farming movements in the Eastern United States. In the Eastern United States, as markets for farm commodities developed, and as taxes and other farming expenses increased and combined with market pressure, this led farmers, out of necessity and as an attempt to stop the further encroachment of the market imperatives into their lives, to specialize and expand.

Parallel to this expansion and specialization was the differentiation and commodification of farm inputs that occurred. Concordantly we also see the beginnings of a process of the development of home goods. Post stated "as Northern farmers were compelled to 'sell to survive', there became a growing home-market for capitalist produced consumer- and capital- goods…Family famers specializing in cash-crops found themselves purchasing a wide variety of consumer-goods (cloth, shoes and boots, etc.) [which] they and their neighbors had previously produced" (Post, 2011, p. 233). This increased reliance on commodified inputs and goods added to the imperatives to sell to survive as the market connections increased. Consumption of more goods required increase cash on hand, which required increased production and sales of farm products and this, in turn, rested on expanding production most often through new technology or expansion of acres farmed, which further increased farmer debt. Here we see the market increasingly taking hold of the economics of small farmers in the regions where this development begins. Post argues that agriculture and the transition from simple production to petty commodity production lay at the root of the US transition from one set of conditions of social reproduction to another as "independent commodity-production posed an obstacle to capitalist production in the antebellum-era because of its ability to provide the conditions of reproduction to the direct producers outside of the capitalist labour-market" (2011, p. 17). By outlining the specific changes in agriculture that constituted the shift in the locus of relations of reproduction he began the process of elucidating the details of the US transition and overcoming the teleological understanding of the progression of technological innovations driving social change.

Post (2011) argued that the rapid mechanization of US agriculture in the two decades preceding the Civil War (mainly the adoption of the mechanical reaper, which I argue actually occurred later, in the late 1850s and 60s) created the conditions for the adoption of capitalist industrialization in the US. However, he also stated: "the complex of industries producing farm-machinery, tools and supplies and processing agricultural raw materials (meat packing, leather tanning, flour milling, and baking) were at the centre of the American industrial revolution" (Post, 2011, p. 99). As Pudup outlines, the transition from localized petty-producers to industrial production of agricultural equipment "reflected the moment when manufacturing within a sector attained maturity as a capitalist enterprise" (1987, p. 45). Her argument rests on the agro-industrialization thesis: that "industrial structure and location have been co-revolutionary" (Pudup, 1987, p. 47). Putting this point to the test requires that Post first show that petty commodity production must lead to agro-industrialization rather than the more historically grounded argument that it was both petty commodity production and the specific industrial innovations that occurred in the Midwest, acting in a symbiotic relationship and building off each other, which produced both industrial development and the expansion of petty commodity agriculture.

While appreciating the breakthrough and accepting the bulk of Post's work, I do find a few points of disagreement and places where detailed historical analysis reveals errors and alternative conclusions. For instance, Post's account of the process is in many ways accurate, however the timing and the role of the history of struggles over land policy, between the interests of independent farmers and investment capital, in the transition to petty commodity production for the majority of Midwestern farmers did not occur until later, and through a greater degree of state intervention and market development. The role of land policy and the mortgages it required of farmers initiated struggles over the process of increased market dependence that played out on the political front. These political struggles over land, its sale, its taxation and improvement, all played an important role. The dynamic capitalist agriculture that emerged in the US Midwest was not only unleashed by an influx of merchant capital, but was part of a social process fed by political struggles over state policies and the development of new institutional forms and institutional capacities in the state to mitigate these struggles.

Departing from Post and his claim that the transition to petty commodity production in the Midwest occurred in the 1840s and 1850s, this study will show how the timing differs from that advanced earlier by North (1961, pp. 146–53), who showed that the majority of farms there only started selling greater than 50 percent of their farm products on the market after 1860. This throws into question what specific forces pushed farmers into market dependency. Post's position is that the transition to petty commodity production produced industrial development while others see the co-development of industrial production as part of the drive that pushes farmers into petty commodity production as the imperatives for these producers shift through an expansion of farm inputs, consumer goods, and the development of markets for their products. Evidence for the co-development, or agro-industrial thesis, includes the relationship between expanding petty commodity production and the development of industrial production.

Others agree that the market imperatives emerged from this dependency and led to increases in the cost of carrying land and enhanced imperatives to growth, they add that this ushered in productivity increases which further strengthened the pull towards market dependency through increased reliance on machinery and the purchasing of home goods, both of which added further incentives towards petty commodity production models (Page and Walker, 1991). The latter development occurred through a corresponding rise in manufacturing, "between 1810 and 1840 there occurred a sevenfold increase in US manufacturing output, most of it in the Northeast" (Clark, 2006, 161).

It is only when the role of state action to support market construction is outlined that a full understanding of the process of agro-industrial development is explicated. This rendition of the agro-industrial thesis adds the commodification pressure towards market involvement that enhanced the imperatives towards market involvement. For example alongside of the pressure towards petty commodity production we see a concomitant growth of the labor supply as agriculture declined in importance and as new consumer markets in process foods emerged (Field, 1978). A more robust and less monocausal version of agro-industrialization does not disarticulate the transition to petty commodity production from the process of industrialization; instead, it highlights the synergistic nature of that development.

Only when we investigate the co-development of petty commodity agriculture and the larger industrial development can we locate the source of the US's unique capitalist and state development. The use of private property in the form of an increasing ownership of land, household and productive goods and machines, which expanded through market pressures to increase the size and scale required to farm in order to maintain farm land, was the deciding factor that made the US case so different from those where peasants were forced through primitive accumulation into market mediated forms.

The agro-industrial revolution both was fed by and fed into this process; the cash crop specialization it induced and that resulted in increased revenue which was returned to manufacturing and produced productivity increases, reduced production costs, and decreased prices for farmers. This "propulsive nature of commercialization", as Page and Walker (1991, p. 11) put it, compelled farmers by the logic of the market to increase productivity and total output, leading to declining prices and propelling farmers further into commercial crops, which, in turn, spurred and impacted overall industrialization. This approach to the development of an agro-industrial complex in the US shifts attention away from the influx of merchant capital or the deus ex-macina of technological development, and instead produces an enhanced understanding of the interplay between competitive, commercial and class dynamics as the motor force of the capitalist development.

This study will substantiate this stronger agro-industrial thesis by proceeding along two main lines. The first, agreeing with much of Post's argument – especially his claim that the constitutional settlement in 1787, with its requirement of farmers to pay taxes and by creating a public lands sales system, set in motion the initial process of agro-industrial development in the Northeast – this study will depart from and augment this interpretation by examining the additional ways the federal state developed to further this process and how this process came to build off of itself by broadening the agro-industrial pressures, this is especially true in the Midwest. Additionally, this study will show the manner in which much of the state building that effectively subsumed farmers into petty commodity production through agro-industrialization emerged in response to agrarian social movement pressure. It will accomplish this by documenting some examples of those movements and outline the states response in institutional capacity building.

Post argues that "elements of independent household-production survived in the trans-Allegheny west through the 1830s" (2011, 192). However as this study will reveal for the majority of territory in what was then called the western US (Midwest), it wasn't until the late 1850s that petty commodity production became hegemonic as the market forces overtook the ability of farmers to meet their needs outside of the market. This study offers a understanding of the unfolding and expanding of petty commodity production through state action to create markets and the associated imperatives. Thus, it will outline the internal relations between state building and agro-industrialization that produced the self-reinforcing market pressures.

An important distinction between this inquiry and that of Post (2011) lies in the recognition of this symbiotic relationship between industrialization and the transition to petty commodity production. While changes in land policy and merchant capital were important early driving forces of capitalist transition, they are insufficient to account fully for the process of transition to petty commodity production. More details on the historic process as it spread from the east to the west, resulting in agrarian resistance leading to state responses, are needed. Too often the transition has been presented as a one-off event, lacking contingency and specificity, as a movement away from 'pre-capitalist' or 'transitionary' forms. Instead, this investigation will uncover the co-developmental process it actually was, thus overcoming the deficient attention on the role of state in tipping the balance of class forces toward market expansion.

The form of state development that took place in colonial and early America sought a means to appease and suppress agrarian social movements while pursuing agricultural and wider economic modernization. Aiding this, while also built of it, was the ideology of a nation formed on independent farmers in opposition to the British crown. The "political origins of the American nation which united petty producers with the commercial and financial bourgeoisie in a common struggle against English colonial rule…[and] left a permanent mark on the ideological representations of American social relations and created political institutions governed by those general principles, which are but legal formalizations of relations of commodity exchange" (Agllietta, 1979, 73). Out of this genesis, the compromise of settler agriculture was arrived at due to the pressures of the emerging capitalist markets.

The missing detail to this process of state building and its relationship with the agrarian transition pivots on farmer responses to encroaching petty commodity relations. The responses frequently took the form of resistance or outright revolt. The state responded through enhanced institutional capacity building in an effort to quell, dismantle, split, or prevent movements, and to direct farmers into reforms fitting capitalist social relations. The state played a "central role in organizing, sanctioning, and legitimizing class domination… [it] exercised power and choice in the organization and development of production and classes" (Panitch, 2004, p. 17).

The transition to fully capitalist production allowed for the replacement of human labor (living) with machinery (dead labor) in the production of foodstuff, thereby raising the productivity of agricultural labor and freeing a portion of the rural population for wage labor. This lowered the costs of feeding the new industrial working class and created a growing market for industrially produced farm machinery, implements and later home goods, which stimulated the transformations in the iron, steel, metalworking and industrial production industries, as well as fueling petty commodity transformations. These developments, in turn, put further pressure on farmers to increase their market dependence. Thus, agricultures transition and the industrial revolution in the US were internally related.

Carville and Hoffman make the case in their rejection of the Habakkuk thesis – the idea that the US adopted technology to industrialize because of a lack of labor and high labor costs – that it was the specific seasonal character of US Midwestern agricultural labor that led to the adoption of technology and to the agro-industrial revolution (Carville and Hoffman, 1980). Agriculture, and specifically grain and corn farming, being seasonal, requires labor for only a limited amount during the year. It is this unique nature of farm labor that helped initiate the technological drive and early adoption of farming mechanization. It is therefore the specific types of crops suitable for Midwestern and Western agriculture that feed into the drive toward technology and petty commodity agriculture. These crops were in part chosen because of the climate, but also dominated because of the large expanses of land they required, made possible by the federal land policy. The seasonal nature of wheat and corn production created the tendency to adopt agricultural technology which put debt pressure on farmers and incentivized acreage expansion.

INTRODUCTION

It may help here to pose a few hypothetical questions: if Midwestern agro-industrialization had not occurred, would petty commodity agriculture have swept the plains as rapidly as it did or would household production agriculture have remained the dominant form and continued to spread westward? Did the land policies by themselves initiate the large scale transition to petty commodity agriculture or was further intervention by the state necessary? These questions help to focus attention on the specificity and contingency of the Midwest in the development of US capitalism with the agro-industrial revolution as the missing and key variable. In light of this, the land policies and influx of merchant capital appear as a necessary but insufficient condition for the transition to petty commodity production. The role of industrial processes that took root during the mid to late 19th Century in the Midwest appears to have aided this change. This isn't to claim that petty commodity production did not pave the road to capitalist development in the US, just that it was an outcome rife with contingency and struggle. Not only was it possible for independent production to survive alongside petty commodity production, but there also remains the possibility within petty commodity production to not transition into industrial capitalism. One can envision a Midwest filled with independent agricultural producers alongside petty commodity producers absent industrial development and this possibility must be considered.

The transition to petty commodity production in the US needs to be understood as a distinct and novel process. To accomplish this, the historical details and contingency of must be elucidated. It is in the details of this process of transformation that we see how it occurred in a relationship with industrialization and through the active participation of the state. If the contingency of the full process of capitalist transition is to be taken seriously, then the details of the social struggles over this process must be central to any understanding.

The strength of the agro-industrial thesis is that it focuses on the distinct process of the transition to capitalism, through the expansion of market imperatives. Only when we investigate the co-development of petty commodity agriculture and the larger agro-industrial development can we locate the source of these unique developments. Furthermore, it is due to the specific form of agriculture in the Midwestern US, the entrenched forms of power, and a specific democratic state that gave rise to the reluctance of independent farming to initially yield to the commodity form, which becomes the source of the dynamic developments of agro-industrialization. While petty commodity family farmers were increasingly compelled to compete with each other in the market place, they resisted the erosion of their independence. The actions of farmers arose out of this drive to maintain their independent ownership of the means of production while coming under increasing pressure to commodify.

The theory of agro-industrialization posits how the use of private property in the form of an increasing ownership of household, machines, and productive goods increased the need to expand the size and scale of farms to maintain private property, leading to increased market reliance. Thus, elucidating this two-way relationship between expanding petty commodity production and industrially produced inputs, tools, and home goods, is paramount.

The development of industry and the movement toward petty commodity production and capitalism in the US were greatly intertwined, as Clark argued: "early industrial labor forces, in other words, were found from among quite subtle and precise variations in the structure and character of rural societies" (2006, p. 166). The very structure of industrial development was strongly influenced by existing and developing social structures and by "the different ways rural economies, household needs, and patterns of regional and international migration shaped labor's availability" (Clark, 2006, p. 167). Initial house-hold production gave way to industrial production only in those areas where agricultural changes allowed for wage workers. Petty commodity productions potential to shed labor, through the changes initiated by state policy and the development of new state institutions to create the markets to instigate the 'freeing up' of labor and the imposition of new imperatives and strategies of reproduction.

Headlee argued that what drove family farmers was the "desire for political independence, for liberty, and for rights secured by private property" (Headlee, 1991, p. 7). Thus, she claims the argument by most American economic historians is incomplete because it rests on the assumption that US family farmers were profit maximizes, leading to the claim that the rise of grain prices fueled specialization, mechanization, and commercialization of family farm production. Post and other political Marxists counted Headlee by claiming that it was the changes in production that created the market imperatives for farmers to become petty commodity producers. However, clearly they are both correct and incorrect. As the US state more and more created the markets and aligned the incentives to connect rights with private property ownership and increased production for markets, the life of farmers shifted from being more independent to being petty commodity producers.[4] The important point being that by focusing exclusively on market forces as causing profit maximizer to alter their lives the changes in the state institutions that were necessary get

---

4 The key point of Political Marxism is to explain the qualitative shift that occurs in social relations and reproduction strategies. In this case, it is the increased need to accumulate capital through expansions in land and mechanization along with the drive to specialize and increase outputs through new techniques that emerges with petty commodity agriculture, which pushes farmers into new social relations.

left out, as will be shown of regions absent this state intervention lacking the agro-industrial development.

Henry Bernstein (2010) has engaged with many of the theoretical issues running through this investigation. He contrasted two conceptions of agrarian capitalism, "one is based on generalization of the original English path and its class structure of capitalist landed property and agrarian capital employing landless wage labor as uniquely definitive of agrarian capitalism....[t]he other is expressed in Banaji's rejection of any single, uniform or 'pure' agrarian capitalism" (p. 35). Key amongst the changes that came with the transition to capitalist agriculture was the associated commodification of both the inputs and outputs (crops) associated with farming. Capitalism's globalizing tendencies, as well as its need to abstract from the use value and generalize, or commodify things in order to facilitate market based exchanges, both contributed to the developmental changes that occurred in farming in the US. Bernstein continues "In capitalism, agriculture becomes increasingly defined as a distinct sector in terms of its place in social divisions of labor and as an object of public policy...[they] link to each other and to that central dynamic emphasized earlier: the commodification of subsistence, through which once largely self-sufficient farmers came to rely increasingly on markets (commodity exchange) for their reproduction" (Bernstein, 2010, p. 65). He highlighted the period from 1870 through today as "one of revolutionary change in the technical conditions of farming" due to the changes brought about by scientific discoveries, technological innovations and the spread of markets (Bernstein, 2010, pp. 65–66). In confirming much of the discussion of Chicago's agro-industrial development, Bernstein discussed how "Chicago pioneered many aspects of modern agribusiness...[and] was central to international agricultural trade and divisions of labour from the 1870s onward...in short, a global division of labour in agricultural production and trade emerged from the 1870s" emanating out of the shifts occurring in the US Midwest (Bernstein, 2010, pp. 67–8).

Important also is the role of the individual freedom ideology of the US social order. Lacking any real long term cultural connections, the new nation's social identity rested more heavily on the ideology of individual rights and personal property, along with the right of most to choose the governmental representatives. Juxtaposing the US case to European farmers, who were themselves forced through primitive accumulation into market mediated forms, in the US we see it was primitive accumulation of land taken from natives, given or sold to farmers, which reveals the specificity of the US process of capitalist transition, industrialization and historical development. This form of colonial-settler development created unique developmental trajectories that influenced the direction of capitalist transition and agro-industrial development.

Also important in the US case are specific geographic and regional differences. The eastern United States witnessed a much earlier transition to reliance on markets for reproduction than where occurring in the Midwest and Western areas of the nation. In these non-Eastern areas, the availability of land due to colonial settler activity continued to allow for agriculture that was not market dependent or market dependent to a much smaller degree. This then allowed for a larger base of social and political opposition to totalizing market forces. While in the South, the impact of slavery and the aftermath of its abolition obviously heavily influenced the direction and speed of capitalist transition and industrialization of agriculture.

For all of the reasons above, the US state played a particularly important and large part in the transition to capitalism and agro-industrial development processes in the US.[5] It was only with the increased involvement of the federal government during and after the Civil War that we see the capacity of the state to even uphold property rights in many parts of the far western US. The previous ubiquitous squatting and general disregard for land rights in the region (Skowronek, 1982; Shannon, 1977), which involved the lack of federal and state enforcement of land rights, fueled independent household production by allowing for expansion into productive land at little to no cost, thereby overcoming the tendency to abuse the soil of its fertility and the demographic crisis most commonly found with this type of agriculture. But after this the state took a much more active role in upholding property ownership rights and in creating the means to develop markets and spur industrial development, and it is only then do we see a transition to petty commodity production and industrial development really taking hold.

Under the intertwined processes of US state formation – including money, banking, land, railroad, canal, and patent policies – the agro-industrial revolution – the technological increases in agricultural productivity, industrial food processing and the new farm consumer goods production, marketing and sales – caused US farms to slowly and increasingly become subsumed under the dictates of the market for survival. The political and economic details of this subsumption, in turn, informed the process of US state institutional capacity building and the US transition to capitalism. As farms were central to the US transition to capitalism they need to be analyzed based on the movement from independent household to petty commodity producing agriculture. What needs to be appreciated is how the changes occurring in agriculture were

---

5   I am separating the transition to capitalism from the agro-industrialization of agriculture largely for heuristic reasons. In actual historical development agro-industrialization was simply the continuation of the expanding and deepening of capitalist social relations.

influencing a whole range of social changes and the direction of state building. This process was filled with contingency and this contingency and agency of farmers should not be taken for granted. Nor should an ahistorical understanding of the inevitable continued expansion of markets be applied posthoc to the development of the United States. Instead, we need to locate how this process moved along, the resistance it encountered, and how this resistance was overcome. The role of the US state in the process is lacking specific detail in much of the groundbreaking work on agro-industrialization. It is this deficiency that this study seeks to remedy.

Transcending State-Market Dichotomies

One of the hurdles in analyzing the role of agriculture in the rise of the US lies in the widespread tendency for scholars to posit a dichotomy between the state and markets.[6] Political Marxist theories of the transition to capitalism, which inform this study, largely avoid this by focusing attention on the role of changing social relations of production in the transition to capitalism. They elucidate the manner in which social property relations are undergirded by market incentives under capitalism and the process of their emergence in the transition to capitalism. Post (2011) claimed political Marxists reject teleological interpretations of history, where some transhistorical dynamic – the growth of markets or the development of the productive forces – explains the transition from one from of social labor to another. Instead, "political Marxism emphasizes the random, unpredictable outcome of class-struggles in preserving, restructuring, or transforming different forms of social labor" (p. 2). This class

---

6 This is prevalent in much of the IPE literature. Ruggie's pivotal article on the embedded nature of the post-war market relied on the notion that "the two international economic orders where quite different: laissez-faire liberalism in the nineteenth century and embedded liberalism in the postwar era" (1982, 1). What Ruggie fails to recognize is that the reforms of the post-war era were "structured so as to be embedded in capitalist social relations" (Panitch and Gindin, 2012, p. 9). This means that the represented institutional developments were intended to further the embedding of society in capitalist relations which enhanced commodification (Lacher, 1999). The liberalism of the post-war era was a means to extend the liberalism of the prior era, not an alternative to it. Stephen Krasner (1985) contrasted two rival views of IPE: 'authoritative allocation', where states played the guiding role and 'market oriented regimes', where a liberal government responded to market forces. Likewise, Benjamin Cohen has claimed "The monopoly power of states has been replaced not by anarchy but by the invisible hand of competition…the power of governance now resides in that social institution we call the market" (1996, p. 146).

struggle takes forms often aided by social movement demands and interventions into the economy as shaped by states and other social actors.

Ellen Meiksins Wood (2002) asserted that "a capitalist economy exists to the extent that it constitutes an integrated market within which market-dependent economic actors are compelled to compete" (p. 33). The important variable she identified rests in the explication of the "historically specific material conditions of social reproduction" (Wood, 2002, p. 18); meaning to uncover the historic details of how people meet their basic needs, the process of the transition away from one way to another through the development of social imperatives or dependence on market forms to meet these needs. Political Marxists (most notably Brenner and Wood) have therefore, outlined an analytical model of the transition to capitalism as well as outlined a methodology for understanding different social property relations in different moments.

Applying the political Marxist approach to the US case was first advanced by Post (1983) when he sought to outline historically when the rules of reproduction shifted in the US. Following O'Conner (1975), Post (2011) argued that agriculture and the transition from simple production to petty commodity production lay at the root of the US transition from one set of conditions of social reproduction to another as "independent commodity-production posed an obstacle to capitalist production in the antebellum-era because of its ability to provide the conditions of reproduction to the direct producers outside of the capitalist labour-market" (p. 17). By outlining the specific changes in agriculture that constituted the shift in the locus of relations of reproduction he began the process of elucidating the details of the US transition and overcoming the teleological understanding of the progression of technological innovations driving social change.

Applying a Political Marxist approach to the US development brings about a discussion of capitalism's requirement of legal rights to own private property, privately own the means of production, and to buy and sell human labor while removing most of the state's responsibility to guarantee a means to meet ones needs. Capitalist social relations are characterized "by individualism and certain conceptions of liberty, freedom and equality backed by laws of private property, rights to appropriation and freedom of contract" (Harvey, 2006, p. 168; Marx, 1973). This is the source of the *market imperatives* that drives capitalists to innovate and constantly seek to reduce the costs of production which produce the continual downward pressure on labor as the class struggle unfolds.

This investigation will describe the processes and struggles of detaching what Wood (1995, p. 210) called the "community forms" from property, in this case mostly land but also credit and debt (cf: Anti-rent and populist movements). The commodification of labor was achieved through this process of detaching the local community and transforming the populace into interchangeable units of labor abstracted from any specific personal or social identity that was connected to land and ownership of means of subsistence and production (Wood, 1995, p. 211). The newly emerging political forms came to subsume many of the older communitarian identities partly through local resistance as it was molded to fit into the liberal democratic system. Thus liberal democracy transformed social identities by disconnecting them from their material linkages and turning them into formal, yet materially weaker, democratic citizen rights (Wood, 1995).

Resistance to this process can actually aid it along its path by taking community forms of identity and reconfiguring them to the requirements of liberal democracy: meaning, detaching them largely from their customary material basis. Liberal ideology's celebration of the 'freeing' of the individual from the state and from custom is in actuality, the glossing over of the historical process of remaking social identities by reconfiguring them into two separate spheres: one political and one economic, thereby detaching class based understandings of identities (Wood, 1995). This new political form is an ideological device to "deny or disguise the more immediate experience of individuals, to disaggregate and delegitimate, or at least to depoliticize, the solidarities that stand between the levels of individual and nation, such as those forged in the workplace, the local community, or in a common class experience" (Wood, 1995, pp. 211–212).

This new liberal democracy allowed a "dissociation of civic identity from socio-economic status which permits the coexistence of formal political equality with class inequality" and also created two distinct planes: one political and one social/economic (Wood, 1995, p. 212). The unique and specific details of how this process occurred in agrarian America will be outlined and what will emerge is an understanding of the interaction and co-production of political identities and distinct market identities. This rendered the US at least partially free from, or in the process of becoming free from, pre-capitalist political and economic institutional forms as the 'rules of reproduction', divided labor and surplus extraction into a 'political' moment and an 'economic' moment (Wood, 1995, p. 197). There is no actual separation of the political and the economic, but an appearance of such that serves the ideological goal of masking the politics involved in market forces. The job of critical political economy is to unmask this relationship, while remaining mindful of the ways this mask informs social development, resistance, and political condensations.

Wood posits capitalist transition as the growth of market imperatives rather than market opportunities: "[t]he question then becomes not how commercial opportunities expanded and economies were freed to take advantage of them, but rather how social arrangements and the production of basic human needs were so fundamentally transformed as to impose compulsions and necessities unlike any that had governed human social life before" (2010, p. 40). This of course should not be taken to mean that the expansion of capitalist markets themselves weren't a social force of transformation of the social order, nor that the arrival of some social compulsions weren't resisted, leading to unique forms of state intervention and forever altering the path of state and social development. By creating and imposing market imperatives the basis of society is transformed while the source of those transformations remain social in origin and, as we will see below, this co-developmental transition to capitalist social property relations and increased commodification of products and labor, are exactly what occurred in the US.

Wood seeks to clarify the point by posing the question as "in what specific conditions do competitive production, profit maximization themselves become survival strategies, the basic condition of subsistence itself" (2010, p. 40). It is only when their strategy of reproduction becomes focused *exclusively* on the reduction of costs of production that Wood claimed the capitalist market imperative has been imposed. However, when or if ever, does the strategy of reproduction become reduced to that of exclusively increasing productivity? Of course it doesn't ever really occur as social life continues to this day to not be entirely subsumed under the logic of capital imperatives.[7] However, her point may be more based on the acceptance of the ideology of the market imperative, or the creation of legitimate forms of domination and subordination, as the point of inflection on the road to capitalism. Clearly there is a moment when the acceptance of the social imperatives of the capitalist market is internalized to the point where they are reified into seemingly natural forces. Short of a crisis of some sort, most of these imperatives of the market go unquestioned in contemporary capitalist society. This is why it is during economic crises when the social forces of capitalism come under increased scrutiny, as well as why much of the goal of the capitalist state becomes one of crisis management. The state bends to the demands of lower classes during crises to fend off the radical cries and to re-establish the normal path of development of increased market imperative driven social relations. It seeks to appease the

---

7 Only in the recent past have childcare, meal preparation and house cleaning increasingly been commodified, resting on market imperatives penetration of family life. Is it possible to say that prior to this social life was not dictated by capitalism? The existence of capitalism does not mean complete rule by the logic of capital imperatives but the hegemony of its domination and its continued expansion into more and more of social life. (See also D'Angelis, 2004).

demands of social movements and to maintain or re-establish the abstraction of the political means to economic power in society (Block, 1987; Jessop, 2008). In this manner, struggles between classes are constitutive of states (Tilly, 1990; Lebowitz, 1992) as capitalist states seek to maintain social equilibrium and will act against the wishes of dominant classes in cases where pressures from below cause the costs of not acting to exceed the costs of reform (cf. Poulantzas, 1978; Therborn, 1983). In instances where it comes down to a choice between control of the state and maintaining control over the means of production the bourgeoisie will choose the latter (Marx, 1876).

Therefore we should focus the transition question to the specific conditions that led agricultural producers to abandon their former survival strategies, or at least diminish their importance to the point of antecedent, for the capitalist forms. What is required is to locate why exactly farmers in the US shifted from safety first agriculture, with limited and intermitted market sales and barter, to a reliance on capitalist markets and what were the details of this transition including the different social forces and actors. This is when US farmers abandoned a class based identity and succumbed to the ideology of market society. Exactly how this occurred is the as yet untold story of the US transition to capitalism.

The US represents one of the exceptions to Brenner's claim that "...agricultural societies, with few if any exceptions, have been predominantly characterized by property relations of a single type" (1986, p. 27). Saturating the entire history of US industrial agriculture development under discussion are multiple class forms of agricultural production, partially reflecting the uneven and combined nature of US agricultural development, as will be seen when we look at the geographical differences in agricultural forms and the specific politics that emerge out of these. The interaction between them, and the class based use of them, greatly aids the efforts to push agro-industrial development. For example, the coexistence of slavery with capitalist production produced both political tensions, as well as economic and social tensions for not only life in the South but across the nation as a whole. These coexisting social forms also, during certain times, aided one another and were used to prevent and push forward capitalist development.

An understanding of agriculture's differences from other sectors of the economy, and particularly US agricultural differences from other geographic locations, are also necessary in order to elucidate the manner in which capitalism interacted with the development of this particular agriculture and vice-versa. One of the keys to understanding the distinctiveness of agriculture in general rests in both its spatial bounded-ness and in its relative lack of surplus value extraction through wage labor. Because capitalism's effect on agriculture in the US was not to introduce wage-labor as a universal form but instead to expand mostly through an expansion of technological innovations, this therefore requires an understanding of how agriculture developed along with capitalism (Goodman and Redclift, 1985). The continued reliance on family labor that persisted in agriculture, with only a small percent of farming based on wage labor, meant that the formal subsumption of labor played a much greater role than the real subsumption of labor. Because of this, agriculture relies more on relative than absolute surplus value extraction, leading to increases through non-human technological advances.

Philip McMichael when outlining the process of the development of capitalist economies around the world labels it the "development project" (2003). In doing so, he is describing "an organized strategy of national economic growth, including an international system of alliances and assistance established within the competitive and militarized terms of the cold war" (2003, p. 345). Describing development as "both a blue print for the world of nation-states and a strategy for world order" he outlines why the epithet project is used to "emphasize that development is something pursued and incomplete, rather than an evolutionary outcome" (2003, p. 23). Similarly, the conception of agroindustrial development utilized in this study rests on the notion of it being multipronged, both a blue print and strategy, along with something pursued as a project or goal rather than a natural outgrowth. For these reasons I am calling this form of agro-industrial development the agro-industrial project. Like the development project the tendency to naturalize the transition to capitalist agriculture and the industrialization of agriculture leads to an insufficient accounting of the state's role, farmer's resistance, and various cultural shifts.

As will be explicated it was both the unique qualities of agricultural production in the US and the resistance to capitalist market imperatives that led to the novel forms of state institutional capacity development in the US and that this, in turn, strengthened the drive toward capitalist development due to the states active hand in directing agricultural development through what I am calling the agro-industrial project. The role of the state, in terms of the agro-industrial project, involved prodding and directing social development and the construction of markets that create imperatives to do the same. This entailed the institutional capacity building of the US state in response to agrarian and capitalist class pressures that continually sought to revolutionize agricultural production between the 1840s and 1940s.

The Food Regimes Approach

The food regimes approach initiated a scholarly inquiry into the role of food and agriculture in reorganizing social forms approach (Friedmann, 1982,

1989, 1990, 1993, 2000, 2004, 2005, 2009; Friedmann and McMichael, 1989; McMichael, 1992, 2004, 2005, 2007, 2009). The 'food regime', Friedmann and McMichael articulated "as a historically significant cluster of global scale food relationships that contributed to stabilizing and underwriting a period of growth in global capitalism" (Campbell and Dixon, 2009, p. 263). A major contribution of the food regimes approach was to highlight those historical periods when a hegemonic power underwrites a given set of agro-food production and trade relations (Prichard, 2009). An offshoot of the 'regulation school of political economy', proponents of this approach described 'food regimes' as "relatively bounded historical period in which complementary expectations govern the behavior of all social actors" including the 'international food order of the post-war era' and the 'global food order' – in order to make connections about the fluidity and global connections between agriculture and industry in the process of growth of the capitalist market (Friedmann and McMichael, 1989). The food regimes approach by locating "the politics of food within stable and transitional periods of capital accumulation", "historicised the global food system; problematizing linear representations of agricultural modernization, underlining the pivotal role of food in global political-economy, and conceptualising key historical contradictions in particular food regimes that produce crisis, transformation and transition" (McMichael, 2009, p. 140). The approach divided the history of agro-food systems into distinct periods with particular policies and relations they claim underpinned them. By investigating the global links between agriculture and industry the approach exposed a "series of key relationships, often enshrined in rule-making and enforcing institutions (including imperial/national policy, trade policy, institutional forms of land use/farming, company regulation, commodity complexes, labour relations, consumption relations in the industrial core)" (Campbell and Dixon, 2009, p. 263). A food regime, for Friedmann, involved a period of "relatively stable sets of relationships" broken up by "unstable periods in between shaped by political contests over a new way forward" (Friedmann, 2005, p. 228). The turn from one 'food order' or 'regime' to the next is said to arise out of crises that emerge because of the built up contradictions of the regime; between the needs of capital and the institutional configurations. For instance, the crisis that emerged in the 1970s resulted in the demise a regime of the 'post-war mercantile food regime' (Friedmann, 1982, 1990, 1993, 2005).

The food regime approach rests on the notion of a two-fold and contradictory analysis of state action. The method used is to describe historically distinct sets of regulatory regimes – a British colonial regime, followed by a Mercantile food-aid regime, giving way to a corporate regime, all with distinct relationships between the market and the state institutional forms – setting up what they claim are contrasting approaches to agricultural policy during the eras, often government involvement is bifurcated into domestically orientated and globally orientated eras (McMichael, 1993; Friedmann, 1982). Through the construction of regimes based on a general domestic or global focus they posit the state and market relationship as zero-sum and alternating in control – the market in one instance and under state control in another. This approach to international agricultural trade and domestic production sometimes explicitly relies on the Polanyian notion of a movement/double movement, in which the market expands, leading to popular induced state responses to offset the social dislocation created. The approach downplays the connections between the market, the state and the broader social institutions. While we must acknowledge that at specific times and in unique institutional arenas different policies were advanced that did represent different goals and produce different, sometimes divergent, outcomes, it is not altogether accurate to see these as outside of an overall globally oriented capitalist project or tendency, as constituted by a more constant state-market relationship that is open to various positions. Therefore, by failing to locate the distinctiveness of the US states rules, roles and results in this process, a failure to account for change as endogenous development, the approach requires a reliance on theories of crisis and distinct food orders or regimes, thus dissecting historical development (Friedmann, 1982; McMichael, 1993).

A major error created by this approach is overemphasizing the disjunction and overlooking the continuity through the artificial imposition of regimes. Out of this, the consistent role of US agriculture in the construction of a global US capitalist empire gets lost, appearing as almost a matter of happenstance or a success because of failure. The expansion of the market is viewed as inducing the double movement popular response, which is seen as the means to rein in the market. This hides the many ways popular responses were part of the fuel for further market expansion and penetration through increased state institutional capacities.

Positing discrete and distinct eras or regimes – resulting from the failures and crises of prior eras or regimes – turns into the playing out of varying degrees of control of the state over the market or the capturing of the state by either the agrarian based social movements or giant US agri-business TNC's. The continuity of state involvement in market building becomes hidden. Thus the notion of a 'regime of accumulation' (Aglietta, 1979) applied to agricultural studies became a hindrance once it began to guide historical analysis and limit the power to locate the kernel of historical development of capitalist agriculture and the continuity that bridges the supposedly distinct 'food regimes'. Therefore, it is important to locate the development of US capitalism, as well

INTRODUCTION 23

as its geopolitical rise, within the specificity of its agricultural production and the social and political struggles this entailed and how these informed state institutional formation. Doing this reveals the flexibility of the US state to respond to the pressures of global capitalism and popular political pressure simultaneously.

Alternatively an engagement with neo-Marxist state theory offers a more accurate picture of the state's continual role in market development. For instance, Jill Quadagno's (1987) claims that the state acted as a mediating body to preserve and enhanced the interests of capital. State policies contributed to the form of reproduction through the mediation of disputes between classes and between competing fractions of capital. For Quadagno (1987) class power "can be derived by analyzing the existing economic and political constraints unique to a particular period and to particular state action, and by assessing how working-class demands get incorporated into state policy" (p. 634). A central argument of Neo-Marxist state theory has been to locate the state as playing a "central role in organizing, sanctioning, and legitimizing class domination within capitalism… A particular configuration of social forces defines in practice the limits or parameters of state purposes, and the modus operandi of state action, defines, in other words, the raison d'état for a particular state … within these parameters, the state exercised power and choice in the organization and development of production and classes" (Panitch, 2010, p. 17).

The agro-industrial project outlined in the investigation clearly reveals how state institutional development set the parameters of both production and classes. By placing the economic change induced agrarian movements and the states response to them at the center, this approach can reveal more clearly the development of the project of agro-industrial development in conjunction with US state building. This clearly reveals the manner in which development of one fed into the developmental trajectory of the others. In the post-war era we see the state also took on the role of "the mediator between the global and the national" (Panitch, 2010, p. 21), which is in response to the prior state institutional development and class formation. This is documented in the push for trade expansion which is the often overlooked aspect of US state institutional development in the USDA. In this manner, the capitalist state organized society to a degree. The state locates power "in the spaces which the bourgeoisie controls, and disempower those spaces which the oppositional movements have the greatest potential to command" (Harvey, 1989, p. 237). This is confirmed in the multiple instances of agrarian resistance that was funneled into reforms based on higher market prices that favored capital through state action. The USDA-research complex is a glaring example of this state capacity, which clearly developed in response to popular agrarian resistance, and which also came to represent the largest state institutional force in aiding capital against the interests of farmers.

The inability or difficulty of capital to fully penetrate and transform agricultural production into a wage-labor based form is due, in part, to the natural attributes of agriculture. One of these attributes in particular is production time. Farmers, for the most part, must invest in the spring and will not take profits on that investment until the fall. This disunity between production and working time was first elucidated by Marx and later expanded on by Mann and Dickenson (1978). The disunity at first appears as a limit to capitalist expansion, excluding capitalist production from agriculture. However, as Harvey (2006) outlined, capitalism turns such limits into mere obstacles and ultimately forces innovations to move around these obstacles. In the case of the disunity of production and labor time in agricultural production this comes through both the expansion of forms and amounts of credit and technological innovation. Both of these occurred in the US case through state intervention. These developments do little to actually aid the farmer, instead they offer up opportunities for others to turn this extended production time into a means to gain. As Henderson (1998) put it, "it is that what works to agriculture's disadvantage vis-à-vis the gaps between working and production times works to someone else's advantage...the very processes that interrupt the circulation of one capital are processes which may be the condition for the circulation of another" (p. 42). The large development and expansion of industrial food manufacturing is a sharp example of this process.

Another limit overcome through state institutional development is in the realm of credit and debt required to facilitate the ever ongoing agro-industrial expansion. Thus, the changes in agriculture and the development of capitalism in America coincided with the rise of sophisticated credit mechanisms and other subsidiary industries to overcome the limits imposed by the natural attributes of agriculture. These limits or obstacles were turned into opportunities. There occurred two key periods of the expansion of debt to farmers during the period under discussion – 1860 to 1875 and 1910 to 1920. During both of these periods we see the amount of farm-mortgage debt doubling. As previously described, both eras were also preceded by major shifts in state policy towards agricultural credit.

Harvey's (2006) delineation of Marx's point about limits turned into opportunities also applied to farmer resistance movements. Farmer reluctance and outright resistance to increasing market dependence was fueled by the changes and loss of autonomy that first appeared with the slow transition to petty commodity production. For most farmers the initial change in direction to selling commodities was viewed as a temporary turn and as a means to re-establish independent, yeoman production. As outlined in the discussions of Shays' Rebellion, the New York State Anti-Rent movement, Midwest Claims Associations, the Grange, Farmers Alliance, and other populist movements,[8] the development of farmer social movements fed the development of the state to deal with and funnel the resistance into forms amendable to the market. It was used as the means to expand the state institutional capacity and in the process strengthen market reliance while creating new opportunities for capital. Exposing the role of the state in overcoming these limits is paramount in developing an understanding of US capitalisms spread, first domestically and later around the globe. Piven and Cloward (1977) demonstrated similar processes of protest leading to reform, which then lead to the rechanneling of the reform once the crisis was surpassed in industrial and low income sectors. Thus they confirmed the thesis that state institutional responses often act to undermine the groups who bring the concerns to light and originally drive the policies (Piven and Cloward, 1977). It also showed the class bias in the state and how even anti-capital social movements could, once in a collaborative relationship with the US state, come to strengthen state institutional capacities to deepen capital's strength.

In order to overcome the limitations of a binary conception of states and markets, a state theory must be utilized that rejects the theoretical separation between state power and class power, as well as, one that also rejects the treatment of politics and economics as distinct categories of enquiry. State and class power must be logically located in the same social relations, as co-determinant, internally related and produced social forces, rather than as distinct and competing. The tendency to ontologize the distinction between state and market must be overcome by understanding the manner in which the state draws its material resources and legitimacy from the relations of production and the social division of labor into classes. State action must also not be seen as narrowly tied to the function of in increasing capital accumulation, as much of the more economistic analysis does, leading to an instrumentalist understanding and a tendency to see state action as either in the interest of capital or against it. Rather, what must be examined and elucidated is the manner in which the state acts to reproduce the class-relevant social formations in a contested arena that is both removed from directly economic activity, but which also, serves to depoliticize the economy

---

8 I use the term populist with a lower case to signal what is discussed in much of the literature as the social movement that emerges in the last quarter of the 19th Century and focused on issues of agrarian economics. This is in contradistinction to Populist Party, which is the party that emerges out of this movement in the last few years of the Century.

through its state apparatuses and institutional shifts, while simultaneously influenced by the balance of class forces produced by economic development and change.

The contradictory role of the state is historically traceable in the institutional configurations through which it both reproduces a class bifurcated society and seeks to depoliticize this bifurcation and its social outcomes. Furthermore, the very formation, existence and reproduction of classes represent one of the key social projects of states, alongside a general maintenance function of the state to create social cohesion (Poulantzas, 1973; Clarke, 1977; Holloway and Picciotto, 1977). The formation, transformation, and reproduction of classes must not be assumed *a priori.* Instead, classes must be traced historically through the institutions which shape them: the economic, political, and ideological crystallisation's in relations and forms of social power that actively inform the process of class production, reproduction, and transformation. Likewise, resistance and struggle must also be understood and analyzed as aspects of, or moments in, the developmental process of history and of state institutional capacities. As Chorev states it, "political struggles, as they shape and reshape institutions, determine the policies that enable (or constrain) future economic trends" (2007, p. 207).

This dissertation will highlight the struggles that developed around agriculture, how these struggles were overcome, and the impacts this had on not only the development of the state and capital but also of the specific form of agricultural production itself. In short, it is an effort to trace the domestic sources of US power through the unique role of agriculture and its impact on economic development, political conflict, and state and global market formation, above all through what Winders (2001) labeled the "USDA-research complex" – the USDA along with the land-grant university system and the State Agricultural Experiment Stations – largely responsible for the development and implementation of agricultural technologies of modernization. Through its support for large-scale scientific agriculture, this complex aided in the construction of the upstream and downstream agribusinesses that would supply the necessary tools, implements, inputs and process of the raw commodity outputs, as well as the development of food products and means to bring them to market, which would fuel rapid increases in farm size and efficiency, through increasingly market dependent relationships (Gilbert and Howe, 1991; Kloppenburg, 1988; Kloppenburg and Buttle, 1987; McMichael, 2003). This agro-industrial project would come through the state institutional capacity enhancement emerging out of the USDA and the other state implemented programs. It would drive productivity gains in agriculture that would ultimately destabilize farmers through overproduction and declining prices rather than help them. The production of food in the US would thus be transformed into its modern industrial model through the USDA along with other state projects of market creation.

The development and growth of the USDA is a clear example of the use of the state to intervene in the economic development of the nation. Tracking this growth reveals how class interests used the state to respond to the discontent of farmers and the threat posed by agrarian movements. It also shows how the development of the USDA funneled agrarian movements and general farmer sentiment into policies that would further the interests of the more powerful and connected. The USDA, as an institution of the US capitalist state, was in the business of 'making two blades of grass grow where one grew before'. This represents a distinctively different task than one seeking to aid farmers in their daily lives, where many of their problems emerged because of modernization and the development of capitalism. That is to say, the USDA served a distinct purpose and its history is about the development of the proper institutional capacity to guide US farmers and the overall agricultural economy down a path of increased productivity through mechanization and toward large scale industrial agribusiness. This doesn't mean that increasing productivity could not have aided struggling farmers, because, in some cases it did. It does mean that increasing productivity doesn't ensure assistance to farmers because that was not the principal purpose of state intervention. The USDA is a successful example of state institutional capacity building to guide the development of the national economy as a whole by harnessing and redirecting farmer movements emerging out of the economic pressures and shifts.

The fact that the USDA led agricultural development down a distinctly capitalist and industrial path did not render it an agency with little farmer support. In fact, though its relationship with farmers was rocky at first, the agency would at various times be quite popular amongst the agrarian class. This occurred through seed distribution, research into pests that ravaged crops, education into how to increase their individual yields, and later the AFBF, combined with the use of a thick layer of farmer aid rhetoric. Ultimately, by the mid-twentieth century, farmers would look to the USDA almost exclusively for help. This was the result of the policies it pushed that were designed to aid farmers with short term economic relief addressing the partiulars of problems, as opposed to class based understandings rooted in a general desire by farmers to maintain or return to an era of less market dependence. Farm groups would over time mostly abandon a social or class based understanding of their social location and troubles, becoming open to any state aid thought to increase commodity prices and improve farm output.

This approach to the development of state institutions like the USDA challenges the state-market dichotomy advanced in the literature that analyzes

New Deal state involvement in the agricultural market through the Agricultural Adjustment Administration (AAA) and other programs (Skocpol and Finegold, 1982, 1995; Weir and Skocpol, 1985). The critical historiographies emerging out of historical sociology generally see US agricultural power as part of a state-market relationship which is bifurcated and oppositional (Skocpol and Finegold, 1995). The state is presented here as vacillating between the market and the problems it produces, between state intervention to correct these problems and the problems of state intervention. This approach has a "tendency to ontologize the distinction between markets and institutions" (Panitch and Konings, 2009, p. 6) and failed to properly grasp how the guiding logic of New Deal state policy contained both a safety-net political stop gate through price floors and other subsidies, along with a form of institutional regulation aimed at increasing the influence of the market directed aspects of agricultural production and expanding international trade, thereby missing the salient point that the state acts as a relatively autonomous player in the construction and maintenance of the capitalist market. Even the most immediately market distorting programs produced outcomes that increased the integration of agricultural production into the market by furthering the penetration of the market logic of increased productivity and competition.

Even during high levels of state intervention on behalf of a push by social movements, the state still put forward polices that encouraged market expansion. Once an increased reliance on the market is developed, the state can become more reliant on creating and propping up these market based means of movement co-option. This process began once farmers moved into market dependence and only increased as they furthered their debt reliance. Indeed, in the US case, the state almost exclusively has focused on market creation and expansion. So even when state policy was influenced by radical agrarian movements, the form of it took ultimately facilitated increased market dependence.

Overview of the Chapters

The second chapter of this thesis will look into the development of Northern US petty commodity agrarian relations through the expansion of the agro-industrialization theory. This will reveal the history of the US transition to capitalism as best understood through a focus on the day-to-day economic realities of farmers, their social movements against the changes coming with capitalist development, and the manner in which the US state aided in overcoming these movements and set up markets that pushed along the transition in the 19th century. The nature of the political and social struggles to maintain an independent and then a petty commodity means of subsistence against the advancing forces of the market reveal a very active state in aiding the reconfiguring of agrarian life and the state's ability to represent and manage class interests. It is these developments in state institutional capacities, unique to the US precisely because of the nature of farming that existed, and the size and political strength of farmers, which represent the source of the US's strength heading into the 20th Century. The long history of the use of land to structure the options of agrarian movements and cut off more radical demands beginning with land policy and the frontier, reveals the active hand of the state constantly shaping not only the lives of farmers but their political responses as well.

The third chapter will investigate the very different nature of Southern agriculture, focusing on the immediate pre and post-civil era which contained many changes for southern farmers. The deployment of slavery, its elimination through the Civil War, and the path of agricultural economic development in the post-war era will be investigated in an effort to locate the changes class structure and state interventions that existed and that were emerging in the late 19th Century. Important in grasping the reorganization of the southern plantation system in the wake of the end of slave labor as the dominant form of agricultural production in the South is that it did not immediately usher in an agro-industrial project similar to that in the North. Instead it gave rise to heightened uneven development with much of the South turning to tenancy, which in turn deeply informed the rise of the radical agrarian class-based populist movement which also drew on the resistance to further commodification by petty commodity producer agriculture in the North.

The fourth chapter offers a historical account of the farmer's movements that emerged, flourished, became powerful and influential, and then dissipated during the last quarter of the 19th and first decade of the 20th Centuries. In response to the shifts occurring due to the transition to petty commodity agriculture – the decline in living standards of farming households, and the rising influence of the agro-industrial project – farmers across the nation began to form and join agrarian social movements. The chapter will trace and show the importance of these agrarian resistances, not least in terms of their effect on the institutional capacity of US state. This lays the basis for further refining the theory of agro-industrial development by showing how ultimately this process led to a stronger and more resilient capitalist state to emerge, while in the process it disarmed opposition movements and integrated them into the developing industrial capitalist social relations. Important in this regard, and highlighted in this chapter, is how the balance of class forces during the last quarter of the 19th and the first quarter of the 20th centuries fuelled the development of the new institutions of the US state. Out of these new institutions emerged the political compromises that favored capital over farmers and helped imbricate them into the expanding capitalist economy while neutering the radical class politics of the farmers and funneling agrarian demands into forms compatible with an expanding industrial capitalism. Concordantly US agriculture also witnessed what is called 'the golden age', as farm prices peaked during the period of 1900–1920. When farm prices crashed in the early 1920s, due mostly to a loss of European markets, combined with ever rising domestic farm productivity, the state institutions and shifts in farmer organizational forms prevented a radical agrarian response.

In the fifth chapter the theory of the agro-industrial project is specifically applied to the development of the United States Department of Agriculture (USDA) It will be shown how the development of the USDA, which began as early as the 1840s, was associated with two main goals: to push farmers into increasingly market dependent forms of production, and to expand the trade necessary to absorb the surpluses that would result from the first. The specific role of the department in advocating for modernizing farms highly dependent on capitalist markets will be traced, as will the introduction and expansion of the USDA-research complex, which came to inform not only the direction of agrarian economic development but also the politics of farming and the development of the industries needed to support modern industrial farming. It will also be shown how the department was engaged in trade promotion, while the USDA-research complex simultaneously pushed agricultural modernization in the US. This will reveal how, through built up institutional capacities, the USDA guided agricultural development and directed farmer responses to the farm prices crises in the 1920s into acceptance of further modernization.

The sixth chapter will focus on the Great Depression and the state policies of the Agricultural Administration Authority and other New Deal polices. It will be shown how the goal of production control was put forward as the guiding New Deal approach to farm trouble during the depression and how this occurred because of the already existing institutional capacities of the state. The specific ways that the programs both benefited larger farms and how they funneled farmers into specific, more market dependent relationships, quelling radical responses will be examined. Once again the theory of agro-industrialization will be modified and tested by focusing on state institutional developments to deal with crisis in agriculture as prices plummeted in the 1930s. This chapter will highlight the states increased role in dealing with the issues facing farmers, as well as, the forms of resistance that emerged and how this produced the heightened state involvement in agriculture prices and supply management that remains to this day. It will be shown that through the funneling of agrarian demands into policies that pushed agro-industrialization, the US state was able to assuage the demands of the agrarian movements through a process that shifted demands toward higher farm product prices, and used the market to discipline farmers and concentrate them under capitalist social forms, while diminishing radical popular opposition.

Chapter 7 focuses on post-1945 institutional developments in the context of the changing balance of class forces, while showing that the forms previously adopted to enable the agro-industrial project domestically now became the basis of the US strategies for global agricultural market reconstruction, beginning with the Food for Peace (PL 480) program. It shows how the domestic process of imbricating farmers and workers through the New Deal programs created both the material basis and the institutional and political blueprints to reconstruct the global market in the American image. It will be argued that the state interventions through the production control policies of the USDA were from their inception geared towards expanding US agricultural trade and reconstructing the global capitalist market. This chapter also offers an historical analysis of the US use of food aid to develop trade, transform societies, and construct the global market will be outlined that pays particular attention to the institutional and political shifts in the nature of the US state. It will stress, against the food regimes claim, that what the food-regimes literature calls the *post-war food regime*, artificially sets up the role of the US state's relationship to agriculture as one centered on what it calls a mercantile approach. Instead, the continuity of US agriculture's role in the post-war US reconstruction and expansion of a global capitalist market will be traced. This then will be the basis for elucidating the limits of the food regime approach and offering an alternative approach that takes the US state, and the large role of agriculture, as the author of globalization through the active involvement of other states in the process of transforming and aligning social relations with a neoliberal globalized form.

It will be argued that the use of state policy to influence the developmental path of other nations and construct a world market was the cornerstone of US policy even through the Keynesian days of the New Deal. As Wood made clear "the bulk of economic assistance from the days of the Marshall Plan to the present has been structured to…promote the expansion of the private sector, both domestic and foreign, and the dominance of market principles of exchange; and to encourage 'outward-looking,' export-oriented types of development" (1986, p. 191).

CHAPTER 2

The Agro-Industrial Roots of the US Capitalist Transition through State Capacity Building: 1830–1870

This chapter will offer a historically grounded analysis of the role that agriculture played in the US transition to capitalism. A key aspect of this transition was the influence of agrarian interests on the path of economic development in combination with the state institutional capacity building response to these interests and how this influenced agrarian economic development. In this regard, the movement from of farmers from simple commodity producers into market dependent petty commodity producers between 1830 and 1870 lies at the heart of this process.[1]

One of the key features of the particular spread of petty commodity production during this period of US history was its expansionary nature, both externally and internally (i.e.: geographically and increasing in scale of the market). This reliance on expansive alongside of intensive forms of development, arises out of the drive by farmers to maintain independence; with some uprooting and moving westward in an effort to reduce their debt burdens and others seeking legal relief. The degree of the expansionary tendencies was relative to the degree of market pressure exerted upon petty commodity producers by capitalist development: meaning that independent and petty commodity production was engaged in a symbiotic relationship with capitalist development. Furthermore, these changes were political in nature, they were built on changes that occurred in the state institutions which were actively constructing the legal basis of and aiding in the development of markets, as well as, resting on the political ideology of the young nation. It is out of the protracted and uneven course of the transition to modern capitalism through the industrial revolution, and the political movements fighting for and against these changes, that the historical trajectory worked itself out. Markets for labor, raw materials, and final products all had to be organized and orchestrated and were done so at differential rates, and in different ways due to the degree of conflict over them. As will be shown, the state had to continually be called on to both

---

[1] I use the terms simple commodity production, independent household production, and yeoman agriculture interchangeably as these terms mean the same thing across the various sources used here.

deal with resistance movements and simple acts of individual resistance that emerged, and to aid in the necessary institutional support aspects required by emerging capitalist firms in the process of market creation.

US Land Policy in the North

Land policy needs to be at the core of any discussion of the development of capitalist agriculture in the US. As first articulated by Madison, the distribution of the population over a large land mass serves as the source of a diminished power of citizenry, a form of "auxiliary precautions" as he called them, which ensures the dominance of the propertied classes and the success of the republic (Madison, 1779). The larger the nation, and the greater the "variety of parties and interests, the more difficult it would be for a mass majority to act in unison": As Madison wrote in Federalist Papers No. 10 "A rage for paper money, for an abolition of debts, for an equal division of property, or for any other wicked project will be less apt to pervade the whole body of the Union than a particular member of it" (Madison, 1779). And further, "To secure the public good and private rights against the danger of such a faction," "and at the same time preserve the spirit and form of popular government is then the great object to which our inquiries are directed" (Madison, 1779). Thus the new Constitution would reflect this effort to enhance and use the federal government to secure the interests of the economically powerful (Beard, 1936). Article I, Section Eight of the Constitution, granting the power to support and regulate commerce and protect property interests, was quickly adopted under little debate (Parenti 1974). Gordon Wood (1969) called the Constitution an "aristocratic document", in that it "gives the Federal Government the power" over measures "of primary concern to investors, merchants, and creditors", including land policies and expansion (Parenti, 1974, p. 9).

Therefore the continued expansion of US territory westward along with the specifics of the land, banking, and debt policies were constructed to strengthen the direct intervention powers of the Federal Government in the economy. The settler colonial expansion of the US territory through the genocide of the indigenous populations was one of the main foundations for the freedoms allowed in the new nation. Early federal policy failed to use the limited federal troops to uphold land claims and prevent squatting. Instead federal troops were used to suppress and extricate native populations, thereby providing the ever expanding land base. This use of the federal government for settler colonial expansion was seen as the more efficient and more politically viable option coming out of the skirmishes of Shays' and the Whiskey Rebellion.

Absent this major source of power in land, the US development path would have been significantly altered. This early state approach informed exactly how future policies and the state institutions would be built, as well as structure the development of the market in agriculture and how it drove farmers to interact with it. This appears as an example of a state policy that did not push a transition to petty commodity production and capitalism. Instead, the goal was to expand the geographic base of the nation and increase the independence of the people through this 'free' land. Even later, when it was becoming clear that absent free productive land to expand into agriculture would transition to petty commodity forms, the federal policy remained committed to further westward land expansion (Clark 1990). That is, as troops were increasingly used to maintain land and property, enforce taxation and aid in pushing farmers into market dependence, the US State also continued to expand westward to maintain the independent ideology of simple commodity producers through 'free' productive land.

The above should not be meant to present the development of land policy in the US as emerging out of a unitary effort to modernize agriculture. On the contrary, land policy wasn't part of a preconceived agro-industrial development policy. As a rule, Federal legislation has been the result of compromises between conflicting factions rather than an expression of a uniform philosophy with coherent and consistent aims. Land policy is no different. Government agencies likewise had a hand in elaborating upon the details of a general policy. Several departments were responsible for the administration of programs or the development of research aimed at influencing the course of agricultural land policy. These departments were not necessarily agreed in their objectives nor were they always models of consistency (Saloutos, 1962, p. 446).

Likewise, there were many competing groups lobbying for a diverse set of land policy approaches. The result of this nexus of competing interests was that little, if any, consideration was given to controlling the settlement of the lands in a manner that would have prevented an over-expansion of agriculture (Saloutos, 1962, p. 446). In fact, jumping ahead that is exactly what we see between 1850 and 1930, as a result of the activities of private groups, and Federal and state legislation, the area of all land in farms more than tripled, and the area of improved land in farms almost quintupled. When this eighty-year period is broken down into smaller time spans, we find that the area opened up to cultivation reached its greatest dimensions during the 1880's and 1890's. Between 1870 and 1900, the total area of all farm lands doubled from 408 to 823 million acres, the improved lands from 189 to 414 million acres, and the improved lands per capita from 4.9 to 5.5 acres (Ely and Wehrwein, 1940, pp. 172–3). This expansion clearly undermined prices, which pushed a specific type of farming. It also went a long way to aid a speculative class. Thus, there was no plan to use land to create a capitalist agriculture. Instead, it was through the working out of policy amongst different interests with varied political pull that federal land policy emerges. The contradictory land policies eventually were turned into one that promoted petty commodity production through a process of political struggle and alongside other social developments.

However, the land policy would come to play a specific and continued role in reshaping the social relations of the nation. It is here that we see the decisive and direct state institutional development and influence over the balance of class forces in agriculture first emerge. These "State and federal policies for disposal of land structured yeoman opportunity to own farms", (Kulikoff, 1992, p. 44), while also, somewhat later, pushing petty commodity production.

One of the most direct interventions of the Federal Government in land policy resulted in the concentration in ownership of land. The majority of new federal land went into the private hands of speculators following 1847 (Gates, 1973). The new Constitution had granted Congress "the Power to dispose of and make all needful Rules and Regulations respecting the Territory or other Property belonging to the United States." Kulikoff (1992, p. 44) argued that "the wealthiest five percent of the population owned between a third and two-fifths of all land in both 1798 and 1860". This means that the doubling and then doubling again of the total land mass of the US territory did little to alter the disparity in land ownership. In fact, federal policy encouraged simultaneously large plots controlled by the wealthy, mostly as investments, and small plots for actual farmers.

Beginning with the Land Ordinance of 1785, there was no restriction placed on the amount of public land any individual could purchase. Land speculation and specifically the speculation that came out of public land auctions, were the first major form of US speculation, occurring thirty years prior to the formation of the New York Stock Exchange (Gates, 1973). Horace Greely (New York Tribune, June 16, 1860) claimed that land speculation led to a five or six million dollar drain on settlers as "tens of thousands have thus paid the government price of their quarter section twice or thrice over before they could call them their own". This structured future class dynamics and shaped the developmental trajectory of the region and the nation by charging a form of ground rent to farmers prior to their farming. Clearly, land policies – and their institutional correlates the General Land Office, Office of Geological Survey, Office of Indian Affairs, as well as indirectly the Federal Military, Court System and Banking institutions – represent one of the earliest and a continued source of US institutional development. The Federal Government actively sought to manage how it developed this land, and the class influence of that development. This was contingent and influenced by how the balance of class forces informed policy decisions. Gates documents 13 major reorganizing pieces of Federal legislation over the century between 1810 and 1910 having to do with land policy reflecting the push and pull of different groups over time. (1973, p. 71).

Beyond this Congress went even further to skew land policy in favor of speculators by offering a ten percent discount for up-front cash sales which favored the wealthy investors over poor farmers and would be farmers (Opie, 1994). This was expanded through the 1785 Land Survey Ordinance and the 1787 Northwest Ordinance, which went even so far as containing the reassurance to speculators that "in no case shall non-resident proprietors be taxed higher than residents" (Opie, 1994, p. 26). The outcome of these policies for many meant simply having to settle on unclaimed land. This land policy orientation can be traced directly back to the Constitution in its call for land disposal at a deliberate speed, "the Constitution thus provided an early indirect subsidy for nationwide capital enterprise" (Opie, 1994, p. 25). Despite this continual backing of speculation the Founding Fathers were actually rather divided on the appropriate land policy for the country. Thomas Jefferson argued that cheap or even free land to settlers would create a flourishing democracy and act as a counterweight to influential moneyed interest in cities and prevent the deteriorization of society as industry spread akin to what he saw in Europe. Despite his urging the actual land policy came to be one of selling off the vast public lands to the highest bidder as a source of revenue for the burgeoning state and as a means to repay wealthy political backers. It would also play a role in creating and expanding a class of land speculators.

The revolution fueled their belief in the democratic promise possible through independent farmers with land to produce (Hammond, 1957; Postel, 2009). The purity of self-reliance of the independent farmer fed the ideology of the new social order by building an economy absent the moral corruption of both wage labor and finance (Konings, 2015). As the economy developed, it was a belief in the power of the democratic state to deliver the necessary credit to farmers to create a democratic economy free of the corruption that plagued Europe (Hammond, 1957; Sanders, 1999). Thus the democratic ethos combined with the 'free' land to instill the independent ideology that both sustained the nation and would threaten it as market forms clashed with it.

This early land policy also aided in the construction of both American individualist ideology and the state's evolving and increasing role in the protection of private property and investment, two not unrelated things. Clearly the policies favored speculation, even if it did not push petty commodity production and capitalist transition directly. As speculators benefited from these land policies, these benefits also led to an increase in their political pull, which in turn

TABLE 1 *US land sales receipts and Federal debt in millions: 1832–1836*

Year	Land Receipts	Federal Debt
1832	2,623	24,322
1834	4,858	4,760
1836	24,877	38

SOURCE: GATES 1968, 276

informed polices to aid this class. Thus, the right of Congress to sell and citizens to buy federal land deposed from native populations, even if just for speculative purposes was enshrined in US law. At its very earliest the US was already using public resources to gather and sell public assets to private individuals, while simultaneously building up a class of political power (see Table 1). This reveals the active hand of the state in economic development through infrastructural power and through the privatization of public assets. The state favored merchant and later industrial capital by creating the means to impose market dependence through its infrastructure support. Federal bias in land policy, canal and road projects, and later railroad projects, all favored the capitalist class relative to the property-less masses. Thus, the infrastructural power given to merchants and capitalists by the federal policies was an active agent affecting the balance of class forces, particularly in the building of agrarian market dependency.

One of the earliest land policy, the Land Act of 1796, called for tracts to be sized at 640-acre sections with credit terms set at a ridiculous five percent down and a full fifty percent due within thirty days and the full balance by the end of the year, based on the minimal size and the $2 per acre minimal price (Opie, 1994). This meant that farmers would have to come up with $64 for the down payment and then an additional $574 within thirty days, along with $640 by the end of the year. Clearly this was out of reach for most farmers and laborers. This early federal land policy also promoted very large farm sizes, and as Veblen (1923) pointed out, led to the practice of farmers purchasing more land than they could cultivate. This increased the farmers need for either labor or baring the necessary population base and capital to pay labor, equipment to cultivate the land and for credit to meet expenses of holding idle and semi-idle land. "All this," wrote Veblen (1923),

> [H]as had the effect of raising the cost of production of farm products; partly by making the individual farm that much more unwieldy as an instrument of production, partly by further enforcing the insufficiency and

the make-shift character of which American farm equipment is justly famed, and partly also by increasing the distances over which the farm supplies and the farm products have had to be moved (p. 136).

If this force slowed production, it also enticed and forced farmers into markets by increasing the pressure to sell by increasing the costs of farming.

From the Land Survey Ordinance of 1785 up until 1816 when Congress granted new exemptions in Ohio, trespassing on public lands was illegal. However, this did not stop hundreds of thousands of land squatters between those dates. The Federal Government had the ability to put in place the Survey System but lacking a standing federal army, no power to enforce it. In 1815, in the face of growing violence between squatters and land owners, Madison threatened to use military force on the "many uniformed or evil-disposed persons" living on unsold land (Opie, 1994, p. 46). In many cases the problems and confusion was simply that the survey teams could not keep up with the expanding farmers, the federal government had a vast resource in land, but was undersized to deal with it in the face of a growing farm population moving west. The general understanding of the time was that squatting was a way to gain land, despite this not actually being the law.

Once the government began to enforce the law and challenge or remove squatters, farmers formed claims clubs and other groups to defend their squatted homesteads. These groups would gather in mass and use the threat of violent reprise to ward off potential rival purchasers for squatted land. Congress acted in the name of stemming the speculation, confusion and growing political tension by passing the Land Act of 1820 requiring the somewhat contradictory policies of full payment for the land at the time of purchase and a reduced price of public lands. The act overall hurt farmers with the full payment requirement which favored speculators. This reduced both the number of land sales and the debt of farmers. After land debt fell from $22 million in 1819 to $6.3 million in 1825, credit sales were once again instituted (Opie, 1994).

The 1830s brought a large land boom to the American West, with 28 million acres moving from public to private ownership in 1834–35 alone. With the land boom came inflation as prices rose 150 percent across the nation in the first six years of the 1830s. A large portion of the boom was fueled by an increased involvement of speculators. One example includes the involvement of the American Land Company, a well-connected company, bankrolled by associates of Andrew Jackson that owned 322,000 acres at one point (Opie, 1994). After numerous newspaper investigations into the large speculators buying up public land on credit President Jackson was forced to intervene with the Specie Currency presidential order in 1836, requiring all land purchases in hard cash.

The resulting crash of the land market was very large and increased the hardship on many western farmers especially in face of the 1837 economic crisis.

The 'panic of 1837', like the one in 1819 before it, helped facilitate large scale changes in the social relations and state institutional forms, specifically by increasing the role of corporations and large investors in the North through new commercial innovations such as credit reporting and new accounting methods which altered the way farmers purchased and held land (Clark, 2006; Post, 2011). As both crises occurred, the prices for agricultural products declined precipitously, leaving farmers to either increase market engagement – by picking up work outside of the farm, selling more of their product or bringing in more putout work for their wives and family- or risk losing their farms to the bank or agent that controlled the mortgage. The back and forth, shifting nature of land policy stimulated various bubbles, which allowed speculators to take advantage of.

Early Farmer Resistance to Market Expansion

Settler colonial land policy had expanded independent commodity production and also increased the social and political power of the class of farmers who engaged in it. In areas where this ability to expand had been exhausted the increase in market pressures and push toward petty commodity production coincided with agrarian resistance. An example of early farmer resistance to the shifting economic pressures occurred in 1786–87 in Massachusetts. After decades of expansion into the 'freed up' land areas, New England farmer's ability to expand or move when productivity waned became increasingly limited. Following the Revolutionary war an economic depression emerged that impacted debt-ridden farmers. The state had imposed land taxes which many farmers could not pay during the depression, resulting in high rates of farm foreclosures. In response, farmers organized and petitioned the state senate for relief in the form of the issuance of paper money, a halting of foreclosures, and the stopping of imprisonment for overdue land taxes. When the state senate, which was filled more with senators whose interest was not in aiding small farmers refused to intervene, armed insurgents rose up in the Western Massachusetts Berkshire Hills and Connecticut Valley. Led by Daniel Shays the insurgents forcibly acted to stop foreclosures and to prevent the courts from ruling against indebted farmers (Minot, 1971).

The forces behind what became known as Shays' Rebellion focused on the high tax rates, the disproportionate influence of merchants in the Massachusetts government and the ever growing social power these merchants wielded over agrarian life in general. The farmers were feeling economic pressure and the only concentrated source of that pressure they could recognize was in the state. Rather than being responsive to the interests of the masses, as the reigning ideology of the time proclaimed, the state was clearly siding with the merchants and had indicated its willingness to use troops against the farmers. The Rebellion occurred just prior to the period Rothenberg (1981) has shown when market prices converged and profit potential became determinant in farmer production decisions in Massachusetts. Thus Massachusetts farmers by the last decade of the 18th Century were for the most part producing for sale in competitive markets with the prices they received being set by these competitive markets (Rothenberg, 1981, 1985, 1988; Clark, 1990; Post, 2011).

The rebellion awoke the new nation to the importance of the federal government in suppressing rebellion and future uprisings. The debate over the federal constitution revolved around the issues that had emerged in Massachusetts: "the interests of merchants, manufacturers, market-oriented farmers, and creditors seemed in conflict with those of the semi-subsistence upland farmers who had supported Shays' Rebellion" (Brown, 1978, p. 122). After Shays' it became clear that farmers were willing to assault contract law, credit, and the courts to maintain their existence and resist market encroachment. The Regulator movement of 1766–1771 in the backcountry North Carolina, as poor and middling farmers directed against the upper classes, added to the sense of social malfunction and gave evidence that Shays' wasn't merely a one off event (Young, 1974, p. 450). These threats to law, order and property were one of the main reasons the constitutional convention was called, the Articles of Confederation was scrapped, and the new constitution was written, which strengthened the federal government, making sure that neither states nor individuals could interfere with contract law or property rights (Summerhill, 2005, p. 18). Importantly it was this very strengthening of the federal government that would enable it to become the key driving force facilitating the transition away from household to petty commodity production. This occurred through the enhanced ability to uphold property rights that came with increased federal troops and the heightened degree of the federal government to regulate a national land policy. Most troublesome to the framers of the Constitution was the insurgent spirit evidenced among the people. In 1787, George Washington wrote to a former comrade-in-arms, "There are combustibles in every State, to which a spark might set fire." Politicians who shortly before the Constitutional Convention had opposed strong federation, now realized an alliance with conservative states would be a safeguard if radicals should capture the state government and they gave up 'state rights' for 'nationalism' (Jenson, 1948, p. 30).

For many small farmers in the north eastern colonies, the colonial era witnessed a tightening of the social conditions that allowed them to meet

TABLE 2   Major 18th and 19th Century Agrarian Movements/Revolts

Year	Location	Movement/Revolt
1737–1759	North Carolina	Green Corn/Anti-land tax riots
1749	New Jersey	New Jersey Land Riots
1750–1760	New York State	Hudson Valley Tenants Riots
1771	North Carolina	Regulators War
1771	Vermont	Green Mountain Boys
1767–1790	Maine	Liberty Men
1786	Massachusetts	Shays' Rebellion
1787–1795	Pennsylvania	Road Closures
1791–1794	Western Pennsylvania	Whiskey Rebellion
1799–1800	Pennsylvania	Fries Rebellion
1846–1851	Up-State New York	Anti-Rent Movement

most of their reproduction needs on their own. Increasingly the forces of the market were encroaching on their existence. The Revolutionary provocateurs played off of these pressures and fears by claiming it was the British colonial tax burden and control over land and commerce causing struggling farmer problems. Land ownership pressures thus created patriots out of many small to middling farmers (Countryman, 1974, p. 41). In fact, the numerous mid-century land riots were one expression of this pressure – in New Jersey, the Hudson Valley, and Northeastern Vermont especially (Countryman, 1974, p. 40). In New Jersey the link between large land holders and the Royal Crown allowed the pressures of emerging PCP agriculture to fuel anti-British sentiment (Countryman, 1974, p. 40).

In New York it was the presence of the "vestiges of medieval tenant subservience, without the owners offering the physical protection that once had presumably justified such subservience" which fueled colonial era unrest and resentments to "add to the atmosphere of general crisis, the sense of many colonists that something was wrong with the standing order" (Countryman, 1974, p. 41,61). In North eastern New York, in what became Vermont, the Green Mountain Boys connected their struggles for land and self-representation antagonistically with the system seen as connected to royal forms of power; as Ethan Allen put it "God Damn your Governor, Laws, King, Council and Assembly" (quoted in Countryman, 1974, p. 47). A combination of radicalism and nostalgia showed themselves in the land riots, in all three affairs – NJ, NY, and Vermont – "a conjuncture of the themes of private property and individualistic acquisition with those of community and fraternity" prevailed and (Countryman, 1974, p. 53).

Under the pressure of mortgages, declining prices, and an increasing reliance on inputs and technology, farmers began to see their lives transformed. Under these pressures, which were undermining their independent natured existence and clashed with the ideology of the new nation, farmers resisted in various political and non-political movements seeking to push back against the encroaching market dependent existence and the political system advancing it.[2] From the North Carolina Regulators, to the Pennsylvania Whiskey Rebels, from the Shaysites to the White Indians of Maine, there was a familiar farmer's hatred for what they called the 'non-producing class' who threatened farmers with the loss of their one productive asset, their land. Similar struggles also occurred across the west as farmers "from Pennsylvania to Georgia resisted land laws and taxes imposed by their faraway state governments" and these struggles led the federal government to centralize political and juridical power (Stock, 1996, p. 44).

It is the "commodification of subsistence" that was a central dynamic of the transition to petty commodity agriculture which emerges as "peasants become petty commodity producers, who have to produce their subsistence (reproduction) through integration into wider social divisions of labour and markets" (Bernstein, 2010, p. 4). These changes produced agrarian resistance movements and struggles. One of the main theses of this investigation is that the imposing market forces led to farmer resistance which spurred government intervention. These interventions to suppress and control agrarian resistance relied on expanding state institutional capacities that would further facilitate market forces. The New Constitution did not abate the agrarian uprisings, even if it was a necessary part of the process of state building that would be required for the national state institutions to eventually guide these movements toward agro-industrial development.

Beginning with the panic of 1837, the "class politics, [that were] elusive during the Jacksonian years, suddenly became a tenable alternative to single-interest society" (Summerhill, 2005, p. 47). The years that followed witnessed resurgence in farmer's movements increasing their impact on the political landscape. The Jacksonian ideology of limited government and local autonomy prevented the party from enacting policies that would benefit farmers and

---

2 I conceive of farmer or agrarian resistance as both formal organization in form and individual in nature. Resistance to market expansion and its dictates took many forms during this era, ranging from political movements to single farmer acts against what were seen as market forces or representatives of those forces (see Scott, 1985; Kulikoff, 1992).

workers once the panic of 1837 hit.[3] This left a political opening for either the Whigs or another party to emerge, particularly in areas more reliant on agriculture. Absent that, there emerged a growing view that the nature of the state was to help those who least needed help. In particular, the rise of "Anti-renters" in upstate New York in 1839 emerged from a series of political conflicts stemming from the rapid social, political and economic changes. As yeoman, artisans, laborers and even some merchants found common cause in political reforms around debtor relief and land redistribution. The panic of 1837 left landlords squeezed to pay back loans. The decreasing value of railroad stocks caused by the sharp decline in investments in western lands by banks left investors searching for liquidity. Some tried to get more from their tenants by seeking back rents for the first time. Meanwhile, the state sought to offset declining tax revenue on the backs of farmer's by raising their taxes (Summerhill, 2005). The farmers, who had little connection to the cash economy, were therefore pushed into commodification and forced to "accept capital-intensive methods as the only way to succeed in a competitive market" (Summerhill, 2005, p. 169).

The movement became famous for preventing government officials from foreclosing and for the Calico Indian practice of tarring and feathering. The Anti-renters newspaper, *The Advocate*, presented the issues in the form of a tenant labor theory of value which sought to nullify the idea of a benevolent republican gentry, while seeking to connect rural and urban problems through the idea that both landed and financial capital were squeezing citizens. As Anti-renter strength grew and they began to take state offices the Whigs sought an alliance that resulted in the compromise that led to a new New York state constitution. In the compromise the Anti-renters gave up land redistribution for a new constitution which was claimed would expand their rights against the state and landowners. It was through this alliance that the anti-renters helped strengthen the merchants and financiers since the new constitution opened the state up to a frenzy of railroad construction, business speculation, and the expansion of commercial agriculture. Electoral victories at the state and local government level, and the requirements of these office holders led to a split among the Anti-renters and the eventual decline of the movement. This occurred just as Whigs reneged on a law that would have strengthened tenant rights. From then on New York legislatures would mostly ignore Anti-renters demands (Summerhill, 2005). By pulling anti-renters into offices and using the state to favor one fraction of the movement against another, the broad coalition that made up the movement was diminished and ultimately nullified.

---

3   This represents an example of the continual contradiction of agrarians who argue for limited government intervention when it hurts them and state help when it might benefit them.

Where farmers did make some headway in gaining possession of land, the new farmers found themselves thrust into the expanding market place where they would increasingly compete with each other. The Anti-renter desire to strip power over the economy away from the landed interests had led not to increased democratic input over the economy or a preservation of their independence as producers; it had instead placed their fortunes and lives more in the hands of the market. The new state constitution, written as a form of compromise between the movement and other interests, paved the way for the state legislature to pass laws allowing the free charter of banks, rail roads, and other corporations and this put new pressure on farmers to reorient themselves towards cash crops, financed through new debt, further curbing their autonomy (Summerhill, 2005, p. 94). What had been held up by many in the movement as a way forward to victory, the focusing on political engagement and pushing for a new constitution (in which many held out the illusion that there would contain land redistribution), ultimately led to defeat and further subordination to the dictates of the market. What resulted was farm concentration, shifts in crops (toward hops and dairy) and increased marketization. Summerhill (2005, pp. 112–113) summarized this:

> The years 1850 to 1865 therefore left a mixed legacy for central New York farmers. At the beginning of the period, they believed that they could achieve agricultural prosperity based on land ownership, limited market production, and the traditional patriarchal household… Remnants of the gentry and the merchant community used the failure of land reform and new economic powers granted after 1846 to leverage farmers into greater market investment, first through tenancy and later credit relations.

Thus, through a similar process as what had occurred after Shays' Rebellion, Maine Liberty Men, Wild Yankees, Frie's Regulators, and the Whiskey Rebellion, and in a form that would become the recurrent process of US economic development, the Anti-rent movement shifted towards a reformist stance through the democratic process and state projects. The state sided with the merchants and large land owners against the small farmers, only appeasing the small farmers by offering them inclusion into expanded market opportunities. This would be the source of pressure to transition farmers to petty commodity production; occurring through market pressure as free land diminished and state policies to uphold land owners and speculators. The differences that we will see between this process in New York and what would come later on in the

Midwest rests on the degree to which the state relied on market forces to push through change and undermine radical movements.

The Anti-rent movement in New York was distinctive only to the degree of agrarian organization it gave rise to, across the country farmers also resisted changes occurring, albeit most often in a more individualized and inchoate manner. State governments across the Midwest and West, faced with rising interest rates on their accrued debt and increasing difficulties to secure new loans turned to increase land taxes significantly, and set an increasing number of collectors and assessors upon the farmers (Post, 2011, p. 89). This put pressure on farmers to increase their market dependence, generating increased organized farmer resistance. This could be seen in the Claim Associations that developed in numerous frontier locations. Following the example of settlers in Elkhorn Creek, Wisconsin who two decades earlier had formed a 'Claim Club' to protect squatters (which was soon followed by settlers in the town of Yankton, South Dakota), in 1854 the Omaha Claim Club (also called the Omaha Township Claim Association and the Omaha Land Company) was organized for the purpose of protecting members' claims in the area. Although it aimed as well at "encouraging the building of a city" the club was most effective at protecting its members' claims, primarily through the use of "mob violence" to enforce its rule (Sheldon, 1904). Established to offset the land policies of the time and in an effort to give squatters rights to the lands they had improved, the Claim Associations' most successful strategy was to intimidate speculators to keep them from bidding on lands that had been squatted. Usually this was done simply to keep the price low and allow the squatting farmer the opportunity to purchase the land. As farmers continued to form Squatters Claims Clubs they began to make demands for a pre-emption law.

The Pre- emption Act of 1841 had done little however to stem land speculation; indeed the 1850s showed the greatest speculation in US lands in history. Gates maintained that "following 1847 an increasing proportion of land being sold was acquired by speculators... reach [ing] a high point in 1854 and 1855 and continued until 1862" (1960, p. 78). He claimed that "a combination of events in the fifties and the lowering of land prices produced a rush for the public domain that surpassed anything in previous history", Eastern money flowed into the West, as "frantic railroad building, particularly in the upper Mississippi valley, the great influx of Germans, Scandinavians, and Easterners into the west, and a new era of banking experiments which greatly increased available credit all contributed to the demand for land" (Gates, 1960, p. 80). Although speculative ownership peaked by the late 1850s, it would be some time until these lands would be resold to farmers with high interest rates, sometimes over sixty percent.

Land, Debt and Speculation

The three peaks in public land speculation – 1818–1819, 1836, and 1855–56 came with favorable balances of trade from the sale of US food and fiber abroad; loose state banking policies that produced large increases in circulating notes and credit; swells in immigration and westward migration; and for the last peak, extraordinary expenditures of public and private funds for internal improvements (Gates, 1960:70). Following each peak was a depression of prices and a general economic downturn. In the wake of these peaks of speculation there occurred liberalizing land policy changes – highlighted first by the Pre-emption Act of 1841 and then the Homestead Act in 1862 – which correlated with increased farmer resistance and organization, through the claims clubs and emerging farmers' political organizations. Following the downturn of 1857, in particular there emerged a new agrarian radicalism that blamed not only the speculative class that it saw as seeking to exploit the hard work of farmers who had risked all to create something from nothing, but also the federal government, from which they sought relief in the form of new laws, particularly a Homestead Law.

Thus, the waves of booms and busts led to resistance followed by changes in state policies. Despite the close connection of 'merchant-capital' to the state during this period (Gates 1960), the policy of land disposal to directly benefit a well-connected wealthy class would continue to be challenged by the small number of settlers who did acquire land, and with it, limited political power. The price of public land was slowly whittled down both due to political pressure and the deteriorating nature of the available parcels – the price declined from $2 per acre in 1800 to $1.25 in 1820, then down to between $.60 and $1.00 in 1850 to free by 1862 (USDA, 1883). During all of this, there were always money lenders willing to borrow the necessary funds to farmers to allow them the means to own the land they required. Lending money with very high interest rates, while still containing high risks, was less risky than outright speculation in land. Due to laws at the time against usury, lenders often would register claims in their names, thus enabling the lender to either take high interest for his loans – 30–40 percent in the thirties and as high as 120 percent in the fifties – and if a lender proved delinquent the lender simply became yet another speculator who owned land hoping for a higher return than invested (Gates, 1960, p. 73). During times of high prices, these loans were rushed into by farmers. However, during downturns the situation proved disastrous for both farmers and lenders as the means to pay disappeared and the value of land decreased while the availability of cheap land increased. Thus, we see how the goals of the agrarian movement to alter land policy often occurred within forms of reform that would ultimately undermine their goals by imbricating them in market dependent relationships.

This same process could also be witnessed in the federal government's move to alleviate the situation of the agrarian class in 1850 with the passage of the Swamp Land Act. It authorized the donation of 64 million acres to the states in the expectation that their governments would supply drainage, improve the lands and then sell them to willing farmers. Instead, the states for the most part turned the land over to private interests, who sold it below minimum land prices and often without any drainage or other improvements (Gates, 1960, p. 73). Whether by design or default, the Act once again fortified elite and speculative ownership of land over small farmers. These both raised farmland prices and increased the debt of farmers.

The geographical divide between the interests of merchants and even farmers in the east and the desire for more cheap land and less speculation called for by those in the west, as documented by Stephenson, persisted right up until the eve of the Civil War (1917). Western settlers regarded the current laws as beneficial to speculators, who due to the policies of the time and the undeveloped nature of their holdings, paid very low taxes, resulting in state budget shortages and higher taxation on farmers (Gates, 1973). Growing political power in the west and the requirement to build coalitions with both the East and the South led to a slow march toward land policy reform. The pre-emption law of 1841 satisfied the West for a short time, but after the increase in the public domain following the Mexican-American War, Western land reform agitation once again increased (Stephenson, 1917, p. 249).

The actually existing land policy was one that expanded federal revenue by selling off land not in a slow and coordinated effort that resulted in increased ownership of land by farmers, but one that encouraged first high prices, second large sales, and third resulted in political favors such as railroad development. Land releases to special interests peaked with land grants to railroad developers. This underlines the general pattern as described by Henry George in 1871, whereby "of the 447,000,000 acres of government land disposed of, not 100,000,000 had passed directly into the hands of farmers" (p. 15). Despite this, the political rhetoric and dominant ideology was of great opportunity for common folks to get free land, work hard and improve it, and thus receive the rewards themselves. While the actual process tended to involve speculative ownership, and only after, sales to individual farmers and with high interest rates. Even in regards to state policy, the objective was always claimed reform to aid farmers, but for the most part it turned out to be as much or even more of a boom to banks and mortgage financiers than to farmers.

As Stephenson argues, any victory by Western land reformers pulled against the interests of other powerful political forces, with capitalists, eastern laborers, merchants and southern plantation owners all pulling in disparate directions (1971). The result was a disappointing compromise that caused the development of an active state whose job, as Madison had outlined, came to be to balance class forces over the issue of land policy. This process of state capacity building once again played a vital role in massaging political movements into a form amendable to the interests of speculators and capitalists.

Canal and Railroad Policy

Canal building brought about significant declines in transportation costs for Midwestern agricultural products. In the Midwest by 1835 canals had reduced the cost of transporting grain down to one to two cents per ton-mile compared with 15 cents per ton-mile for wagon loads (North, 1961, p. 111). While the development of inter-sectional canals was first to occur, connecting the Midwest to the eastern markets, it was the intra-regional canals that created the greatest impact in opening up large areas of commercial transactions. The Erie in New York, first developed in 1825 and expanded and improved for the next few decades was the first major intra-regional canal. Ohio developed the first major successful canal system in the Midwest with a 917 mile system that opened up over 18,000 square miles of farmland by the mid-1840s for commercial exploitation by creating a one day round trip connection to markets for farmers (Meyer, 1989, p. 927). This was followed by the Wabash in Indiana, and the Illinois and Michigan Canals which were all completed by 1848 (Taylor, 1950). Similar impacts on efficient market access accompanied the Wabash, Erie, Illinois, and Michigan canals (Meyer, 1989). Government expenditures on the canal systems reduced the cost and time of travel for agricultural commodities, thereby linking simple commodity producers with distant markets for the first time.

Between 1830 and 1840 the city of Chicago sought to construct a canal and protect it with piers on either side. The city convinced the Federal Government to fund the project and the US Government invested a quarter of a million dollars to dredge and maintain the canal, which would allow large cargo ships to enter the port (Cronon, 1991). Overall, this created a huge advantage for Chicago as large ships could now come to port. This federal investment would influence economic activity and future projects, partially solidifying Chicago's future as the Midwestern hub city for the export of raw materials and agricultural goods. The changes in Chicago that occurred between 1840 and the end of the Century were directly influenced by this federal investment which focused and gave a boost to the economic activity of the city as a transportation hub linking the Midwest, west and the East.

The work of Canal building set to remake the Midwest through the agro-industrial process by which markets were created and enhancing market dependence. As Nemi summarized "if the canals worked as developmental instruments, as most certainly seems to be the case, given the distribution of population and labor force in the period before 1820, then their role was one, not of integrating markets, but rather of creating markets" (1970, p. 504). The canal process was one of the initial geneses of agro-industrialization it sparked the creation of markets for other commodities in a relationship with the newly expanding shipping of agricultural commodities, while also stimulating agricultural expansion. In Ohio counties with canal, five years after the canals were built, the percent change of total economic activity accounted for by agriculture declined by 15.2 percent, while manufacturing and commerce increased by 58.2 and 271.4 percent respectively (Nemi, 1970, p. 507). As production and transport costs were reduced in agriculture, the stimulus to ancillary industrial production produced expansion greater than in agriculture itself. Comparing the Ohio counties with canals with the non-canal counties, we can make the case even stronger that the development of the canals led to increased overall economic activity. This reveals how the markets for consumer goods and the development of a specialized industrial manufacturing sector of agricultural implements occurred through a process of state supported market creation. As Nemi put it: "...rather than fostering a concentration on the primary sector, the direct stimulus seems to have been to encourage activities intended to satisfy demand in the newly developing areas" (Nemi, 1970, p. 511). Comparatively there is a lack of development of ancillary industries in other regions which are absent the state created transportation system or other means of state support to construct a market for agricultural commodities. This helps to explain the scale of Midwestern development relative to the prior development in the East.

Canals were financed by a mix of private and public funds. However, most of the private investors understood the significant grants, tax breaks, and other forms of state support that hid behind the veil of private ownership. Overall, the canal system that developed was the second wave of massive state investment, following land policy, in the facilitation of expanding commerce. All told four million acres were granted for the construction of various wagon roads, and another four and a half million for the construction of canals; but by far the largest grants were to railroads, beginning in 1850, when six sections per mile, or in all 2.6 million acres, were granted for the construction of the Illinois Central road (George, 1904, p. 20). – "the amount given to these companies within the last ten years (1850–1860) aggregating nearly one half as much as all the public lands disposed of in other ways since the formation of the Government" (George, 1904, pp. 19–20).

Railroads quickly surpassed canals for volume of goods and replaced the canal systems soon after its completion, by the early-to mid-1860s. Having tried and failed at direct state funded rail projects, most states turned to grants of land and municipal securities to railroad corporations who built the rails, which became the norm after the 1830s. This innovation in public-private partnerships undergirds the later processes of monopolization and the specific nature of rail development, as land grants and very large sections of the west fell under control of the newly formed railroad companies (many formed for the specific intent to get land grants and then transfer ownership to its board members and disband as a unit).

The impact of the railroad system after 1850 in opening up vast areas not reached by the canal systems cannot be over-stated, as the amount of railroad track in the Midwest jumped from just 1000 miles to over 10,000 miles during the 1850s alone (Fishlow, 1965). However, the growth of rail lines did more to increase intra-Midwest trade of goods than to produce inter-regional US trade due to the lack of an integrated East–west rail network prior to 1880 – emerging mostly because of the largely private and unplanned development that led to gauge differences, gaps between lines, unbridged rivers, and uncoordinated freight movements.

Large land grants to the railroads represent the third, major involvement of the US Federal government in aiding in the construction of capitalist markets and creating agricultural modernization through the agro-industrial project. The Illinois Central Railroad received a grant of 2.6 million acres of land to aid in the construction of a central railroad through the heart of Illinois, which Gates called "the greatest capitalistic enterprise in the West at the time" (1973, p. 264). After the Civil War, with southern obstructionism removed, Congress quickly set to grant land for the building of the transcontinental line, the key infrastructural foundation for a fully national market for agricultural goods. All told the legislation to create this line provided 2,720 miles of right-of-way and surrendered 34.5 million acres of public land to private hands (Opie, 1987). The granting of power to the Railroad was greatly increased in 1865 when the General Land Office granted the Burlington and Missouri Railroad free range "over the nation's entire public domain: the company could select land from geographically distant regions unrelated to the railroad lines" (Opie, 1987, p. 76). This combined with the military bounties and grants to states of land doomed wet, swampy or in an overflow area, and led to the end of the era of public domain in Illinois years prior to the enactment of the Homestead Act

(Gates, 1973). With free land to work with, the Illinois Central Railroad could hold out for the highest possible price for its huge tracts of land, often seeking $5–$10 per acre for its better land (Gates, 1934). Many farmers who took the railroad terms were hammered by the 1857 downturn and ended up taking very small parcel settlements in return for back rent payments, which rendered them unable to meet their needs through farming alone or meant borrowing more money to purchase more land (Gates, 1934).

Alfred Chandler (1965) outlined the concentration in railroads and the railway supply industry in the wake of the 1837 crisis, as those that survived concentrated they required financial innovations to fund their larger scale investments, projects and purchases, in a climate of tighter credit. One such innovation was in the development of note brokerage that began to draw some merchants away from buying and selling goods and into buying and selling specialized notes, which became indispensable to manufactures (Porter and Livesay, 1971). An example is the railroad supply industry, which before the 1837 crisis was made up of mostly small, localized producers, but after the crisis, with its concentrating and eliminating effect, left the railroad supply industry as an important site of innovative in the area of finance (Porter and Livesay, 1971). The financial innovations that emerged in the railroad supply industry, due to the consolidation and requirements to control for risk after the crises, were the sales of securities for self-finance and direct sales, through traveling salesmen, without middlemen (Porter and Livesay, 1971).

With renewed railway construction, one of the first industries to recover after the crisis due to the heavy state investment, as this period ranks second only to the major land grant push for new rail lines of the 1850–1860 era and there occurred another general boom. Other industries would lag behind railroad supplies, but would come to adapt, build on and innovate off these new methods. This reveals the path of development through state intervention, crisis, and more state intervention towards the initial development of Midwestern industrial production.

Early State Involvement in Agriculture

Absent a large Federal government role in the economy in the pre-Civil War era, individual states were more involved in the development of markets and in the assistance to private enterprises, including agriculture. State Warehouses were some of the earliest ways individual states got involved in agricultural marketing. States also spent funds researching solutions to common agricultural pests (Shannon, 1960). In the late 1830s, both Maine and Massachusetts paid farmers a bounty, basically a subsidy, to grow wheat in an effort to stop the trend of its declining production and prevent a reliance on importation from neighboring states (Pabst, 1940). There was also state funded research into the production of silk during the boom, and Massachusetts sought to stimulate sugar beet production through a similar bounty. When the Pleuropneumonia epidemic struck Cattle in 1859, the Massachusetts Governor called a special session of the state legislature and "never before had government moved so swiftly and so effectively to meet a calamity" (Shannon, 1960, p. 318). Public warehouses were funded across the South for tobacco storage, the State of New York set up an inspection system for flour that was to be shipped to other countries, and Louisiana and Kentucky established state standards and inspections for meat packing (Shannon, 1960). These actions at the individual state level brought "farmers' issues out into the open, to marshal support for common ends and to exert influence on the federal government on behalf of measures designed to aid specific interests" which led to the idea that "the government should aid agriculture through grants to farmers' education, experimental work, the collection of agricultural statistics, and distribution of new seeds and plants" (Shannon, 1960, p. 321).

I was southern planters who first urged the Federal government to get involved directly in agriculture, with the first programs beginning at the behest of tobacco and cotton producers who were seeking lower tariffs. When the demand for bat guano became an eight million dollar per year industry, the Federal government looked into using the Navy to make a claim to the Peruvian island of Lobos. In 1836 through the agitation of farm association journals – one, the Cultivator stating that "Agriculture should be patronized by the Government" – the US patent office began surveying methods to improve agricultural production (Shannon, 1960, p. 272). This included studies by entomologists, and discussions of the best varieties of crops. Commencing in 1837 the United States Patent Office began to distribute seeds and plants of species new or rare (Harding, 1947). The move was favorably received, and in 1839 Congress began to support the work with small appropriations and a designated Division of Agriculture was organized in the Patten Office, which was moved to the Department of the Interior in 1849.

In the 1840s as commissioner of the Agricultural Department of the Patent Office Henry Leavitt Ellsworth saw the future in mechanized agriculture and the development of seeds with higher yields (Harding, 1947, p. 9). He encouraged hybrid seed development in an effort to increase the productivity, believing that a twenty percent increase would raise farmer incomes by $15–20 million annually (Harding, 1947, p. 10). Ellsworth's approach, and his overall influence on the development of government agricultural intervention, rested on pushing an ever increasing productivity on agriculture, effectively involving what Bernstein outlines as a transition from "farming" to "agriculture" (Bernstein, 2010). Ellsworth was able to convince Congress of the benefit of this approach, leading to its first allocation for agriculture – at least apart from that used for land and money spent to maintain the property of slave owners – of $1000 in 1839, a sum which would triple by 1845 (Harding, 1947, p. 10).

By the early 1840s, Ellsworth was using Congressional funds in a drive to create sugar out of corn, thereby encouraging the process of turning crops into commodities that could be used for a larger variety of food inputs, which came to form a major part of the later agro-industrial project emanating out of the USDA. Ellsworth advanced the goal of expanding foreign agricultural markets, including the sponsoring of a study on the effects of the British Corn Laws on US crop exports (Harding, 1947, p. 11). This too would later be a constant concern of the USDA. Recognizing this should dispel the notion that trade promotion by the state only came once massive surpluses were created through government programs after the New Deal. Instead the USDA orientation was always based in an agro-industrial project that included expanding exports and foreign market creation as part of the process of modernized agriculture.

These early government interventions, although arising from farmer advocacy groups, were used as the means to push a specific type of agriculture. Horace Greeley was among the early critics of federal involvement and one of the first to locate the states drive toward agro-industrialization emerging from federal involvement (Shannon, 1960). As Gates (1960) affirmed about Greeley's critique of the Federal project to control and direct agricultural production:

> Horace Greeley maintained that the Agricultural Branch of the Patent Office, by spending taxpayers' money in compiling material for the annual volume, and printing, binding, and conveying hundreds of thousands of copies of it to people in all parts of the country, was undermining and threatening to destroy by unfair competition the agricultural press (pp. 332–334).

Despite these and other critics of the Federal involvement, Congress increased the appropriations for the Patent Office agricultural work by 250 percent between 1847 and 1857 (USDA 1935). By the mid-1850s, a short 15 years after the initial funding, the congressional allocation to the agricultural Department of the Patent Office had risen to $35,000, from its meager $1000 in 1840 (Harding, 1947).

It is clear that the early work of Ellsworth set the federal government's involvement down a path of pursuing agricultural technology for productivity gains as the solution to farmer's problems. In the 1862 Agricultural Division of the Patent Office Manual the main focus is the call for scientific investigations and the improvement of agricultural tools to improve production. This early work would lead to other problems for agriculture as it was transformed to fit within a capitalist social production system. The need for increased access to credit for farmers, along with the chosen federal land policy favoring speculation to drive up land prices, is a clear result of this focus on developing and spreading agricultural technology. The policy approached by early state intervention resulted in merely shifting problems and contradictions while promoting an industrial capitalist agriculture. Early state funded research into agriculture sought its modernization through new techniques, tools and seeds. Frustrated farmers adopted these as an attempt to maintain their ownership of their farm and some semblance of independence.

In 1852 when the United States Agricultural Society (USAS) was formed, Daniel Lee, favorably known to farmers across the country as editor of the periodical the Genesee Farmer, was elected secretary of the new advocacy group. Lee served as secretary of the society during its formative period, as the Society sought to push greater state involvement in agriculture (Carrier, 1937, p. 284). The near single purpose of this organization, the USAS, was to lobby for the establishment of a stand-alone department of agriculture. The opening salvo of its literature proclaimed "this society would not solicit but demand the establishment of what they believed to be their rights... they should not solicit anybody, not even Congress" (USAS Journal, 1860). "The evidence would also seem to justify the conclusion that without the support given to the bill by an influential national organization such as the United States Agricultural Society there would have been little, if any, likelihood of its passage" (Carrier, 1937, pp. 283–284). The USAS was mostly comprised of wealthy farmers, and early on most common farmers resisted its influence and that of the wealthy landowners and gentlemen farmers through the US government funding (Kloppenburg, 2004:58; Gates, 1960:313; Danbom, 1979: 17). There was also a geographic split emerging around support for state funded research centered on eastern farmers issues focused on soil fertility and their increasing integration into markets, which differed from the main concerns of the South, still locked out of agro-industrial development (Kloppenburg, 2004, p. 59). Here we witness a growing sectional divide that arose out of the uneven development of capitalist agriculture in the US, as the North and the South's natural crop differences combined with their different production models were pulling the state in different directions. In 1856, after the House of Representatives proposed appropriation of funds to the Patent Office's agricultural branch for obtaining cuttings and seeds to collect agricultural statistics, a sectional debate over government support erupted as

> ... strict constructionists from Missouri, Virginia, Arkansas, Kentucky, and Georgia opposed the item, while northern representatives from Pennsylvania, Indiana, Maine, and New York favored it. Later, in the same session, an appropriation of $75,000 was voted for the identical purpose but without discussion...the Pierce Administration seemed to favor the use of enlarged appropriation for the encouragement of the cultivation of tea and, more important, the improvement of the sugar industry, neither offering anything to the North.
> GATES 1960, pp. 325–326; See also HARDING, 1947

The Patent Office was transferred to the Department of the Interior in 1849 with a separate agricultural division and eventually in 1862 the Agricultural Division of the Patent Office was elevated to a separate Department of Agriculture (True, 1929). This left the Patent Office free to focus on other industrially produced products. The action of the Federal Patent Office played a large role in not only the development of the industrial system of manufacturing but also in the geographical patterning of industrial production sites (Nemi, 1987).[4]

The key resolution passed in 1857 by USAS in the push for a national department to be created read as follows: "That the United States Agricultural Society appoint a Committee of five, to memoiralize [sic] Congress, asking in the name of the Farmers of the Republic the organization of a Department of Agriculture, with a Secretary at its head entitled to a seat and a voice in the Cabinet" (USAS Journal, 1856). And indeed, it was shortly after this, "to avert the storm of protest that was being directed at the Patent Office, the Secretary of the Interior proposed in his annual report for 1858 that a bureau of agriculture separate from the Patent Office be created in his Department" (Carrier, 1937, p. 286). This recommendation put strong political influence on Congress, and the United States Department of Agriculture was soon finally created (see Chapter 5) with a commissioner at its head who was directly responsible to the President of the United States. Farmer's influence on the direction of institutional capacity development in the US going forward would take on a particularly direct role through the expansion of the USDA.

---

4 Nemi argued "patents played a central role in the development and location of farm machinery production during the workshop/manufacture stage, specifically because of the ways patents contributed to the industry's competitive structure" (1987, p. 215).

At the behest of what was originally a small group of agricultural advocates for vocational education and against the general desire for a limited government role by most farmers at the time, the first rudimentary forms of agricultural education began to appear in the mid-1840s. The original push for scientific research to aid agriculture mostly came in the form of ways to modernize agriculture and adapt it to industrial forms: specialization, increased scale, and mechanization. To the detriment of any attempt to create a market for private seeds, the US Patent Office would distribute over 1 million seed packets by 1855 (Kloppenburg, 2004, p. 56). The new plant varieties which were developed through government research or acquired from outside the US through government funds, were largely tested by farmers on their plots after being highlighted at seed fairs and through agricultural education programs. Eventually this agricultural education program would expand into a major political and become the central projects to overcome radical agrarian movements connecting farmers with the state and introducing them to commodity markets for both inputs and the outputs from their farms. This also acted to construct authority in the state in the expertise of agricultural production while convincing farmers that their problems arose out of a lack of productivity rather than economic relationships. It advocated for technological fixes to socio-economic problems.

There was also a substantial shift in legal structures that aided in the facilitation of the emergence of industrial capitalism during the mid-19th Century. The economic transformation of an agrarian into an industrial capitalist society posed hard problems for the law and its inherited doctrine of property rights (Morton, 1951). There was an increasing autonomy of the legal profession, changes in the doctrine of eminent domain, an increase in the power of judges relative to juries, and a shift in protection of property away from small to large holders, or a general "forging of an alliance between legal and commercial interests" (Horwitz, 1977, p. 140). The forging of these types of alliances appeared as legal shifts in the economy and were perceived by many as 'non-political' in their push for economic development of an industrial capitalist kind.

Agro-Industrial Development

The other major component to the agro-industrial project was the development of the means to industrially produce the needed machinery to mechanize agriculture. The development of industrial production that emerges in the Midwest is equal partner in the co-development of industry and agriculture. This co-development process really starts to come into its own in the Midwest between 1850 and 1865. By this time the Western and Midwestern US came to manufacture almost half (48.4%) of the total US production of implements and machinery geared toward agriculture (Nemi, 1987, p. 19). It was these technological advances in agriculture that led to the decreasing price pressure that enhanced the market incentives towards industrial agriculture. Deeper analysis also shows that not only was the Midwest rapidly increasing its manufacturing of agricultural machines and implements in the 1850s–1860s but that it also contributed to national value added in a few other areas – namely resource processing industries such as lumber and wood products, flour and meal, liquors, and packing house products (Nemi, 1987, p. 5,8,13) Confirming this agro-industrial co-developmental process is the fact that a large amount of the total products produced in any specific industry were produced for local markets (Nemi, 1987, p. 19). The notion that industrial capitalist transition of the Midwest was complete by the 1860s is not confirmed in Nemi's work, which involves comparing the level of industrial development in 1860 to that in 1900 by region and state. Nemi's data revealed that the major transition to industrial capitalism in the Midwest comes after the Civil War. In Illinois the manufactured value added to food products increased from $8,074,900 in 1860 to $132,268,000 in 1900 (Nemi, 1987, pp. 114–120). Similarly, the production of non-electric machinery increased from $1,552,000 in 1860 to $47,360,000 in 1900 and transportation equipment grew from a mere $954,000 to over $22,000,000 in the same period (Nemi, 1987, pp. 114–120). Therefore the process of agro-industrial development, while beginning in the 1840s, takes off only in the 1850s and has its largest growth in the 1860s, 70s and through to the 19th Century, that it really gains steam. This coincided with the already mentioned transition to market dependence for farm product sales, which also occurred after 1850 in much of the Midwest (North, 1961, pp. 146–53).

To take food production, as an example, it witnessed one of the greatest increases in capital investment in the Midwest, after 1860 (Figure 1). Meyer confirmed the point claiming that: "industrial growth accelerated somewhat after the mid-1840s as both the intra- and interregional railroad network improved, but there was little shift from primary to secondary activity by 1840" (1989, p. 922). The key period of Midwestern industrial development was between 1860 and 1880, during which absolute and percentage increases in manufacturing employment occurred – growth in employment climbed 283 percent (Meyer, 1989, p. 923). Furthermore, the Midwest's share of the nation's food manufacturing increased dramatically during the 1860s (Figure 2).

Midwestern firms had a window of opportunity to develop ahead of Eastern firms due to these factors and their development relied more extensively on new innovations uniquely situated to take advantage of the situation. The specific nature of state policies and the particularities of their development in

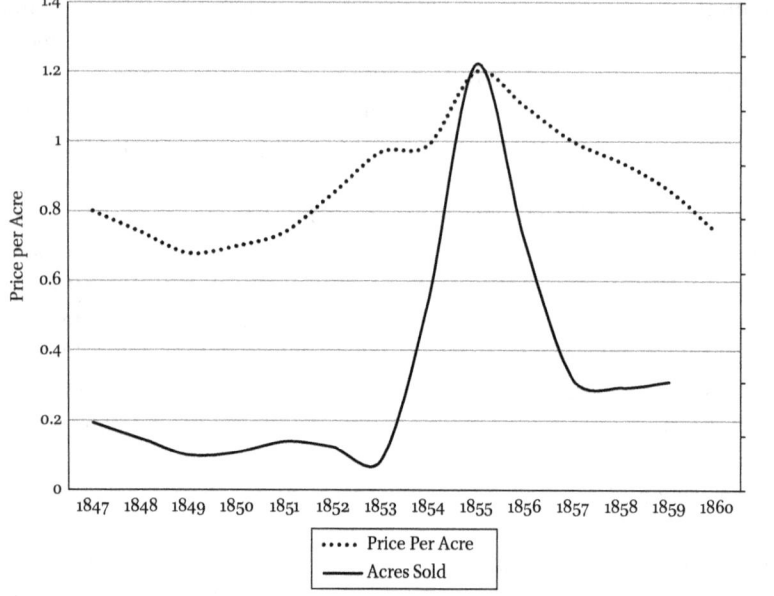

FIGURE 1   Public land sales per year by price and acres sold: 1847–1860
SOURCE: GATES 1968, 28, 278

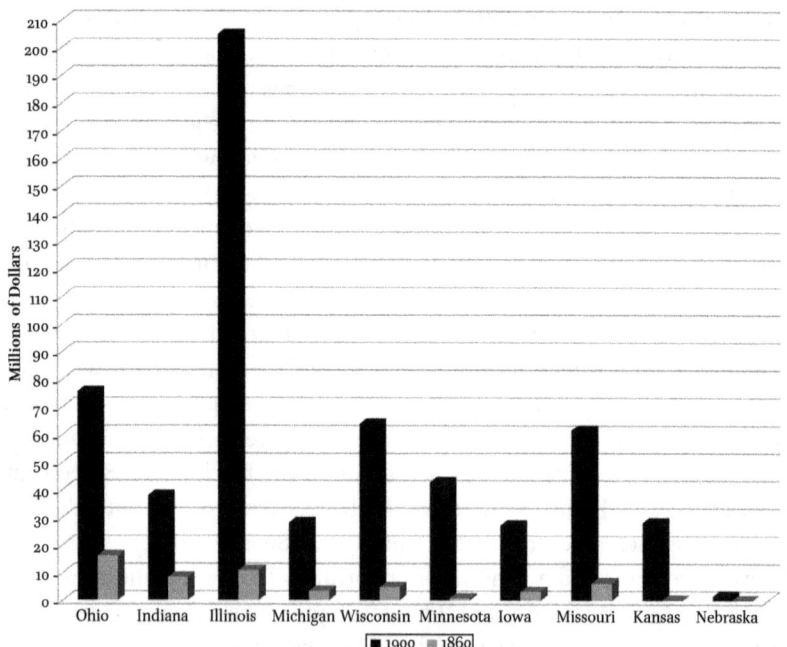

FIGURE 2   Capital invested in food manufacturing: 1860 and 1900
SOURCE: USDA, 1934

concert with the transformation of agriculture in the Midwest marked different trajectory and produced a distinct speed of transformation. Midwestern total factor productivity grew at annual rates of 2.1 percent from 1820 to 1850 and 2.4 percent from 1850 to 1860, while labor productivity grew at annual rates of 2.3 percent from 1820 to 1850 and 3.2 percent from 1850 to 1860 (Meyer, 1989, p. 923). It was these very revolutions in production which were fueled by a shift in agricultural production towards petty commodity relations. This shift was the effect of the forces of commodification and the resistance to it by farmers, combined with the very nature of the western geography and the natural proclivities of agriculture that required capital penetration up and down stream of production.

Page and Walker argue that capitalism spread into the Midwest because resistance was "little developed" thus giving the balance of class forces "a new face" from that in the East (1991, p. 282). However, it wasn't the weak resistance by farmers but rather the strength of their resistance requiring the entire apparatus of the state to develop new institutional forms and actively work to shift the balance away from agrarians and towards industrialists and merchants. Unlike in the earlier examples of Shays' Rebellion, the Whiskey Rebellion, and the Anti-Renters, where eruptions of violence ended quickly as farmers were easily forced into new forms of agriculture in the Midwest, where the farmer's strength required greater state intervention. While the farmer social movements did not as organized did not take on an as organized form in the Midwest during this era, due in part to the disbursed nature of land settlement and isolation of farmers, they were much more numerous and constituted a large portion of the population. This, along with their larger role in the overall economy, combined to give these farmers more political weight than farmers in the East had earlier.

There is also ample data to show that during this period there was overall, and even more specifically in the Midwest, a movement towards more localized markets for manufactured goods (Nemi, 1987, p. 59). The distinct model of Midwestern development lies in the relationship between industry and agriculture, and between agriculture and markets. Already by the middle of the 19th Century in New England and the mid-Atlantic regions over 40 percent of the population lived in cities, with the agricultural areas serving the needs of the urban centers. In the Midwest, however, where less than 20 percent of the population was as yet urbanized, the cities grew in relation to and depended upon the agriculture and natural resources surrounding them (Sanders, 1999, p. 16). The distinction is important for an understanding of the process of agro-industrialization. The Midwest cities grew more out of the needs of the rural agrarians – the need for specialized tools and implements, and home products – or in a symbiotic, co-developmental relationship (Page and Walker,

1991, p. 1). The sheer size of farms in the Midwest dwarfed those in the East, which combined with a lack of labor and contributed to the need for mechanization. This is confirmed by the data on the increase in localization of manufacturing between 1860 and 1900 in the Midwestern dominated industries: a decrease in interregional trade in the manufactured products dominated by the Midwest from 22 to 14 percent (Nemi, 1987, pp. 19–21).

Related to technological development was the movement towards specialization that occurred in the Northeast and the diversification that was occurring during this phase in the Midwest (Nemi, 1987, pp. 45–46). A small group of eastern states dominated interstate export of manufactured goods in 1860, with Massachusetts, Rhode Island, Connecticut, New York, New Jersey, and Pennsylvania generating over 75 percent of the interregional export of manufactured goods in all but a few industries (Nemi, 1987, p. 59). The northeast region actually increased its share of total manufacturing value added from 14.3% in 1860 to over a quarter of all US manufacturing, 25.9%, by 1900 (Nemi, 1974, p. 16). Thus, the Midwestern industrialization occurred in a regionally based manner that produced a unique diversification due to the lack of early, pre-1860s, connection between Eastern and Midwestern markets.

William Cronon (1991) has shown how this diversification arose in Chicago around the grain elevators and stockyards, with the emergence of restaurants, hotels, bars, general stores and brothels locating themselves near these agricultural processing industries and having their economic lifeblood tied to them, or as Louis Hacker recognized, American agriculture as the "cats-paw for our industrial capitalism" for the same reason (1980, p. 399). This development of local industrial production to meet the needs of an increasingly market dependent and commodified agriculture increased pressure not only on those remnants of simple commodity production in the region but also those farmers in neighboring and even nearby regions. Therefore the development of petty commodity production for a portion of the farms in the area spurred industrial production of farm inputs and processing of farm products, which acted as a stimulus for further development of other farms and eventually a majority of farms were operating in a manner informed by market imperatives serving productivity advances.

The market for agricultural implements was central to the industrial development process. There was virtually no market for wheat reapers in the Midwest prior to 1855 and the history of the development of the reaper market shows the long and protracted process of creating, developing and expanding this market (Headlee, 1991; Cronon, 1991; Gates, 1973). One specific aspect of this was the innovation of using credit to allow farmers to purchase farm machinery developed by the McCormick Corporation. This innovation in credit emerged alongside McCormick's discovery that they had to develop an entirely new form of marketing to sell the large and expensive product. McCormick formed a team of agents who would take the machines to county fairs and courthouse squares and offer demonstrations on the use of the mechanical reaper (Cronon, 1991; Henderson, 1998; Gates, 1973).

Mechanical reapers were also too large and heavy to transport, making their transportation to farms scattered across the vast prairies expensive prior to the railroad system development. This system didn't reach deep into farm country until after 1854 when it finally crossed the Mississippi River and subsequently the distribution of the reapers spread out rapidly (Cronon, 1991). It wasn't until after 1855 that McCormick began to sell more than 3000 reapers per year, in a nation with over 4 million farms (Headlee, 1991, p. 81). Furthermore, the production of the reaper and its widespread purchase by farmers did not rely on the previous adoption of the profit motive and capital expansion as the main driving force behind the majority of Midwestern farms (Mann, 1990, pp. 28–46; Post, 2011, p. 96). Instead, it was one of the means by which, through the taking of credit to purchase the machines and to expand the area of production, farmers adopted a petty commodity production approach (Headlee, 1991). Some subsistence farming did continue to exist and was mixed with these market sales and equipment purchases during this period. This means that the developments of the production and marketing techniques of McCormick aided farmers while also increasing market dependence through the innovations in credit and the development of the delivery system and farmer education around their use in production.

The evidence to back up the claim that petty commodity production everywhere preceded the industrial developments in the Midwest seems to be absent. Instead, we see state intervention fueling the developments of industrial products for, and with, agricultural products at the same time, and these changes proved instrumental to the farmers transitioning to a petty commodity existence. Innovations in industrial production, credit, transportation, and farming were all part of the transition to petty commodity production and the commodification of agricultural.

Further evidence can be seen in the fact that during the 1860s the bulk of the economic gains were in the major metro areas, which were relatively better situated within the existing transportation system. The twenty largest cities in the Midwest's industrial employment grew on average 144.6 percent for the decade of the 1860s, with three cities growing by more than 400 percent while this growth slows to 60.5 percent in the next decade, without any growing more than 200 percent (Gates, 1973). With only one exception – Minneapolis – all of these rapidly growing industrial centers were railroad hubs. Agreeing with Page and Walker, Meyer argues that despite the conventional portrayal, the Midwest was not merely a raw materials processing center, but instead was a highly diversified industrial production area (1989). There were many factors that limited the ability of Midwestern manufactures from expanding and selling in a wider market and that kept a lot of Eastern manufactured goods out of the Midwest (Meyer, 1989). Among them are: lack of efficient transportation system; closeness to raw materials, underdeveloped marketing and wholesale industries.

Here we can delineate some clear similarities and differences in the process of agro-industrialization in different areas, especially if we compare this Midwestern form from that which occurred earlier, in New York and Massachusetts for example. While in the later agro-industrial development – exemplified in the Midwestern US – we see the state engaged in propping up aspects of the market as the means to address the movements and to increase the commodification and industrialization of farms through more totalizing reliance on markets for both inputs and goods. In the earlier New York case it was more about setting up a rudimentary form of petty commodity agriculture. In the latter, we see the development of technology, the increased investment in canal projects and the state-led development of new crop markets incorporated a larger and more resistant group of farmers.

The limited reach of the federal government and the lack of federal investment in infrastructure in the Midwest prior to the 1850s determined the timing of the transition to petty commodity production as farmers were compelled to improve by the logic of the market to increase productivity and total output through increasing land holdings and purchasing farm inputs and implements. These changes led to downward pressure on farm commodity prices, further compelling farmers to improve and commercialize their operations. Therefore the market imperative to become petty commodity producers was maintained and strengthened through these changes in federal policies. Prior to the revolutions in mechanical agriculture and home items, some of these farmers were connected to markets, and therefore came under the market imperatives to compete in the marketplace, however the agro-industrial development that really took off after 1850 in the Midwest went further, forcing even more farms into commodified forms of production, as well as removing the last strongholds and vestiges of the notion of household production. As Page and Walker made clear, the industrial processing and producing, occurring up and down the production chain, proceeded as quickly as the developments on the farms themselves in changing the nature of the farmer's relationship with the market (1991, p. 11). Post's 'Merchant-capital' does indeed play a significant role in the transition to petty commodity production. However, it is doubtful that this "subordination of self-organized commodity-production to the dictates of the law of value, through the activities of merchant-capital and merchant-sponsored state-policies, had been completed by the late 1830s" as he claims (2011, p. 24). Instead it appears to have been just beginning in much of the Midwestern and Western United States and would continue through to the 1870s.

There are legions of examples of the differentiation of agricultural production and the commodification of agricultural products that occurs in the Midwest following the 1850s. Cronon uses the example of corn to make the point about the industrial innovations occurring that could turn raw materials into industrial products through agro-industrialization: "corn in particular becomes more profitable in its travels by undergoing an alchemical transmutation into denser, more valuable substances: kegs filled with whisky or animals that could carry themselves to market" (1998, p. 208). Flour milling is also exemplary in revealing this process, as it tended to lead the agro-industrialization process: between 1850 and 1860, it was the nation's leading industry in terms of the total value of products produced; in 1860 its capital to output ratio exceeded that of all other manufacturing by two to one; productivity per workers was likewise twice that of manufacturing as a whole (Fishlow, 1964). On the input side, agricultural machine manufacturing grew by 1870 to account for 25.5 percent of the value added of all US manufacturing (Pudup, 1987). This makes clear how a great deal of the large increases in the industrial markets for agricultural inputs and outputs really began to take hold of agriculture in the second half of the 19th Century.

If we take Chicago and the area around it as an example, we see this process of agro-industrialization, or the co-development of petty commodity agriculture and industrial production at play. Against Turner (1920), we need to see cities not as the end of the frontier, but as growing in a symbiotic relationship with them. The major developments in and around Chicago – specifically the development of railroad tracks, shipping canals, roads, and the industrial capacity to process the material resources of the surrounding prairies – were barely even started prior to the crisis of 1837. Some, including a major canal project and railroad project were planned and cancelled because of the crisis, if only to re-emerge in the 1840s. Despite this relatively late start, by 1852 over half of the city's wheat arrived from the farms around by the two major rail lines built in the 1840s (Cronon, 1991). It was after that, 1852 when two rails finally linked by direct route Chicago to New York City. We shouldn't underestimate the impact of railroads to transform, as one Chicagoan stated:

> [R]ailroads are talismanic wands. They have a charming power. They do wonders – they work miracles. They are better than laws; they are essentially, politically and religiously – the pioneer, and vanguard of civilization.
> quoted in CRONON, 1991, p. 72

They also quickly surpassed the canal system around the city that was completed only a few decades before. These new lines decreased the travel time from New York City to Chicago from 3 weeks to 2 days between 1830 and 1857 (Cronon, 1991, p. 76). The railroads were uniquely supported by non-civic capital with much of it from the East and Europe. However, this does not relinquish state involvement as most railroads did depend on some Federal support in the way of land grants. To entice the building of railroad lines, there occurred a restructuring of land policies regarding the plot size and surveys, as well as infrastructure requirements (Gates, 1934). Although rail dominance in the Midwest around Chicago, in in linking Chicago to the West was already in place by the Civil War, around 90 percent of wheat that was traveling east from there still traveled by water in the antebellum era (Cronon, 1991).

More important is the fact that even at mid-century the movement of wheat, corn and other cereal crops was done without disrupting the link between grain as a physical object and grain as a saleable commodity. It was moved in bags that kept the individual, distinct qualities of the specific grain connected to the individual farm that produced it. So although farmers were selling their products as commodities they had yet not been fully commodified, at least not in an industrial sense, which shows the degree to which farmers still asserted some control over the quality and price. This control could not be fully dissolved until grain grading and mixing became the norm.

The revolution in grain trade that would in part usher in the second industrial revolution occurred through the transformation of grain into a commodity. This reveals the general process of the co-development of agrarian capitalism with industrial capitalism. As Chicago emerged as the epicenter of agricultural commodity processing and shipping, the movement away from specific individual bags of grains reflected the changes in shipping methods that were occurring. As Cronon noted, "the city [Chicago] and its merchants changed forever the way prairie farmers could sell their crops… And at the same time, the farmers and their crops fundamentally altered Chicago's markets" (1991, p. 110).

The process of commodification of grains occurred both through the sheer volume of Chicago's market and through the particularities of its co-development with agricultural production for the market. Railroad cars stuffed to the brim with bags full of wheat soon came to be understood less as individual bags and more as full cars of wheat. And farmers themselves – who increasingly during the second half of the 19th Century reaped their wheat on a mechanical device – were less intimate with their crop than when they used a scythe. Chicago's geographic and socially produced position at the epicentre of grain trade meant that the volume of grain rendered its individual qualities superfluous to its volume.

The invention of the device that Cronon called the "most important yet least acknowledged in the history of American agriculture", the steam-powered grain elevator, led "the way toward a transformation of grain marketing worldwide" (1991, p. 111). This device, which was developed singularly in Chicago due to its particular geographical attributes, replaced human handling of small amounts of grain with machine handling of large amounts of grain. By the end of the 1850s there were more than a dozen large elevators with a combined capacity to store four million bushels, which was more than the entire yearly shipment of grain out of the next biggest port of St. Louis (US Treasury, 1958). This began the process of rendering large amounts of grain intermixable. This process took another step when grain warehouses and dealers began defining standards in terms of weight rather than volume (Taylor, 1917). This occurred as a result of the innovation of the grain elevator, as it required the grain to be sack less to move up the conveyor belt and into the elevator, a productive innovation that led to grain movements that required "little labor, except that of machinery" (Chicago Daily Press, 1857). Decreasing the amount of human labor involved in the movement of grain and the general drive to further commodify grain put added pressure on farmers by both equalizing and decreasing prices. Of course this is a fluid relationship rather than a mono- causal event; as grain production and market involvement increased, innovations occurred in the storing and shipping of grains through the process of market pressures on the storing and shipping industries, putting further pressure on famers to compete in the expanding markets.

Cronon highlights how these innovations called into question the entire legal system as previously existed because to maintain and enhance efficiencies, grain storers and shippers insisted on filling bins that required mixing small batches of individual farmer's crops together. This comingling of grain rendered moot the legal ownership of grain by the individual farmer. He merely was given a receipt for said amount of grain, and the legal contract of the grain shipper to deliver the actual grain purchased as more or less meaningless. Effectively this was the commodification of the farmer's product and the alienation of the farmer from the product of his labor in one action done for the efficiency of the market.

The Chicago Board of Trade (CBT) designated three categories of wheat and set standards for the quality of each; "the grading system allowed elevators to sever the link between ownership rights and physical grain" (Cronon, 1991, p. 116). Elevator receipts for grain began to be treated as a form of currency as the physical tie between the grain purchased was released by the standards established by the CBT, as Cronon wrote: "elevator receipts, as traded on the floor of the 'change, accomplished the transmutation of one of humanity's oldest foods, obscuring its physical identity and displacing it into the symbolic world of capital" (1991, p. 120). With this grading system and the guarantee of value it created, in effect grain became fully commodified, no longer was the use value of grain as a means to fulfill our need from food the central focus of the industry. Instead there began to emerge an ever larger group of speculators whose sole interest in grain was as a means to increase wealth. As elevator receipts for grain became a new form of currency rendered valuable through state action in the name of capitals need for efficiency and the dictates of the market place, so too did new speculative devices emerge.

Among international developments affecting the timing of this transition to agro-industrlialization in the US was the Crimean War, which is often cited as the driving force in commodification due to its first doubling and then trebling of wheat exports, along with a 50 percent rise in prices (Fornari, 1973). The war's disruptions of Ukrainian wheat exports were felt around the world. This exposes how the increasingly interconnected world market, as Chicago saw prices climb and had the capacity to meet the increasing demand due to the industrial shifts occurring, as well as this increased demand, helped to feed the shifts in agricultural production. This brought with it new found influence and power to the CBT as the total amount of grain leaving Chicago more than tripled between 1853 and 1856 (Boyle, 1922). Again, these changes occurred in a relationship with the increase in grain production in the Midwest in a response to state policies that spurred rapid productivity gains. This along with the changes occurring in the storing and shipping of grain together had a large impact on the further incorporation of farmers into market dependence. As the effects of the Crimean War hit the fields of the Midwest, with increased prices and demand, farmers who previously had merely dabbled in markets were further enticed to specialize, grow their operations, and sell more to markets. Because of the changes in the transportation and storage of grain, as well as the research and dissemination of seed and production technology and innovations in mechanical planting and harvesting, farmers were able to rapidly increase their production.

Table 3 reveals the major agricultural changes that occurred during the 1850s, as the full force of agro-industrialization played out on petty commodity producers across the nation. After the industrialization of the East Coast, the depression of 1837–1843, and the expansion of canal and rail transport, which connected the family farms with the world market, the transition of most early nineteenth century Midwestern farms from simple household to petty commodity forms was largely completed in this decade (Headlee, 1998, p. 5).

With the onset of the economic downturn in 1857 (spring wheat prices fell by more than half in 1856 and into 1857), US farmers began to take advantage

TABLE 3 *Agro-industrial development in the 1850s*

	Percent increase 1850 to 1860
Total farm acres	45
Improved acres	80
Capital formation	158
Wheat productivity	102
Value of farm implements	90
Value of farm	62
Production of wheat per farm	26
Wheat production in dollars	27.5
Mechanical reaper production	1000
Farm wages	13
Wheat specialization	10
Wheat harvested by mechanical reaper	22

SOURCE: USDA 1883

of the new weight based system of grain prices by intentionally not cleaning or mixing cheaper grains into their deposits at the elevators to increase the weight and therefore the amount received for their crops (Cronon, 1991, p. 117). This resistance to the dictates of the market by farmers led to new innovations in the grain storage industry in the form of the grading system developed by the CBT which produced a negative association between Chicago and wheat quality. The imperatives of a commodified grain economy now put further pressure on farmers to compete, while state policies pushed markets and land expansion to further increase the market imperative pressures facing farmers.

Cronon points to three major developments in Chicago that greatly enhanced the commodification of grain, and in turn the market dependence of farmers: one, the development of the grading system due to both market pressures to innovate technologically and to farmers resistance to the effects of commodification; two, the technological development of the grain elevator and new forms of shipping and storing grain, sans bags; and three, the "privately regulated central market governed by the CTB" (Cronon, 1991, p. 120). Taken together these developments have been called "the most important step in the history of the grain trade" by historian Henry Crosby Emery (1896, p. 53).

The state's active role in the commodification or development of market dependence could be seen in the very important legal changes in 1859 that allowed Chicago through the granting of quasi-judicial powers to the CBT, to grade grain (Cronon, 1991, p. 119), as well as in state involvement in the shipping and telegraph innovations of the time. These two developments, which once again should not be viewed as occurring independently of agrarian market dependence development, allowed for the equalization of grain prices in what where once separate and localized markets. Thus through the distanciation that occurred by innovations in telegraphy technology and shipping efficiencies, a local crop failure, for example, did not necessarily lead to increased prices because buyers would simply use the telegraph to check prices in other locales and then use the new railroad shipping system to deliver grain at a nationally set price. These developments aided the process of "making the Chicago Board of Trade one of the key grain markets in the world" (Cronon, 1991, p. 122). With the availability of telegraphic orders – which came from the numerous innovations occurring in Chicago – there occurred a sharp rise in "to arrive" contracts, simply contracts for future delivery of a set amount and standard of grain. Following this development, banks began to offer loans to farmers and shippers on the basis of these contracts – adding to the loans on elevator receipts that they already were making – thus altering significantly their credit requirements (Cronon, 1991, p. 123). Out of these developments would emerge Chicago's greatest innovation in grade trade: the commodities futures market. The full-fledged futures market came into being during the Civil War due to Union demand which developed a speculative market in those commodities and morphed "to arrive" contracts into futures. The CBT adopted its first rules governing futures contracts in 1865 (Cronon, 1991, p. 124).

Headlee stressed the roll of the specific form of agriculture in the Midwest as influencing the development of industry, as well as the timing of the two as important contingent forces in this process.: "without the farm machinery, the food needs of the US industrialization probably would not have been met... [b]ut without the family farm system, the mass production of that machinery probably would not have been taken on by American Entrepreneurial capitalists" (1991, p. 5). In Illinois the value of agricultural implements manufactures rose 212 percent between 1850 and 1860, population of the state rose 101 percent and value of agricultural implements increased 417.6 percent (Gates, 1968, p. xvi). Between 1850 and 1860 the total cash value of farms under cultivation in the US increased 103 percent; while the amount of capital invested in implements and machinery increased by 63 percent during the decade; and production of implements increased by 156 percent (Gates, 1968, p. xv). In 1850 the US exported just under 2 million bushels worth of wheat and wheat flour worth $7.6 million, by 1862 the US exported 76 million bushels worth $88 million, with almost half of it going to Great Britain and Ireland (Gates, 1968, p. exxxvii).

TABLE 4 *Midwestern Agro-industrial development: Early 1850s to Early 1860s*

	Early 1850s	Early 1860s
Annual Chicago flour and wheat shipments	1.38 million bushels	20.4 million bushels
Annual Milwaukie Wheat shipments	0.5 million bushels	13.70 million bushels
Number of railroad miles six states	1,275 miles	10,394 miles
Annual US wheat and flour production	100 million bushels	173 million bushels
Annual US wheat and flour export	7.5 million bushels	17.2 million bushels
Annual Receipts of flour & grain at Buffalo	17.7 million bushels	68.7 million bushels
Annual Receipts of wheat at Cincinnati	0.38 million bushels	1.7 million bushels
Annual Production of Wheat in five states	39.3 million bushels	79.8 million bushels
Agricultural Machinery value	$6.8 million	$17.4 million

Five States: OH, ILL, IN, MI, WI; Six States: Five + Iowa
SOURCE: USDA (1864) EXLIII–ELX

Meyer (1989) and others claim that the bulk of Midwestern industrial development took place from 1850–1890, with the "key period being 1860 to 1880" (p. 921; see also Nemi, 1974; Taylor, 1950). The 1860s in particular saw the Midwest's industrial production growth rise faster than the eastern part of the country, with almost half of the Midwest's industrial growth for the period of 1860–1920 occurring during the 1860s alone (Meyer, 1989). Figure 4 shows the specific changes in the Midwest during the period of the early 1850s and the early 1860s. Weather this industrialization occurred in the late 1850s or mostly after that in the 1860s depends on which region is the focus of investigation. However, the point still holds that the Midwest witnessed a massive agro-industrial development during the 1850–1870 era. It was in those twenty years, not the twenty before, that the social transformation occurred that swept all farmers in the region into petty commodity production.

The growth in manufacturing in the Midwest was an index of the increasing coordination of activities across urban and rural sector, as markets for agricultural and manufacturing goods became integrated and mutually dependent and as towns, merchants, and manufacturers linked them together through state infrastructure development (Clark, 2006, p. 168). However, despite this steady increase in existing farm productivity there was also westward expansion of agriculture, with an increase of over eight percent in farm labor for the north and south central area of the US between 1820 and 1840, and an associated decrease in US farm labor in the North east and south Atlantic regions by 9.2 percent over the same period (David, 1967, p. 195). Wheat and corn production increased almost three-fold between 1859 and 1889 as farmland expanded and the number of US farms doubled between 1860 and 1900 (Winders, 2009). We see a steady transformation as farmers are increasingly pushed into industrial forms, as mono crop agriculture dependent on inputs and mechanization due to size becomes dominant, through the competitive market pressures towards change.

Conclusion

This chapter explicated the process of the transition to petty commodity production and the details of the agro-industrial project. It linked the transition to petty commodity production agriculture with the post-1840s development in the Midwest and West by documenting how the transition of farmers to petty-commodity production combined with the agro-industrial project of state institutions.

Federal policy was shown as the initial drive that produced "the rapid transformation of land into a commodity during the 1830s" and its impact on the reproduction strategies of farmers who now had to incur higher land prices, increasing tax rates, and declining commodity prices (Post, 1995, p. 425). These rising 'farm-building' costs led to new strategies to maintain control over the means of existence and required either relocation westward to "free land", or as these options became less tenable, successful commodity production for the market: transforming farms from simple household into petty commodity producers, and then from farming into agriculture. As Headlee stated, this transformation in land created an economic relationship "between family farming and fledgling industrial capitalism in the mid-nineteenth century... [which] promoted the transition to capitalism by fostering simultaneous industrial and agricultural revolutions that resulted in the creation of an agro-industrial complex" (1991, p. 1). As cash crop specialization resulted in increased revenue that was returned to manufacturing to produce the means, as well as the requirement, for further productivity increases, farms were compelled by the logic of the market to increase productivity and total output, which led to further declining prices and propelling farmers further into commercialization. The development of Midwestern industrial production did not follow the processes of change occurring in agriculture, they were integral to those changes; "industry did not follow the plough, it built the plough" (Page and Walker, 1991, p. 1). As some farmers began to adopt petty commodity production this began to infuse agricultural markets with a new competitive pressures. These competitive pressures were emanating from the expanding markets fed by the increasing productivity of mechanized agriculture, as well as, producing the growth of the industrial market. Headlee confirmed this view:

> The backward link from agricultural development to the growth in the sector of the capitalist manufacture of farm machinery was crucial. Without the farm machinery, the food needs of the US industrialization probably would not have been met. But without the family farm system, the mass production of that machinery probably would not have been taken on by American entrepreneurial capitalists (1998, p. 5).

Land policy acted as the first major source of this drive toward petty commodity agriculture while also creating the imperatives toward industrial development. Part-time industrial production, done mostly at first in farm workshops, led to some putting-out networks or to small manufacturing workshops, this grew into an increased specialization and a growth in the division of labor. From this emerged a shift in the division of agricultural labor, away from simple household production towards a regional based linkage with wider capitalist development. Out of this development grew a whole set of new industries to feed the needs of the agrarian petty commodity producers, as "commercial farming eagerly absorbed new farm implements and machines that raised labor productivity, and welcomed any fall in cost due to industrial processing of fertilizers or improvements in transportation" (Page and Walker, 1991, p. 292). This then acted as a spur to competitive and dynamic improvements in industrial production and agriculture alike.

This localized development of agriculture fed into capitalist industry by offering a source of expansion and led to increases in agricultural technology in many aspects including inputs such as fertilizers and later herbicides and pesticides, mechanization and farm implements, as well as output food processing industries such as flour milling, distilleries, meatpacking and leather tanning (Page and Walker, 1991; Cronon, 1998; Wade, 1987). It is this symbiotic link with the growth of industry in localized settings that is crucial, as is the way the state developed the institutional capacities to deal with the diversity and uneven development of US agricultural production and the emerging industrial producers. The thesis of the agro-industrial project put forward here locates the state as integral to the agro-industrial development in the Midwest. This could be seen from the early land policies that concentrated and integrated farmers into markets through mortgage debts, to the canals and railroad policies that connected farmers to regional markets, to the new developments in seeds and farming techniques that began to commodify farm production inputs and the increased the availability and use of farm implements in a growing competitive market. This refined agro-industrialization thesis reveals how the resistance to capitalist development in the US was incorporated into the development of state institutions and how this fueled a more dynamic development. Ultimately this led to a stronger and more resilient capitalist state to emerge while disarming opposition movements. This reveals and highlights the role of the state as an important site in the battle between class forces and the various ways the state intervenes to aid capital in this contest. Amidst shifts in the balance of class forces during the last quarter of the 19th Century new institutions of the US state emerged to facilitate the political compromises that favored capitalist 'agriculture' over 'farming', while helping to neutering opposition to this imbricate farmers in the expanding capitalist economy.

CHAPTER 3

The End of Slavery and Southern Agricultural Class Structure

As I have previously shown, the role of agriculture in the Northern and Midwestern US during the middle of the 19th Century was increasingly transformed by the movement from simple household agriculture to petty commodity production as compelled by the increasing development of state induced regional markets encouraging industrialization. Meanwhile in the southern US, agro-industrial development did not take place for the most part. This was due not only to the power of the entrenched planter class who intentionally blocked industrialization, but also to the economic, social, and material circumstances of its slave-based labor system which lacked many of the imperatives of capitalist market development despite being highly integrated into global circuits of capital through the cotton trade.

The particular configuration of class forces is important when enquiring into what emerged after the Civil War. As will be shown, what transpired was the emergence of a highly independent, fragmented, and disjointed agriculture that lacked the underlying industrial organizing forces as those that had developed in the North. Instead of encouraging commercial markets, the planter class prevented the agro-industrial project due through its entrenched economic and political power. This combined with a lack of free social mobility along a rigid race-based hierarchical class structure that prevented a wage labor system. Instead of organized capital based commercial ventures, it was large land owners who fought to maintain a stubborn land plantation system and a general distrust of larger industrial scale ventures and state initiatives. Thus, what emerged instead of agro-industrial development was a form of tenant and cropper agriculture that impoverished not only farmers but the entire economic and social development of the South, at least until the Populist revolt surfaced.

Finally, in this chapter's enquiry into the factors that prevented industrial development, especially in agriculture in the antebellum and the Post-War South as compared with the North, I will highlight the differences between the northern and southern class structures, offering a comparison of how the particular balance of class forces at any given time informed the involvement or lack of involvement of the state in agricultural development. This represented a key variable in the historical development of industry and agriculture in the US.

Slavery, the Civil War and the Transition

As outlined in Chapter 2, the conflict between the North and the South over westward expansion came to a head during the late 1850s for two main reasons. First, because the political power of the North was growing as the agro-industrial development process was beginning to unfold which the South sought to stifle. Second, it erupted because of the simple commodity production farming requirement for westward expansion by northern farmers. A constant stream of farmers took up simple commodity producer homesteads in western lands, expanding the population and eventually, petty commodity production moved into the Midwest. This tendency created the tension over the future of western development between the North and the South. Alongside this there was also one of the state's main forces of market integration through land policies. The state used land policy to integrate farmers into market dependent relations as well as a source of anti-market dependent ideology. Also important was the existing speculative capital that was interested in continuing its favorable relationship with the US state through its expansive land policy. In the mix of all of these competing class interests the state formed a policy based on westward expansion and opposed a slave based economy in Western lands.

Pressure both in the North and the South for westward expansion emerged because of the particular historical dictates, not because of the competing economic modes of production of slavery and petty commodity production alone. It is only in the particular social setting at that time – under slave production methods, facing world market competition, with diminishing and increasingly costly human capital (slave labor), and under political pressure from the North – that we can analyze to what degree internal expansion in the South was available or whether geographic expansion westward was necessary for plantation slavery to survive. Neither slavery nor petty commodity production in the West required extensive expansion.[1] Analyzed within the given social reality of the historical period, westward expansion of slavery appears mostly as a political demand. The promise of westward expansion was not entirely able to remedy the shortcomings of slavery or meet the requirements for its continued existence. However, it did serve an ideological purpose as the center of a rallying cry against Northern interests preventing the 'greatness of the South' from being fully realized.

---

1 See Hirst and Hidess (1975, pp. 162–70) for a detailed historical analysis of the lack of a relationship between slave property relations and soil exhaustion and therefore extensive expansion.

Any structural antagonism between capitalism and slavery emerged within the specific political and social relations of the time. The battle that emerged in the specific historical situation between the North and the South rested on the political developments of the time; that is they rested on the political inability to continue the shift of the contradictory forces of capitalism and slavery. Furthermore, to remove any functionalism from our understanding we must locate the political and social struggles that set the parameters of the available responses that ultimately led to the War. Under different social and political situations, the co-existence of capitalism and plantation slavery could have continued. The Civil War wasn't entirely caused by the economic structures of the time because economic structures don't exist independent of social existence or outside political struggles. However much the class structures differed in the North and South, it was the way these informed the political and social realities of the time that led them to move along a path of civil war.

The South's internally funded credit markets reduced or eliminated the kinds of pressures on farmers witnessed in the North in the antebellum decades, as increasing debt loads fed the incentives towards agro-industrialization. In the plantation south, the planters maintained control over vast areas of land and over slaves as a form of property and therefore collateral or sunk capital. The incentives and market pressures to compete, plantation against plantation, towards labor saving innovations was absent due to the sunken capital and the lack of self-exploitation relative to petty commodity producers.

Having invested in the means to subordinate and maintain a slave based labor supply, the south created an incentive to purchase more slaves rather than invest in labor saving technology (Genovese, 1965). This is not to say the competition to sell and market imperatives of the capitalist world market were not present in the South, as slavery was linked to the world market. In fact, at the time southern plantation slavery was more integrated into the capitalist world market than the majority of petty commodity farmers in the North. However in response to these capitalist produced imperatives of competition, slavery based producers could respond differently than capitalist and petty commodity producers due to the type of labor employed and the class based imperatives and politics this informed. This isn't an economic determinist understanding, as it shows the political and social parameters faced in the South at the time. These parameters did not limit all options; therefore the specific political realities of the conjuncture remain a necessary variable while recognizing the class based realties and sources of those options. It is, as neo-Marxist state theory articulates, the class based power that produces the different state institutions as the politics of the day are in an internal relationship with the balance of class forces.

Post (2009) viewed the growing divide between the economic-capital controlled North and plantation slavery's barrier to capital formation in the South as the cause of the Civil War. On this he is only partially correct, as the pressures emanating from the North were more and more coming to bear on the South. However, the economic structures of the South could have held tight absent the political and social pressures from the North as cotton from the South was still intricately connected to a strong world market, and, as will be seen, the plantation owners' influence on the politics of the South was still very strong. At the time just prior to the Civil War plantation slavery was economically successful and expanding, in terms of both acres and numbers of slaves (Baptist, 2014).

Alternatively, it could be argued that it was less the barrier to capitalist development that the South posed than the unevenness of national economic development and the trajectories of the specific region that led to the Civil War (Nemi, 1974). Similar to Beard's thesis (1927), but going beyond Beard's overestimation of the power of Northern industrialists to push their drive for increased tariffs to the point of a Civil War, Nemi sees the war as the outcome of political struggles, informed and influenced by economic changes between the increasingly powerful North, as it developed industrially, and the South and their struggle to grab the allegiance of the west to expand slavery.

Insofar as we regard such economic pressures as integrated with political and social forces, not as separated from them, we can appreciate how the growing strength of the North in national politics, arising from the success of its economy in light of its transition to capitalism, was increasingly impinging on the South, not least as the state pushed through changes that would not benefit the South. As Sanders (1999) outlined, "New England's political representatives embraced the protective tariff, cheap land, and the military expenditures demanded by western sections" and used these to build a coalition against this (p. 13). Likewise, Headlee (1991) argued that amidst the "simultaneous industrial and agricultural revolutions that resulted in the creation of an agro-industrial complex" there emerged a "political alliance between family farmers and industrial capitalists in the form of the Republican Party, which enabled the industrial capitalists to take control of the state from the democratic party of the southern plantation slave owners" (p. 1).

The North–south divide was also furthered by the moral arguments emerging around slavery, which were juxtaposed against the 'freedom' of petty commodity producers and wage laborers. As will be shown, ideology played a big role in this divide as Northern capitalists pushed of 'free labor' as a means to overcome the everyday problems faced by farmers. It was class struggle and the ideological political rhetoric of class obfuscation, not simply some abstract the technical logic of the development of the different modes of production, which ultimately led to the Civil War.

The geographically differentiated uneven development between the North and the South can also be tracked back to the particular crops grown in the two areas and the associated markets that either developed or didn't develop around the sale of the commodities produced. In the US during the period of 1800–1860, the production of regional agricultural staples, determined by the amount rural laborers earned, governed the process of economic development, urbanization, and industrialization. The cost of unskilled urban labor was a function of rural labor's earnings: where rural laborers did poorly, urban labor was cheap; where rural laborers did well, urban labor was expensive. This 'transfer wage', not immigration, determined urban unskilled wage rates- "since the cost of rural labor was determined primarily by the forces of seasonality, immigration had minimal effect in lowering the transfer wage by narrowing the differential between the annual earnings of rural and urban labor" due to the migration from the countryside (Carville and Hoffman, 1980 pp. 1064–65). The Midwest's heavy reliance on wheat, corn, and livestock meant sporadic labor demand that in turn meant increased labor availability and decreased labor cost when comparing the Midwest, South and English agriculture – full time year-round needs for agricultural labor had increased labor costs in both England and the US South, while staying constant or decreasing in the US Midwest. Therefore, the influence of agricultural economic forces on urban labor, particularly in the emerging industrial centers, was a factor in the different political positions. Decreased industrial labor costs combined with increased productivity meant increasing capitalist power in the North, while increasing costs of labor and slaves and constant productivity prevented planter economic power ascendency.

The North's political reliance on the continued westward expansion of the nation, an expansion that was also not necessary but politically expedient, increased with the Homestead Bill. The US House of Representatives finally, after decades of farmer pressure passed the Homestead Bill in 1862 by a two to one vote, with many members who opposed the bill reluctant to vote against it out of fear of the political fallout (Stephenson, 1917). Stephenson (1917) outlined the bill's political significance this way:

> The course of the homestead bill in Congress in 1862 is significant chiefly for two things: First, it shows that Homestead was of such great importance that both of the old parties were hedging in order not to injure their chances in a presidential election; and, second, the South was becoming a unit in opposition. This ultimately transformed the issue from one on

which the West and labor were lined up against the old States into a contest between the North and South (p. 146).

In this we see how the agitation for and growing importance of homestead held the possibility of disrupting the Northern alliance around issues of class, but was ideologically transformed into a North–south sectional issue. In the process it fanned the flames of the dispute over slavery and forced the North's hand to move against the South. It was the dispute over the Homestead Act that ultimately brought the very large number of German immigrants in the Midwest over to a Republican Party that they had previously disliked because of the strong influence and connection with the anti-immigrant Know-Nothing Party (Stephenson, 1917).

It was the North's rhetorical use of agrarian self-sufficiency, with its calls for 'free soil and free labor' that enabled the Republican Party to win majorities and move its platform forward. Thus, the reliance on the nostalgic ideology was aligned with the party and the North, not because it was capitalist and allowed for 'free individuals' but because it was still in the midst of transitioning to capitalism, with an existing class of simple household producers, and to a greater degree the memory of household production and the relative independence it had. The binary of slavery and "free labor" was used to overcome the differences between 'free' individuals in the North, differences between simple household, petty commodity producers, merchants, capitalists and wage laborers. Under this ideology wage labor – which was once socially understood as "disreputable and as a mark of dependence" – was transformed, by the late 1840s, into "one archetype of an ideal 'free labor' system" (Clark, 2006, p. 140). It was through the juxtaposition of slavery versus 'free labor' that the growing class conflict of the north was transformed into a united political movement against slavery. Much of the unity attained by the Republican platform rested on this ideological obfuscation of class differences and, as Clark noted, the "growing political conflict over slavery and its expansion in the 1840s and 1850s tightened further the association between wage labor and 'freedom' by grouping all of the Northern class differences in opposition to southern slavery" (p. 229). Only through this political rhetoric and dichotomously produce-dideology could farmers in the North with 40 times the wealth of wage laborers be viewed as social and political equals.[2] With abolitionists insisting that "poverty is not slavery", to drive home the message that the North had

---

[2] Clark (2006: 230) stated that in 1850 farmers on average had 18 times the mean wealth of wage laborers and by 1860 this grew to forty times.

political equality while the South had a two caste system, the "complex regional differences became resolved into sharp contrasts in social structures" (Clark, 2006, p. 233).

This wedge between yeomen and plantation slave owners was effectively wielded by Lincoln himself through his continual claims during his 1860 presidential campaign that wage work was merely a temporary condition, as the means to pull oneself up to land ownership and independence. Lincoln picked up the Jeffersonian mantle and played into farmers' discomfort with the emerging market forces in their lives, claiming that "stopping the expansion of slavery would be the only way to protect the small farmer from being overtaken by aristocratic planters who exploited the labor of others" (Clark, 2006, p. 244). Others too, most notably Senator Seward, claimed that the South sought to replace the free labor system in the North and spread slavery (Bensel, 1990). Thus, the Republican Party sutured petty commodity production to their campaign by using the very real pressures and anxieties of small farmers, many of whom were in the process of transitioning to petty commodity production or were still filled with the memory of that transition. This allowed them to co-opt and refocus much of the angst and resistance felt and apply it to the slave south, the social dislocation and a loss of autonomy for the farmers was articulated within the drive against the South.

It was not slavery's weakness but its strength that lead to the conflict with the North as cotton, sugar, rice, and tobacco production all expanded in the South along with the total number of slaves through the 1850s (Clark, 2006). In fact, it was the South's political strength that represented more of a threat to the Northern bourgeoisie than its weakness. During the 1840s and 1850s the South was strong, both economically and politically. Cotton alone accounted for three-fifths of all US exports in 1860 and cotton production had increased 173 percent over the previous 20 years (Hammond, 1897). It was the confluence of increasing economic expansion and the conflicts between policies beneficial to southern plantation owners or to northern capitalists that undergirded the main vicissitudes of the Civil War.

Like the North, the South was also witnessing rising income inequality amongst white social groups. This, in part was due in part to a rising price of slaves since the slave trade was outlawed, resulting in a shrinking absolute number of white southern slave owners through concentration of plantation and slave ownership. Also, as in the North, Southern elites tried to create political cohesion amongst the increasingly disparate class locations and maintain the confidence of independent yeomen farmers by claiming it was the North that was attempting to force wage labor on the South. As Clark (2006) summarized:

> The two visions, the Southern one of identity between farmers and planters, and the free-soil one of an egalitarian society of family farmers untroubled by interference from planters or their slaves, each adapted the realities of a household-based rural economy – but each reached radically different conclusions. The differences helped turn the debate on slavery into a wedge between North and South, and to turn the discussion of regional variety into a conflict over sectional difference (p. 245).

Here Clark put too much stress on the regional aspects of the US economy while downplaying the class divisions both across and within regions of the developing nation. However his point on the class nature of sectionalism was poignant: in both the North and the South the scapegoating of the other, while not completely determining state action, was a means to conceal increasing class differences and stitch together a political coalition. Bensel's work (1990) sustains this assessment, showing that the North resisted the loss of the South in part because it would have "created a new political economy in which the basis of Republican-led alliance of eastern industry and western yeoman agriculture would have rapidly dissolved as the two wings of the party struggled over the competing interests of industrial expansion and agricultural settlement" (p. 93).[3] Yet Bensel's argument (1990) is also flawed in that it posited the source of the South's antagonism as the North's threat of capitalist expansion, when in reality the threat was not nearly so imminent; the rhetorical use of threat in the South was designed to drum up ideological unity between planters and farmers.[4]

Meanwhile, in the North the agitations against slavery were also in large part driven by the ideological construction of political unity between classes, as capitalism and in turn wage labor expanded. The relative position of merchants, manufacturers, farmers and laborers shifted and were realigned due to this political displacement of class conflict into a North versus South antagonism (Clark, 2006). Sectionalist politics came to suppress class issues and would continue to do for decades. Indeed, the war was as much the product of the growing tensions between capitalists and petty commodity producers as it was about conflicts between capitalists and plantation slavery. Struggling

---

3 This is not simply to repeat Barrington Moore's analysis (1967) and claim that the North and the South's differences were mostly sociological – the North's bourgeois versus the South's aristocratic ideology. Instead it is to point out how class dynamics inform the social totality.

4 The mostly ideological nature of the threat is revealed by the lack of capitalist development in the South following the war. In fact, it wouldn't be until the mid-20th Century before industrial capitalism finally became dominant in the US South.

petty commodity producers were told that their problems and the main threat to their survival stemmed from the slavery of the South. The problems of the agrarian economy, along with the increasing tension between industrial workers and capitalists, were displaced onto slavery through the creation of a class unity of Northern farmers, workers and capitalists. In an effort to explain away class dominance, agrarian and industrial capitalists used the slavery issue to deflect attention and to build a political alliance between the classes. In a word they sought to construct hegemony out of the slavery divide.

The Civil War and State Institutional Expansion

While the spread of capitalism was more of a political threat to the South than an economic one, it is true that the war itself aided in the spread of capitalist social relations. This occurred in two main ways: first, through the glossing over or displacement of emerging class conflict and complaints of petty commodity producers; and two, through the increase in state involvement in market construction in the North. The war itself initiated major developments in state capacity building. This process of increased state formation lies at the heart of the process of capitalist development that was greatly enlarged through the war. Even as the war was just beginning, Bensel (1990) highlighted how "secession itself was an enormously facilitating event in American state formation because disunion ensured the identification of the Republican Party with the central state and brought on a massive enlargement of governmental authority in the North" (p. 92). The state was able to push through changes under the guise of defeating the South, which had previously been prevented by farmers and laborers.[5]

Far from being complete, the agro-industrial development in the North was aided by the Civil War. One very important shift the war caused was an increase in Government demand for credit. This provided the final drive for a section of the economy away from merchants and toward new forms of finance and sales as "the balance of financial power shifted from the merchant's house to the factory office" during the war and in its immediate aftermath (Porter and Livesay, 1971, p. 119). As credit contracted during the war many manufacturers moved to cash or monthly terms, which allowed them to receive their sales proceeds sooner, diminishing the amount of working capital required to sustain production (Hedges, 1935; Klien, 1911; Porter and

---

5   Although it should not be exaggerated or applied to all situations as the only force, there is something to Tilly's (1990) claim that war making is state making.

Livesay, 1971). This also made it possible for manufacturers to pay off their suppliers sooner, thus reducing interest payments and increasing profits; "The Civil War presented many manufacturers with a long-awaited opportunity to get off the credit treadmill" (Porter and Livesay, 1971, p. 122). This disintermediation of merchants and wholesalers through increased direct sales meant that manufacturers now had greater financial flexibility over pricing and credit terms, decreased competition and increased profit potential. The availability of capital was also increased due to the war, with large amounts of public expenditure going to manufacturers through what Sylla (1967) described as the "great catalyst of capital market development: the Civil War" (p. 657). The growth of a national banking system (and economies of scale) occurring because the war diminished private banking development and increased monopolistic control over agricultural loans, which simultaneously shifted the receivers and increasing the amount of loans towards manufacturers and railroad companies. The increasing access by manufacturers to the pool of capital formed by private savings was accompanied by a steady growth of bank loans (Porter and Livesay, 1971). This spur to capitalist development in the North did not occur in the same way in the South.

Both during, and in the wake of the War, there occurred widespread, both at the state and federal level, institutional development to facilitate the modernization and commodification of agriculture. The concentration of power in the North following succession, removed the influence of the Planters in national government, for a time, freeing up the more capitalist and industrial focused North to push through agro-industrial policies – the Morrill Land-Grant College Act, the Homestead Act, the Pacific Railway Act, and the most important agricultural institutional development, the act establishment of the United States Department of Agriculture.

With the passage of these laws in the immediate absence of Southern political opposition, we see clearly how the South had blocked the full use of the federal government to aid in the transition of Midwestern and Western farmers and the overall economy towards petty commodity production. The Homestead Act and Pacific Railway Act themselves would become major forces in moving the remaining simple commodity producing farmers of the Midwest and West into market mediated social relations. Likewise these two acts, as already outlined in the case of Chicago, spurred industrial developments that enhanced the capacity to further commodify agricultural products. The state institutional developments in the USDA and land grant system would also become long-term forces for the differentiation and commodification of agriculture for the next Century.

Postbellum Southern Agriculture

The path toward state institutional involvement in agriculture is a long and winding one. The removal of slavery did not immediately free Southern agriculture from Planter control and quickly usher in capitalist agrarian social relations. Instead it gave rise to heightened uneven development with much of the South moving to tenancy to overcome the problems in the War's aftermath. This was due to the nature of the state, the economy and the balance of class forces at the time, including the importance of tenancy as a key factor in the rise of Populism.

Cotton prices decreased to a third of the price per pound between 1870 and 1897. Simultaneously the costs of seeds, fertilizers and supplies rose, due, in part, to the tariffs the North was able to pass with a weakened Southern opposition. For a number of reasons the division of land ownership in the South shifted only slightly following the Civil War and the subsequent decades and there occurred a doubling of the number of small farms amidst a large reduction of large plantations during the decade following the war (Bruce, 1905; Hammond, 1897; Hawk, 1934). This appears to sustain Post's claim that there occurred a major break-up of large plantations in the immediate post-war era. However, the opening up of public and unused lands – particularly in Florida, Alabama, Mississippi, Louisiana, and Arkansas – skews the data (Shannon, 1973), while there was also landholders who were double counted – including both those who owned the land and those who were sharecropping the acreage (Brooks, 1914).

Instead, the tendency in the immediate decade after the war was, in fact, for the average acreage holding to increase, not decrease in size (Shannon, 1973). In Louisiana, the class struggle in the aftermath of the war led to a threefold increase in the number of plantations over 100 acres between 1860 and 1880, and by 1900 plantations of over 100 acres enclosed half the cultivated land in the state (Shugg, 1939). This consolidation of land through the expansion of large plantations occurred because merchants increased their loans to landowners, who were now absent the slaves that had formed their main source of collateral, leaving plantation owners only their land to put up. This combined with the diminished price of cotton to sharply increase foreclosures and consolidate smaller farms into larger ones. With the shift toward tenancy and sharecropping, combined with the increased concentration of land ownership in merchant's hands, the value of Southern agricultural land diminished greatly: by 1870 farming land was worth fifty two percent of its pre-war value or a drop from $1,479,000,000 to $764,000,000 for all lands in cultivation (Shannon, 1973).

The breakup of the plantation system, – Shannon (1973) called it the "supposed breakup" -that did occur in much of the South came from the "transference from gang labour to tenancy" – the movement from hired forms of labor to farmers renting land (p. 95). With the freeing of the slaves, farmers that lacked capital turned to sharecropping and tenancy instead of hired labor or petty commodity production.

In the immediate aftermath of the Civil War, the plantation system came to an abrupt end and the question of what would replace it quickly emerged as the focus of intense struggle. To fully answer why capitalist agriculture did not fill the void left by slavery's end, we need to look at the class power and take into account how social classes at the time wielded influence over the state and how the particularities of agriculture informed these processes. The class structure dominant in the South after the Civil War was one in which "a large class of landlords and merchants, ruling a still larger number of tenants, croppers, and day labourers" dominated (Shannon, 1973, p. 97). This runs counter to those who claim the South's non-capitalist production ended and give way to petty commodity production immediately after the War (Post, 2009). Instead, petty commodity agriculture doesn't really come to play a major role in the South until much later and only after planters have been stripped as a class of their political power.

The compromise reached over the type of agrarian production did give landlords significant power, but it also granted some limited control to the croppers over their own labor power McMath (1992). By insisting that the cropper's labor was now a commodity, McMath opposed those who viewed the sharecropper relationship as non-capitalist (Lenin, 1974; Mann, 1990; Rochester, 1940). I too am making a distinction between tenant farming and petty commodity production because of the different market imperatives present. While both are producing agricultural goods for markets, the means of responding to market produced competitive pressures is quite dissimilar. The petty commodity agricultural production in the North was driven by the competitive market towards innovation through the market imperatives imposed on individual producers in the form of land and other debt that increased the drive toward increasing production. In an effort to remain competitive to maintain ownership of the means of production – the agricultural land – petty commodity farmers were forced to innovate and investing in specialization, expansion and labor saving technology.

Conversely, tenancy is marked by an absence of ownership of the land by the direct producer. Therefore the market incentives driven by land debt, in an effort to maintain ownership of the means of production, are absent. This means that the market imperatives towards expansion are also missing, as are the imperatives to adapt labor saving technology to expand or to increase productivity. This difference emerges because of a lack of both land and a source of credit. The point being that there were different market incentives created under petty commodity production where the land was owned and tenant farming or sharecropping, where the land was rented. These differences influenced owner-tenant social relationships and production behaviour in very distinct ways.

Friedmann (1980) has claimed that sharecropping is not capitalist because the reproduction of sharecropping farms was not based on direct market relations but instead rested on factor monopolies and coercion rather than market imperatives. Likewise, market coercion under sharecropping did not produce the same necessities for technological innovation and increased productivity as petty commodity production. Instead the particularities of the US situation produced what Blackburn (2011) calls "hybrid forms of labour" in the New World – indentured servitude, slavery, sharecropping and petty commodity production. As Wolf (1982) argued, capitalism historically came into symbiotic relationships with other forms of social relations without immediately creating capitalist social relations. And Jairus Banaji (2010) noted:

> Relations of production are simply not reducible to forms of exploitation [such as slavery], both because modes of production embrace a wider range of relationships than those in their immediate process of production and because the deployment of labor, the organization and control of the labor-process, "correlates" with historical relations of production in complex ways. (p. 41)

This correlation of forms of labor or symbiotic or hybrid class relationships with different relations of production thus requires historic elaboration.

If understanding slavery as a system based on a non-capitalist mode of production that was nevertheless connected with the increasingly capitalist world market is accepted, then so too must the persistence of the sharecropping system that dominated the South during the 1870s and 1880s be understood in a similar way. They both relied on the dictates of the world market for cotton and tobacco produced that were almost exclusively produced due to the influence of merchants; they both responded to the imperatives of the capitalist market through very specific and non-capitalist responses to market competition; and neither of them contained the class based imperatives to innovation and market development witnessed in the North. Neither slavery nor sharecropping contained the market based imperatives that drove technological innovation as a means to out compete, as witnessed in the historical absence of such innovation.

With slavery swept aside by the Civil War and the Thirteenth Amendment, what replaced it would not be agriculture based on capitalist wage labor or petty commodity production but would instead be tenancy and sharecropping. Even in the emerging industrial areas of the South, the dominance of the company store and the truck system of wage payment prevented farmers from becoming petty commodity producers because of the familiarity of that structure to both merchants, who were mostly former landlords or landlord sons, and the former croppers who migrated into cities to take jobs (Bruce, 1905). This situation might have been altered had the requisite capital investment from the North been available for farmers to borrow and purchase land and the radical reconstruction would have broken up the large plantations and revoked their political power as a class. Instead, the reliance on the little capital available from internal, Southern sources, mainly from merchants or country stores, retarded the development of petty commodity agriculture and labor markets in the classical sense. The lack of federal investment in infrastructure and land grants to any degree as those witnessed in the North and the failure to immediately dismantle the planter system led ultimately to tenancy and sharecropper agriculture.

Needless to say, the Southern economic recovery was slow to come. Foner (1984) laid some of the blame on the inability to do the "required assault on the plantation" (p. 98). He outlined what he saw as the weaknesses of plantation systems throughout the world: "Geared toward producing agricultural staples for the world market, they have weak internal markets and planter classes use their political power to prevent the emergence of alternative economic enterprises that might threaten their control of the labor force" (pp. 98–99). Very similar developments occurred in the South both during and after the overthrow of the slave system. Thus, though they wanted economic development, the planters of the South, who held tightly as they could to their former power, actively prevented the economic development of the south in the immediate post war era through, amongst other things the black codes (discussed in more detail below), their tight grip over land, and the manner in which they leveraged that into a type of control over labor. To achieve full scale economic development would have required the dissolution of the planter class. Opting to maintain immediate sources of power instead of economic development the Southern planters locked the South into a development trajectory that painted the historical process of the entire nation for the next few decades.

Following the Civil War a large mass of property less, poor laborers were unleashed into the economy. Mann (1990) has posed the provocative question of why despite the post war south's situation, which appeared to be ripe for capitalist wage labor to become dominant, it did not travel down this path.

The answers many have proposed highlights some of the obstacles to capitalist development in agriculture that are both universal, as well as some that are socially and historically unique to the South in that particular conjuncture. Absent capital, credit and marketing facilities, which had been damaged by the war with the collapse of the southern banking system and the decline in agricultural output, most southern landowners did not have and could not attract the necessary requirements to produce capitalistically (Shannon, 1945; Ransom and Sutch, 1972). Because a large amount of southern capital was tied up in the form of slaves, the freeing of them meant that most planters lost the collateral used to get the necessary capital to plant and run their plantations. This lack of capital meant planters could not cover the operating costs for the season. These plantation owners fought to keep their hold on land and for the most part won (Dubois, 1935). This ability to keep control over the majority of fertile land was greatly diminished by the loss of the labor necessary for production (Ransom and Sutch, 1972). Reconstruction did not bring about a redistribution of land in the South, and in fact, concentration of land was greater in 1880 than before the war (Saloutos, 1960). Henry Grady quipped that the planters were "still lords of acres, though not of slaves" (quoted in Birchman, 1939, p. 345). The history of land ownership in the South, informed by decades of slavery, would be a major influence on social and economic development for a long time even after slavery itself was removed. Planters held tight to class power despite having lost the economic ability to reproduce that power.

Related to this was the rise of croppers and tenant farmers. The extent of tenancy in this era is not precisely known, as there is little clear data and the US Census did not count tenants until the 1880 census (Ferleger, 1942). One estimate has Alabama croppers in 1880 as constituting thirty five percent of all farmers, with owners making up forty percent and hired laborers being just over twenty percent (Black and Allen, 1937). The number of croppers increases by 1890 to constitute forty percent, with a slight increase in owners and a five percent decline in laborers (Black and Allen, 1937). Black and Allen (1937) compare this to Northern states and in Wisconsin for example, we see the ownership rate at 75 percent, labor making up 19 percent and croppers only constituting six percent in 1880.

The planters hold over large quantities of land and political power would appear to be a situation ripe for capitalist wage labor in the absence of slave relations. In the South, unlike in the North, large landowners dominated, and wage labor would have offered them the ability to continue to produce on a large scale. Instead a system of family sharecropping became dominant (Jaynes, 1986). One of the things that prevented the immediate transition to capitalist agriculture and wage labor was the power of the landowners and their continued influence over state policy in the south. Planters actively worked to maintain the structures that served as the basis of their power and used state laws and customs to subordinate the market to their concerns. Only slowly was the role of the state reconfigured to enact changes in the class structures of the South. This shift eventually occurred as the balance of class forces first began to favour merchants over planters and the state incorporating and enacting populist reforms. The complete economic shift from merchants to capitalists only came much later still, really only occurring after the end of Jim Crow.[6]

In the immediate post bellum period, the freed slaves lacked the means to the land they required to become independent producers and the landowners could not get the freed slaves to adapt to labor market requirements. This was due in part to the freed slave's resistance to that form of labor, but also because of planters who did not wish to abide by market forces themselves or lacked the capital to proceed as large capitalist wage based producers (Math, 1992). Although lacking land and capital, the freed black laborers were in a position to create problems for the landowners and effectively prevented this dominant class from imposing labor markets to maintain a centralized control over cotton production (Royce, 1985). Foner sees the freedman's demands for improved working and economic conditions that ensured that for "the majority of planters, as for their former slaves, the Confederacy's defeat and the end of slavery ushered in a difficult adjustment to new race and class relations and new ways of organizing labor", as the paternalist ethos of the slave mode had no place in "a social order in which labor relations were mediated by the impersonal market and blacks aggressively pressed claims to autonomy and equality" (Foner, 1984, p. 59; see also Shannon, p. 87). The 'freedom' of labor required for capitalist social property relations were incapable of occurring within the racially bifurcated society of the South. While no longer slaves, blacks in the South lacked the social freedom required to facilitate the imperatives of work on which capitalism rests. Mann has dug deepest into the specificity of agriculture and particularly cotton production, which she argued precludes easy transition to capitalist wage labor. The deep structural "problems at the root of the failure of wage labor to adequately substitute for slavery… [which was] centered on the inability of landowners to ensure an immobile, stable labor force both on a day-to-day basis and throughout the

---

6   The political developments in the South traced Marx's prediction that the first order of business in the South was to clear away the remnants of the slave system, before the consolidation of the capitalist class system could complete its development (Nimtz, 2003). Marx was incorrect that the Civil War would immediately remove this barrier.

production cycle" led to the haphazard and slow drift toward sharecropping in the South (Mann, 1990, p. 78).

There exist many competing explanations of why wage labour did not fill the vacuum left by the Civil War. Those who view the outcome of a shift to sharecropping as the result of the strength of the landowners able to maintain control over freedmen through laws and civil pressure despite the loss of their main asset (Saloutos, 1960; Zeichner, 1939) stand opposed to those who view the strength of the freedmen in an industry that required a stable labour force because of the nature of the crop with its long season (Davis, 1982; Mandle, 1978; Mann, 1990; Ransom and Sutch, 1977; Weiner, 1978). Either way, there can be no doubt that the transition to a new form of labor was widely recognized as the decisive question facing the South at the time. As William H. Trescot explained to South Carolina's Governor in December 1865, "you will find that this question of the control of labor underlies every other question of state interest" (quoted in Foner, 1990, p. 93).

The labor scarcity that emerged after the war, as the supply of black labor dropped by about one third, emerged largely because former slaves worked fewer hours and because many former slave women and children removed themselves from the fields (Foner, 1984). Also important was the unwillingness of white laborers to work next to black freedmen and the increasing use of the criminal justice system to incarcerate freed slaves (Blackmon, 2008). Prejudice prevented economic development and a smooth transition to capitalist labor markets, as many of the southern states passed discrimination laws to continue the subordination of blacks to whites and the white privilege of the South. In the spring and summer of 1865, military commanders issued stringent orders to stem the influx of freedmen into Southern cities, as "Military regulations forbade blacks to travel without passes from their employers or be on the streets at night and prohibited 'insubordination' on their part" (Foner, 1984, p. 69). Thus, the infamous Black Codes, summarized in Table 5, were instituted across many states in the south, as both a means to stop this migration and to uphold the white supremacy and psychological wages this gave poor whites (Foner, 1984; Shannon, 1945; Debois, 1935).

Many legal changes were required in the wake of the Civil War across the South. Emancipation made the law of master and slave irrelevant; "existing law concerning tenancy and free labor proved incomplete and in-adequate to meet the needs of the new social relations" (Woodman, 1979, p. 320). Not only was it necessary to alter the nature of contracts to deal with the emancipation of a large portion of the population, but also the law would be used to maintain white control during this process. With the two classes trying to pull the economic relations in either direction "The ensuing conflict produced new

TABLE 5 *Selected southern black codes*

In South Carolina blacks had to present written authorization from their "masters" before selling farm produce.

In most southern states black's rights to hunt, fish and to free graze were severely restricted after the war.

Poll taxes and unfair land taxes led to further discrimination.

Militia officers patrolled mostly plantation areas, not the upland country dominated by poor white yeomen, and many continued to wear their grays or confederacy uniforms while on duty.

Gun and dog ownership was restricted or illegal for blacks.

Laws were enforced by an all-white police and judicial system.

Freedmen were forbidden from renting homes or land in urban areas.

There were strict laws against vagrancy and petty theft, which were the result of an increase in homeless freedmen who were driven off their former plantations by landowners to prevent the break-up and dispersion to the former slaves of their holdings.

Black laborers who left their jobs prior to the completion of the contract were subject to arrest by any white male.

In South Carolina blacks had to pay an annual tax from $10–$100 if they wished to follow any occupation other than farmer or servant.

Apprenticeship laws required all black minors to work without pay for planters.

In Louisiana and Texas labor contracts specified that the contracts "shall embrace the labor of all the members of the family able to work."

Mississippi required all blacks to possess written evidence of employment.

In Virginia the definition of vagrancy was defined to include anyone not willing to work for the common and usual wage.

SOURCE: FONER, 1984; SHANNON, 1973

laws and customs which determined the basic features of southern agriculture until well into the twentieth century" (Woodman, 1979, p. 324). Sharecropping became the South's new peculiar institution – a unique form of wage labor that grew up on the war-created debris of the old peculiar institution.

During the high cotton prices of the late 1860s and early 1870s the sharecropping system offered a glimmer of hope for freed blacks to move into a position of economic freedom and possibly one day own the land that the family worked (McMath, 1990). Two things emerged to crush, or at least forestall, those dreams.[7] The first was the end of Reconstruction, radical or otherwise, coming with the Compromise of 1877 across the entire region and arriving as early as 1871 in some areas (McMath, 1990). This meant the planters could more openly use race to maintain control and suppress sharecroppers without fear of federal reprisal. The second blow to the dream of equality came with the collapse of cotton prices in the wake of the 1873 crisis, which would stay depressed for over two decades. This greatly reduced profits, leaving what little profit to be made for the class with the control over the means of production (land) in the system.

Yet another impediment to immediate capitalist development in the South was the 'one crop evil', the ill effects on economic and social relations because of the domination of cotton production in the South (Hicks, 1955).[8] Because of its ubiquity, and as a source of its ubiquity, cotton was used as a virtual currency in the south. Having the qualities of money – durability, constant marketability, lacking a use value, and relatively uniform – it was widely used to barter across the South (Hicks, 1955). Because of this, it became a crop that was desired by merchants and farmers alike. Merchants would offer the farmer's store credit based on the number of acres planted in cotton, unlike corn, wheat, or potatoes. Farmers in debt were required to grow only cotton, as it was viewed as the only stable crop in the region (Goodwyn, 1978; Hicks, 1955). Thus the drive to specialize was part of the social order of the time and should be viewed as an economic compulsion despite its effect of diminishing self-sufficiency of farmers.

---

7 The literature on the Agricultural ladder outlines the emergence of a new 'rung' in the latter to full ownership of farm land through tenancy and/or sharecropping- see: Attack (1989b); Black and Allen (1937); Bogue (1959); Curti (1959); Gates (1936); Le Duc (1950); Saloutos (1962); and Winters (1978).
8 The phrase impediment to capitalist development should be taken with a grain of salt. As one of the key distinctions of the approach I am advocating for is the understanding that capitalist development is not an automatic occurrence, but requires an active state to build.

This reveals the lack of control over production that remained even in petty commodity forms of agriculture. Merchants insisted on cotton being planted for reasons other than just the stability of the demand. They also sought to discourage the growing of other crops for self-sufficiency thereby creating a more dependent relationship. Likewise the practice of leaving fields fallow or growing crops to rebuild fertility was viewed as something that would cut into fertilizer sales. The compulsion to plant every acre in the south with cotton was rooted partially in the need for ever more and ever cheaper cotton to fuel the capitalist Northeastern and English mills, which was reinforcing merchant power across the South as it had for the previous almost 200 years, while undermining plantation power. Here we see clearly the sharp distinction between the merchant forced class dynamics in the South and the construction of market based demand that occurred in the North, reflecting the continuation of the uneven development of the economy in the US at the time. In the North the state's actions occurred along the agro-industrial project while in the South the entrenched power of the plantation class prevented state policies that would create petty commodity production and its industrializing incentives. It wasn't the lack of influence of capitalism or the lack of market imperatives – planters in the South were pushed to expand production and reduce production costs. Instead, it was the existing political power and nature of the class structure that produced the divergent outcomes between the North and South.

Coming out of the Civil War, for reasons already discussed, credit and capital necessary to invest in the years crops and make regular wage payments for work to wage laborers, along with the payments for supplies, was impossible for many planters. "The lengthy production time of the cotton crop exacerbated the already severe problems of lack of capital and increased the necessity of post-harvest payment based systems" (Mann, 1990, p. 85). In these conditions, "the quintessence of most financial dealings in southern agriculture was waiting" for what was known as "long pay", so that "from the poorest laborer to the large planter and merchant, the problem of obtaining cash and credit on the basis of crops which would not be sold until the end of the year proved paramount" (Jaynes, 1986, p. 225). These natural attributes of cotton production were compounded in 1866 and 1887 by natural disasters in the form of an overly wet year that wreaked havoc on the crop which was followed by a drought and then more flooding and then by first the boll worm and then the cotton caterpillar invasions (Wiener, 1978). In the face of these natural barriers for many landowners there was an advantage in sharecropping over wage payments, as croppers became a form of insurance or risk sharing alongside the landowners. There were also advantages for freedmen as the tendency for planters to either throw laborers off the land after a bad harvest or to not pay them, or both, was removed when they were given a share of the crop. Again the legal system in the South at the time was tilted in favor of landowners and there was little recourse in the wage system for laborers to recover unpaid wages (Mann, 1990).

The long season of the crop also enabled the rise of the crop-lien system for many small landowners and planters alike. There have been similar credit monopoly systems in other sectors and even in industrial production, yet they appear mostly in isolated areas or during crises moments in an industry or in the credit system, rather than widespread and preferred, as in cotton production (Mann, 1990). Furthermore, when the cotton South is compared to the wheat growing Midwest, where there was an even longer production time, we see how the rapid emergence of local and state banks and mortgage companies crushed the monopolistic local credit merchants, illustrating the interaction between natural attributes and the proclivities of the individual and the local political struggles they inform (Mann, 1990). The unique nature of Southern development therefore, led to an uneven yet combined development of productive forces that severed as an impediment to agro-industrial development in the South.

The gang labor systems across the south did initially settle in those areas where plantation owners were able to gather the necessary capital, but by 1867 the gang system all but disappeared from the cotton fields (Foner, 1984). The advantages of allowing more independence for the croppers through sharecropping were that it offered freedmen an escape from gang labor and day-to-day supervision; it also reduced cost and labor supervision for planters and allowed them to share the risks with croppers; and most importantly it stabilized the work force by utilizing all family members and giving croppers a vested interest in staying around until the harvest (Foner, 1984; Jayne, 1986). Sharecropping also allowed freed black males a patriarchal and paternal role, as control over households let freedmen have some form of or feeling of control over their destiny, while at the same time reversing the trend toward the removal of female and children from field work that was occurring through the attempts at wage systems (Mann, 1990).

There is evidence that the civil war slowly pushed many southwestern farmers into machine adoption, by first limiting the availability of labor and forcing capitalist wage farming (Mann, 1990). In the North the farm labour shortage created by the war, along with the increased demand for products, high prices, and general technological advance resulted in a precipitous rise in farm machinery sales and use between 1862 and 1865. The number of mowers manufactured rose from 20,000 to 70,000. Associated with these sales were demonstrations on the use of such devices and the acquisition of materials and publications related to their use. It also increased the use of biological, chemical, genetic and mechanical advances in agriculture, which should be viewed as the "social modification or reduction of natural obstacles to capitalist production" or what others have called "appropriationism" (Mann, 1990, p. 116; Goodman, Sorj and Wilkinson, 1987). This particular confluence of events put pressure on the state to advance technological development in agriculture as a means to solve the immediate problems.

The cost of agricultural labor required to grow the major crops declined rapidly after the Civil War due to the increase in paid labor available for hire with the demise of the slave system. The labor cost of producing a bushel of wheat in 1830 was $0.19 and dropped to $0.10 by 1896; for corn a bushel fell from being worth $0.13 in 1850 to $0.08 in 1894; for cotton the cost in 1841 was $1.23 and in 1895 it had dropped to $0.94; over an average of twenty-seven different crops the labor cost for machine versus strict hand labor produced crops was about half as much (US Commission of Labor, 1898, pp. 24–25). Tobacco was the only industry that hadn't had a major technological breakthrough sufficient to cause a large reduction in labor costs, seeing a rise between 1853 and 1895 by 15 cents per 100 lbs. This is confirmed by the Census data of 1900 that showed a reduction for labor costs in all major crops by 46 percent over a 44-year period (USDA, 1936). Furthermore, the percent of the price of a crop that labor costs accounted for also dropped; in that wheat it fell from 38.34 percent in 1830 to just 6.75 percent going to labor by 1896; in cotton it fell from labor costs making up roughly 246 percent of the cost of production in 1841 to 94 percent in 1895 (Shannon, 1945).[9]

The planters that did try to implement a wage labour system after the war largely failed (Zeichner, 1939). This is why McMath (1990) called sharecropping "a rough and unequal compromise between the desire of the planter for control and that freedman for independence" (p. 31). Foner (1984) summarized the drawn-out class restructuring:

> It was an economic transformation that would culminate, long after the end of Reconstruction, in the consolidation of a rural proletariat composed of the descendants of former slaves and white yeomen, and

---

9 There is some ambiguity caused by the dates for the data available. Since the antebellum numbers are for a full decade or two prior to the war, it is possible technological improvements occurred in the 1850s. Shannon (1945) noted, "some of the gains, above mentioned, came before 1860, but most of them were achieved afterward" (p. 145). Regardless, the numbers come from 1830 or later, so this sustains the argument that the transition to capitalist agriculture came about after the 1840s.

of a new owning class of planters and merchants, itself subordinate to Northern financiers and industrialists (p. 78).

A rural proletariat would be a long time coming and would first have to pass through sharecropping. Overall tenancy rates in the entire US increased by just fewer than ten percent for the two decades after 1870 (Shannon, 1945, p. 418). There were eleven states that had increases over ten percent with three states having greater than twenty percent increased rates in tenancy: Louisiana, Oklahoma, and South Dakota. In the South in general there was a 12.4 percent increase and the West had only a 2.6 percent increase during the last 20 years of the century (Shannon, 1945). These numbers on the rates of change hide the absolute percentages, which in seven states topped fifty percent, with Mississippi and South Carolina having over sixty percent of farmers in tenant relations (Shannon, 1945).

Uneven Development across the South

By 1930 less than thirty percent of US cotton farms would rely on wage labor for production (US Census Bureau, 1930) and already by 1890, about 40 percent of all farmers in the south were tenants, with tenancy rates at about 20 percent across the north (Gates, 1973). Between 1865 and 1880, sharecropping spread beyond the plantation belt and into predominantly white farming areas (Mann, 1990). The Cotton Belt witnessed a concentration of wealth and an increase in social stratification between the 1830s and 1860s (McMath, 1990). However this seemingly rapid rise in tenancy, similar to one occurring simultaneously on a smaller scale in the Northern prairies, when viewed in the long history of the US reveals a steady trend of increased tenancy alongside petty commodity production and increasing stratification (Gates, 1973).

The shift to sharecropping and tenancy that occurred across much of the plantation areas failed to take root in some pockets of the South. In the upcountry regions, the relative isolation from the market of farmers in the upper piedmont areas of the Carolinas, Georgia, Alabama, and Mississippi, and in the thinly settled Wire-grass regions of the Georgia-Alabama coastal plain that had led to a kind of rural self-sufficiency, began to break down in the 1870s (McMath, 1990). During the 1870s in these regions the balance shifted from self-sufficiency in foodstuffs toward cotton or tobacco production for the market as farmers increasingly becoming dependent on the whim of alien forces outside of their community. In the upcountry, where less than one quarter of citizens were black, the wealth distribution was more similar to the North than in the south, where concentrations of wealth and property were higher. Some counties of the Georgian upcountry had farms that were over seventy-five percent non-slave and amongst those with slaves, around 80 percent had fewer than ten. McMath stated: "the world of the upcountry yeomen was one in which production of consumption focused on the household; in which kinship rather than the marketplace mediated most productive relations; in which general farming prevailed and family self-sufficiency proved the fundamental concern; and in which networks of exchange proliferated" (p. 29). Hahn argues the upcountry South "renders somewhat artificial the neat categories of subsistence and commercial agriculture, pointing instead to an entire system of productive organization – paralleled elsewhere in early America – that combined features of each within an overriding logic of its own" (2006, p. 29; see also Clark 1979; Henretta, 1978). What Shannon calls a yeoman-farmer class, "in between the landlord-capitalist and landless-farmer (cropper) groups continued after the war" (1973, p. 98). These yeoman families looked to securing most of life's necessities "through their own efforts", yet, most farmers also exchanged some products for others (Hahn, 2006, pp. 29–33). The incentive to increase production to pay off debt to maintain control of the land was largely absent in these pockets in the immediate postbellum South.

In a similar process as had occurred in the Midwestern and Western railroad line construction, Southern construction also generated right of way controversies, along with, speculative land dealings and increased attention to market production that would undermine self-sufficiency and independence (Weiman, 1983). Merchants and craftsman located in the upcountry areas also feared the lines would disrupt their way of life by connecting them to outside markets, thus increasing the desire for purchased goods.

These upcountry family farms that had been weakly connected to national and international markets had their independence undermined by military destruction and the economic and political policies of the Confederacy during the war. In the post war 1870s further developments removed this relative isolation. There occurred a marked decline of self-sufficiency not only in food stuffs but in other household items. One example is the decline in spinning wheels in Georgia upcountry counties from being in seven of ten households in 1850 down to two in ten by the 1880s, as these upcountry yeoman families increasingly became reliant on markets for clothes (Hahn, 1983, p. 186).

Again, much like in the north during the 1850s and 1860s, the expansion of the market for home items in the 1870s and 1880s pulled in simple commodity producers across the southern upcountry and created an increased reliance on the market for farm input, outputs and home goods. Southern market dependence emerged through three interrelated developments: one, the spread of railroads into the area, linking producers with markets; two, shops emerging as merchants moved in, providing connections for farmers to buy inputs and to sell their products; three, both of the above brought phosphate fertilizer into the region allowing them to produce cotton on commercial scales at a reduced cost (McMath, p. 34). This meant increased class power for those who produced and sold goods both to farmers and those who made products out of farm commodities, while a decrease in power to those who were increasingly reliant on the dictates of the market to both sell their corps and buy inputs and products. Shannon (1973) reduced the number of classes down to two because of these developments:

> As far as income is concerned, in the cotton belt there was little difference between croppers, tenants, and small freeholders. All were victim to the crop-lien system wherever it prevailed. Hence there were essentially two classes: on the one hand, the landlord-merchant-banker-capitalist group, numbering approximately a sixth of the total population and having all the political power; on the other, the great bulk of field workers, living from enfeebled hand to empty mouth (p. 99).

The changes occurring, minus the impact of the war itself, all appear on the surface to be entirely market driven. Two points are worth mentioning here: first, that undergirding all of the southern activity were state actions; and second, that none of the changes really led directly to a capitalist southern agricultural economy. The railroads had been granted land in exchange by the state for laying lines and without which they probably wouldn't have risked the capital. Merchants relied on these rail lines for their very existence and also benefited from the racial policies that kept black sharecroppers out of the upcountry and allowed the white majority of independent landowners to become dependent on the merchant's shops for agricultural inputs and as a marketing source for products. Therefore, "[s]outhern public policy was all on the side of the crop-lien credit system...[which] was maintained to almost total neglect of banking and the building of a sound financial structure", as well as the racial divisions through the Black Codes (Shannon, 1973, 99). Here we witness the active hand of the state, influenced by the remnants of the power of the planter class, in the maintenance of non-capitalist social property relations that were inhibiting the full development of the labor and capital markets.

In the region along the Virginia-North Carolina border the transformation came through technological changes facilitating a transition from self-sufficient cotton farming towards flue-cured bright-leaf tobacco production for markets. This new crop strain, the rising demand for which came from the increasing popularity of cigarettes, when combined with commercial fertilizer allowed extensive production in this region, hitching these farmers to commercial markets in a new way. Prior to the widespread availability of commercial fertilizer, tobacco required crop rotation and fallowing, and this in turn, required extensive land holdings with limited commercial linkages or debt. Much like the up-country farmers switch to cotton had initiated the adoption of widespread monoculture; bright-leaf tobacco in the region led the formerly independent agrarians increasingly under the yoke of debt and the dictates of distant markets and tobacco warehouses towards ever chasing productivity gains. Similarly, it strengthened the small-town merchant who was no longer just a neighbor but became the link in the commercial chain between the farmers and the wholesale centers and the commercial source of farm inputs – seeds and fertilizer (McMath, 1990). The important role of commercial fertilizer in pushing cotton and tobacco farmers into market dependence is very similar to the process achieved by mechanization of grain production in the North, "but this chemical technology, like the mechanical technologies of the Great Plains, locked the up-country farmer ever more tightly into a cycle of indebtedness" because almost all small producers of "cotton and tobacco bought their fertilizer on credit" (McMath, 1990, p. 37). Again the former slave relations had depressed cotton prices to the point where the fertility of the soil was neglected in an effort to secure a marketable crop and make a profit to pay off the requisite loans, all of which fed into the need for increased chemical inputs and the resulting indebtedness to merchants.

Yet another force pushing the up-country yeoman into market dependence was their ability to expand, however limited, into the broken up plantations that offered better soil and growing conditions. This extensive expansion further demonstrated the non-capitalist nature of some of the decisions made in these relationships as the newly petty commodity farmers held to their prior thinking about increased production through new land. Rather than investment in new forms of production, technology, or increased wage laborers, the tendency was to expand the holding, plant and work more acreage with the same family labor, and utilizing the same methods of production in an effort to maintain simple or limited petty commodity production. Apart from the adaption of a new form of tobacco and shift in some production methods, the major movements were to expand the area farmed and to increase the self-exploitation of their own and their family's labor. This sort of *extensive* growth based on the absolute growth of surplus labor is typical of non-capitalist forms of social labor (Marx, 1976; Brenner, 1977, Shaikh, 1978). There was little evidence of gains in productivity through the replacement of labor with new and more complex tools and machinery – the "increase in *relative* surplus labor extraction that typifies capitalist agriculture and industry" (Post, 2006, p. 7). The movement to extensive expansion of yeoman agriculture in the post-bellum South was more the exception than the rule. Much more common were failed attempts at land acquisition and ownership, or the drive toward sharecropping through debt.

Tenancy and the Class Politics of Reconstruction

In this vortex of failed dreams of both the freedmen to be independent farmers, and of the planters to maintain complete control over the labor required for their crops, emerged the crop lien system representing another class in the south seeking to squeeze a profit out of hard times: the merchant. Shannon (1945) described the emergence of the crop-lien system and merchant power thusly:

> The landlord no longer could mortgage his labor supply for credit, and the uncertainties of crops in the period of transition made necessary some other means of financing the croppers during the season. So the workers, and sometimes the owners as well, turned to the local country storekeepers whom they were acquainted (p. 89).

With Southern banking still in a shambles from the war, as it would remain until at least 1875, Southern farmers were desperate for the necessary capital to plant and produce a crop. The lack of banks was so extreme in some areas, as in the twenty-three counties of Georgia where there wasn't even a single bank, the merchants were the only people being given any sort of credit, which they in turn advanced to farmers (Hicks, 1931). Often this arrangement took the form of merchants lending out the necessary goods and inputs to farmers so they could plant a crop and live until the next harvest through a lien on the product produced and often backed up by the very land upon which it was to grow serving as collateral. This practice was facilitated by quick changes in the laws making the practice legal in most southern states (Hicks, 1931). As a testament to the decline in planter political power, the planters failed at an attempt to legally limit the capacity to grant liens to anyone but property owners. This over-ruling by the strengthening merchant class, who benefitted in granting lien contracts to croppers, reveals the shifting balance of class forces or class fractions (Brooks, 1914). The tendency was for the two classes to merge as plantation owner after plantation owner failed to meet his debt obligations to the merchants, leading to merchant consolidation of cropland. This situation produced a few distinct advantages for merchant landowners over the planters. The first was that tenants preferred absent ownership that allowed for greater autonomy in production. The second was the ability of merchants to grant debt to tenants. And finally, merchants tended to raise prices and charge high interest rates on the products and debt they made available to both tenants and planters (Foner, 1990; Hicks, 1931; McMath, 1992; Shannon, 1973;).

All of the changes worked in the interest of merchants and steadily strengthened their position in the new South: "the effect of the crop liens was to establish a condition of peonage throughout the cotton south...the farmer who gave a lien on his crop delivered himself over to the tender mercies of the merchant who held the mortgage" (Hicks, 1931, p. 43). The reasons why farmers, croppers and planters might enter into crop liens were twofold: first, they often had no choice because they lacked the necessary resources to plant that year's crop; and second, similar to the rise of sharecropping, the relationship transferred some of the risk onto the merchants (Shannon, 1973). As it did to former planters and poor landless whites across the south, the credit system and crop-lien arrangements quickly undermined the promise of autonomy made to freed slaves (Foner, 1990).

The crop-lien system worked well for the merchants despite years of bad crops in the late 1860s. One reason for this was because of price weighting, where the price of the goods consumed by the farmers was dependent on the financial needs of the merchants. Many of the goods sold by merchants never had a set cash price, since almost all of the merchants business was on credit, and the price would rise alongside the assumed risk, so that many farmers were perpetually barely able to clear their yearly liens after harvest (Shannon, 1973). Once in debt past a season the situation most often became even more inescapable as no other stores would carry the farmer once a lien was in place granting the holder of the lien power to raise prices at will on the farmer with no recourse, setting in motion the trajectory leading to an eventual loss of the very land they became indebted to save (Shannon, 1973). Thus the remnants of class power held by planters effected the development trajectory of the South in the aftermath of the Civil War and pushed the structure of the economy not into an emergent capitalist class, but towards a merchant class ascendance.

What emerged were three capitalist fractions within the postbellum Republican Party. The first was based in the banking and financial interests who formed a national association in 1869 to advocate for increased inflationary policies and a return to the gold standard. A second was based in the tariff-sensitive industries, most predominantly Pennsylvania iron, and those who relied on iron, most importantly railroads. A third capitalist fraction aligned within the Republican Party represented Western and Southern periphery interests. In opposition to both the rising protectionism and the idea of a resumption of species payment and deflationary monetary policy, this fraction, while less influential, did help to deepen the growing rift in the party, which ultimately undermined Reconstruction. The Republican Party of the era was effectively a "hegemonic coalition in the northern section of the country", where the different powerful interests lobbied for their positions in an attempt to influence the program of the party (Bensel, 1990, p. 311), but differences within it nevertheless ran deep over the financial issues of the day. Between 1865 and 1871 there were ten congressional bills that clearly revealed the influence of the financial sector (Timberlake, 1978).[10] All this legislative activity reflected the financial sector attempting to tip the balance of class forces "members from districts with relatively high allocations of national bank notes ('capital-rich' districts) delivered much more support for the finance capital position than did members from districts with smaller shares of circulation (relatively 'capital-poor' districts)" (Bensel, 1990, p. 323).

The failure of Reconstruction was rooted in how the Republican Party fragmented into, first two separate factions under the circumstances of the Postbellum era. The financial wing of the party sought financial stability, a return to the gold standard, the reestablishment of cotton cultivation, and a strong administrative capacity in the treasury. On the other side were those pushing for a radical Reconstruction, mostly freed blacks and radical northerners, were who had previously aligned around tariff issues and their objection to southern slavery, who now threatened southern plantation owner's rights to own land as well as many of the interests of financial capital. The fear that Reconstruction would spread over to state confiscation of white yeoman land, as much as the very idea that land could be appropriated and redistributed by the state – an idea actively popularized by plantation owners and others who opposed radical Reconstruction – pushed many to abandon reconstruction. Reconstruction completely collapsed by 1871. Its failure and the subsequent split it caused in the party served to crush the electoral viability of the Republican Party in much of the South for a long time.

---

10   They were: The Bankruptcy act of 1867; the bill to Ban counterfeiting public securities; a bill to dissolve the national banking system; bills that led to the public sale of treasury gold; the rejection of a bill to tax bank capital and circulation; the bills that came to be known as the Public Credit Act, which ensured that the US would pay its debt in full to creditors; the failure of efforts to expand Greenback circulation; a bill failed that sought to overturn aspects of the Public Credit Act; the National Bank Currency Act seeking to turn the US' debt into long-term securities similar to the British consoles or French rents; and the Refund act of 1870, which redeemed the currencies known as the 5/20's that had been put into circulation during the war (Timberlake, 1978).

Reconstruction was effectively ended with the compromise of 1877 when the Southern ruling class ceded federal power over to Northern capital in exchange for sectional and political control through the revival of institutional racism in the form of black codes and the end of the Freedman's Bureaus power (Dowd, 1974; O'Conner, 1975). The steady rise of Jim Crow out of this situation was a desperate attempt to hold onto power in the face of shifting class forces by the remaining plantation elite, while simultaneously undermining radical reconstruction and southern black Republican power. Thus, as James O'Conner (1975) pointed out "capitalism did not need Jim Crow so much economically as politically, given the uneven development of the US economy as a whole" (p. 48). In fact, economically segregation set back the south for decades to come. Yet the inability of southern planters to transform their class position and the social relations of agriculture into capitalist forms, combined with the ongoing transformation of northern farmers due to market expansion and their convergence with capitalist social relations, eventually fueling the rise of popular sentiments against these socially disruptive changes. The situation was ripe for a political movement that could unite Northern and Southern farmers of all types.

Conclusion

We have seen that even after the Civil War, severe obstacles to the implantation of fully capitalist social relations remained in place. Capitalism, Mann (1990) wrote, "is neither invincible nor inevitable" (p. 128). The history of US agriculture reveals how the path of capitalist development was still often blocked and that the removal of these barriers was often accomplished through extra-economic intervention or through non-capitalist social relations being propped up. The arrival of capitalism as the hegemonic social order in the US occurred only with the decline of power held by the class of simple commodity producers and plantation slave owners. The class struggle between these classes, as Marx early on recognized, is key to understanding the history of the US development of capitalism (O'Conner, 1974). This class struggle was still ongoing after the Civil War ended and only really was resolved, or more accurately arrived at its respite from the acute nature of the struggle, with the increased control by merchants, bankers and later corporations of the 20th century.

We also can see the role of the state in passing legislation and aiding in the perpetuation of planter power, as well as aiding in the rise of merchant power in the South. The rise of tenancy amidst particularities of southern agriculture and the situation of the class struggle, informed the operation of state institutions, and this in turn gave rise to new social struggles that eventually played out with the emergence of the populist movement. The many changes in the South would increasingly render farmers under the control of merchants through the rise of tenancy and sharecropping. The inability of Planters after the war to access the capital necessary to run their operations in the South pushed many large landowners off of the land. Meanwhile the political power of the plantation class stalled the necessary legal changes and state policies to create equitable contracts with small farmers and blocked agro-industrial policies that would've hastened the rise of a class of petty commodity farmers. Simultaneously, landless farm laborers emerged who were put to work as tenants instead of wage earners by this same lack of capital and the racially segregated nature of the social order. These two processes, obviously linked backward to slavery's impact on the social, political and economic uneven development across the region, would inflict a brutal pressure on farmers that would eventually fuel the populist movement.

So while the Civil War officially ended slavery in the South it did not usher in an alignment of Southern agriculture with that in the North through industrial capitalism and modernization through petty commodity farming; the only exception being in the up-country region that did begin to move into petty commodity forms of production. Due to the continued political strength but lack of requisite capital of the planter class, what emerged was a compromise between that still entrenched but diminishing planter class and the newly freedmen and white, property-less tenant farmers. The increasing tenancy and share-cropping rates in the South throughout the postbellum era stood in sharp contrast to the continuing success of the economic development in the North.

In its stead, there emerged a strengthened merchant class that used tenancy and control of capital, most frequently in the form of farming inputs and day-to-day necessities, to increase its standing against the politically powerful planter class. Occasionally the latter morphed into the former, but most often the planters lost their land to merchants who then rented it to tenants, croppers or the very same former landowners. This lack of a capitalist market in farm labor meant an underdevelopment of the social incentives that are witnessed in petty commodity agriculture, with its drive toward increasing mechanization, specialization and reliance on inputs. Instead, what little development of agriculture did occur in the South during the immediate postbellum era was simply through borrowed technology from the North and its continued connection to expanding capitalist markets for its agricultural products.

The lack of development in the South, of both industrial and agricultural varieties, and the power of the plantation class and the emerging merchant class would come to play an important role in the agrarian revolt that emerged with the Populist movement, although as we shall also now see, the ongoing racial divide in the South would come to ill serve the Populist movement.

CHAPTER 4

Agrarian Populism: The Rise and Fall of Populism

The chapter addresses the important role that agrarian resistance played in the institutional capacity building of the US state between 1870 and 1920. We shall see that the resistance to capitalist development in the US was incorporated into the development of state institutions through state policy and institution formation, producing a more dynamic developmental trajectory. Ultimately this process enabled a stronger and more resilient capitalist state to emerge, while in the process co-opting and disarming opposition movements by integrating them into developing industrial capitalist social relations. The path toward state institutional involvement in agriculture will be outlined with historic detail.

The removal of slavery, as was shown, did not usher in an instant turn toward capitalist agriculture production, let alone large-scale led agricultural and industrial development across the South. Instead it gave rise to heightened uneven development, with much of the South principally turning to plantation tenancy due to the nature of the state, the economy and the balance of class forces left in slaveries wake. Meanwhile, the dynamic system of industrial production continued to pick up steam in the North, and the federal political system tilted more and more toward the interests of capital over both labor and petty-commodity production (Beard and Beard, 1930; Saloutos, 1982; Williams, 1961). Geographic differences between North and South persisted, reflected in the continuation of different crops and styles of farming as well as the social relations of agriculture, which gave rise to the infamous and lasting sectorial political divides that characterized the post-civil war era. The uneven nature of the development of the economy in the US during this era produced a complex mix of different regional agrarian concerns and sources of frustration. The importance of this for the emergence of the populist movement will be examined in detail in this chapter.

Farmers and Farming in the Late 19th Century USA

As farmers became increasingly tied to markets and began to increase their level of indebtedness out of a drive to increase productivity in the postbellum era, the over-producing tendencies of agriculture recurrently asserted themselves. For a period of time immediately following the end of the Civil war the prices of agricultural goods rose, and with that Northern farmers reinvested in technological innovations, growing their land holdings and increasing the division of labor through differentiation and specialization. This altered the nature of farm life and tied farmers into ever-increasing market dependent relationships. This arose out of the increasing connection to the market and its imperative for competitive growth that put the squeeze on some farmers who were forced to either quit or increase the speed at which they turned the treadmill of production. That is, they had to further specialize, increase their acreage and reinvest in more technology to enhance their productivity or be left behind their competitors; but these investments came with a high price, i.e., they had to produce more crop tonnage to increase their revenues so they would be able to service the debt they incurred.

The many downturns in commodity prices during the late 19th century increased the debt and would severely squeeze farmers. With the population of American cities growing 59 percent between 1860 and 1870, and 42 percent between 1870 and 1880, urban demand for foodstuffs grew at least as rapidly, and receipts of livestock and other commodities at seaboard cities increased steadily over the period 1869 to 1880 (US Census, 1930). In 1870 for example, 125,922 bushels of grain were received at northeastern ocean ports; and in 1880, receipts more than doubled to total 315,497 bushels (US Census, 1930). Much of the increase was consumed in the 939 (mostly northeastern) cities that were home to 28 percent of the American population in 1880 (US Census, 1930). Thus, there was an expanding market for agricultural goods compared to the expansion of agricultural production.

The Civil War offered many additional spurs to economic and capitalist development. First of all, it not only promoted the return of securities from Europe, it also flooded financial markets with Union bonds and notes to the point that the issuance of private stocks and bonds were greatly diminished (Bensel, 1990). This expansion of government issued credit relieved the pressure that arose from private sources of financing.

During and after the Civil War there was a major increase in the role of the federal government through policy shifts, investment in infrastructure and in its authority arising from an increased use of force through an expanded federal military. This increased role of the federal government represents another reason why the effect of the war's end while a boon to industry, also increased the role of the state and after a shift in class and political alliances. Additionally, transatlantic trade absorbed a growing share of agricultural products after the Civil War. The volume of wheat exported from the US grew by a factor of five from 1865–69 to 1880–84, and wheat and wheat flour exports from the North Central States grew precipitously from about $20 million in 1870 to $127 million in 1880 (Gregson, 1993). The Republican promise to farmers of increased agricultural exports appears to have occurred in the immediate aftermath of the War.

Despite the rising industrial workforce, farmers in 1870 still made up the majority of workers in the US, with manufacturing, trade and transportation accounting for only 30 percent (Shannon, 1973). Following the war, military bounties totaling sixty one million acres were given to former soldiers, most of whom had no desire to move west and instead sold their warrants to brokers and speculators (Gates, 1973). These war bounty warrants significantly increased the supply of land for sale, temporarily forcing lower prices and making it possible in turn, for speculators to purchase twice as much land before driving prices upwards in frenzied land trading (Gates, 1973). Once again we see Federal land policy, fueling speculation in Western lands, thereby driving up farm starting costs and increasing indebtedness.

Major production gains in agriculture also came about during the 40 year period following the Civil War. Almost all of the increases in production can be attributed to just a few factors, such as the increase in the number of farms, a rising productivity of staple crops due to technological innovations, with some crops seeing reductions of 50 percent or more in man-hours required to produce crops, and increases in agricultural lands brought under cultivation – with between 15 and 25 million acres added just in the period between 1890 and 1910 (Saloutos, 1982). This expansion of production was fueled by the expansion of trade and by the increase of credit made available to agriculture; fueling both increases in size of operations and in the use of technology.

Meanwhile in the South, cotton production expanded both westward into the new territories and, to a lesser extent, into the upcountry areas of the South (Hahn, 1983). In the North the continued westward expansion of cropland combined with new techniques, seeds, and machinery to greatly increase output. In the North as petty commodity production continued to replace independent household production and harvest sizes grew due to mechanization, combined with the increased number of farms and acres farmed, the outcome was a glut of farm commodities and eventually led to a major drop in prices. After the labor shortages during the war and the associated high farm prices, leading to expanded production, the end of the War brought a glut of labor and production. The "tremendous expansion of production, particularly of the staple crops" that occurred in agriculture following the civil war, created an era of "bitter depression" for farmers across the country (Buck, 1920, p. 19). With the demobilization of the armies, ending of war industries, more immigration, improved machinery adoption, and the rails linking markets together the frontier moved ever westward (Buck, 1920). The Increased crop acreage and production depressed prices, throwing farmers into increasingly difficult situations.

Amid surplus production and during periods of nominal currency, debt became unpayable (Prasad, 2012). Adding to this downward economic pressure on prices was the handing of the baton of sectorial hegemony from agriculture to industrial manufacturing with the value added by agriculture declining from 50 percent of the total in 1859 to just 33 percent in 1899, while manufacturing increased its share of the total from 32 percent in 1859 to 49 percent by 1899 (Phillips, 2002). The increased use of food inputs to industrial manufacturing operations by emerging food manufacturers represented part of the process of differentiation that occurred. This led to, and combined with, a decline in actual consumption of staple crops such as wheat and corn, which dropped from 224 to 176 and 120 to 46 pounds per person respectively between the periods of 1827 to 1902 and 1922 to 1927 (Saloutos, 1982).

Here we see the working out of the process of capitalist transformation of agriculture, not only in the manner in which it produced raw materials directly, but also through the changing of social diets to accommodate an increase in consumer products and corporate activity. This differentiation of food production into constituent elements based on commodities is one means of capturing value from agriculture outside of the immediate growing process. It rests on the commodification of farm products occurring through market imperatives of commodification of crops.

In the South cotton prices decreased to a third of the price per pound between 1870 and 1897, while simultaneously the costs of seeds, fertilizers and supplies rose. Prices received by farmers for wheat, cotton, and corn all fell between the 1850s and 1894 as wheat fell from $1.53 per bushel to a low of $0.49, cotton fell from $0.32 per pound to $0.06, and corn from $0.47 per bushel to $0.25 (US Census, 1910). However, these prices represented the peak for the year, usually just before harvest, and most farmers sold their crops far below this price, usually as soon as they were harvested when the market was saturated and prices were lowest Shannon (1973). Thus the ability of farmers to gainfully plant and harvest crops, let alone carve out enough profit to improve their economic position, was undermined in most of the country by excessive oversupply, deflationary pressures of the currency regime, and a lack of the many market controlling mechanisms in place today designed to prevent such an outcome.

Money and banking greatly added to the negative pressure on farmers. Bankers and other holders of government bonds wanted a return to the gold standard after the war because the oversupply of paper money 'greenbacks' had, in their view, depreciated the currency. As Goodwyn (1978, p. 11) explained "A government decision to begin paying coin for its obligations would mean that, though the Civil War had been fought with fifty-cent dollars, the cost would be paid in one-hundred-cent dollars... taxpayers would pay the difference to the banking community holding the bonds". The return to hard money, Goodwyn argued, could only be achieved in one of two ways: first, by raising taxes and using the proceeds to pay back wartime bonds; or second, by ending greenback issuance, and contracting the currency by holding the existing money supply at current levels for a long period of time. The second route would mean that farmers would see the price they received for their products reduced as the value of the currency regained its buying power. In the near term, indebted farmers with short-term loans would face a situation that required them to immediately grow two to three times as much to pay off their debts incurred before the change in monetary policy. The greenback movement was born in opposition to the policy of holding the monetary circulation steady and letting the currency value climb, which is what was adopted and implemented. The outcome of this federal policy led to a drop in the total amount of money in circulation from $30.35 per capita in 1865 to $19.36 by 1880 (Goodwyn, 1978, p. 15). This monetary appreciation, affecting the value of all goods and services, would fuel the currency based arguments through the 1870s, including those of the Greenbackers and later the Farmers Alliance (Sanders, 1999).

Late 19th Century Agrarian Political Economy

The crisis that emerged in the fall of 1873, and the 'great deflation' that followed it in the 1880s, pushed the country to the brink of economic ruin and placed further pressure on already downtrodden farmers for decades. Farmers who had for years struggled to make ends meet, or worse those who were deep in debt, suddenly found either a lack of credit, or loans called in by creditors who demanded immediate payment (Buck, 1920). Outside the South, agricultural production had expanded rapidly in the immediate period during and after the Civil War, creating a period of overproduction and falling prices by the 1870s. The fluctuation of currency during and after the war, combined with a high tariff meant that farmers were producers of export crops but consumers of domestic machinery and inputs (Buck, 1920).

Although the claim of unsatisfied industrial workers from the east moving west to start farms has been overstated by many historians, there was a palpable westward movement (Turner, 1893). The source of this movement was likely more from Midwestern farmers fleeing the pressures to turn to petty commodity production, or new immigrants drawn by railroad companies and others, instead of eastern industrial workers. In any case, between 1870 and 1880 the population of the Dakota Territory expanded by 853 percent, that of

Nebraska by 268 percent and Kansas by 173 percent (US Census, 1900). This continuous expansion of farm acres put further downward pressures on commodity prices and increased land prices through the 1870s.

The lack of banks and capital in the west complicated the requirement for capital because "competition for markets made necessary large acreages of land and a continuous process of increased mechanization"; enabling money lenders to charge unsustainably high interest rates (Shannon, 1945, p. 303). Barry Eichengreen (1984) has argued that the interest rates extended to farmers during this period were commensurate with the risk assumed by lenders given the risky nature of farming, while Sarah Quinn (2010) has made the case that even if land was free, which only a very small percent of it was, the need to borrow to start and maintain a farm was still present. Going further into debt appeared as the only solution to avoid the loss of the farm. However, the depressed prices of the next few decades combined with the mortgage rates often twice as high as national average rates (Prasad, 2012, pp. 72–73). This undermined the capacity to repay the loans and the expansion of acreage and the situation was exacerbated by increased mechanization that led to ever larger harvests that further depressed prices (Shannon, 1945).

Worsening the problem was the deflationary pressure caused by the ongoing restriction of the money supply in the post-war era. This compounded the problem as the farmer who borrowed in the early 1860s had to pay back with money worth twice as much as that borrowed in the late 1870s (Shannon, 1945). Many of the problems in the West grew out of the rapid nature of its development, basing the price and profit structure of the region on the basis of continued scarcity in everything except agricultural production (Shannon, 1945). Also important is the cycle of booms and busts in land that occurred there as outlined in Chapter 1, which brought with it booms and busts in the burgeoning Western banking industry, all of which gave rise to a great skepticism in the farmers of the era (Prasad, 2012). Additionally, as argued, it may not have been the deflationary pressure on the prices they received for their crops or the high interest rates alone, but the fact that market prices were increasingly putting new pressure on farmers and coercing them through the growing market imperatives (Mayhew, 1972).

If there was one recognizable trend in the US during the last quarter of the nineteenth century it was the boom and bust cycles, not the least of which was seen in the availability of credit. Occurring in the Midwest during the 1880s there was what Hicks (1931) called an "avalanche of credit" (p. 23). This fed a rash of overinvestment and speculation that aided by a few years of bumper crops, high prices, and rising land values. This speculation and over-investment took place in land, for both investors and farmers of all kinds, but it also led to a rush to invest in new breeds of animal stock and the purchasing of the best and newest available equipment (Hicks, 1931). Census data shows that the states with some of the most rapid population expansions – i.e., Kansas, Nebraska, the Dakotas, and Minnesota – had the highest mortgage debt per capita while also being some of the poorest regions of the nation (US Census, 1890). As Hicks (1931) stated, most of these Western states were "literally mortgaged for all they were worth" and sometimes much beyond that (p. 24). The peak of land speculation in this cycle came in 1887. Caught up in the boom were many federal, state and local offices that passed bond measures for investments in public and private enterprises, enhancing the booms while helping to lead to their inevitable bust.

By late 1887 the strength of the boom in land expansion and prices waned just as a draught ensued – an unexpected environmental shock that would continue for the next ten seasons. Between 1887 and 1897, in fact, there were only two seasons during which the central and western areas received adequate rainfall to produce good harvests, and for five of the ten years there was virtually no crop at all (Hicks, 1931). This drought led to crop failures and a further escalation of debt. The resulting land value slump helped to push down the entire economy of the Midwest and West. Towns that had sprung up like mushrooms on the prairie disappeared as quickly, leaving behind abandoned ghost towns. Farms across the region were foreclosed or abandoned. In Kansas alone between 1889 and 1893, over eleven thousand farms were foreclosed with some counties seeing 90 percent of the agricultural land changing hands (Hicks, 1931). Thus, the vicissitudes of uneven development in this region of the nation continued to plague agriculture worse than other areas of the economy and would, as we shall see, fuel a strong social movement. As Hofstadter (1955) stated, "the collapse of this [land] boom provides the immediate background of western populism" (p. 56), the boom had rested on rising prices for commodities and land due to the uneven nature of development, which was the source of the contradictions that helped end the boom. The boom and bust cycles, that plagued the US economy in the last quarter of the 19th Century served to grow the agrarian unrest just as this social group was near its peak in terms of both size and strength.

The Rise of Populism

The uneven development of US agriculture, the particular state and federal institutional responses to this uneven development, the agrarian social movements that formed, and the balance of class forces, all came to inform and propel the emergence of the populist movement toward the end of the 19th Century. In the North the deepening market dependence expanded with petty commodity agriculture. Simultaneously, in the South the expansion of tenancy and sharecropping created growing farmer indebtedness. These two forces combined with the economic crisis from 1872–1890 creating an acute agrarian political struggle.

Just as these struggles on the land were advancing, the antagonism between classes was commanding a greater degree of attention in national politics. In the late 19th century tensions between them led to the US Senate opening the first ever comprehensive investigation of the "relations between labor and capital". They were joined by "newspaper editors, ministers, local politicians, and other members of the elite in making 'class conflict' part of the American political vocabulary as never before" and this occurred just as "the social and political thrust of the Gilded Age met staunch popular challenges" (Hahn, 1983, p. 1). The highlights of the hearing related to the recurring theme of the lack of contract law in the South, with many, from differing class locations, testifying that stricter laws and enforcement of farm labor contracts would have eased many of the recurring problems in southern agriculture and the drive towards tenancy (US Congress, 1885). In response to the lack of contract law, the entrenched strength of the plantation owners, the use of white supremacy, and the lack of an effective agro-industrial project, the South emerged as a hotbed of the radical agrarian movement, beginning with the Grange.

This recognition of the acute nature of political struggles over changing class relations is the starting point of analysis of the populist movements. "To describe the origins of Populism in one sentence, the cooperative movement recruited American farmers, and their subsequent experience within the cooperatives radically altered their political consciousness… The agrarian revolt cannot be understood outside the framework of the economic crusade that not only was its source but also created the culture of the movement itself" (Goodwyn, 1978, p. xvii).

The great debate over the essential nature of agrarian reform and populism of the late 1800s is best represented by the work of Richard Hofstadter (1955) and Lawrence Goodwyn (1978). For Hofstadter, populists suffered from irrational status anxiety in a changing world; Populism was unjustified extremism. For Goodwyn, the agrarian movement was entirely rational having identified several financial structures and practices as leading to unfair outcomes for farmers.

The Grange, officially referred to as The National Grange of the Order of Patrons of Husbandry, was a fraternal organization in the United States that encouraged families to band together to promote the economic and political well-being of the community and agriculture. The Granger movement, while beginning in 1867, really took off in 1872 and between then and the following spring the number of Grange chapters quadrupled. The rapid growth continued, and by the end of 1873 the organization had come to penetrate all but four states – Connecticut, Rhode Island, Delaware, and Nevada (Buck, 1920). The Grange was not a political party, nor did it even profess to be involved in politics. Instead, it presented itself only as an association that worked to advance the common interests of farmers. After a brief attempt at running cooperative marketing schemes, and even a few attempts at manufacturing their own farm implements, they turned to more overtly political aims (McMath, 1992). Specifically, according to Buck (1920), they sought to:

> find practical applications in efforts to enhance the comfort and attractions of homes, maintain the laws, to advance agricultural and industrial education, to diversify crops, to systematize farm work, to establish cooperative buying and selling, to suppress personal, local, sectional, and national prejudices, and to discountenance the credit system, the fashion system, and every other system tending to prodigality and bankruptcy (p. 28)

The prior accomplishments of the Farmers' Cooperative Demonstration Work (FCDW) acted as a model and laid the ground work for the push by the Grange. Yet despite their timid and avowed non-political approach, the establishment of the Grange marked the definitive entrance of poor white farmers as a class into politics at a national level (Buck, 1920). By determining early on that to become effective they needed to attract all members of the farming "class" the Grange became one of the first mass based farmers' movements in the US. To accomplish this task required first approaching issues with broad support, such as railroad monopolies, even if they had not yet grasped how their approach would alienate sharecroppers and most black farm laborers.

In the upcountry of the South the Granger movement would come to align with conservative Democrats in a convenient 'marriage' of strange bedfellows. The grievances of most southern yeoman, and newly turned sharecroppers shared much in common with the rest of the movement. However, Hahn showed how a large basis of upcountry Granger support came from large landowners who joined in an effort to stop the advance of the merchants. The first Grange locals were established not in the South but in New York and Minnesota, although the movement found more fertile ground in the South due to the high number of tenants and poor state of the rural economy.

The first few truly political actions of the Grange were numerous attempts to get laws passed to regulate railroads, specifically seeking to set rates charged to farmers for freight. The earliest political successes came in Illinois during the late 1860s and early 1870s. Due to the agitation of the Grange in the late 1860s the new Illinois State Constitution of 1870 contained a provision directing the state legislature to pass laws to prevent extortion and unjust discrimination in railway charges, only to have the state supreme court declare it unconstitutional in 1873 (Buck, 1920). But the following year Granger members flocked to the state legislature convincing them to pass even stricter laws, and in June they flocked to the polls and "retired" the deciding judge in the prior state Supreme Court case (Buck, 1920). Thus it became clear that a political stance aimed at the economic interests the farmers easily understood and that placed their class interest in an antagonistic relationship with a definable and recognizable opposing class as being responsible for their plight was an effective approach to politics for the Grange.

The lasting impacts of the Grange's ability to mobilize farmers can be seen in the many other laws passed to regulate railroads and a good many higher court cases involved the rights of states to regulate railroad rates: laws passed in Wisconsin, Minnesota and Illinois that became known as the Granger Laws (Buck, 1920).[1] The Grange sought federal regulations to improve roads and deliver parcels; provide for the direct election of US senators (in an effort to remove railroad influence); women's suffrage; and offer agricultural education. At the peak of their agitation, they even forced the US Senate to take up railroad regulation concerns and there were numerous federal railroad regulations that emerged directly from these Granger campaigns of the 1870s (Skowronek, 1982). State railroad regulations came in most prominently in those states with the largest and most effective Granger movements (Buck, 1913). George Miller (1971) argued that the federal railroad regulations based on the Illinois Commission of 1873 was a conservative attempt at co-opting and containing the more radical agrarian organization demands.

Granger successes at pushing issues and getting candidates elected inspired others mostly in the Midwest, to follow suit and move into the electoral politics arena. Short lived, spontaneous third parties emerged all across the prairies around numerous issues – tariff rates, civil service systems and the currency – however, most had at the center of their platform railroad regulation (Buck, 1920). These early attempts were but harbingers of the national movement that would come later once these movements gained political maturity, but they planted the seed by showing that "solidarity could be obtained among the

---

1   The Illinois Granger laws focused primarily on eliminating the discrimination between long haul and short haul rates of railroads and regulating the maximum price charged by grain storage facilities.

agricultural class" through the advocacy of immediate economic interests (Buck, 1920, p. 35).

More than merely prophetic though, some of the figures and movements to emerge would come to exhibit real staying power and would play a prominent role in later farmers' movements. One such figure was Ignatius Donnelly, who in 1873 was elected to the Minnesota State Senate on the Anti-Monopoly party ticket and started the newspaper – *The Anti-Monopolist*. Donnelly's influence would continue to play a role in agrarian politics despite the fading Granger movement that transformed into the populist political movement (Buck, 1920) in light of the desperate situation farmers found themselves facing.[2]

Although only forming the very early ruminations of the process, the Grangers did initiate a shift in the administration of federal institutions, one that moved away from the legislature to an administrative body and the courts (Skowronek, 1982). This would pick up speed later on, after the tide of populism receded, in an effort to insulate institutional development from expanding agrarian electoral power.

The Granger movement reached its high water mark in 1874, after which it receded "as quickly as it had grown" (Buck, 1920, p. 14; Goodwyn, 1978). Many who had turned to the Grange in hopes of seeing immediate improvements in their affairs left when this did not materialize as rapidly as they had expected. Government regulation of railroads had turned out to aid railroads and pushed farmers further into commodified market reliance instead of eliminating their problems. Moreover, local businessmen joined the Grange and hoped to make connections to politicians who latched on to the emerging political movement out of self serving interests, all of which tended to alienate many farmers who felt that the organization was drifting from its core role. The failure of numerous cooperative attempts also helped undermine Granger support, as did the continued debate between the National Grange and the local chapters. Unlike the Farmers Alliance that was to follow, the cooperative efforts of the Grange were viewed as a means of circumventing the railroad monopolies, which were little affected by the "Granger Laws" (Buck, 1920). Once railroad regulations were put in place, in the mid to late 1870s, (however watered-down), the solidarity of the movement quickly receded and along with them thorough critiques of the banking system.

Picking up some of the momentum was the small emerging Greenbacker movement. The Greenback argument for fiat currency, rather than a gold

---

2 Iowa farmers who were forced to burn their corn crops for fuel because the going rate was only fifteen cents a bushel, which was less than the cost of coal while the same corn sold in the east for over a dollar a bushel.

standard, and the expansion of the money supply to aid farmers, was not at first accepted by much of the agrarian movement associated with the Grange. Granger leader Donnelly had denounced the Greenbackers in 1873 in a pamphlet in which he argued: "there is too much paper money… The currency is diluted – watered – weakened…we have no interest in an inflated money market…species payments would practically add eighteen cents to the price of every bushel of wheat" (Buck, 1920, p. 81). It was around this "financial question" that American politics would begin to break free of some of the hold of sectional affiliations that lay in the division between the North and the South and the legacy of the Civil War. It would also smooth over some of the clashes between different cultural and political norms that existed between the East and the West. Furthermore it was through the financial question that a single aim of raising prices would coalesce. This occurred through an argument for agricultural parity prices, or the idea that agricultural cost of production should determine commodity prices instead of market supply and demand. However as the Grange showed, while allowing for the rapid building of a political movement, the financial question could also undermine the movement by opening it up to reforms within commodity agriculture. Ultimately, higher prices for crops fed into agro-industrial pressures rather than highlighting the class basis of these rising pressures.

Meanwhile, the crop lien system continued to spread across the southern half of the country. The transition to sharecropping rather than a sign of a shift in forms of labor represented the increasing influence of credit over the balance of class forces in agriculture. With the enlarging role of credit, farmers' movements began to focus increasingly on financial questions within existing economic structures. Enhanced by the currency contraction policies, the crop lien system would feed off of the inability of farmers to acquire sufficient capital, making them dependent on high interest and the vagaries of crop lien (Goodwyn, 1978). For most farmers this meant the eventual loss of their land. With farm tenancy increasing in the South Central US from 36.2 percent in 1880 to 48.6 percent by 1900, crop lien/credit problems hastened the demise of the simple household farmers and continued to undermine planters, fueling the growth of the movement in this region (Snowden, 1987). These developments combined with the effects of the Civil War in the "export-based agricultural economy in a rapidly industrializing nation trapped the South in a downward spiral of poverty and near-colonial dependence" (Sanders, 1999, p. 112). As the main thing the majority of the people of the south knew how to do, farming, rested on the increasingly impossible necessity of owning land in a region severely lacking credit, the populist basis of a movement for money and bank reform was solidified by the 1880s (Sanders, 1999). It would be in Texas that the crop lien would give rise to an agrarian movement unlike any before or since. But even then the populist movement should be located in the trajectory of farmer agitation that began with the Grange, it was only because of this footing that the agrarian movement was able to develop and grow out of the maldevelopment of the South (Goodwyn, 1978).

Meanwhile in the North it wasn't crop liens that were gobbling up farmers but mortgages. The imperative to continually expand production due to agro-industrial development was driving farmers further and further into debt. The high level of indebtedness of Midwestern farmers was compounded by the crisis of 1887 that caused interest rates to rise precipitously. Reluctant to bear the burden themselves, the banks and holders of mortgages merely passed their hardship onto those lacking the power to resist the financial haircut. Mortgage rates on farmland climbed to averages of eighteen to twenty four percent, with forty percent not being unheard of (Hicks, 1931). An editor of the Farmers Alliance Newspaper (1890) opined:

> There are three great crops raised in Nebraska. One is a crop of corn, one a crop of freight rates, and one a crop of interest. One is produced by farmers who by sweat and toil farm the land. The other two are produced by men who sit in their offices and behind their bank counters and farm the farmers (p. 3).

Adding insult to injury was the fact that railroads were being allowed to refinance their debt to reduce their interest payments through special help of state governments (Hicks, 1931). Tax policy also favored the railroads; they could avoid paying taxes on their very large land-granted holdings by not claiming them until the time of sale. This further solidified the notion that the state was working for the interests of the banks and railroads at great cost to the farmer. This occurred not through the direct favoring of one class over another but by structuring the possibilities in ways that fed market mediated social relations, and in these relations one class had the upper hand. In the North this was part and parcel of the process of petty commodity expansion and increased debt. In the South the lack of agro-industrial development and the particularities of the Southern economy, led to reliance on tenancy and sharecropping that fueled rising indebtedness or loss of farms. In both areas, the position of farmers – both economically and politically – was being undermined at a time when they still constituted the majority of the population.

Monica Prasad (2012, p. 93) argues that the US had a form of "mortgage Keynesianism" in which mortgage credit was used to finance consumer expansion. She convincingly makes the case that this "mortgage Keynesianism" grew out of the progressive era farmers' movements (Prasad, 2012). Farmers fought the attempt to create a national sales tax in 1921 by getting Midwestern republicans to vote against their party on the issue. Again in 1932 and 1942 farmers were the major obstacle to a national sales tax. Populists backed bankruptcy law changes and progressive income taxes, and were also instrumental in getting the Interstate Commerce Commission (ICC) established to regulate railroad rates. After numerous agrarian pushed House bills garnished no action in the Senate the Interstate Commerce Act emerged from the Senate as a means to push through regulations that were more capital friendly. "Thus, at each stage in the story – the rise of the initial grievance, the solution of delegation, and the strengthening of the ICC- the unique features of American state formation in the in the context of rapid economic growth channeled politics down the line of independent regulatory agencies" (Prasad, 2012, p. 194). This sort of 'market Keynesian' needs to be understood in relation to agro-industrial project by the US state.

Populist Politics

The sectional loyalties that existed in the postbellum era, in which most tended to 'vote as they shot', overrode class interests across most of the South. On top of sectional issues, the class interests of the parties differed by region, and based on this so too did the need of the ruling class to align its voting bloc. These political allegiances were strongest in the South amongst the white plantation owners whose loyalty to the 'bloody shirts' would remain unscathed through the 19th century. Meanwhile, many less loyal Northern and Western farmers voted Republican more out of the ability of elected representatives to ensure post war pensions and offer other economic benefits to farmers. However, the Republican Party's main class base would increasingly be in the ascendant capitalist class. As time passed the Northern base of the GOP would waver in its support of Reconstruction, or at least the radical version of it, which had been driven by Northern abolitionists and Southern blacks. As the Old South fought back, and the Party's base among amongst southern blacks fell to the rise of Jim Crow, moderate members of the party regained control and tried to align themselves with the interests of the capitalist class (Foner, 1988; Goodwyn, 1978).

The sectional pro-business direction of both major parties not only became the animating political cause of the emergence of populism, but the almost wholly non-ideological climate created by sectional politics was also to prove the third party's principle obstacle (Goodwyn, 1978, p. 8). Only with the development of the populist movement of the Farmers Alliance could the sectional divides in the county be completely broken (Goodwyn, 1978; Hahn, 1983). With the capacity to break the sectional hold on US politics serving as the decisive factor in the success or failure of the Populists, it meant that the creation of a unifying political ideology was necessary. This was no easy task at the time.

In fact, the original Farmers Alliance group, that emerged in 1877 in Lampasas County, Texas, first as the Knights of Reliance, lasted only until 1880 as the members split along sectional lines, with the political allegiances in the group shifting to either the Greenback party or the Democrats (Buck, 1920; Goodwyn, 1973). So from its inception the movement's success or failure rested on the ability to forge a class movement by overcoming divisions around racial lines and Civil War issues. However, all around Texas the crop lien system produced sufficient problems to overcome the immediate sectional divide. Despite the short-lived nature of the original alliance in Lampasas County, 120 new alliances soon sprung up in the twelve surrounding counties. The agitators learned from that initial failure to avoid immediate political insurgency because of the deep roots of sectionalism. Instead the Alliance set its initial goal to merely address the immediate needs of farmers: to aid in credit and to help farmers buy the necessary inputs by breaking the monopoly of the merchants through cooperatives. They sought to align the class interests of farmers by transcending the independent agrarian ideology that had atomized farmers through advancing cooperative ideas and goals.

Whether or not the cooperative movement should be viewed as the end in itself, or the means to the end is debatable. On the one hand, the ability of the coopcratives and the aim of pooling farmers together to meet their needs and to break the bonds of the crop lien had been the basis of many earlier movements. On the other hand, all of these movements had for the most part failed to solve the problems faced by the farmers. Many of the early Alliance members knew this and approached the cooperative goals as a means to educate their members and to break the hold of sectionalism. Also important was the strong role of education within the Alliance. Clearly they understood the need to break the sectional hold on politics and to unite as wide a section of agrarians as possible. The cooperative push would serve to educate farmers on their shared interests as a class and aid in overcoming the class disunity. Similar to the efforts of the Grange, they sought to show individualized producers their shared problems and interests which could be advanced through unity and cooperation. Focusing on large problems of the political system, the parties, and the economic structures would have worked against the movements' goal of attracting a broad base of farmer's and creating unity amongst them. Conversely, efforts aimed at immediate issues, such as railroad regulation or co-operatives to bypass merchants, resonated and opened the political space for unity that could later be applied to larger issues.

The early 'traveling lectures' of S.O. Daws emphasized the role of credit merchants, railroads, trusts, the money power and capitalists in the problems facing rural people and stressed a solution in the Alliance and the creation of cooperatives. These new forms of social interaction and political movement building, what Goodwyn (1973) called "experimenting with a new kind of mass autonomy" (p. 33), and the development of individual self-respect and collective self-confidence or class-consciousness, would flower into a new politics known as populism. By focusing the movement on the immediate problems, the populists were able to cast a wider political net and use the movement itself as a pedagogical tool. Put quite simply, the idea that through the action of the movement the class would become ever more self-aware, rather than the alternative of educating the class and achieving class consciousness prior to movement formation, served as the unspoken proxy of the Populists.

At about the same time the farmers in the Northwest were also organizing. However, here it was occurring around more radical, class based goals. The National Farmers' Alliance, or the Northwest Alliance, mostly through the action of the editor of the *Western Rural*, Milton George, grew to 100,000 members in two short years after its start in 1880 (Shannon, 1945). A national organization was formed in Chicago in October of 1880. The following year in Chicago, they set out their official platform. Evidence of the Northwest Alliance's growing focus on class-consciousness is seen in their cooperation with the Knights of Labor at the 1887 Convention in Minneapolis. Indeed Shannon (1945) went as far as to claim "by 1890, the Midwest farmers were thoroughly class conscious" (p. 313). The politicization of the movement had reached a critical mass by 1887, when they adopted a resolution that stands in stark contrast to the one from 1881, arguing for ownership of transportation lines by the government and the immediate acquisition of the Union Pacific Railroad Company (Buck, 1920). The radicalization could be seen at the 1886 convention in Cleburne, Texas, where seventeen demands were put forward, with five dealing with labor issues, three with the power of railroads, two with the financial problems, and six relating to agricultural specifically, five focused on land policy and the sixth on commodity dealings in the futures market (Goodwyn, 1978).

There were numerous material changes that aided in the expansion of the movement in the 1880s and 90s. These included the price of cotton staying below ten cents for a decade after 1881, the nationwide economic crisis of 1893, the popping of the land bubble in the West that caused a rise in interest rates, the price of plows and other implements increased by as much as double. Also impacting farmers was the increasing rates of interest from the declining availability of credit, rising tax rates due to a shrinking tax base caused by the increase in foreclosures, along with the aforementioned increase in tenancy rates (Shannon, 1945). Material changes of course don't automatically lead to the emergence of social movements, much less guarantee movement success; instead it was the already present nature of the agrarian movements that enabled them to channel growing frustration with farmers' economic problems into an effective force for changing the balance of class forces.

As stated above, the cooperative efforts of the Alliance movement should be viewed more as pedagogical or politically unifying efforts – the means to unity as the first goal of the movement – than as attempts to directly alter the economy of rural life. Similar to the efforts of the Grange, they sought to show a mostly individualized group of producers, that they had common problems and a shared purpose, and that only through unity and cooperation could they reach their common goals. This also focused attention on the downstream and upstream processes that would come to take larger and larger portions of the incomes of farmers. At first the cooperative schemes sought to meet immediate needs and manifest problems facing farmers. Speaking directly of the problems of the political system, the parties, and the larger political economic structures would have prevented it from its goal of attracting a large number of farmer's attention and creating a unified movement. Conversely, efforts aimed at immediate issues, such as railroad regulation or overcoming the problems of the merchant crop-lien through cooperatives, resonated and opened the political space for unity which could later be applied to larger political and economic issues.

The Alliance also remained relevant by adapting to local conditions and issues. Again this diversity far from initially undermining unity, acted to create lively and democratic debate that helped propel the movement forward. California offers the perfect example of this diversity. Coming late to populism and the Alliance, the state was nonetheless ripe for it as the wheat boom which had led to the establishment of many farms in the San Joaquin and Salinas valleys ended with prices declining and the area's farms shifting to fruit production during the 1880s (McMath, 1992). The California Alliance flourished in this time of economic transition and grew rapidly. Both because of its late birth and because of the particularities of the local issues, its success led to the establishment of cooperatives, centralized control of irrigation and favourable railroad regulation. Yet this took the wind out of the more radical elements of the movement and it quickly turned against small producers in the coming decades because the political movements dissipated and left them open for capture by big agribusiness.

The Great Southwest Strike of 1886 would allow a more radical fraction of the National Farmers Alliance to come to the fore under the leadership of William Lamb. The Knights of labor had forced Jay Gould to honor a labor contract in what they thought was a major victory (Goodwyn, 1978). After the surge in union numbers coming out of the victory Gould responded by trying to crush the union and the emboldened union moved to strike in East Texas. The Great Southwest Strike pitted armed strikebreakers against armed union members as it spread across the West. Lamb insisted that the Farmer's Alliance back labor and push for a farm-labor coalition more aligned with the approach of the Northwest Alliance and against the demands of the more conservative national leadership. Lamb abandoned the ideology of the farmer as Jeffersonian independent producer, instead seeing them as workers in an emerging capitalist economy, requiring that they "build a farm-labour coalition to restructure American politics" (Goodwyn, 1978, p. 36). This radical break with prior agrarian movements – by casting farmer interests as part of the larger class struggle between owners and workers, with the "labour question as central" – was a departure from the approach seeking to slowly build a class consciousness in farmers through cooperatives (Goodwyn, 1978, p. 39). This would allow many of the conservative tendencies of the movement to be shed, as well as position farmers so as not as easily undermined by increased market prices and technological development. This especially aided in exposing the limits of the Democratic Party for many southern members of the Alliance.

Despite the failure of the Great Southwest Strike, and it being the deathblow to the Knights of Labour, the Alliance grew ever stronger based on its new ideological understanding of farmers as members of the working class in a battle against business. The newly granted leader of the movement, C.O. Daws, devised a plan for what he saw as "non-political" politics. Coming out of the failure of the strike, he put forward a plan to rely on the creation of anti-monopoly leagues and the running of independent candidates in areas where the demands of the Alliance fell on deaf ears in the two main parties. Along with this, "farmers and workers fielded independent tickets in at least twenty counties across northern Texas in 1886" (McMath, 1992, p. 77). The Cleburne demands set forth in 1887 only added to the distinctiveness of the new political movement by weaving together enough traditional themes of 'producerism' with other 'class struggle' demands and effectively casting a wide enough tent to draw in the disaffected from a very diverse political standing. Thus, the turn both appealed to many and sought to sharpen the contradictions of traditional parties and their platforms. This is often missed by those analysts who cast the populists as merely another in the long list of provincial, conservative agrarian movements seeking to maintain their social location through a return to privileged status. Hofstadter (1955) certainly missed this point when he claimed, "the utopia of the Populists was in the past, not the future" (p. 62).

The distinction between the Alliance and most agrarian movements before rests in their radicalized class-consciousness and in the fact that they began to push demands that the two corporate parties could not incorporate, while simultaneously having enough reformist goals to maintain a coalition with the more moderate members of the movement. The Alliance's demands – 'greenbackism', ownership of railroad lines, and particular political reforms – were not palatable, at least initially nor ever in their entirety, to either main party. The main parties would eventually come to pick one or two demands and incorporate them into their platform. Most effectively this adoption of some aspects populist polices occurred with William Jennings Bryan's promotion of greenbackism even while failing to swallow the entirety of Alliance demands. The inability of the main parties to swallow the demands of the Farmer's Alliance (FA) in their entirety reveals how movements outside of the existing power structures can often circumvent the patterns of class representation institutionalized by the state apparatuses and achieve greater reforms (Piven and Cloward, 1977). Simultaneously, we see how it was the narrow economic interests that drove the movement, and how these narrow interests eventually facilitated cooptation as the major parties began advocating some of the more moderate demands, splitting and undermining the movement (McConnell, 1953). Yet, the populist movement was successful in shifting the balance of class forces requiring new institutional forms for the maintenance of capitalist class control. With the demand of confiscation of the means of production put into real play by the rise of populism, the state quickly pushed through the necessary changes to prevent this undermining of the true source of power.

Populist Fractures

To be sure the movement was not completely unified by any means. The internal contradictions of the movement were bitter and sharp. One of the populist leaders, Macune, who is often portrayed as a reformist, clearly understood the internal contradictions of the movement as his sub-treasury plan sought to suture together the wings of the movement by offering a grand reform that could address the immediate economic problems of the farmers. Therefore, the plan sought to use the internal contradictions to sharpen the contradictions in the broader social order. His ability to tie together radicals and reformists within a single movement allowed the Alliance to proceed with demands indigestible to the two major parties in their entirety.

The sub-treasury plan put forward in 1889 would have allowed farmers to store their harvest at federal warehouses during periods of low prices, and to obtain federal loans worth 80 percent of the crops' market value. The plan's intention was to enable farmers to keep commodities off the market when prices were low and support themselves with loans until they rebounded. It was well suited to cotton, which did not spoil in storage, and was most popular among southern populists. Despite its tenuous economic prescripts, Macune's plan was an inspired political attempt to both meet the immediate economic needs of farmers and workers while also offering a political tool that rested right in the apex of radical and reformist agendas. The plan called for the use of government purchases and warehousing of surplus crops to serve as a currency used to invest in rural economies. This plan took root in most areas, from the generally conservative base of the Grangers and the Southern Alliance to the more radical areas. As Thomas Gaines, one of the architects of the Alliance and associate of Lamb explained, the Alliance would stand in relation to political parties just as the Jacobin Clubs had stood in relation to the new democratic parliamentary government of France. This forced the major parties to scramble to adopt portions of the Alliances platforms in an attempt to split the movement along the competing factions.

Ultimately, the task of containing all of the contradictions within one movement proved too great, however. The problem arose first in the electoral sphere where the movement was unable to establish a common set of goals or a common party platform as its membership swelled. The movement's support varied and fractured by local issues. In much of the old South the Alliance tended to support the Democratic Party, except for the Colored Alliance. In the Great Plains the politics were still different, where they once favored the Republican Party; local "Alliance ticket" candidates began to challenge the dominance of the two-party stranglehold. McMath (1992) locates the disparity between these Great Plains breaks and the Southern Democratic allegiance in the increased desperation of the plains farmers, the history of third party Greenback support, and the differences in the two party approach to the Alliance: the Republican ridicule versus the Democrats supportive platitudes. Harris (1976) outlines the break from hard-money by Southern Democrats in Congress to align themselves with Western and Midwestern silver advocates as early as the 43rd Congress of 1873. Sanders (1999) agrees with Harris, and cites the Southern Democrats movement toward free silver in the 1870s as playing a key role in blunting subsequent third party attempts in the region. Others, most notably Foner (1988), claimed the racial tensions still present in the South served as a key reason why the farmers failed to fully break with the Democrats.

Both race and sectional loyalties, along with partisan traditions, were simply aspects of the political and social ideology of the US at the time as constituted, in part by state apparatuses that maintained the divides to shift the balance of class forces through division. The failure to hold together the different geographic regions within an umbrella group emerged out of both the divergent economic circumstances and the differing politics of the areas. In Kansas in 1890 a meeting of alliance, Knights of Labour, Farmers' Mutual Benefit Association, and Single Tax clubs launched the Peoples Party. After an impressive number of victories in their first election cycle the party quickly expanded beyond Kansas. The main problem for the party was in the South – the real birth place of the Alliance – where the co-opting of many local Democrats and the racial tensions prevented the complete abandonment of the Democrats for the new Peoples Party. The Southern Alliance pushed many Democratic office-holders on some of their issues, but this endangered the drive for an independent party (McMath, 1992). In fact, in some places the Alliance had completely captured the Democratic Party making more difficult the effort to persuade its members to shift to the Peoples Party in the South.

By 1896 the populist organization was in even more turmoil than that of Democrats. Two main factions had appeared. One party – the fusion Populists – sought to merge with the Democrats, using the threat of independent organization to force changes in the major party's platform. The populist organization in Kansas had already "fused" over the bitter protest of those who considered this a sell-out. Fusionists argued that the regionally based third party could never hold national power; thus, the best strategy was to influence a major party that could. The second faction, called "mid-roaders," suspected that Democratic leaders wanted to destroy the third-party threat. Fusion, they argued would play right into this plot to co-opt the populist movement. Instead, they advocated staying out of the two larger parties, and not merging. These populists tended to be more radical and held to their convictions, while the fusionists were more willing to compromise on some party platforms in order to win over more people. The radicals declared fusion to be the road to ruin for the populists, as this statement by that faction declared:

> The burning question of today is, shall we fuse with the democrats[sic]? Shall all the reform elements of this country drop every other reform issue, except free coinage of gold and silver, join hands with the free silver Democrats and fight the common enemy – plutocratic republicanism?.... We forced them into making free coinage the issue; shall we then drop all other reform issues and run to meet them with open arms?... No, my

brother; the Democratic Party cannot swallow me down unless it swallows all the populist reform issues. (1896, pp. 7–8).

Just as the populists were battling over the issue of fusion or a third party, the two major parties started to pick up more and more of the Alliance's demands. In choosing some of the farmer's demands, the major parties added pressure to the internal fractures of the party. The "fusion" politics that emerged most stridently in Nebraska, sought to trim down the Populist Party platform into a few of its constituent parts. William Jennings Bryan became the "fusionist" extraordinary as he came to adopt the "free silver" platform that came to define what Goodwyn (1978) described as the shadow movement within populism. Bryan's opportunism is revealed by an 1892 speech where he admitted he did not "know anything about free silver…the people of Nebraska are for free silver and I am for free silver….I will look up the arguments later" (Quoted in Goodwyn, 1978, p. 228).

The worst part was not that Bryan was using the free silver platform to undermine the Peoples Party and win votes, but that the free silver argument was coming to define the entire populist movement. The drive to use credit as the means to overcome the problems of farmers was not new, however; and, as we have and will continue to see, it actually had the effect of eventually driving farmers into further market dependence. With the siphoning of some platform positions came the removal or watering down of others until the entire edifice of the populists rested only on free silver (Goodwyn, 1978). Even in Kansas, the birthplace of the third party, they moved into a fusion with Democrats for political expedience. Likewise in Alabama, after electoral defeats in many traditional Democratic areas, the Party began to adapt the only aspect of the Populist Party platform that was palatable: i.e., "free silver". The fractures also emerged out of political opportunism, as "the third party's internal struggle was a contest between a cooperating group of political office-seekers on the one hand and the Populist movement on the other" (Goodwyn, 1978, p. 231). Only where the movement had a long history with deep roots, did it resist the tendency to seek immediate electoral gains through the fusion with Democrats and the abandonment of most of their distinctly populist goals (Goodwyn, 1978).

The Decline of Populism

The Presidential election of 1896 was the closest thing that radical agrarianism ever had to taking hold of real structural power and that it would ever come to winning the presidency with William Jennings Bryan who captured about six and a half million votes. With the Republican candidate William McKinley, the continuation of President Grover Cleveland's monetary policy was ensured. With this, the free silver cause that had helped to unite the Northern and Southern Farmers' Alliances lost it momentum. The return of higher agricultural prices effectively sounded the death knell to the movement, as it split the coalition of diversity by solving the immediate economic needs of the reformists, pulling them away from the more radical members.

This movement also succumbed due to the jingoist response to the explosion on the USS Maine. As Hofstadter noted "jingoism was confined to no class, section, or party; but the populists stood in the vanguard, and their pressure went far to bring about a needless war...[as] the blare of the bugle drowned the voice of the reformer" (1955, pp. 90–91). However, this both overstated the impact of the populists and understated the role of the ruling class in drumming up the jingoist zeitgeist, especially the role of yellow journalism. The insurgency in Cuba, like most, had its roots in social changes occurring at a rapid pace and Spain's inability to politically ameliorate the tensions that arose. Global sugar production was rapidly industrializing and a concordant explosion in sugar supply was increasing competition and depressing the value. Cuban sugar production was desperately in need of capital to compete with a growing industrialization of cane production and a challenging sugar beet industry; while Spain was struggling with internal political conflict US capital began to infuse Cuban sugar production (Hennessey, 1999). US corporate capital penetration caused a rapid consolidation of farms and processing facilities and a proletarianization of Cuban campesinos. By 1894, 87% of all Cuban exports were headed for the US. The Wilson-Gorman tariff act of 1894 eliminated the US market and intensified the immiseration of the Cuban agrarians, feeding the revolutionary ferment of the populace by reversing the 1890 McKinley tariff concessions on Cuban imports (Crapol and Schonberger, 1972). By 1896 the island was engaged in a civil conflict that would be used to justify an imperial America. Conversely, the war solved some of the demands of the movement at home in the US by increasing farm product prices. It also allowed for the use of state institutions to construct a fix to the economic problems that were undergirding the class divides and fuelling the movement by creating unity across classes through the coming Spanish-American War.

The demise of the populist's movement also rested with the removal of agrarian problems by the revival of prosperity. There was an easing of credit amidst the increased global circulation of money following the end of the crisis in 1897, and prices of farm products rose (albeit) slowly in the years around the turn of the century. All this caused farmers to "drift back into the Republican and Democratic lines", and as they did so all the hard political issues raised by Bryan's old question of "Shall the people rule?" also faded away, suggesting that the "mass of the Populist voters brooded over these matters only when their expenses exceeded their incomes" (Shannon, 1945, p. 327). Most farmers involved in the movement "sought no fundamental social and economic reorganization...they wanted higher prices for their crops, and after 1900 they were getting them" (p. 327). The conservative wing of the populists movement were easily swayed by this increase in prices, while others lost the standing of their critique as the energy waned from the movement in the later years.

This view begs the question of if it is too simplistic and too materialist, or does it take for granted the source of the higher prices in the return of prosperity through the market. That is, does it assume the policy shifts that led to the return of prosperity and higher farm product prices did not come from the very social movement that sought just that; or at the very least, were they the means to co-opt the momentum through more capital friendly policies that still sought minimal reform? It is true that the return of higher cotton prices in the South did lead to the resumption of even more racial practices. Once higher prices returned to the fields, the use of racial strategies by white laborers to distinguish their labor from that of blacks became even more prevalent as class issues were glossed over by Jim Crow (Shannon, 1945, pp. 327–328).

Hofstadter (1955) claimed that the populists were one of the most successful failures in the history of US political movements. He cited many who saw them as a failure for having not obtained their own stated goals. However he also mentioned the long list of populist demands that eventually became policy. He located the source of this contradiction in what he calls the soft versus hard side of the farmer's movement, which centered on the structural differences that occurred after the populists direct influence diminished then subsequently arose. He then determined that another reason for their failure as a radical movement was the base of their support in the rural poor sections, having failed to rouse sufficient support from labor due to its dissociation. However despite the conservative nature of the two major parties during this time, there was enough local autonomy within them to allow for specific candidates to pick up a proposal or two from the populists and take the wind out of their sails. And with this the populists fulfilled their function as they saw most of their program become law, albeit through the demise of the movement with the Democratic party pick off issue after issue from their platform. As Hofstadter noted: "[p]opulists had the satisfaction of seeing plank after plank of their platforms made law by the parties whose leaders had once dismissed them as lunatics...It transformed one of the major parties, had a sharp impact on the other" (1955, p. 108). In fact, one would have to scan out for a longer-term view to fully grasp the true impact of the populists on the direction of the country. Over the course of the next 50 years the nation would first pick up much of the populist platform on what the state could do to aid agriculture, and then it would use some of the same approaches to fix the failing industrial system during the depression. In the long arc of state institutional formation, the populists played a major role despite their failure to grasp complete political control over their own fate. The proper focus to evaluate the populists, and the correct focus for political analysis of the movement, is on the state institutions that were altered due to their impact on the class struggles. The effects of the populist social movement on state policy resulted in modest reforms that would bear short-term fruit for farmers but would also serve as the seeds for increased market dependence and another round of agrarian political movements.

One key test of influence of state involvement on different classes can be seen in how the farmers quickly lost their unifying class orientation once prices rose – during wars which at the same time stoked their nationalist sentiments. The states also successfully diverted farmers from the previously radical goals to which they had earlier been attracted through modest reforms. The memory of the strength of the agrarian movement explains why its reforms continued to be rolled out during the Progressive era, even after the movement itself subsided (McConnell, 1955). Not only had new state institutional support for farmers been established and agrarian political power advanced, but the memory of the radical threat informed the balance of class forces, and most importantly state institutional capacity development.

Shannon (1945) asserted that it was a case of "government catching up with the social and economic needs of the preceding generation" (p. 328) that resulted in the nullification of any class based agrarian movement. Therefore, he argues "the development of a deeply rooted class philosophy for the farmers was not to emerge from only a single generation of hard times" (Shannon, 1945, p. 328). The reforms of the government not only undermined and fractured the radical movements, but they also increased the market penetration. Thereby, these reforms continued to undermine farmer class based understandings and inserted an economic market ontology based on achieving a higher price for crops. Almost immediately after the fateful year that "McKinley and Hanna inflicted their overwhelming defeat on the forces of agrarianism, the American commercial farmer entered upon the longest sustained period of peacetime prosperity he has ever enjoyed" (Hofstadter, 1955, p. 109), what came to be known as the "golden age" of US agriculture arrived. Alongside rising prices, the impact of technological advances enabled gigantic gains in productivity. But this came at the expense of increased farm specialization, debt, and commodification, which eventually meant that the 'golden age' only temporarily mediated the contradictions between the situation of petty commodity producers in agriculture and their entrapment in an industrial capitalism that was expanding, even if still in an uneven form, across the agrarian landscape.

The first two decades of the 20th Century witnessed a calming of agrarian movements alongside a generally better economy for farm products. It also contained a few important state institutional program developments that sought to continue the push toward capitalist agrarian relations. Many viewed the improved economic conditions and the lack of mention of agrarian issues in major political campaigns as a sign of the demise of agrarian movements. However, Sanders (1999) rejected the common theme of an end to agrarian radicalism with the new century and the idea of a bourgeoisie pushed progressive era.[3] She located four factors "that sustained the agrarian reform program in national politics after 1896" – a new wave of farmer organization; the direct primary; the national Democratic Party leadership of William Jennings Bryan; and most fundamentally, regional political economy (p. 149).

In Sander's analysis, there was a clear line of populist continuity between the rise of the Grange and the rise of the Farmers' Union (FU) which arose out of the efforts of former Farmers Alliance members in 1902. By 1906 the FU claimed to have over 900,000 members which outnumbered the AFL at the time (Sanders, 1999). Originally set out to be non-political and to focus on cooperatives, slowly, like the FA before them, the FU moved into political campaigns again after attempts at cooperative alternatives mostly failed (Hurt, 2002). Despite their more conservative beginnings, by 1915, Sanders (1999) stated, "there was scarcely a radical reform – from nationalizing essential natural resources to outlawing child labour – that the FU did not advocate" (p. 151). The FU was "certainly less frightening to the political and economic elites" of its time than the Alliance and the Populist Party had been. This was due as much to the "extent to which agrarian positions of the 1890s had been absorbed into a regional ideology" as it was to the timid nature of the organization. But there can be little doubt that much of the transmission of the populist demands into actual state policies in the 20th century rests on the fusionists and on Bryan, who like other popular leaders before him, straddled the divide between radical demands and middle of the road reformist. The words of the new Oklahoma State constitution, which Bryan played a large role in drafting, were both only used to fuel "the nations' strongest Socialist Party", but were also combined with the Nebraska state Democratic party platform as well as with various planks borrowed directly from the American Federation of Labour (AFL) to inform the Democratic party platform for the 1908 elections (Sanders

---

3   On the latter see Kolko (1963) and Sklar (1988).

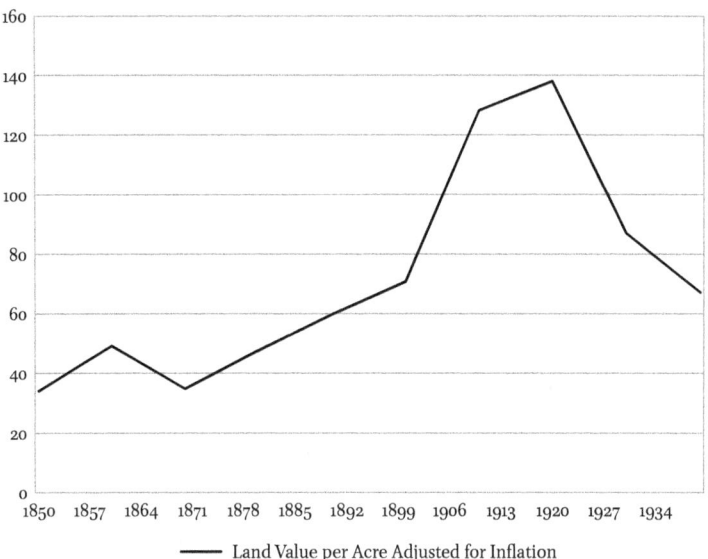

FIGURE 3   *Land value per acre adjusted for inflation: 1850–1940*
ADAPTED FROM USDA CENSUS ERS 2005

1999, p. 157). And it was Bryan, who then pushed the Democrats to persuade the President to move on antitrust, labor, banking, currency, farm credit, and Philippine independence.

According to Hurt (2002) "[b]etween 1900 and 1920 agricultural production rose by 30 percent while the national population increased 40 percent" (p. 12) as the 1900 farm price index of 69 for 1910–1914 rose to 104 by 1910, peaked in 1919 at 217 before falling after WWI to 211. Even though agricultural productivity climbed rapidly, from 100 in 1870 to 151 in 1900 and up to 218 by 1929, demand expanded enough to keep the up prices (McConnell, 1945, p. 15). The prices farmers received also increased relative to the prices they paid for inputs (Hurt, 2002). Accordingly, the average income per farm increased between 1910 and 1920 from $652 to $1,196 in constant dollars (Hurt, 2002). Also increasing was the value of their land, as can be seen in Figure 3. The result was that "[t]he decade of fastest appreciation [of farm land values] was 1900–1910, that Golden Era in which the farmer's terms of trade rose to the all-time peak in 1910–1914...in the first decade of this century, the real price of farm land jumped six percent a year, the fastest decadal rate in US history except for the 1970s (and possibly the 1790s)" (Lindert, 1988, p. 5). During the "Golden Age" there was once again a renewal of mechanization of agriculture at a rapid rate that went along with increasing land values (ERS/USDA, 2005). This expansion

TABLE 6 Shifts in numbers employed on Farms (1,000 males): 1880 and 1930

	1880	1930	Change	1880	1930	Change
	Kansas			Iowa		
Owners	715	427	−288	630	375	−255
Laborers	146	258	112	173	389	116
Tenants	139	315	176	197	336	139
	Ohio			Wisconsin		
Owners	593	517	−76	743	566	−177
Laborers	266	300	34	183	308	125
Tenants	141	183	42	74	126	52
	New Jersey			California		
Owners	473	386	−87	580	348	−232
Laborers	373	544	171	277	577	300
Tenants	154	70	−84	143	75	−68
	North Carolina			Alabama		
Owners	474	382	−92	388	277	−111
Laborers	289	252	−37	270	221	−49
Tenants	237	366	129	342	502	160

ADAPTED FROM BLACK AND ALLEN 1937, P. 403

of mechanization in agriculture occurred in part due to the development of "several key institutions to facilitate the democratization of credit", including the use of amortized loans for the first time in response to farmer pressure and the Federal Farm Loan Act of 1916 (Prasad, 2012, p. 199; see also Quinn, 2010). This crucially informed the future direction of US capacity building and agricultural development.

Despite the 'Golden Age' farmers' ability to climb the 'agricultural ladder'[4] and move from landless laborer up to farmer owner/operator, changed. Rather than a shorter ladder consisting of laborer to yeoman to petty commodity producer, the increased cost of production and necessary capital requirements appeared to produce another rung of cropper or tenant farmer (see Table 6). Clearly the growth of each category of farmer was dependent upon

---

4 On the agricultural ladder see Attack (1989); Black & Allen (1937); Bogue (1959); Curti (1959); Gates (1936); Le Duc (1950); Saloutos (1962); and Winters (1978).

local labor markets and types of crops grown, but the overall pattern shows an increase in laborers and in croppers as another rung was added.

While the return of rising prices and access to credit undermined the populists, the standing of farmers and the political economic system undergirding their struggles changed only slightly. Despite the generally high prices of the era, farm tenancy moved from 38 and 80 percent for white and black farmers respectively in 1910 to 50 and 81 percent by 1930, while the amount of wealth in the periphery states – the South Atlantic, west-north-central, and mountain regions – declined or showed no significant increase between 1890 and 1912 (US Census, 1933; BLS, 1933). Yet the periphery locations that contained the agricultural, timber, and mining regions held the largest block of members in all four congresses from 1910 to 1917, with 47 percent of House seats and 57–58 percent of the Senate. This reveals how the Progressive politicians appeared to work for the interests of the agrarian population while the policies that developed only aided in their demise.

All told, during the administrations of President Woodrow Wilson (1913–21), more agricultural legislation passed than ever before (Hurt, 2002). As ruling class elites caught up with the shift that had occurred in the agrarian movements during the twenty or thirty years prior, they accepted and pushed through lower tariff acts, strengthened railroad regulations, created a new banking system with some dispersed regional power and granted the authority to determine agricultural prices to the executive branch (Hanson, 1991). All of these were indications that the ideology of the nation had "clearly moved away from the Jeffersonian ideal that championed minimal government and maximum personal independence" (Hurt, 2002, p. 39). Again we should be careful not to read back into those agrarian movements the eventual statist and market oriented outcomes but instead focus on how the political parties created and used this shift in ideals to maintain. The shift in ideals emerging from the agrarian revolt of the populists became ubiquitous enough to demand a reconfiguration of hegemony based upon these ideals. It pushed forward an increase in the use of state capacities through the construction of new institutional forms to address the demands of the agrarian movements in a manner that would corral them into the market. In effect then, farmers became co-authors of the new basis of a hegemonic social order resting on the statist reconstruction of the American government and the forging of new state institutional designs based directly in agro-industrialization. The limits of the possible confined the accomplishments of the movement while opening up enough space to undermine the radical nature of the social movement.

American farmers benefited greatly from World War I. During the War US farmers saw the price they received for products rise along the international demand spiked. The prices of cotton, corn and wheat all more than doubled in price, with cotton prices rising five-fold (Winders, 2009). This led to gross farm income also climbing from $7.6 million to $17.7 million (USDA, 1942). When the Armistice came in 1918, dairy products were priced 70 percent higher than before the war and cotton witnessed a four-fold increase per pound (USDA, 1933). High prices brought a boom to western state expansion, as North Dakota, Montana and other western states rapidly became major wheat producers due to war time prices. The end of the war brought a sudden collapse of prices and it was the first agricultural depression since the 1890s, as Europe began to produce its own food again, US farm exports declined from $3.8 to $1.9 billion (Hurt, 2002). In the summer of 1920 prices for agricultural goods declined sharply – 78 percent for corn, 64 percent for wheat, and 57 percent for cotton (Hurt, 2002). Most farmers responded by planting more and the mounting surplus helped to reduce prices even more, with net farm income falling from the $9 billion it had been in 1919 to $3.3 billion in 1921 – a decline in income for most farmers by almost two thirds (Hurt, 2002). Once prices did recover to approximately 30 percent higher than prewar levels, the level of debt incurred by farmers, both before the downturn in the economically good times of the war and during the downturn to simply stay afloat, became a debilitating pressure (Hurt, 2002; Paarlberg, 2000). The response by the Non-partisan League and other more radical farm groups was for an even larger government role in keeping prices up. However, this abandonment of a class based understanding by farmer's, turning them towards seeking higher profits that quickly becoming the basis for state institutional development which helped secure higher prices in the interim and greater market dependence in the long run.

The American Farm Bureau Federation

The Farm Bureau 'movement' officially started in 1911 when John Barron, a farmer who graduated from Cornell University and worked as an extension agent in Broome County, New York, received an advance of funds from the United States Department of Agriculture, which got the funds from the Lackawanna Railroad through the Chamber of Commerce. Barron served as a "Farm Bureau" representative for farmers who was paid by the Binghamton, New York Chamber of Commerce. The effort to start the Bureau was. The 'movement' expanded with Farmers meeting in Saline County, Missouri, forming the first a state-wide Farm Bureau in 1915 (Buck, 1920). The other key support came from the Federal funding of county agents who, since the passing of the Smith-Lever Act which created the county extension agent farm education programs in

1914, were paid to be public figures in organizing farmers into the Bureau. Prior to this most funding had come from private sources, with some of this private money continuing, with the Smith-Lever Act "explicitly permitted continuation of the system of paying the agent from separately administered public and private funds" (McConnell, 1953, p. 44). Thus, it is another early example of a private-public partnership with the county agent being a "paid organizer of the American Farm Bureau Federation (AFBF)" (p. 47). The Extension Agents were to be supported by the 'Bureaus' who were to find independent funding and members (USDA, 1915). The Federal Government continued to aid the growth of the AFBF by instructing County Agents to organize Bureaus and in 1919 Secretary of Agriculture Houston called on farmers to join Bureaus to fend off Bolshevism (McConnell, 1953).

The AFBF was well positioned when the agricultural depression set in during the first few years of the 1920s, since it had already emerged as the lead farm organization, although its deliberately high dues and vocational approach combined to keep its actual membership numbers low and of a certain type. Despite this its political reach was ascendant. This political strength without mass membership was possible due to the source of its funding, as businesses had effectively colluded with the state to preempt radical agrarians through the organizations founding. The response to the first agricultural downturn in the 20th Century would be one driven by a "responsible" organization, with strong ties to the state and business, and crouched in the expanding state institutional capacities pushing productivity advances as solution. With the support of the state and corporate backers the AFBF actively sought to undermine radical farm groups such as the Nonpartisan League, the National Farmers Union and the Farmer-Labour Party (McConnell, 1969). The creation of the county Extension Service, and the AFBF that would emerge out of it, linked the state to the most prosperous farmers and actively promoted the methods they engaged in that represented the large farming interests (Kolko, 1976; Domhoff and Weber, 2011).

The emergence in May 1921 of the Farm Bloc – a group of agrarian centered members of Congress – was a turning point in this relationship between farm movements and Congress.[5] Under the guidance of the American Farm Bureau Federation leadership of Gray Silver, a new Farm Bloc formed to push market-oriented answers to the farming crisis (Hanson, 1991). The

---

5 The "Farm Bloc" refers to an organization formed by representatives and senators form farm states pushed by the Farm Bureau. It was formed in 1921 and lasted until 1923. It is not to be confused with the farm bloc, which is a generic term for more informal and temporary alliances (Hanson, 1991).

Farm Bloc represented farm organizations becoming a part of the political establishment, pushing their demands and lobbying independent of political parties (Hansen, 1991). The Farm Bloc at the time was called "the most effective organized force in Congress" (Barnes, 1922, p. 52). In brazen moves that were based on AFBF members making demands on their members of Congress, the farm bloc fought and beat back party leadership demands when it came to agricultural bills. However the Bloc was short lived and was not reconvened in 1923, only two short years after its first victories (Hansen, 1991). It was however, a very strong show of farm organization strength and portended the future role of these organizations driving policy, even against party, into a reformist state institutional build up. By seeming to be a very powerful mass farmer movement, with deep political ties and strength, the AFBF blocked alternatives, and with it more radical class based movements from emerging during the farm depression of the 1920s. According to Domhoff and Weber (2011), the AFBF was "the organization that spoke for the agricultural segment of the nationwide ownership class by the outset of the New Deal" (p. 63). The AFBF revealed most clearly the understanding by powerful forces that through the industrialization of agriculture and concentrated ownership, an increase in capitalist power over it emerged. It revealed, from the original Rockefeller funding of the extension service program which was the basis through which the AFBF connected with farmers, how elites understood the role that agro-industrialization would play in enhancing class power and control over agriculture (Domhoff and Weber, 2012; McConnell, 1953).

None of these reformist state interventions in agriculture turned out to be enough to prevent or even temper the effects of the loss of agricultural trade that began in the early 1920s. With the US agricultural trade balance slipping into a deficit in 1923, combined with crop prices declining by 40 percent, net farm income fell to half what it had been (Paarlberg and Paarlberg, 2000). US farm exports declined sharply from $3.8 billion in 1920 to $1.9 billion in 1922, or a 50 percent reduction in two years (Hurt, 2002). The federal response to this downturn in agricultural prosperity was "a minimalist one" (Paarlberg and Paarlberg, 2000, p. 139). The state's response to populists and progressive demands for intervention in the preceding few decades had funneled farmers into increasingly industrial agricultural forms that were reliant on market prices and vulnerable to its swings. In fact, the domination of industrial interests of the time blocked efforts to raise farm commodity prices due to their fear that this would drive up food prices, thus, driving up industrial wage demands (Paarlberg and Paarlberg, 2000).

Conclusion

As the nation emerged from the Civil War numerous changes in both the South and the North occurred that, in aggregate, had mostly a negative impact on farmers. In the South the inability to access the capital necessary to run their operations, combined with entrenched planter class power, would push many large land owners off of the land. Simultaneously, landless farm laborers emerged and were put to work as tenants instead of wage laborers. These two processes – linked backward to the impact of slavery on the social, political and economic uneven development across the south inflicted a brutal pressure on farmers, eventually leading to the farmer's backlash in the populist movement.

Likewise in the North the further spreading of petty commodity agriculture created a level of desperation as indebtedness and overproduction set in to make the situation ripe for the emergence of an agrarian class based social movement. Building off the earlier mechanical advances in labor saving technologies of the agrarian-industrial revolution this process continued to spread in an uneven fashion and added downward pressure on farm prices. Out of this emerged land augmenting technologies developed during the first part of the 20th century that would increase productivity, along with farmer debt and consolidation (McConnell, 1969; Mundlak, 2005; Olmstead and Rhode, 2002). These developments came out of the state funded agricultural research of the land grant colleges created in the 1862 Morrill Act and experimental stations coming out of the 1887 Hatch Act, that produced "a stream of new crops, new strains, new techniques, and even new concepts of farming" (McConnell, 1969, p. 13). Therefore, the federal funding of agricultural research (discussed in more detail in the next chapter) was mostly a response to populist and mass farmers' movement demands. The increased state involvement would come to play a vital role in the growth of the agro-business sector occurring after WWII that continued the trend towards the capturing of the upstream and downstream aspects of the agricultural production process by corporations (Olmstead and Rhode, 2002). This represented a deflection of the demands of the populists into state responses that sought to avoid nationalization of railways and banks along with other proposals opposed to the social dislocation of market expansion. Instead, the state was used to facilitate the deepening of capitalism's penetration into agrarian production. The continuation and expansion of the earlier use of land as a tool to infuse the rural petty commodity production social relations with capital, as well as, farm and consumer products binding farmers through debt and market imperative. The use of the state to smooth over the immediate social dislocations of the changes occurring through forms of market regulation went a long way to integrate agrarian unrest into an expansive and dynamic form of capitalist development. The outcome of these processes would be the populist movement. Yet despite this political energy and the advanced level of organizing that occurred, the outcome was viewed by most as a failure.

Because of this, we can see a two-fold approach of first using the state to create political acquiescence to perpetuate markets, as well as the development of the objective capacities for capital to do so. Hurt (2002) summarized the outcome of the 'statist' turn by farmers in the first quarter of the twentieth century as one in which farmers sought a "fundamental and major expansion of government aid, which involved greater regulation of agriculture" (p. 31). But this statist turn took a very particular form as the state built the institutional capacity to aid farmers in particular, market friendly, agro-industrial means. Thus, the resistance of the farmers to further commodification was overcome by the active involvement of the state in various ways, both as a means to increase the economic position of farmers and to mute their more radical demands through state incorporation. The attempt by the state to expand and reproduce capitalist class control while congruently seeking to incorporate enough of the agrarian movements' demands to mute them required increasing its overall reach. This reveals the dialectical co-development of the US state and the economy arising out of barriers and resistance it encountered and overcame by creating a more dynamic form of capitalist state.

The increased influence of capital during the decade of the 1920s revealed the shift in the balance of class forces that had taken place in the ebb of the agrarian movements as well as the limits of the state institutional shifts that had come from the farmer's groups' demands for higher prices. The reforms of the Progressive era amounted to providing institutional support for the expansion of industrial agriculture. The easing up of credit and the farmer education all pushed the farmers further into market based social relations and the competitive drive of industrial capitalism. Furthermore, during the "golden age" farmers had expanded their production with loans for equipment and more acres, revealing the outcome of the agro-industrial based policies of the progressives (Hurt, 2002). Farmers had also expanded their household items, with a growing reliance on telephones and automobiles during the golden age of the boom. And once again the incentives of the market system pushed farmers to plant more acres as the prices dropped rapidly in the post-war era, thus making the crisis even worse. In light of the reduced farmer organization outside of reformist models and absent agrarian agitation the initial response by the states was to do little (Hamilton, 1991).

The political history of agrarian movements from the Civil War to the 1920s revealed a slow but steady shift towards this statist approach clearly structured by the confines of the possible within capitalist control as the state increasingly moved to fulfill its requirements as a capitalist state. With the increasing success of the FA and populists to suture together radicals and reformers and to articulate a class-consciousness, the need of the state to intervene and shift the balance of class forces away from the radicals increased. The AFBF represented a major step forward in the prophylactic state institutional capacities, which would expand exponentially in the next few decades with the USDA as is discussed in the next chapter.

CHAPTER 5

State Institutional Capacity Building of the USDA-Research Complex

> It should be the aim of every young farmer to do not only as well as his father, but to do his best to make two blades of grass grow where but one grew before.
> HENRY LEAVITT ELLSWORTH, First Head of the USDA

In response to the farmers' movements and price swings of the late 19th and early 20th centuries, agricultural state institutional capacity was greatly expanded. This chapter will outline this growth, which began in the second half of the 19th Century with the events leading up to the creation of the US Department of Agriciulture (USDA). The role of the federal government in building markets and pushing industrial agriculture will be shown as a response to the agrarian social movements and as the means to reinforce market based forms of social relations. The state responded to the various class pressures at different moments, revealing a large range of flexibility, with the majority of this state institutional development aiding in agro-industrial development. This chapter will focus on the nature of state policy and institutional development which overcame, incorporated and diminished the farmer populist movements that emerged as a strong force in the 1890–1920 era. This capacity of the state to shift the balance of class forces back toward capitalist hegemony through state institutional interventions emerged through the process of interaction with class forces, as it built up the ability to guide and alleviate class tensions while facilitating market imperatives. The institutional development that emerges in the form of the USDA mostly coalesces around a broad based technological expertise that is developed in the USDA-research complex.

The important variable in this process was its continuation of the agro-industrial project that increased productivy moving farmers further and further into modernizing forms of production. Starting with the agrarian state institutional build up that began with the initial drive to have a federal agricultural agency; this chapter will locate the source of this drive and the nature of the agency that emerged. It will be outlined how the USDA structure pushed an agribusiness model through research into technological innovations that enhanced agricultural productivity. Next, moving beyond the USDA, I will look into the nature of state experimental services and agricultural training. This will highlight the role of industry and private funding in guiding this research as well as the federalization of state experimental education programs and research. Through this program of educational outreach farmers were exposed to the latest agricultural technologies, while simultaneously, the US state effectively enlarged its institutional capacities to imbricate farmers with industrial commodity markets. Because of the technological innovations developed at USDA research facilities, family farming would increasingly be subdued under those fractions of capital that could capture value up-stream and down-stream of production by offering productivity increasing technology inputs, mortgages, and the development of the capacities to process raw commodities into value added products.

Simultaneously, these developments impelled these farmers towards increased market mediation of their relations. During the "golden age" of US farming – the first two decades of the twentieth century – the policies put in place, although arising out of pressures from the agrarian class, in practice pushed farmers further into market mediated social forms. Likewise, once the crisis of the 1920s began, state institutional response varied in its support of large and small farmers. Ultimately these policies would co-opt agrarian movements and aid the agro-industrial project. Specific areas of agriculture in places such as California had already moved quite a distance along into these forms of appropriation but were still under similar pressures.

By analyzing this history and the manner in which the state interacted with the uneven development of agriculture the strength of the US state's capitalist bias can be determined while overcoming the common mistake of juxtaposing states and markets – a phenomenon usually expressed as eras of less or more state involvement in the market. The USDA and this era during which it arose, is usually understood as one in which big government intervened in the market to aid farmers who were struggling. In fact this is the very response that many farmers fought for. The state's ability to funnel agrarian demands into policies that produced agro-industrial imperatives, the US state created the capacity to assuage the demands of the agrarian movements. As a result of the US state first merging reformist movement demands toward higher farm product prices, farmers came to favor particular development patterns that could use the market to discipline farmers and concentrate them under capitalist social forms. In other words by pursuing a more capitalist market dependent form of agriculture, the US state diminished radical popular opposition while appearing to act in the interest of saving or helping farmers.

Institutional Response to Agrarian Movements

The roots of the USDA go back to the early 19th century in the US Patent Office (Harding, 1947). Prior to formation of the USDA, the Patent Office's Agricultural Department, which was part of the Department of State, had been tasked with issuing pamphlets and disseminating information to farmers about seeds, plants and farm inventions and technologies. Commencing in 1837 the United States Patent Office began to collect new or rare species of plants and seeds from around the world to distribute to farmers. The move was favorably received, and in 1839 Congress began to support the work through small appropriations. Finally, a Division of Agriculture within the Patent Office was created based on this success.

A major force in the push for the application of science to agriculture was the US Patent Office under the directions of Henry Leavitt Ellsworth. As the commissioner of the Agricultural Department of the Patent Office, he was a staunch advocate for agricultural technology and distributed new seeds as early as 1836, claiming that the future laid in mechanized agriculture and the development of seeds with higher yields (Harding, 1947). He encouraged hybrid seed development in wheat and corn in an effort to increase the productivity, believing that a twenty percent increase would raise farmer incomes by $15–20 million annually. Ellsworth's approach, and his overall influence on the development of state agricultural intervention, revealed the early origins of the role of the department in the agro-industrial project. This approach rested on striving for an ever increasing agricultural productivity through technological advancement arrived at through scientific research and its dissemination. Ellsworth was able to convince the US Congress of the benefit of this approach, leading to the first congressional allocation of $1,000 in 1839 for agriculture – apart from that used for land and money spent to maintain the property of slave owners. This sum would increase rapidly and triple by 1845 (Harding, 1947). As the agrarian unrest described in the previous chapter intensified, the support for this approach gained steam among businessmen and political backing.

One example of how agricultural research funds were used is in early attempts at extracting sugar from corn beginning in 1841. This revealed the very early drive to turn crops into commodities that could be used for a larger variety of food inputs in an industrial production model. This approach, to use research to find the means to commodify agriculture and push the adoption of this technology, would eventually come to form a major part of the agrarian push through state policies emanating out of the USDA-research complex; and it began even prior to the formation of the USDA as a stand-alone agency.

Importantly another longstanding and central goal of the USDA, dating back to 1842 at least, was Commissioner Ellsworth's focus on expanding foreign agricultural markets around the world. An early example being a study of the effects of the British Corn Laws on US exports (Harding, 1947). This focus would constitute a constant theme extending the entire history of the USDA as the agency would increasingly work to expand markets outside of the US. These external markets would sop up the excess production coming from the adoption of new techniques resulting from USDA research and education that would help to quell agrarian unrest.

Clearly then, expanded international trade was integral to the initial institutional build up around government purchases of surplus crops and was not an afterthought or a shift in orientation that emerges after the depression, as the food regimes approach claims (Friedmann, 1993, 2003; McMichael, 1992, 2000). The USDA was actively involved in trade promotion from its inception and, like the expansion of home goods domestically, this promotion constituted a cornerstone of the state institution led move to modernize agriculture while dealing with the effects of the surpluses this created. The drive to modernize farms, increase productivity and expand agriculture always required and was institutionally tied with expanding markets both at home and around the world.

In 1844 Ellsworth increased his predictions of the impact of an increase in productivity from the application of science to agriculture, claiming that it would lead to a $30 million increase in farmers' annual incomes (Harding, 1947). It is out of Commissioner Ellsworth's work and those around him that "Agricultural science got its start in the federal government" (Harding, 1947, p. 12). By the mid-1850s, just over a decade after the initial funding the Agricultural Department of the Patent Office had risen from its initial $1,000 congressional allocation to $35,000. This drastic increase in funding was in recognition that in 1850 there were 11,680,000 farm residents making up half of the population of the United States and 64 percent of the labor force, with a full 80 percent of all US exports coming from agriculture (Rasmussen, 1969). Farmers played both a major role in the economy and increasingly held more political influence.

It is clear that the early work of Commissioner Ellsworth set the federal government's involvement down a path of pushing agricultural technology for productivity gains; often presented as the solution to farmers' problems, and contradictorily, often fueling problems on the farms. In the 1862 Agricultural Division of the Patent Office Manual the main focus is the call for scientific investigations and the improvement of agricultural tools to improve production (Hadwiger, 1982). This particular focus of governmental involvement produced other problems for agriculture as it transformed it to fit within an industrial capitalist production system. The need for increased access to credit for farmers emerged as one consequence of this policy of pushing the development and spreading of agricultural technology.

In 1852 when the United States Agricultural Society (USAS) was formed, Daniel Lee – well known to the farmers of the country as editor of the periodical *The Genesee Farmer* – was elected secretary of the new advocacy group. Lee served as secretary of the society during its formative period, as the Society sought to push greater state involvement in agriculture (Carrier, 1937). The primary purpose for the formation of the USAS was to push for the establishment of a stand-alone department of agriculture. The position of the Society was that Federal Government support for agriculture was a right of the citizenry of the United States and they would demand an agency: "This society would not solicit but demand the establishment of what they believed to be their rights… they should not solicit anybody, not even Congress" (USAS Journal, 1860, p. 290).

The USAS took a strong stance in 1856: "Resolved, That the United States Agricultural Society appoint a Committee of five, to memor[i]alize Congress, asking in the name of the Farmers of the Republic the organization of a Department of Agriculture, with a Secretary at its head entitled to a seat and a voice in the Cabinet" (USAS Journal, 1856, p. 7). Out of the strength of the society, and additionally, as a means to stem more radical movements "in order to avert the storm of protest…the Secretary of the Interior proposed in his annual report for 1858 that a bureau of agriculture separate from the Patent Office be created in his Department" (Carrier, 1937, p. 286). The resolution of the society and Interior Secretary Clemson's recommendation clearly put strong political influence to bear on Congress as evidenced by the fact that the United States Department of Agriculture was later created with a commissioner at its head who was directly responsible to the President of the United States. Their support proved to be a major impetus for the creation of the USDA and served to form the parameters of the states response; "The evidence would also seem to justify the conclusion that without the support given to the bill by an influential national organization such as the United States Agricultural Society there would have been little, if any, likelihood of its passage" (Carrier, 1937, pp. 283–284). The USAS thus played an important part in securing two significant enactments by Congress. The first was the Land Grant Act for the support of colleges of agriculture and mechanic arts, and the second was the law creating the United States Department of Agriculture (Carrier, 1937). Together they form the basis of the USDA-research complex that would become fundamental to the agro-industrial project.

In 1862, in part as payback for farmer support for the Republican party and with the departure of most of the Southern States from the Union, Congress passed and President Lincoln signed into law four bills publically described as aimed at helping struggling farmers: the Homestead Act, The Morrill Land-Grant College Act, the Pacific Railway Act, and the act establishing the United States Department of Agriculture. Isaac Newton of Pennsylvania, whose election as vice president of the United States Agricultural Society six years earlier had disturbed the amicable relations between the society and the Patent Office, was appointed the first Commissioner of Agriculture (Carrier, 1937, p. 287).

The USDA had a humble beginning in 1862, with three employees of the Agricultural Division of the Patent Office becoming the first USDA employees. And although created in 1862, the Department did not attain cabinet status until 1889. From its beginning it was focused almost exclusively on the application of science in agriculture, as Commissioner Isaac Newton (1862) stated "nothing is impossible to labour aided by science." With its success USDA funding would climb from the 1899 level of $2.8 Million to $28 Million by 1917 and by the end of WWI it was second only to the Treasury in federal employees (Hurt, 2002, p. 36).

The early USDA work centered on the distribution of untested seeds and pork-barrel style research projects (Carpenter, 2001). In this it was continuing the path laid out by the Agricultural Division of the Patent Office that had distributed over 2.4 million seed packets between 1839 and 1861 (Kloppenburg, 1988, p. 61). The Patent Office had been invested in disseminating new seed varieties, and even sending representatives to Europe to search for new varieties. Up until around 1860 this created little competition with private seed companies as there existed so few patentable seed strains to support this industry. As more and more seed varieties and hybrids were developed, "this nascent capitalist seed sector was thoroughly alarmed by the explosive growth of what they regarded as the government seed business" (Kloppenburg, 1988, p. 62). Yet the early Patent Office and later USDA seed distribution program would continue until the mid-1890s and represented an area where the twin goals of state institutions to aid farmers and to modernize the farms coexisted with state support and the building of private markets for commodified agricultural inputs directly. The state institutional development was more responsive to immediate farming problems during these early years, most likely due to the agrarian movement's impact on the balance of class forces. This does not mean that the agro-industrial pressure was not the guiding force for seed distribution, just that it was not the exclusive one. More to the point, this shows how many farmers had already turned the corner and abandoned class based understandings of the impact of modernization on the class and accepted the goal of improved production and prices, mainly coming through increased technology.

The South was not immune from the interventions of the rising federal turn toward agricultural institutional development. Cotton producers continued to worry about the state of their production on the world market (Nettles, 1962). In response to an 1856 Congressional resolution, the Department of State analyzed tariff duties and customs regulations on cotton. In 1857 Congress allocated $3,500 to the Commissioner of Patents to study cotton consumption in industrialized nations (US Census, 1937). Also in 1856, the House of Representatives proposed appropriation of funds to the Patent Office's agricultural branch for obtaining cuttings and seeds to collect agricultural statistics and support Southern Agriculture as the Pierce Administration favored appropriations to encourage the cultivation of "tea and the improvement of the sugar industry, neither offering anything to the North." (Gates, 1960, pp. 325–326). In the South, were a general attitude of less government involvement in markets helped obfuscate state institutional support for market construction, Tobacco and rice planters sought government help in lowering tariff rates on their products abroad. Before the industry wide work of the Patent Office Agricultural Division on trade promotion, tobacco planters convinced Congress to establish a committee to review tobacco trade and appoint agents to seek better treatment for American tobacco. Gray (1958) writes that: "In 1836 the tobacco producing interests secured a resolution in Congress directing the President to instruct American diplomatic representatives to negotiate for diminution of duties and other burdens on American tobacco" (pp. 763–764). These early agricultural lobbying groups advocated retaliation in trade policy as well: "It was urged that in case negotiations should fail, resort be had to countervailing duties" (Gray, 1958, p. 764).

Another specific instance was federal government sponsorship of imported Mexican cotton. This variety of cotton was not disposed to rotting, the bolls opened wide, and it produced longer fibers that were more easily gathered. A worker could harvest several times more of the Mexican cotton in one day than he could of the old upland cotton. "Next to the cotton gin" this work on cotton breeding, later called Petit Gulf, "was the most important development in spreading cotton cultivation throughout the Deep South" (Gates, 1960, p. 301). Planters seeking solutions to the poor cotton prices and diminishing returns of the 1840s looked to the new varieties for miraculous results. Southern agriculture would continue to benefit from government institutional capacity building and specifically the expansion of trade and would slowly pass through its own agro-industrial development. The existence of a seed distribution project, initially housed in the Patent Office, was formed in this nexus as it helped farmers economically while aiding in the transition to market dependence by increasing yields and reliance on technical production.

Thus the roots of the expansion of state institutional capacity in the USDA clearly rested in the nexus of a drive to modernize farms, pushing the transition from farming to agriculture, combined with the shifts in the nature of farmer movements away from class and towards narrow economic demands. The result of productivity gains meant growing surpluses and the USDA-research complexes solution for this problem, from the very beginning, rested in state institutional development of trade promotion. From very early on the federal government sponsored experiments using agricultural imports from other countries in an effort to develop new varieties. In 1827 the Secretary of the Treasury directed American consuls in other countries to obtain seeds, plants and cuttings for shipment back to the US, they were "instructed to collect forest trees useful for timber'; grain of any description; fruit trees, vegetables for the table, esculent root; and in short, plants" useful for US agricultural development (Gates, 1960, p. 298). In 1830, the House of Representatives asked the Navy Department to bring new sugar cane varieties from the West Indies and sent the cuttings to Florida. Lima beans were brought from Peru in 1824 and alfalfa imported in the 1820s (Gates, 1960, p. 298). Wilkes Expedition of 1839–1842 collected 40,000 plant specimens in South America, the Pacific coast, the Hawaiian and other Pacific Islands, and Singapore which were given to the new National Institute for the Promotion of Science (Gates, 1960, pp. 298–300). Not only did the state seek out sees and plants, it also sought out markets for US agricultural products abroad.

Importantly the USDA drove to expand both domestic and export markets. Thus the increased productivity resulting from farm modernization could be absorbed by these exports and domestic markets. This drive also supported the other aspect of the agro-industrial project – keeping food prices low to maintain cheap consumer goods through industrial production. In fact, as will be discussed in Chapter 7, these two goals of agricultural export and cheap food to fuel industrial production coalesced in the post-WWII era to facilitate the rise of the US internationally and the reconstruction of a world capitalist market. Beyond seed technology and expanding trade, the state institutional agro-industrial project also advanced through USDA research into other areas.

The Agro-Industrial Project in Research

The USDA institutional model was one of semi-separate divisions and over time this would evolve and expand to more than thirty in total. In 1862 one of these divisions, the US Department of Agriculture's Division of Chemistry was established. It would publish piles of papers and conduct thousands of studies dealing with agricultural inputs and agricultural products. This little known departmental division would be a major influence on the future direction of agriculture. Harvey Wiley argued in 1899 that "we find chemistry intimately associated with nearly every line of agricultural progress and pointing the way to still greater advancement" as at least half of all federal money spent "for strict scientific investigations has been for chemical studies" (Wiley, 1899, p. 158). The agency would prove important for the trajectory of the development of agricultural production in the US going forward. USDA investigations into chemistry would come to play a major role in transforming agriculture and lead to the rapid advances in agricultural productivity over the next century through the development of new chemical fertilizers and pesticides.

The main thrust of early USDA work was in the collection and dissemination of data. Similar to the Division of Chemistry, the Division of Statistics, created in 1863, spent its budget collecting data on agricultural production (Shannon, 1945). Everything from data on harvests, conditions of crops, rates of fertilizer use, and livestock numbers were amassed and published in an effort to inform producers of market conditions and best production practices, along with helping to guide further research.

Also created in 1863, the USDA Division of Entomology furthered the work of earlier piecemeal attempts to understand and combat specific insect invasions. This Division was the predecessor to the work of the Hatch Act that would enable the creation of experiment stations. The importance of this work should not be underestimated. The approach pushed entomology to overcome the pests that gained the upper hand as crops became more concentrated and isolated on modern industrial farms. Thus, the work would enable the development of the mono-crop system that industrial agriculture would come to rely on and that allowed the major technological innovations in agriculture. This division would also provide outreach to farmers and win many over to the USDA through its work at helping them overcome pest problems they were encountering; again, most often as a result of the industrialization of farms (Kloppenburg, 1988).

The 1887 Hatch Act provided the first nation-wide subsidized funding of agricultural research to be carried out at land-grant colleges created by the Morrill Act. It also set up the state experiment stations. At the time of the establishment of these agencies farms across the country were battling several massive infestations of bug and disease outbreaks leading to large crop failures. These occurred in part because of the ongoing transition to a more concentrated mono-crop industrial form of agriculture and the interconnections between distant farms and markets that were developing. The scientific breakthroughs at the USDA research facilities and land-grant universities were in effect producing the need for further science to solve the problems they created, forcing more farmers to use scientific methods to overcome the problems from their neighbors farms and their own industrial agricultural methods, creating a cycle of increasing technological dependence.

An early report from the Commissioner of Agriculture in 1862 discussed the case of the introduction of sorghum as a crop to the US (Newton, 1862). The report claimed that since the Agricultural Bureau of Patent office had introduced the crop in 1835 its use had spread widely to the point where by 1862 40,000,000 gallons of sorghum syrup had been produced in the United States and that two mills had been built in Illinois to process its fiber into paper products (Newton, 1862). The report went on to claim that:

> As soon as arrangements now being made in the labouratory [sic] are completed, the chemist will enter into the analysis of the various grasses and grains of the United States, in order to learn which will produce the greatest amount of fat, flesh, muscle and bone; also of soils, manures, and the constituents of plants, with special reference to restoring fertility to exhausted farms.
> NEWTON, 1862, p. 23

The early focus of the Department's research into increasing the output of farms and turning crops into commodities is already present and overt in this early report from the first Head of the Department. This report also discussed the role of expanding agricultural surpluses on the culture of products of the nation:

> The surplus of agriculture not only allows the farmer to pay his debts and accumulate wealth, but also does the same for the nation....[t]o increase this surplus, therefore, to develop and bring out the vast resources of our soil, and thus create new additional capital, should be the great object of the Department of Agriculture and of legislation.
> NEWTON, 1862, p. 26

Clearly increasing farm productivity did not lead farmers paying their debts and accumulating wealth in large part. This is why the second part of this statement is so important; it articulates the goal of the department, despite the rhetoric of the first part of the statement, as using agro-industrial development to aid in the economic development of the nation.

The report went on to discuss improvements in the production of cotton and how this had expanded the US exports of the crop, along with the transformations in processing and product innovations (Newton, 1862).

The report also focused on the progress of research into tobacco, wheat and flax and how because of this progress new manufacturing opportunities had opened up (Newton, 1862). From this it can be deduced that the surplus created by the technological innovations coming out of the USDA-research complex were not seen as a problem; to the contrary, this was the goal of the research. The solution put forward by the state agency to any problems this increase in productivity created was more research to find the means to dispose of the commodities through new industrial production or through market expansion, both of which would emerge from expanding state institutional capacities.

By 1868 the USDA had 47 employees – statisticians, entomologists, chemists, and a superintendent of the experimental garden. By 1876 it contained divisions of chemistry, horticulture, entomology, statistics, seeds and botany. However, the drive for new food commodity products was creating not only the rise of a new mass consumer base but with it repeated problems of food adulteration and safety. With the expansion of industrial food production technologies, came the requirement for state institutions to oversee the developing markets, to insure food safety and protect not only to consumers but to the legitimacy of the fragile market itself. Into this void of insufficient institutional regulation of food safety stepped the USDA. Recognizing the link between the development of food processing and transportation methods, along with food additives and the development of chemical processes of food production that was emerging out of the work at the USDA, the Commissioner of the USDA Daniel Le Duc argued it only natural that the USDA also expand into food safety regulation (Harding, 1947).

After a 1883 USDA study determined that an effort by the federal government to prohibit certain types of butter adulteration would greatly benefit dairy producers as it would "aid the dairy interest in establishing a standard of good butter", the USDA entered into the regulation of foods, not only on the grounds of protecting consumers, but also on the grounds of effective marketing (Harding, 1947, p. 33). The department would go on to do research leading to major breakthroughs in producing food industrially while maintaining food safety, out of which would eventually grow giant food companies capable of turning a small number of inputs into thousands of food products with long shelf lives made possible through chemical input developed through USDA research.

So there was also an internal benefit to the Department that arose out of the transition to an industrial food system; as the food system industrialized because of the advances in production and processing worked out in USDA labs, the need for inspection and regulation of food increased, as did the need for more research into dealing with pests and crop problems caused by industrial agriculture. This should not be dismissed as another case of institutional mission creep. Instead it emerged in response to the demands of agrarian movement and out of the problems that grew out of the particular path of state institutional intervention. Agro-industrial development ensured an expanding need for state institutional involvement in the increasingly complex market for agricultural goods.

Other divisions of the USDA also sprang up during this era as the state's role expanded in an effort to stem part of the downward pressure on farmers, quell agrarian unrest and integrate agriculture into a capitalist economy. The USDA's expansion through the creation of the division of Botany, Section on Mycology, Division of Microscopy, divisions of Plant Pathology, Pomology, Dairy, Biological Survey and Plant Science, and Bureau of Plant Industry all worked to improve agricultural production during an era of vast overproduction. Also in 1891, the Weather Bureau was transferred from the Department of War to the USDA (Shannon, 1945). The creation of these divisions should be viewed as both the means to transition the agriculture of the country towards a market oriented, industrial form, thereby feeding the increasing urban industrial workforce with ever cheaper food and also as the means to pre-empt the demands of the growing agrarian radicals and distressed farmers. In both ways it served as a clear aid to the ongoing transition to industrial capitalism in both the farming and manufacturing sectors.

The Department's early communications, issued as annual reports, brought little excitement in the agricultural press at the time. The Department undertook an effort to make their research and reports more usable and accessible to the average farmer, causing their popularity to increase sharply. In 1889 they began issuing Farmers Bulletins and the annual report became the *Yearbook of Agriculture* in 1894 (Rasmussen, 1989). Alongside their more pedestrian presentation style, these reports and bulletins both pushed agricultural technology as the solution to farmers' problems and a market based understanding of farmer problems. This quantification of farm issues aligned with and aided in a shift away from a focus on the deep rooted problems of farmers, including the specific class dynamics at work, and into concerns over prices and productivity, as well as the technical aspects of crop production. This depoliticization of the market represents a substantial goal undergirding much federal support of agriculture as well as the drive of major reformist groups such as the AFBF and the Progressives. It represents a major goal of the USDA as an institution in the US State

With an initial appropriation of $10,000 for food investigations in 1894 Nutritional research within the USDA became a site of expanding market construction. The lead instigator in the push for this research funding was Wilbur

Atwater, who became the Chief of Nutritional Investigation in the USDA's Office of Experiment Stations (Dupont, 2009). In the ten years that he headed the program, Atwater coordinated and conducted experiments in four different areas: types and amounts of foods, effects of cooking and food processing on nutritional quality, chemical composition of food, and types and amounts of nutrients required for optimal health (Dupont, 2009).

A full and complete history of the influence of nutritional research and its impact on the direction of agriculture and food products is beyond the scope of this investigation. However, even a cursory assessment of the project reveals how this research helped to further the technological and industrial form of agriculture. While expanding consumer demand for industrially produced agricultural products, USDA nutritional research also established a limited and specific knowledge of food role in health, which would aid in the industrialization of agriculture and food by spreading an understanding of food based on reducing it down to the nutrients contained in certain foods. This approach rendered diets, and importantly traditional diets, less important than eating the nutrient content of the foods. This then dislodged food cultures and replaced them with various food products said to meet the desired nutrient intake to maintain optimal health (Pollan, 2007). The ability to expand food products and eventually fortify food and create tens of thousands of industrial food products out of a handful of agricultural crops emerged out of this early USDA work. The USDA food and nutrient databases provided the basic infrastructure for food and nutrition research, nutrition monitoring, policy, and dietary practice having had a long history that goes back to 1892 (Ahuja et al., 2013). This public domain database provided the necessary information for tens of thousands of food corporation innovations throughout its existence. Nutrition information coming out of the USDA would come to play a major role in transforming American, and by extension, international diets.

In the 1880s the decentralization of congressional appropriations helped politicians channel federal funds back home to their districts and this altered the direction of state institutional support for agriculture. Created in 1867, the House Appropriations Committee was designed to defend the Treasury; the committee often reduced federal spending to the chagrin of representatives in search of government pork and who were facing rising hostility from farmers in their districts. By the late 1870s, critics complained of the committee's power over budgetary decisions and the negative effects of limited state intervention. In 1880, a House revolt against this power resulted in a shift of authority from the Appropriations Committee to individual Congressional Committees. By 1885, virtually all power over spending decisions was in the hands of these committees. Stewart (1987) referred to these changes as a process of "expansionary fragmentation" – institutional changes that decentralized authority in order to promote increased federal spending (pp. 585–605).

One of the first committees to gain control over its own appropriations in 1880 was the House Agriculture Committee. Not surprisingly, the annual budget of the Department of Agriculture increased rapidly thereafter through "expansionary fragmentation". This shift in the political structures increased reliance on individual members of Congress who would respond to pressures at home through the allocation of funds to USDA projects in their districts. Thus we see one of the mechanisms by which agrarian discontent was channelled through state apparatus and institutions to push agro-industrialization. Furthermore, this enlargement of the USDA budget through a shift in appropriations enhanced federal state institutional ability to coordinate the direction of agricultural development across the nation while simultaneously diffusing social input into individual congressional districts.

Of the many cases of USDA research into areas which increased the commercial viability of crops, the research into durum wheat serves as a good example because it allowed the production of processed pasta and led to an increase from the sale of seven million bushels of wheat in 1903 to 50 million bushels in 1906 (Harding, 1947). New varieties of wheat were developed from the hardy Russian and Turkish wheat varieties which had been brought to the US through the USDA work overseas. The US Department of Agriculture's Experiment Stations took the lead in developing wheat varieties for different regions. For example, in the Columbia River Basin new varieties raised yields from an average of 19.1 bushels per acre in 1913–22 to 23.1 bushels per acre in 1933–42 (Shepherd, 1980). In another example, early work on soybeans came in 1907 and would transform this crop into a major source of oils and industrial food inputs (Harding, 1947).

Similarly, USDA work on hybrid corn would eventually develop hybrid forms which increased yields from an average of 40 bushels per acre to 100 to 120 bushels per acre. These developments in corn varieties – worked out through USDA research – would not only transform the Midwestern states into the world producers of corn but also make them "absolutely fundamental to the rapid growth of the American seed industry and increase the availability and price of meat that has transformed diets in the 20th Century" (Kloppenburg, 1988, p. 94).

There was also research into new ways to dehydrate, store and transport fruit and vegetables along with the development of technologies in freezing, canning, freeze drying, and methods for shipment, including refrigeration, chemical rot retardants, ripening agents for produce picked early for better resistance to damage during shipping, which occurring in USDA research facilities funded by federal dollars (Harding, 1947). USDA researchers also worked to develop ways to deal with agricultural waste, by transforming them into profitable by-products. For example, USDA research found a use for the culled citrus fruit by developing the processes for manufacturing citric acid, pectin, lemon oil, orange oil and other valuable by-products that would spur the industrial food system (Harding, 1947). The discovery that ethylene gas would loosen walnut hulls, ripen fruit, add desired fruit color and other industrial food uses, most of which made products more shippable, more saleable by making them last longer and was all discovered at USDA research facilities (Harding, 1947).

All of this research was part of the drive to commodify agricultural products through differentiation of non-farm production of marketable consumer food products. That is to say, USDA led research created new means to create both commodified farm products and products that were inputs to the industrial manufacturing of food products. The state was engaged in appropriation through the transfer of value beyond the farm into industrial production, a business context that was open to surplus extraction through capital investment (Kloppenburg, 1988). The work of the USDA aided in "the displacement of production activities off-farm and into circumstances in which fully developed capitalist realization of production can be imposed" (Kloppenburg, 1988, p. 31). These technological innovations, forged in the emerging relationship between industry and agriculture, fostered the ability of industrial capitalism to overcome both natural and social barriers to capitalist agricultural development through a process that would increasingly by-pass or diminish the influence and power of small farmers. The ability of capitalism to turn farming into the mass production of raw materials for industrial processing through the use of other industrially produced input materials, would allow for the continued advance of industrial production of cheaper food. Simultaneously it created the market imperatives to propel farmers into large industrial production and diminish the overall share of profits they received.

According to Harding (1947, p. 32) the "Department's policy of making two blades of grass grow where one grew before, while eminently successful, did not suffice to solve farmers' problems". Indeed, as early as 1890, with the frontier gone and as agricultural overproduction became a threat, there was a growing recognition of overproduction. Yet the Department's "sole remedy was to evolve scientific methods which further increased production or else decreased per-unit cost of production" (Harding, 1947, p. 33). "Farmers intensified their efforts, followed instructions, made their land yield just as much as possible, yet did not always prosper" (Harding, 1947, p. 33).

During the first thirty to forty years of its existence the USDA research was not regarded by most farmers as in their particular interest (Gates, 1960;

Hadwiger, 1982). The drive of the 19th century farmers' movements rested in a pursuit of social reform rather than the seeking of agricultural science. Some have claimed it was the backward orientation of small farmers that caused their objections to agricultural science and a misinterpretation of how increased production as a threat to farmers' lives and existence (Hadwiger, 1982). The fact that the populist movement reformers in Kansas and other areas sought, and for a brief time convinced, the experiment station managers and agricultural college professors to focus their work on economic issues rather than the scientific improvement of agricultural production could be viewed as evidence of the naivety of the benefits to farmers that could come from scientific advance. But it could also be viewed as the product of a more class based ideology emerging from their lived experiences and their longing to return to the era when they had more control over their lives and were generally more prosperous.

Battles over whose needs and what goals the United States Department of Agriculture's programs should serve have continued to take place at every corner of the institution. There were men and women within farm organizations – the land grant colleges and the USDA – who viewed the benefits of a dynamic, expanding, capitalist economy as the best hope for farmers. They believed in the use of the tools of science and social science to increase production, trade, and consumption, advocating for research into new technologies to increase production and promoting capital intensive agribusiness. At the same time, however, populist programs lay behind efforts to develop social and economic institutions that would protect farmers and their communities from the many threats to their existence being caused by this emerging form of industrial agriculture, or at least help farmers to transition in a less jarring manner. Efforts to establish a counterbalance to market forces included the regulation of the railroads, meat packers, and futures trading. However, even these were approached in such a way as to ease the agro-industrial model onto farmers. The USDA would hold the hands of farmers as they made the difficult transition to industrial agribusiness; and groups such as the AFBF would help to convince farmers that their best hope lay in technological innovation, improved productivity and expanding markets.

State Capacity Building in Trade and Banking

As previously discussed, during and immediately after the Civil War the federal government rapidly expanded its institutional capacity. The Civil War Congress almost immediately passed bills that provided five spurs to industrial capitalism: first, in 1862 it granted the charters for the first transcontinental railroads; next, it passed the Homestead Act of 1862 and began the sale of railroad land, which ensured that the vast territory would be filled by farmers who would become large markets for industrial goods; then, it acted to protect these growing markets through tariffs enacted in 1861 and kept high through the rest of the 19th century industrialization processes; following that, Congress set up a national currency system and a system of national banks in 1863 and 1864 to aid capital formation; and finally, the federal government liberalized immigration procedures in 1864 to provide the increases in labor necessary for the industrializing nation (Headlee, 1991). The legislation passed during these four short years went a long way to shape the future direction of development of the nation for decades to come.

Along with these spurs to industry, banking laws were also altered to meet the institutional demands of the times. Although many of the reforms emerged due to agrarian movements and were presented as the means to solve the issues and problems they faced. These reforms would both disarm the agrarian critics and help expand market mediated social relations. Despite its populist origins the banking reforms would become one of the foundations of moving farmers further into commodification. Additionally, after the war Treasury policy shifts encouraged the transfer of accumulated capital from the government to the construction of railroads. In the immediate four years following the war more than $500 million in new railroad and canal securities entered the financial markets, seeking to liquidate state and federal debt (Bensel, 1990). The expansion of railways would further integrate local markets and intensify market competition by linking together agricultural commodities markets.

Because of the debt incurred during the Civil War the Legal Tender Act of 1862 was passed. This act mandated that paper money be issued and accepted in lieu of gold and silver coins or greenbacks. It was modeled on state "free banking" principles which emerged between 1852 and 1863 by which all states, with the exception of Texas and Oregon, had already taken up the policies (Hammond, 1957). In response to long held farmer critiques of the problems of state and local banks, the 1862 Act turned many state owned banks over to the federal government – the number of national banks rose from sixty-six immediately after the Act to 7,473 in 1913. This rise in national banking came at the expense of state banking – the number of state banks dwindled from 1,466 in 1863 to 247 in 1868. The 1864 act required national banks to maintain a minimum of $50,000 of capital stock in towns under 6,000 people and $100,000 of capital stock in population from 6,000–50,000 and $200,000 in cities with greater than 50,000 people (Huntington and Mawinney, 1910). A subsequent act in 1865 imposed a tax of ten percent on the notes of state banks to take effect on July 1, 1866. Similar to previous taxes, this effectively forced all non-federal currency from circulation. It also resulted in the creation of demand deposit accounts, and encouraged banks to join the national system, thus increasing the number of national banks substantially.

Headlee (1991) cited these banking changes as the source of the rise of "new banking capital" in the post-war era, as industrial capitalism defeated merchant capitalism. With the increased role of the federal government in banking and the decline in state banking, an increase in regulation occurred. The farm movements were demanding a large, government subsidized, rural banking system. Examples of how the political compromises abound between the organized farmers and corporations fed into agro-industrial market dependence. The federal regulation of banks is one example of this process. The injection of federal loans regulated by the state facilitated improvements in production by providing needed capital to farmers, but it also made them dependent upon a web of debt and federal government involvement in agriculture. The populist movements opposition to a central bank was therefore partially overcome through the granting of state responses to other issues related to agriculture, mostly in the form of cooperative efforts, some credit based on land, and some regulation of railroads. The reason the state was so responsive to this particular agrarian demand was because it fit into the emerging institutional arrangement of the transitioning of farming into agriculture (Bernstein, 2010). It was credit that would help to facilitate the modernization of farms and fuel the expansion of agro-business.

As the new Federal banking regulations played out they had the effect of ensuring that banking capital would slowly come to dominate over merchant capital. This was the most important impacts of the the 1913 Federal Reserve Act – ironically one of the greatest reforms of the Progressive Era. The Act, which created twelve regional banks under the guidance of the Federal Reserve Board, helped to spread liquidity to regional banks and regulate interest rates. Even with this change farmers still needed long term low-interest credit. Their continued pressure on President Wilson eventually got him to push for the Federal Farm Loan Bill that in 1916 created twelve Federal Land Banks modeled after the Federal Reserve System (Hurt, 2002). The act allowed farmers to borrow from the federal government against their land and commodities as security, thus allowing them to hold the commodities until the market became less saturated and prices rose. The Fed was assuming the major risk in the credit system, which was essentially a huge help to the banking industry and helped to loosen farm credit.

The creation of the Federal Reserve also began the process of internationalizing the US dollar in a "fusion of financial and government power" (Chernow,

1990, p. 131; Panitch and Gindin, 2012, p. 43). This act served to remove issues of "money, banking and currency from political significance" related to farming (Livingston, 1986, p. 26). By effectively ending the class war over credit between banks and farmers as the US state signaled its intentions to finance and nudge the US into an expanding world market. On the other side farmers acquiesced to the modernizing drive which meant farmer's credit needs would be met and they could borrow from the federal government against their only assets, land and commodities. This not only undermined many of the agrarians demands, it also imbricated them into the emerging world market through the further commodification of their crops and by allowing them to borrow for industrial agricultural expansion.

What emerged after the long and ongoing history of the construction of US institutional capacity was a capitalist state able to manage the demands of the opposing classes by incorporating their demands in a modified form into the very structure of the state institutional capacities. It is a clear example of the working out of the construction of the US capitalist state and its particular institutional strengths. Also important was the unevenness that was caused, in part by the geographic differences and the crops they supported. Crops that were easily commodified created different social pressures than perishable agricultural products, especially before mass refrigeration and pasteurization.

The agro-industrial project was furthered by changes in tariff policy as well. Midwestern and Western farmers had consistently pushed for the elimination of tariffs, and specifically had vociferously opposed the 1897 Dingley Tariff that imposed a 52 percent import tax. The rates on agricultural input imports shifted wildly between 1890 and 1930. From the late 19th Century until 1913 a protectionist approach was pushed through by a coalition of agricultural and industrial capitalists alike (Winders, 2009). This shifted with the 1913 Underwood Tariff Act – the result in good part of farmer political activities – "reduced rates on manufactured goods to pre-Civil War levels, with agricultural machinery placed on the free list" (Hurt, 2002, p. 25). Farmers victories on the tariff issue in this era both raised prices and expanded markets, which was something farmers had already come around to accept as a solution to their problems thanks to the decades long work of reformers within agrarian movements in pushing industrial agriculture as the means to improve the lives of farmers.

Agro-Industrialization through Farmer Education

Initially the drive toward practical farmer education was at the genesis of the founding of the Patrons of the Grange. The organizations that were emerging mostly championed education as a means to improve farmers' lives. This support was combined with the assistance of ruling class philanthropy seeking technological education and research that would influence both farm organizations and the direction of state intervention into agricultural education. In 1850 and 1851, Jonathan B. Turner of Illinois delivered a series of lectures on industrial education which served to crystallize a widespread sentiment for the introduction of agricultural subjects into the school curricula (Schmidt, 1920). Turner published in the annual report of the United States Patent Office for 1851 a plan for an industrial university (James, 1910). It would be more than a decade later before Morrill Act would be referred to congressional committee, passing on June 17, 1862 and sent to President Lincoln for signing on July 2, 1862. As finally enacted it provided for a grant of 30,000 acres of land for each Senator and Representative according to the apportionment for the Census of 1860 (True, 1929). The land was to be sold for the purpose of creating Colleges of Agriculture.

Despite the help from some farmers' movements in the drive for farmer education, the early support was mostly linked to wealthy and well-connected elites who advocated for a government centered educational program directed at an ever more industrial farming model. "Government employees played a crucial role in establishing the Grangers just as they did the Farm Bureau" with

> Oliver Kelley was working as a clerk for the Agriculture Bureau in 1867 when he organized six other men (five of whom were government clerks) and his niece to join him in founding the Patrons of Husbandry. A man with an extra-ordinary ear for messages that would resonate with his audiences, Kelley approached his colleagues in Washington with the idea that a mass organization of farmers would promote scientific agriculture and vastly increase the Agriculture Department's influence and funding.
> SUMMERS, 1996, P. 402

The influence on farmers' organizations that would be consolidated in farmer education occurred the means to neutralize more radical agrarian groups. Despite this influence, early attempts were often tempered by the sheer number of farmers who felt differently and opposed an education and technology centered solution. As Turner recognized: "The idea of discussions upon how to raise crops is stale. They all want some plan of work to oppose the infernal monopolies." (Summers, 1996, p. 402). As previously outlined, the main program of the 19th century farmers' movements lay in a pursuit of social reform, not the seeking of agricultural science and farm modernization. Most of the farmers of the populist era were eager for a political response to the problems that capitalist development was causing, with its monopolies and powerful industries. For the most part, this battle between reformists and radicals in farmer organizations of the late 19th century had ended with a defeat of the more social based demands and the increased acceptance of the economic modernization approach. At least for a time however, the Populist movements in Kansas and other areas where able to shift the focus of experiment stations and agricultural colleges on to economic issues rather than the scientific improvement of agricultural production (Hadwiger, 1982). This focus was short lived however, and was eventually redirected toward price increases that the agricultural institutions of the nation convincingly argued could be achieved through technological advances occurring through research and education.

In an effort to improve the research capacity and the image of the land-grant colleges, Commissioner of Agriculture George Loring asked Seaman Knapp of the Iowa Agricultural College to draft a proposal for a system of agricultural experiment stations. Knapp, who submitted his plan to a convention of land-grant college administrators in 1882, envisioned a system of experiment stations that would operate "under the general control of the agricultural colleges" (True, 1929, p. 51). Knapp insisted that "the general character of the work and of the experiments to be performed at each station shall be determined by the Commissioner of Agriculture." Knapp argued, this federal guidance would "systemize their [the stations'] work throughout the United States and will avoid too much repetition of experiments at different stations" (True, 1929, p. 52). Here was an attempt to create a research network that linked state and federal institutions under the guidance of a commissioner in Washington D.C. This would allow it to deal with the particular issues facing different locations, while also creating an overarching institutional basis for agricultural industrialization.

The Knapp proposal was introduced in Congress in 1883. However, the proposed role of the USDA raised immediate objections. Some college administrators voiced objections to the apparent subordination of the stations to the USDA. While Knapp's plan languished in committee, a substitute bill, recommended favorably by the House Agriculture Committee, placed the new experiment stations under the control of state governments with the stations directly affiliated with existing agricultural colleges and reporting directly to each state government. The bill went so far as to emphasize that nothing "shall be construed to authorize [the] Commissioner to control or direct the work or management of any such station" (True, 1929, p. 96). In the end, the 1887 Hatch Act bore little resemblance to the system of agricultural research stations envisioned by Knapp. Although the act created a means to fund a system of experiment stations for agricultural research, neither the USDA nor the land-grant colleges exercised much control over their operation and states remained at the helm of the research and education they engaged in. The fate of the proposal reveals the inability of a national push towards agro-industrial national institutions to dictate policies during this particular balance of class forces. Although the relationship between them would grow to intertwine, the USDA would not have much of a direct say in state experiment stations.

In 1908 President Theodore Roosevelt said that "Successful manufacturing depends primarily on cheap food" (Hurt, 2002, p. 14). To this end he appointed the Commission on Country Life to study the problems of rural life because, in his words "the problems of country life is in the truest sense a national problem" (Hurt, 2002, pp. 15–16). This perspective represented recognition of one of the agrarian movements' central ideas – that rural farm life was the lifeblood of the nation and it should not be allowed to be degraded by the growth of urban centers and big corporations. The commission, in fact, was initiated in response to the country life movement seeking a combination of a celebration of some rural traditional lifestyles and increased agricultural technology to safeguard the economy necessary for these lifestyles. Despite its rural focus, the movement was started and maintained by mostly wealthy, well educated urbanites (Bowers, 1974, p. 34). In opposition to its rhetoric of aiding rural peoples, the true motivation for the movement was a Malthusian based attempt to combat an alleged slowing of agricultural productivity. Accordingly, major backers and funders of the movement were industries that relied on agriculture (Kloppenburg, 2004). What these groups Advocates for the movement spanned a diverse set of interests from USDA scientists to titans of the railroads and shared an interest in the rationalization of agriculture through science. "If the agricultural scientists were motivated by a vision of a transformed and improved rural society, the business interests were unambiguously interested in restoring productivity advance as a necessary condition for their own continued capital accumulation" (Kloppenburg, 2004, p. 74). The commission Teddy Roosevelt set up included sociologist Kenyon Butterfield, Gifford Pinchot, and the future Secretary of Agriculture Henry Wallace (Swanson, 1977, p. 360). When the commission recommendations came back they echoed the more timid reforms put forward by the populist and FA movements – low interest loans, aid in marketing of crops, a national agricultural extension service, and a national agency devoted to rural progress – and were absent any proposals that didn't represent state policies that advanced industrial agriculture and the associated industrial developments that went along with it. The recommendations to aid rural livelihood rested mainly on education of the farmer on technological innovations and best practices to maintain advances in agricultural productivity.

The recommendations of the Commission on Country Life reflected the timing of the commission, coming during relatively prosperous times for farmers, as well as the desires of more conservative elements and big philanthropic groups for education and voluntary groups as the solution to agrarian problems (McConnell, 1935). The Rockefeller-endowed General Education Board was advocating for the land-grant universities to adopt agricultural demonstrations and a systematic approach to extension (McConnell, 1953). Another important factor lie in the appointment of the conservative Liberty Hyde Bailey (1918) as the chair of the commission, who made his contempt for the populist and progressive farm movements clear when he stated "I must point out the dangers in those kinds of organized efforts that seek to gain their ends by force of numbers, by compulsion and strategy... I trust that we will avoid class legislation" (pp. 102–103). What emerged is a set of state policies aimed at elevating some of the farmer's hardships and responding to democratic pressure, while pursuing agricultural development in an industrial direction.

This "'bureaucratic remedy' spoke to all who were fearful of socialists and agrarian radicals" while maintaining the acceptable balance of "industrial capitalism and support for democracy" (Skowronek, 1982, p. 165). Fitting the expansion of industrial capitalism within the confines of the American system of democracy and capitalism required the reconfiguration of agriculture to meet the demands of that system. A focus on agricultural technology advancement and education was one means to this end. It also served to obscure and obfuscate the class differences behind experts and the gains in efficiency they promised. Aligning the goals of industry and agriculture would occur through the technological transformation of agriculture. Just as during the anti-rent movement in the state of New York over eighty years prior, the commissions recommendation and federal policy responses were a move to use the state, and its reconfiguration, as a means to undermine the radical movements that sought more significant social change by drawing them into believing that state apparatuses could meet their demands through productivity gains. Thus creating the idea that the national state was responsive to farmer's needs (Hanson, 1991), while simultaneously pushing the policies of agro-industrialization.

During the Progressive era, the Federal Government underwent a major expansion and reorganization. The expansion of administrative power, and I would argue the concurrent granting of political autonomy to institutional apparatuses, should be viewed as an outgrowth of Teddy Roosevelt's progressivism represented a clear opposition to populism. The fact that Roosevelt's move to heighten administrative power rested on granting a measure of 'neutrality' to the layers of federal agencies undermined his party's ability to use government offices for future political gains and meant that he quickly created enemies in his own party (Skowronek, 1982). The back-lash this created, and his response to it, represented a significant portion of his credentials as a reformer and independent thinker. The rest came from his inclusion of some of the demands for the government to move against the big "trusts" of the day. However this too shared the goal of neutering radical movements as driving the decisions more than the lofty ideals of those movements. Like FDR after him, Teddy Roosevelt was a master at understanding how to use interest group politics to steer radicals into acceptable policies and thereby neutralize the radical appeal. It was a move "toward the construction of an entirely new system of civil administration and a reconstitution of institutional power relationships" as the shape of state institutional capacity shifted through the addition of a layer of independent or autonomous state power between the classes (Skowronek, 1982, p. 180).

The effort to use state power and institutional reforms to depoliticize agricultural class issues during the era went all the way up to the executive. Through his actions, Teddy Roosevelt was "driving a wedge between national administration and local politics, he jolted long-established governing arrangements and permanently altered national institutional politics", which did not go unnoticed to members of his party and others whose power was undermined by his moves (Skowronek, 1982, p. 186). These policies would lead to a backlash first as party unity fell apart, creating a very momentary partnership between Democrats and Republicans in opposition. The success of populist reformers such as Robert LaFollette rested on the unity created among the widespread local opposition to the expansion of federal administrative power. But this backlash should not be seen (as Skowronek does) as effectively undermining the administrative reform. Instead, both administrative efficiency and the taming of the radical movements was achieved. The use of and the ability to shift between these levels or levers of power, is a unique and powerful capacity of the US power structure. Teddy Roosevelt very effectively used both federal power and local power to his advantage to push through institutional changes in industrial capitalist development.

The improvements in rural life that came, in part, from the response of the Federal Government to the report by the Commission on Rural Living, were used as the means to keep food prices low and to spur industrial development. Despite Teddy Roosevelt's disguised agro-industrial goals, by 1910 the Progressive movement had achieved a laundry list of the more moderate agrarian goals first set forward three decades earlier. The key question is just exactly how were these demands transformed into state policies? By describing the steps we can reveal the process by which agrarian demands were remade into forms aligned with the interests of capitalist class power through state institutional capacity building.

There was a whole parade of Congressional Acts coming during the Progressive era aimed at assuaging the demands of farmers through the federal government: the 1914 Cotton Futures Act, 1914 Smith-Lever Agricultural Extension Act, 1916 Grain Standards Act, 1916 Warehouse Act, and the 1917 Smith-Hughes Act, to name just a few. Also accruing during the first few decades of the 20th Century was the USDA's development and transformation of itself from an information gathering agency into a "bureaucratic regulatory agency with considerable powers" (Hurt, 2002, p. 35). USDA funding would climb from the 1899 level of $2.8 Million to $28 Million by 1917, and by the end of WWI it was second only to the Treasury in the number of federal employees (Hurt, 2002).

The Cotton Futures and Grain Standards act of 1916 standardized the grading of certain commodities, while also restricting some speculation and market manipulation, and ending fraudulent practices (Winders, 2009). As discussed in Chapter 4, the farmers' and populists' demands for some means to deal with the questionable practices of grain warehouses was eventually responded to by policies standardizing grain grading and setting rules on practices (Cronon, 1991). Despite its populist roots, the functioning of the law ended up being much more about the grading of grain that helped marketers and streamlined commercialization of the crops, than it ever was about helping farmers deal with dishonest grain buyers (McConnell, 1966). The grading system would become part of the culture of grain farming that led to a new orientation of farmers towards the "marketability" of their crops.[1]

The Grain Standards Act of 1916 represented a clear example of the building of agro-industrial state institutional capacities to structure the rules to guide behavior and development. There had been many independent attempts by local Chambers of Commerce, boards of trade, and major grain corporations to develop grain standards to reduce the confusion and corruption that characterized the trade. These efforts had largely failed because of inequalities among markets and differing standards. Thus a drive for federal legislation to set industry wide standards emerged. As a result, the Department of Agriculture over time had established labouratory tests and conducted numerous interviews and hearings to identify the most urgent needs of the grain industry. The information became the basis for the legislation that was adopted. This aided in turning grain into a commodity by constructing a unified grading system thus facilitating and easing market transitions. The application of science combined with social science interviews by the USDA led to a set of standards

---

1 See Chapter 2 for a discussion of the early adoption of grain standards in Chicago that emerged out of the demands of the Chicago Mercantile Association.

that benefited the grain industry. This then would inform the planting decisions of farmers around the nation.

The other aspect of the commodification of agriculture into industrial inputs was the growth of the market for consumer food products that would lead the way, along with helping to fuel production through cheap food, to the industrial consumer product boom (Prasad, 2012; Cohen, 2003; Cronon, 1991; Maier, 1977). Again agriculture serves as both the blueprint for the expansion of consumer products and as the cheap food inputs which increased disposable income of labor to purchase these products (not to mention the preparation time many of these food products saved, which either turned into more workable hours or into leisure time to use many of the new consumer products).

In the early 20th century two patterns of clientele support aided the growth of agricultural research and teaching: the first was the producers of particular commodities, who "did much to shape, or misshape, teaching curriculums and research agendas as well as the intellectual environment of the colleges" (Hadwiger, 1982, p. 20). At the federal level it was most often an interest in a particular commodity that drove cooperation between bureau chiefs and congressional leaders (Hadwiger, 1982). Similarly, at the state level it was the major commodity interests that drove research (Hadwiger,1982). Industrialists who were impatient with the federal pace of agricultural education rollout pushed ahead with their own versions of agricultural education programs. By 1910, most major railroad companies had established their own agricultural departments to "promote better agricultural methods among our farmers, interest them in the scientific side of the work, and…prevail on them to adopt it," as a Frisco Line executive put it (Scott, 1962, p. 14). There were many of these traveling agricultural demonstration railcars that sought to protect the growth of the rail industry by pushing the continued commodification of agriculture (Kloppenburg, 2004; Scott, 1962).

Based on the extensive lobbying of industry and a shift in the balance of class forces make it possible, a national governmental institution to work to educate farmers was created in 1914, thereby establishing a governmental agency to take over the work started by the private agricultural technology education extension programs (Kloppenburg, 2004). An act to establish county extension agents came to be law, with little direct support from farmers. as North Dakota Senator Asle Gronna underscored by stating on the Senate floor that he had "yet to find the first farmer who has asked for this appropriation" (Danbom, 1979, p. 73). The Smith-Lever Act of 1914 funded the employment of county-level extension agents to distribute research findings to farmers. Extension agents recruited farmers into county associations called farm bureaus, which grew to be corporatist affiliates of the AFBF – a national farm organization – in order to overcome the reluctance of farmers. (Hadwiger, 1982; McConnell, 1953). Importantly McConnell (1953) outlined the public-private funding behind the Smith-Lever Act, as major business associations – including the American Bankers' Association, the Council of North American Grain Exchangers, and the fertilizer funded interest group the National Soil Fertility League – funded by railroad, bank and manufacturing interests pushed for and provided private grants for the agricultural education policies (pp. 29–34). Through the act banking and business interests combined with large farms to create a state institution to push agro-industrial models (McConnell, 1955). The act moved to federalize local and state agricultural programs, alongside incorporation of private associations into a federally funded system of agricultural extension (McConnell, 1953). In this way it also represents a consolidation of power in the federal government. The USDA in concert with the land grant universities would be in charge of the extension service work (Rasmusson, 1989).

County Agents were pushed to be nonpartisan and seemingly apolitical by decree, in an attempt to depoliticize the market while pushing the agro-industrialization engaged in by the state (McConnell, 1966). The Extension Agents also sought to build up local chapters who could, through their organization and socializing environment, aid in "teaching" the latest methods in farming to members (McConnell, 1966). These volunteer groups, and the extension service, represented the battlefield of the class war in agriculture and together formed "the most powerful private pressure group agriculture has ever produced" (McConnell, 1966, p. 76). The agricultural colleges almost exclusively stressed efficiency and productivity as the means for achieving agricultural well-being, along with providing the informational and technological guidance triggering advances in agriculture that focused on specialization, concentration, mechanization and enlargement of farms (Goodman and Redclift, 1991; Harding, 1955; Hightower, 1972; Hurt, 2002, McConnell, 1953). The system set up "imposed the rule that research should be useful to commercial agriculture and in no way embarrassing to or in competition with it" (Hadwiger, 1982, p. 22).

The Smith-Hughes Act of 1917, organized and passed by non-agrarian interests to neutralize radical agrarian demands, sought to set up vocational education by establishing agricultural schools, the agricultural extension service, and Federally funded education related to agriculture (Winders, 2009). American citizens who lived in this time period also witnessed an increase in Federal involvement in agriculture through the the 1917 Food Protection Act that placed USDA demonstration agents in every agricultural county; also in 1917 the Food Control Act created the US Food Administration run by Herbert Hoover, who set a minimal price for wheat and encouraged maximum production

(Hurt, 2002). Similar to the Standards Act and the Vocational Education Act, these projects of state institutional development were responses to farmers' demands for government intervention into the market. Yet the increased state institutional capacity that this entailed further embedded farmers in market relations.

The growth of county extension agent work was swift – funding grew more than 300% from just under $3.6 million in 1915 to over $11 million by 1918 and $17 million by 1920. This was fueled, in part, by passage of emergency funding through the Food Production Act that would grant $6.1 million to the Extension Service. Accordingly, the number of counties having agents rose from 928 in 1914 to 2,434 in 1918 and total extension staff increased from 2,601 to 6,728 in the same four year period (Rasmusson, 1989).

This was part of the reorganization of the USDA during David Houston's tenure as Secretary of Agriculture from 1913–1920. This reorganization was explicitly designed to deal with the economic and social problems long ignored by the Department. Houston established a new Cooperative Extension Service, an Office of Information, and an Office of Markets. He initiated a study of rural credit and agricultural marketing facilities and later an inquiry on how to overcome economic problems by producing agricultural commodities of higher quality that greater added value to food products. An unusual amount of agricultural legislation was passed during the seven years Houston held the office: the Smith-Lever Act (agricultural extension), the Farm Loan Act, the Warehouse Act, and the Federal Aid Road Act, which for the first time established effective cooperation between the states and the federal government in the building of national highways. Houston opposed direct Federal aid to the poor, instead preferring programs that enabled greater access to credit and the building of greater opportunities through various market mechanisms.

Also created around this time was the Bureau of Home Economics in 1923. In 1930 it was headed by Louise Stanley who was the Chief of the Food and Nutrition Division, and Hazel Stiebeling who was the head of the section on Food Economics. Stiebeling initiated a program of research to investigate the nutritional value of US diets. Included in this research was the first nationwide consumer purchase survey in 1935–36 (Hadwiger, 1982). The study's results lead to President Franklin Roosevelt's famous statement that "one third of our nation is ill-fed, ill-housed and ill-clothed." The USDA research facilities ameliorated a portion of this problem by developing and then requiring the enrichment of flour and bread with iron and three separate B vitamins (USDA, 1939). The Department also launched a vigorous and widespread nutrition education and a school lunch programs. The attempt to quantify the nutritional needs of the citizenry represented a shift in focus that held the potential to open up the ability of the state to direct both the diets of Americans as well as the types of food products produced and sold.

The result was that, increasingly "farmers thus placed greater reliance on the federal government to do what they lacked the resources and expertise to accomplish for themselves" (Hurt, 2002, p. 34). The state's new institutional capacities reinforced the structure of the capitalist system and increase the standing of the capitalist class by setting the parameters of industrial agricultural production. This came about despite the impetus for reforms, revealing how US state institutional capacity was being constructed through co-opting popular resistance based demands. What emerged after the long and ongoing history of the construction of US institutional capacity was a capitalist state that was able to manage the demands of farmers by incorporating their demands in a modified form into the very structure of the state institutions.

This could especially be seen in the growing interconnection between the AFBF and agro-industrial policies. Strengthened through the establishment of the Agricultural Extension Service, the AFBF increasingly grew politically stronger. The group's strength though, did not rest in its mass membership base (as discussed in Chapter 4), but instead relied on its tight connections with both the USDA and Congressional representatives of the 'farm bloc'.

State Responses to the Agricultural Crisis of the 1920s

In the second half of the 1920s the federal government would do little in the way of expansion of new agricultural institutions apart from those aimed at establishing cooperatives through grants. This was the major policy being initiated with the Agricultural Marketing Act (Benedict, 1953). "The policy response from Washington during this decade of crisis was to continue its long-standing practice of protecting industry (mostly through high tariffs on competing imports), while offering little to agriculture" (Paarlberg and Paarlberg, 2000, p. 240).

There were two important things that occurred needing to be pointed out. The first was the desire at the time to keep agricultural prices low. After the consensus of agrarian movements was transformed into a focus on prices, it was increasingly hard to aid farmers in any manner other than policies aimed at raising prices. Industry however balked at this rise in agricultural prices due to the effect this would have on industrial wage demands, developing industries and the rest of the economy. The second, and sometimes conflicting, sometimes complementary reason to oppose price increases was due to the agro-industrial project: the desire to transition farmers into larger, more capital intensive forms of agriculture as the basis of all policy approaches. This meant that simply intervening to prop up prices would counteract the pressure towards agro-industrialization.

Paradoxically, low prices, absent ever expanding debt opportunities, also prevented farmers from purchasing new equipment and expanding their land holdings in the absence of access to cheap credit. In the end, the large increase in farm efficiency and agro-industrialization that had occurred during the boom years of 1914–1918, when net farm income doubled in nominal terms, was seen as sufficient in the short run to spur agro-industrialization (Paarlberg and Paarlberg, 2000). In the absence of radical demands the state mostly sought to help farmers achieve greater productivity by improving access to loans to facilitate the purchasing of new agriculture technology.

An excellent example of this process was the McNary-Haugen proposal advanced by agricultural economists as a solution to the farm problem and pushed by the farm equipment manufacturer turned Presidential advisor, George Peek. To raise farm prices relative to industrial prices, McNary-Haugen would set a tariff on imports of agricultural goods, and pay out an "equalization fee" for the difference between domestic and international prices to farmers that would create a benefit to farmers who sold their crops in the US (Hurt, 2002). In its drive to raise farm prices, McNary-Haugen appeared in direct opposition to the goals of industry, however its sponsors explicitly understood their role as combating radical agrarianism by creating modest reform policies (Fite, 1954). Agriculture Committee Chairman Gilbert Haugen's support for the bill followed his reformist bill to regulate the meat industry, and was embraced by the packers as a lesser evil than more radical bills that were being proposed (Hansen, 1991). Large farms, farm commodity processors, and capitalist farms opposed McNary-Haugen both out of an ideological belief in limiting government control over commodity prices and out of direct economic gains they stood to lose.

In the end even this meager level of support for farmers could not win. During the three failed attempts to pass the bill the southern Democrats voted against it because the price of cotton had been rising and therefore it was not necessary for their constituents at the time: seventy percent of southern Democrats voted against the bill in the first round (Winders, 2009). They were joined in opposition to the bill by President Coolidge, Secretary of Commerce Herbert Hoover, grain traders, millers, bankers, the US Chamber of Commerce, many newspaper editors, and a number of farm leaders (Winders, 2009). However, once the price of cotton began to decline in 1926, and farmers managed to organize into the American Council of Agriculture, the bill passed both houses, failing only through two successive vetoes by President Coolidge.

The push for McNary-Haugen effectively illuminated the shift a majority of farmers' movements had already taken towards a focus on raising prices, which held more benefits for larger industrial farmers than smaller ones (McConnell, 1953). Coolidge's veto revealed how the bill set up a choice between pro-market and more pro-market options, with real radical positions absent from consideration. The public manner in which the bill had been debated and shot down three times instilled in the public the notion of an actual fight and democratic debate over how a major overhaul of the agricultural system and a shift in state policy was to occur. In fact it was another attempt by the state to move farmers into enhanced market mediation through legislation. The failure of McNary-Haugen showed the growing strength of capital, and the state's response in the form of loan legislation fueling the drive towards agro-industrialization. This outcome is traceable directly back to the balance of class forces and the degree to which the AFBF undermined radical impulses while offering a road through Congress. The majority of farmers' organizations at the time were calling for a policy of agricultural parity through the McNary-Haugen bill or other approaches to raise agricultural prices. It is only after a shift to the middle by the AFBF and the growth of agrarian pressure all around that Congress opened itself up to the AFBF's "middle of the road" input (Hanson, 1991).

The depression in agriculture began before the Great Depression, emerging in the second half of the 1920s. When the crash of 1929 hit the rest of the economy it heightened the distress on the farm, as farm prices fell more than 50 percent between 1929 and 1932, the parity ratio plummeted from 89 to 55, and farm income dropped by 40 percent (Schlesinger, 1958; Winders, 2011). The bottom for agriculture would come in 1932 as wheat prices declined 70 percent relative to 1925, cotton dropped 75 percent and corn declined by 70 percent (USDA, 1957). Farm prices and farmer income fell to even lower levels than the trough of the 1920s crisis; gross farm income would drop 54 percent over seven years and the rate of farm foreclosures would more than double, reaching as high as half of all Midwestern farms being threatened by foreclosure (Gilbert and Howe, 1991; USDA, 1957). The rise in foreclosures and general crisis in agriculture was attributable to both the decline in prices, the overcapitalization of farmers coming on the back of strong prices, and the effect of the agro-industrial project to modernize and expand (Clarke, 1994; Kolko, 1976). A crisis in farm credit emerged as farmers went further into debt as the index of land values dropped from 116 in 1929 to 86 by 1932, farm mortgage debt payments exceeded the value of most farms leading to an increase in forced sales from 130,000 in 1929 to more than double that amount in 1931 (USDA, 1933).

As McConnell (1958) correctly suggested, "this was the first agricultural depression since the nineties [and] judging from the experience of the nineteenth century, a resurgence of agrarian organization might have been expected" (p. 55). In response to the crisis, protests sprang up first across the Midwest in the form of foreclosure stoppages and protests along the highways against produce shipments. This prompted Edward O'Neal, head of the AFBF to warn a Senate committee: "Unless something is done for the American Farmer we will have revolution in the countryside within less than twelve months" (Schlesinger, 1958, p. 27). Secretary of Agriculture Henry Wallace said "When former civilizations have fallen, there is a strong reason for believing that they fell because they could not achieve the necessary balance between city and country" (Schlesinger, 1958, p. 35). Wallace saw this balance as being upset by the economic vulnerability in agriculture. FDR seemed to agree when he commented "that's the fellow you've got to build up, the farmer" (Schlesinger, 1958, p. 27). The twin blows to agriculture – the loss of export markets and the depression – had left it as the most vulnerable industry, with rural poverty reaching levels twice that of urban areas. Due largely to the above mentioned twin crisis "the farmer's dollar, based on wheat, corn, hogs, and cotton, bought only half as many city products as it used to, while the city dollar, based on gold, bought more farm products than before" (Schlesinger, 1958, pp. 35–36). However, this time, unlike what had happened in the late 19th century, resistance gained little traction due in large part to the AFBF and the states quick response (Kolko, 1976).

The strong agro-industrial push under the Republican Presidencies of Harding (1920–1923), Coolidge (1923–1928), and Hoover (1928–1932) included a policy of allowing cooperatives to organize production and increase marketing of products by allowing farmers to pool together. Farmers would also benefit by cutting out the middle man and achieving a more sustainable future without direct government interference in the market. Once the depression hit, President Hoover signed into law the Agricultural Marketing Act (AMA) of 1929 that focused on federal support to cooperatives to relieve farmers from seasonal and yearly ups and downs in market prices (Hamilton, 1991). The Act allotted $500 million in federal loans to cooperatives, while also creating the Federal Farm Board (FFB) (Fite, 1954; Hurt, 2002). The FFB under the AMA was granted the authority to follow Hoover's advice and create "stabilization corporations" that could purchase surplus commodities in an effort to stabilize prices. The FFB put in place funding to support regional cooperatives as the it initially only purchasing excess commodities from cooperatives affiliated with the Farmers National Grain Corporation (FNGC), pitting FNGC affiliated cooperatives against non-affiliated cooperatives and private grain handlers. Problems with the FNGC lay in the top down manner in which they were constructed. The large regional chapters of the FNGC were set up across the country, many in areas with strong existing cooperatives, and some in areas without those social forces. The sheer size and regional nature led to a lack of control by local farmers. Many farmers came to view the FNGC cooperatives as no different from the large private dealers who had been profiting as they suffered for years (Hamilton, 1991). Notably Kolko (1976) saw the FFB as mostly set up to aid banks that were heavily invested in agricultural mortgages.

Importantly the AMA did not seek to raise prices to "parity" or to control production, only to stabilize market prices through cooperatives and the FFB (Winders, 2009). Thus lacking production controls, and given reduced exports and rising productivity, the AMA failed to overcome the immediate problems facing agrarians: with farmers increasing production to compensate for decreased prices, worsening overall market conditions for farmers (Hurt, 2002). The immediate result of the AMA and the FFB was a worsening position for farmers as prices continued to decline alongside farmer incomes (USDA, 1957).

Conclusion

Between the mid-19th century and 1930, the US state built a sophisticated and wide ranging set of institutional capacities to aid in the agro-industrial development. At the pinnacle of this development was the USDA-research complex. The two primary aspects of this complex were the USDA with its expanding research and publication divisions, and the extension service and land-grant universities seeking to disseminate the USDA technological developments to the farming masses. This state institutional build up came as a response to the agrarian movements of the late 19th century. Early on these movements contained a high degree of radical, class based activists, threatening the expanding dominance of capital these posed resulted in numerous attempts to co-opt and defang farming movements by pushing them towards goals attainable within the emerging market based industrial system.

Early state support for farmers is seen in the work of the Census Bureau's Agricultural Department. Through the support of reformist farm groups and business interests this eventually expanded to form the stand alone agency of the USDA. As shown from its inception, the USDA sought to use the state to develop agricultural technology to aid in the agro-industrial project to transition farmers into industrial and market mediated agriculture. The sophistication and scope of this USDA research expanded through the twists and turns of the late 19th and early 20th centuries. Thus, farm groups slowly came to rely on and become integrated within the vision of the USDA, thereby accepting its industrial agricultural model accomplished through technological innovation and expanding agricultural productivity.

The institutional capacity to reach farmers was enhanced as the state moved to expand into farming education. Similar to the formation of the USDA itself, the development of state experimental educational facilities emerged through prodding and funnelling by private business interests. Despite the business roots of this educational work, it greatly expanded the acceptance of USDA and its technological innovations among farmers; mainly accomplished through its promise of higher prices for atomized individual producers. This process was aided by the emergence of the AFBF, who came to form a rearguard against radical farm groups through its political strength and connections with the extension service and the USDA. Thus we see the connection between reformist organizations and the state in an effort to neutralize radical, class based responses through agro-industrial development institutional projects.

Farmers increasingly enhance their technology and mechanization over this period moved them closer toward an industrial agriculture model advocated by the many USDA research and development programs. From this it is clear how the state institutional response to the agrarian movements were successful in steering them first into the hands of the state and then into acceptance of solutions that led them deeper into industrial capitalism. This came to a head in the 1920s as the farm productivity advances ultimately producing a crisis of farm commodity overproduction aided by the lack of export potential emerging from the inter-war collapse of the world market, despite the USDA's efforts at export promotion. The dominance of the AFBF among farm groups emerged as the only solution with their productionist oriented approach that did not offer a challenge the existing industrial system. The solutions on the table during the 1920s – cooperative support, the Agricultural Marketing Act and the Federal Farm Board – proved too weak to overcome the worsening agricultural crisis as the floor dropped out with the crash of 1929 and the coming depression.

As the economy moved into the Great Depression, the USDA became the source of hope for farmers. But this rested on previous farmer acceptance of the form of agriculture the USDA had been pushing for decades and the overcoming and suppression of class based agricultural movements. This reveals the success of the state's institutional capacity building during the era of the emergence and growth of the USDA: for as the Depression raged on, there emerged few effective radical agrarian movements that sought solutions outside of these state institutions. Thus, the USDA had effectively established the hegemony of the agro-industrial project as all solutions came to fully rest on improving prices.

CHAPTER 6

The New Deal and Agricultural State Institutional Capacity Building

As the US entered the Great Depression in the late 1920s, farmers had already been in a depressed state in most regions of the nation for almost a decade. The collapse of the stock market in 1929, the rising unemployment and depression that beset the entire economy simply exacerbated the already existing farm crisis. Because of this and the continued political strength and economic importance of agriculture, one of the first responses by the US government to the Depression would come in the form of agricultural institutional development.

The Agricultural Adjustment Act (AAA) emerged as the primary New Deal policy aimed at agriculture. The Act sought to reduce agricultural production, called production control or the domestic allotment, by paying farmers subsidies not to plant on part of their land. It also would pay farmers to kill off livestock. Its purpose was to reduce crop surplus and therefore effectively raise the value of crops. The plan was based strongly on input from the AFBF, as the AAA at least rhetorically incorporated the goals of raising farm prices to a parity level, meaning the price received would cover the cost of production. Its success really lies in its ability to blunt any farm movements that may emerge around more radically orientated movements by incorporating and neutralizing them within the Democratic Party and the policy put forward. The success of the AFBF and the USDA – research complex in co-opting farmers into a state led approach seeking to raise farm prices is therefore clearly evident and must be the starting point for any thorough analysis of the New Deal agricultural programs.

This chapter will examine not only the policies that emanated from the AAA, but also the specific politics behind these policies. It is important to stress the different impact of the AAA on northern and southern agriculture; especially the diverse approach taken in each region to pushing forward agro-industrial development. The case of Southern sharecroppers and tenancy will be given particular attention as it revealed how the state responded to agrarian movements during this era, proving its openness to the influences of a shift in the balance of class forces. It will also look into the specific case of California, which due to its greater degree of capitalist development at the time as its unique climate and crops created a different response to the Great Depression and the New Deal Policies than the rest of the nation. The chapter will go on to investigate a few leading theories of the New Deal in an effort to highlight how the class based, agro-industrial centered approach of this inquiry differs and offers a more accurate and total picture of the social developments of the era. Finally an outline will be suggested describing the influence of New Deal agricultural policies on state institutional capacity building in general, as well as the agro-industrial project more specifically. This will include an assessment of the agro-industrial projects influence on the broader program of expanding consumption of goods as the means to construct a healthy capitalist economy in the post-Depression era.

The Politics of the Agricultural Adjustment Act

On the back of a decade of crisis in agriculture the impact of the great depression on agriculture moved the situation from desperate to dire. With the election of Franklin Delano Roosevelt came an abrupt transition in the federal approach to agriculture. The pivot from attempting to remain outside of direct intervention in the market, as demand by the prior administration through the pushing of cooperatives into the New Deal state projects of the Agricultural Adjustment Act is indicative of the degree of desperation.

The lack of demand for the very large harvests of agricultural goods stood as the source of the immediate crisis in agriculture. Ironically the problem – increasingly conceived as one of overproduction – would become the near singular focus of New Deal agricultural policy. This was ironic in that the USDA, whose main focus and reason for existence was to increase agricultural productivity, would be tasked with reducing the reason for its very creation.

It will be shown that the AAA fit squarely into the agro-industrial project, representing the further advancement of the state institutional capacity building through the USDA. The AAA program, as passed, had a goal of restoring farm purchasing power by increasing the prices of agricultural commodities; or the fair exchange value of a commodity based upon price relative to the prewar 1909–14 level. This was to be accomplished by the Secretary of Agriculture through the use of a number of policy mechanisms:

> These included the authorization (1) to secure voluntary reduction of the acreage in basic crops through agreements with producers and use of direct payments for participation in acreage control programs; (2) to regulate marketing through voluntary agreements with processors, associations or producers, and other handlers of agricultural commodities or products; (3) to license processors, associations of producers, and others

handling agricultural commodities to eliminate unfair practices or charges; (4) to determine the necessity for and the rate or processing taxes; and (5) to use the proceeds of taxes and appropriate funds for the cost of adjustment operations, for the expansion of markets, and for the removal or agricultural surpluses.

USDA, 1976, p. 2

In this way the AAA used the language of the oft failed McNary-Haugan plan and the bottom up push for parity prices, 'relative to prewar 1909–14 level', without specifically providing any real mechanism to approach parity prices. The decision over how to achieve parity was left up to the Secretary of Agriculture and not spelled out in any direct way. The rhetoric of seeking parity was either enough to convince many that the state and this plan could fix what ailed agriculture, or the situation of farmers was so desperate for any alternative that they took what they could get. Specifically though, this appeal to parity as an abstract goal of the AAA got the AFBF to both drop its long-standing push for McNary-Haugan and deliver many farmers to the AAA. This includes large scale producers who both recognized the degree of panic and also the degree to which the AAA, as written would benefit them.

Despite this seeming acquiescence of farm movements to the goals of the AAA, it is important to understand that the initial debate within farm groups, particularly the AFBF, which had come to take on the role of official farm group during New Deal discussions, had already acquiesced to agro-industrial based plans of either price supports or production controls to increase prices (McConnell, 1958). Therefore already by 1930, radical farm groups had been sidelined and approaches to agricultural problems left off the policy agenda. The AFBF was pushing the program it had been advancing for a decade or more: price supports to bring parity between prices of farm inputs and what farmers received for their products. Conversely, FDR's agricultural economists were pushing for a system of production controls. As Domhoff and Weber (2011, p. 99) put it, the "domestic allotment and parity price plans were actually two rival business-sponsored plans for dealing with agricultural surpluses, one more nationalistic in orientation, the other more sensitive to creating an international economy". Absent a strong, well organized radical agricultural movement, both plans were attempting overcome farm problems by understanding them as a price problem, leaving the solution as more agro-industrialization.

The very fact that both sides of the debate narrowed their focuses to only prices meant they fit squarely within the agro-industrial drive. It was the production control model that fit better with the increasingly powerful corporate class in the US as production control had the capacity to leave existing large landowners intact while creating the market imperative towards increased mechanization and agro-industrialization more broadly (Kolko, 1976, p. 147). Production control could create rising prices and payments for acreage reductions, leading to increased incentives towards mechanization and its efficiencies. Thus it was able to cloak the continuance of the agro-industrial project behind rising prices and government payments.

FDR's solution to the debate over the two approaches was to create a plan that included parts of both (Saloutos, 1982). As Hamilton (1991) correctly outlined in the case of Farm Bureau and National Grange counter positions on the issues, "faced with new calls for a farm strike and a dire political crisis, FDR skillfully deflected the protests with political compromises" (p. 248). The decision by FDR to include more than just production controls in the initial Agricultural Adjustment Act was designed to reduce resistance and stymie both radical and corporate interests organizing against it. Despite this rhetoric of a mix of approaches, it was the domestic allotment, production control policy that would be the only plan implemented. This occurred through a loophole placed in the law allowing the Secretary of Agriculture the discretion to choose how much of each proposal to use (McConnell, 1958; Saloutos, 1956; Schlesinger, 1958, p. 38). After its passage the USDA came to focus a great deal of its attention on the domestic allotment plan to control production.

The domestic allotment plan – crop acreage reduction achieved by offering farmers payments in return for a reduction in their acreage of certain crops – rubbed conservatives the wrong way and went against the 20 year argument for McNary-Haugerism that would have propped up inefficient farms by acting against the agro-industrial project (Schlesinger, 1958). Grassroots groups and radicals over time came to recognize the AAA as a handout to large farms (McConnell, 1953). Despite the decades of fighting for a farm plan based on McNary-Haugen, opposed as it was again and again by capitalist farmers and industry, farmers ended up getting something much different – something that would expand trade in time, but meanwhile rewarded those farmers who were most efficient, and who moved towards industrial based efficiencies. Thus while the focus, goals, and ultimate aims of moving US agriculture towards a more efficient, larger, and market mediated corporate agriculture system was a thread running through all of the New Deal agricultural programs, production control (the so called 'domestic allotment') were chosen. This is because it had the ability to raise prices for all and avoid opposition while rewarding large agriculture, moving everyone closer to a large agricultural system of production. In this it represented neither a complete sellout of farm movements for small farmers nor a victory for them as they did benefit in the interim.

The USDA during the New Deal would maintain its focus on modernizing agriculture and the domestic allotment, while forestalling that drive a bit by propping up smaller farms with increased prices. Importantly none of this approach undermined the agro-industrial project. In fact the long struggle over price supports or production control both fit squarely within the agro-industrial approach. Neither was a radical proposal and the outcries by capitalists in the press about government overreach effectively obfuscated the productionist basis of the plan. The institutionalized development around agriculture that came out of the AAA would go a long way to further construct markets and to push agro-industrial solutions.

Voluntary production controls also worked to shift more conservative farmers towards a unified call for more government involvement and regulation in the following ways. Those who volunteered for restricting their production received subsidies, while at the same time everyone else benefited from rising prices, even those who actually increased their acreage. This left those who did volunteer – a very high percentage of whom had large farms growing major commodities – to increase their demand for the government to mandate required production controls (Hamilton, 1991). Thus farmers, along with more free market farm groups, began advocating for increased government involvement, and in the case of three major crops – cotton, tobacco, and potatoes – the government responded with a large tax that effectively made the production controls mandatory (Hamilton, 1991).

FDR's remarkable political strength during the New Deal was due to the complete control enjoyed by the Democratic Party, most importantly based in the South (Katznelson, 2014). It was the racially-based, overwhelmingly Democratic southern majority whose power was unified and was required in presidential elections. For a third of a century, between 1896 and 1928, 84.5 percent of the total Electoral College votes for all Democratic presidential candidates came from the South, with the exception of Woodrow Wilson (Domhoff and Weber, 2011). In Congress, the power of Southern Democrats was perhaps even greater because of their seniority and therefore dominant positions on congressional committees (Potter, 1972). The structural constraint the reliance on Southern Democrats put on FDR carried important consequences for New Deal agricultural programs as southern plantation owners enjoyed an enhanced input in the formulation of proposals (Potter, 1972; Winders, 2007; Katznelson, 2013). In fact, the political importance of the Southern states to the Democratic Party and Roosevelt's win gave them an inflated influence on federal policy that was coupled with extraordinary power in the overall national agricultural economy. The support for production control polices was greater in the South due to their legacy of experience with similar state programs in Louisiana, South

Carolina, Texas, Arkansas, and Mississippi. Thus, the South's greater influence easily dominated that of other regions, with profound national effects despite the particularly exaggerated racial divide and the agricultural class dynamics the tenancy tradition created in the South. The agricultural associations represented linked the interests of specific crop producers with banking and merchant interests, and this, along with the control of plantation capitalists over agriculture, made these associations tools for capitalist power while also sources of integration between their demands and that of petty commodity producers (Saloutos, 1960).

With the inclusion of production controls in the AAA, the AFBF got fully behind it, in turn, the bureau would greatly benefited from the AAA. It was the southern plantation owners, and therefore, Southern Democrats and those chapters of the AFBF that supported the production control aspects of the plan who would reap the most benefits (Saloutos, 1960). As Domhoff and Weber (2011) put it, "Northern corporate moderates and Southern planters were the key power actors in creating the context in which Roosevelt was receptive to a last-minute push for introducing the Agricultural Adjustment Act into the special session of Congress" (p. 100). The pain being felt by farmers combined with the inclusion of payments to increase participation in the acreage reductions meant this act "was as certain to be approved as any law could be" (Domhoff and Weber, 2011, p. 100).

The economic power of large agricultural interests to use institutional forms and farm groups to their advantage was most evident in the AFBF as it was "the organization that spoke for the agricultural segment of the nationwide ownership class by the outset of the New Deal" (Domhoff and Weber, 2011, p. 63). The AFBF revealed most clearly the understanding by powerful forces that through the industrialization of agriculture and concentrated ownership of farms, an increase in capitalist power would emerge. The organizations very beginnings through the Rockefeller funding of the extension service program – which served as the basis through which the AFBF connection with farmers and its strength was built – showed how members of the upper class understood the role that agro-industrialization would play in enhancing class power and control over agriculture (Domhoff and Weber, 2012; McConnell, 1953). In conjunction with this there was emerging an ideological hegemony of state market creation that would later become both the norm domestically and the basis for US projection of this model of development around the world.

It was the Smith-Lever Act of 1914 that increased federal spending on county extension services and made the land grant colleges subsidiaries of this system placing the AFBF as the key articulation site of farmer/state interaction (McConnell, 1956). It was through the AFBF that connections between southern plantation capitalists, corn and hog farmers in the Midwest, and large agribusiness interests and ranchers in California built an alliance in the 1920s and 1930s, in part, through the work of AFBF President Edward A. O'Neal (Domhoff and Weber, 2012). Thus on the eve of the Great Depression and New Deal policies, the AFBF had come to play a hegemonic role in agricultural movements. During the New Deal, the AAA programs that would emerge were heavily influenced by the AFBF who played a key role in the dissemination of information, coordination of state programs, most importantly delivery subsidies and government payments (Kolko, 1976). The AFBF throughout the years of the depression acted to both divert farm organizations away from radical demands, push modernization on farmers and through this simultaneously reproduce capitalist class dominance in the political and economic realm (McConnell, 1956).

The AAA program of production control was conceived around the notion that county extension agents could coordinate groups of local associations and county production control boards to oversee the AAA program as quickly as possible. The AFBF was extensively involved in the process of developing the county production control boards, "in many communities the local farm bureaus 'literally took over' the task of organizing AAA committees" (McConnell, 1956, p. 75). After a decade of agricultural crisis the AFBF was in a clear position to offer help to farmers by facilitating the federal program bringing money to farmers. Finally, the AFBF came to basically write the new farm programs that emerged in 1938 as the Bureau and federal agencies became more intimate than ever (AFBF, 1936).

Even though the AFBF was able to dominate most agrarian movements and thereby mute most radical groups, there were some that managed to cause a stir. One such group – the Farmers' Holiday Association – threatened to halt farm production with an agricultural strike. The passage of the Emergency Farm Mortgage Act of 1933 was the direct result of the militant protests of the Farmers' Holiday Association and others to push the Roosevelt administration to do something beyond the New Deal proposal to reduce acreage. The passage of this law revealed the quick response of the state to the shifts in the balance of class forces that radical groups, combined with the economic reality of the times, could produced. To be clear though, the overall balance of class forces was never tilted to a strong enough degree towards agrarian or working classes during this era to warrant revolutionary changes. This is evident by the manner in which the AAA programs were implemented, with many business leaders coming to occupy positions within the institution and the management of the program by AFBF connected agents (Saloutos, 1982). It is also witnessed in how the AAA never dismantled the institutions of the agro-industrial

THE NEW DEAL AND AGRICULTURAL STATE INSTITUTIONS   181

project or it worked to counter that direction, in fact, it strengthened them in the long term.

The dominance of the AFBF and the associated County Extension Services in the application of the AAA is well documented: the degree of AFBF involvement in the AAA in 1936 stood at 117 out of 169 (69 percent) of state committee members, and in some states "90 percent or more of the county and township committeemen were Farm Bureau members" (McConnell, 1953, p. 78). Additionally, the fact that the management and implementation of the AAA programs occurred not solely through state institutions but also through the public/private partnership of the AFBF and County Extension services showed the reluctance of capital to leave the program in the hands of state agents due to the uncertain balance of class forces during the depression (Domhoff and Weber, 2011). The state was able to maintain its relative autonomy by creating a program that could function through this public-private partnership and reproduce class dominance from a distance and for a long enough time to diminish the radical threat.

The AAA took effect in 1933 by imposing supply controls on seven basic commodities: wheat, corn, rice, tobacco, cotton, hogs, and milk products. It authorized "rental" payments to farmers for the reduction of 35 million acres of productive land (Paarlberg and Paarlberg, 2000). The administration of this program, coming as it did in a relatively quick manner for its size, was through the establishment of more than 4,200 county-level production control committees created by the USDA (Schlesinger, 1958). The development of these county production control committees fell to the AFBF who "found it easy to dominate and used them effectively as a setting in which to recruit and organize new dues-paying members," with AFBF membership nearly tripling during the 1930s (Paarlberg and Paarlberg, 2000, p. 141). Gross farm income rose between 1932 and 1934 from $6.4 billion to $8.4 (Hamilton, 1991). However, 1935 farm prices had only risen by 6% while prices for agricultural inputs had gone up by 26%, meaning the situation had grown more desperate for farmers in the early years of the New Deal (USDA, 1936).

Yet this apparent lack of progress didn't stop Secretary Wallace from claiming success: "four of every five persons reemployed in urban industry since spring of 1933 owed the recovery of their jobs to improvements in farm conditions" (Saloutos, 1960, p. 125). Some specific crop reductions for 1934–35: wheat declined by 20 percent; cotton 40 percent; tobacco 30 percent; and corn-hog (hogs and the corn to feed them combined) 20 percent (USDA, 1936). Looking at cotton for example we see that at the start of 1933 the unsold 1932 cotton supply in the US was greater than the entire world consumption of US cotton and growers had planted four million more acres for the next season than they had in the previous year (Badger, 1989). This left policy planners no choice but to seek the destruction of some of the crop already planted. Farmers thus destroyed 10.5 million acres of cotton and the price rose after the 1933 harvest by 10 cents a pound, fetching farmers an additional $114 million dollars (Badger, 1989). Declining corn prices had led to an increase in hog production, which was bringing a glut to that market. As a result of these AAA programs, the government bought and slaughtered 8.5 million pigs. This disposal of food during a period of acute economic hardship reveals the lengths policy makers went to maintain the agro-industrial project as the state intervened to prop up prices and markets for the commodities.

In 1936 the Supreme Court ruled the AAA unconstitutional due to its tax on processors. The Soil Conservation and Domestic Allotment Act (SCDAA) of 1936 replaced the AAA and had a few minor differences. The new act sought to get farmers to parity income instead of seeking parity prices for goods by reestablishing "the [1909–1914] ratio between the purchasing power of the net income per person on farms and that of the income per person not on farms" (Hurt, 2002, p. 46). Some claimed that this move shifted those who benefitted the most from the program away from large farms to smaller farmers by taking more land out of the equation (Hurt, 2002). However the act did more to move farmers towards greater efficacy in production than it did to stabilize small farms. Farmers with more land would receive greater benefit by the higher prices if they made those lands as productive as possible. They would also benefit by having the extra land available to set aside under the conservation programs while still having enough land to produce a large crop. Thus, the USDA's agro-industrial drive remained oriented towards the removal of smaller, less efficient farms. As Hurt puts it: "The USDA recognized that too many farmers (including tenants and sharecroppers) remained on the land for all of them to prosper ... [and the]... agency was committed to encouraging small-scale farmers to leave agriculture" (Hurt, 2002, p. 82).

The AFBF influence also led to a few key changes to the AAA in 1935 and again in 1938 further adding to the AFBF benefits from the program (Campbell, 1962). As McConnell (1953) outlined:

> First, administrative organization was now general and not broken along commodity lines. Second, it paralleled the local Farm Bureau structure. Third, it was more amenable to direction through the county agents. In the South the county agent automatically became the secretary of the local association (p. 78).

The AFBF actually drafted many of the changes to the 1938 law and were a major force in lobbying the amended law through Congress (Saloutos, 1982).

Out of this the AFBF "had accomplished its basic legislative program" by placing the domestic allotment at "the service of the plantation capitalists and other commercial farmers to the tune of many hundreds of millions of dollars each year in the 1930s and several billion dollars a year thereafter" (Domhoff and Weber, 2011, p. 188).

The New Deal Farm Credit Program was created in 1933 to use the federal government to guarantee land bank bonds. Like much of the New Deal agricultural acts, despite its rhetoric about aid to struggling farmers, it represented a massive bailout of commercial farming and commercial farm lending institutions (Hamilton, 1991). All told the program would "refinance one-fifth of all farm mortgages, reduce the interest rate on its loans to 3.5 percent, and extend in less than three years about $800,000,000 in long-term 'rescue' loans" (Hamilton, 1991, p. 245). Out of this, the federal land banks ended up holding nearly 40 percent of all farm mortgage debt by the end of the 1930s, three times higher than during the previous decade (USDA, 1942). This propping up of farm land values, while coming to the aid of struggling farms was also an aid to the banking industry as it took over the highest risk farm loans.

Attached as Title III to the Act, the Thomas Amendment became the 'third horse' in the New Deal's farm relief bill. Drafted by Senator Elmer Thomas of Oklahoma, the amendment blended populist easy-money views with the theories of the New Economics, "Thomas wanted a stabilized 'honest dollar', one that would be fair to debtor and creditor alike" (Webb, 1977, p. 43). The Amendment said that whenever the President desired currency expansion, he must first authorize the Federal Open Market Committee of the Federal Reserve to purchase up to $3 billion of federal obligations. Should open market operations prove insufficient, the President had several options. He could have the US Treasury issue up to $3 billion in greenbacks, reduce the gold content of the dollar by as much as 50 percent, or accept 100 million dollars in silver at a price not to exceed fifty cents per ounce in payment of World War I debts owed by European nations (Webb, 1977). The Thomas Amendment was used sparingly, however armed with the Amendment Roosevelt ratified the Pittman London Silver Amendment on December 21, 1933, ordering the United States mints to buy the entire domestic production of newly mined silver at 64.5¢ per ounce. Roosevelt's most dramatic use of the Thomas amendment came on January 31, 1934, when he decreased the gold content of the dollar to 40.94 percent (Webb, 1977). However, wholesale prices still continued to climb. Possibly the most significant expansion brought on by the Thomas Amendment may have been the growth of governmental power over monetary policy. The impact of this amendment was to reduce the amount of silver that was being held by private citizens (presumably as a hedge against inflation or collapse of the financial system) and increase the amount of circulating currency to stimulate economic activity and discourage savings. This also had the effect of driving down the debt obligations of farmers by decreasing the value of the dollar, even if only slightly.

The state institutional development through the New Deal, although claiming to be a break with a drive to increase the market mediation of social relations, actually worked to increase the market dependency and drive toward industrial farming. The role of the AFBF, with its particular bias and connection, was one of the main mechanisms through which this occurred. As we will see, it was not without its critics and the state was even responsive to some degree to these critiques.

Southern Tenants and the AAA

As the AAA began to take effect there emerged a problem in its implementation through the county agents composed of AFBF and county extension agent recruits. The problem was that landlords had begun accepting AAA payments for acreage reductions, pocketing the money, and kicking the croppers and tenants off the land (Schlesinger, 1958). The program in effect created incentives to remove tenants from the land through government subsidies. Here we see the influence of Southern planters and other large land owners on the AAA, namely the way it was formed and instituted through the AFBF and the county extension agents. The AAA was increasing the class power of landlords through its programs (Kolko, 1976).

The displacement of tenants was but one aspect of the act favoring large, industrial farmers over smaller ones. The act heightened the crisis for the croppers and tenants, so much so that they began to organize, forming the Southern Tenants Farmers Union (STFU). STFU was created in 1934 specifically to combat some of the injustices of the New Deal agricultural programs; they carried out protests and organized those tenants who had their leases terminated due to the AAA (Mann, 1990; Bernstein, 2010; Saloutos, 1973). In 1935 STFU carried out its first strike as cotton pickers demanded higher pay. Through this and a host of other protests and strikes the Union brought attention to the issues facing southern tenant farmers and effectively shifted the balance of class forces and with it, government policy.

It is telling that just one year after the formation of the STFU Congress created the Bankhead-Jones Farm Tenant Act in 1935 with its stated goal of "reducing farm tenancy and sharecropping by strengthening the financial viability of farm families through 'rehabilitation' loans" (Schlesinger, 1958, p. 380). This act revealed the manner in which the New Deal state institutional development program operated on a razor's edge balance between pushing too hard for agro-industrialization and the need to respond to farm movements during the crisis. Secretary Wallace himself became interested in the plight of tenants and croppers stating "I know of no better means of reconstructing our agriculture on a thoroughly sound and permanently desirable basis than to make as its foundation the family-size, owner-operated farm" (Schlesinger, 1958, p. 380). Some locate Wallace's conversion to a trip through the South at the insistence of Tugwell, despite the fact that Tugwell later became a strong opponent to transitioning tenants and croppers to family farmers (Schlesinger, 1958). This example of the manner in which the balance of class forces influenced state policy revealed how the STFU was able to pull the state into the kind of action that was more autonomous than capitalist agriculture in the South could produce. However, this lasted only as long as the STFU remained an aggressive force. Once the balance of class forces shifted – a shift influenced by state action to some degree – the state revoked most of the gains achieved by the STFU or aligned them more with the interests of agribusiness and renewed the drive to modernize and expel small farmers.

Although the STFU was successful in bringing about protections for tenant farmers and sharecroppers under the SCDAA of 1938, its success and influence was short-lived. The more radical actions and demands of STFU continued only until there was some slight regress to their demands, upon which this radical group moved to the center while losing the majority of its members (Fite, 1984; Gilbert and Howe, 1988; Kirby, 1987; Saloutos, 1973;). There occurred a backlash to this aid to sharecroppers, centered in the AFBF, which caused the ending of many of the programs aimed to help sharecroppers and tenants and leading to a purge of the USDA of most of its progressives at the direction of the AFBF connected policy elites (Gilbert and Howe, 1988; Hooks, 1986; Kirby, 1987). The overall outcome of the New Deal on Southern sharecroppers and tenants was a negative one, much as it was on small farms in general (Fite, 1984; Kolko, 1976).

The AAA liberals and the entire AAA Legal Division and Consumers' Counsel Division, who were sympathetic to the tenants, were purged in 1935 as a result of their push to get legal standing for tenants and croppers who were being forced off the land by landlords who were getting subsidies for not planting crops (McConnell, 1958). The Resettlement Administration that later became the Farm Service Administration (FSA), sought to integrate tenants into the emerging agricultural system but not on terms that organized workers along class lines as the STFU had done (Skocpol and Finegold, 1995). In the AAA battle over southern landlord/tenant relations – spurred on by the recalcitrance of southern tenants' organizations, most influentially STFU, led "these agency leaders from the triple alliance of Extension Services, Farm Bureau, and land-grant colleges [to] side entirely with the dominant agricultural classes" (Gilbert and Howe, 1991, p. 211). The AAA programs clearly favored landlords over tenants because they released surplus labor from small farms onto the market, thereby lowering the cost of production, while they simultaneously rechanneled discontent away from radical demands by applying market rule, which was perceived as being apolitical (McClellan, 1991). This outcome of the New Deal agricultural policies of hurting small farmer's more than big ones was a product of the class biases built into the state capacities by agricultural capitalists, represented in the AFBF (Gilbert and Howe, 1991).

The decades immediately following the Great Depression would entail a transformation of southern agriculture on a scale so large that some have compared its significance to the British enclosure (Daniel, 1985; Kirby, 1987). During the middle decades of the 20th century, over eight million southern sharecroppers and tenant farmers were forced off the land (Bartley, 1987; Kirby, 1987). What occurred in the South was the demise of sharecropping and the rise of capitalist cotton farms (Mann, 1990). This represented a direct reversal of the trend that had been occurring; between 1880 and 1900 the number of sharecroppers and tenants had doubled, and almost doubled again over the next three decades, coming to comprise half of all farms in the Old South by 1930 (Rochester, 1940).

After the peak in 1930 a complete reversal of the long trend towards an increase in sharecroppers and tenants occurred as the number of sharecroppers in the South was cut in half Over the next two decades (US Bureau of Census, 1964). By 1959 there were less than 130,000 sharecroppers in the South, which is a six-fold decline (US Bureau of Census, 1964). By the 1960s the number of sharecroppers was deemed too insignificant by the Census Bureau to warrant counting (Kirby, 1987). The outcome of a reduction in sharecropping in the South was the rise of wage labor: with only 28 percent of all cotton farms using wage labor in the South in 1930 shifting to 65 percent by 1964 (US Bureau of Census, 1964). Land in the South became more concentrated during this period and the size of farms also increased (Daniel, 1985). Mann (1990) located the forces behind this shift in the impact of New Deal policies, advances in agricultural technology, labor shortages created by World War II along with a rise in foreign cotton production, and an increase in synthetic fabric use.[1]

---

1 Fite (1984) claimed that competition from other cotton producers brought down the share of the market the US commanded, "in 1941 the US produced only 38 percent of world production compared to 72 percent back in 1911" and in addition the growth of synthetics ate into cotton production as well, "between 1919 and 1943 the share of the fiber market taken over by rayon rose from 0.3 to 10.6 percent" (p. 175). The outcome of this was a competitive drive to increase the efficiency of Southern cotton production which had been mostly absent before.

It was also due to the effects of the long awaited breakdown of the planter structure in the South as farmers begun to enlarge and mechanize. This reveals both the impact of the populist movement and the influence of the New Deal state institutional capacity building on large-scale agro-industrial development in the South. It is the state led transition of the South into industrial capitalism.

Goran Therborn (1978) argued that agricultural capitalists were in a stronger position before the New Deal than industrial capitalists were, as agricultural workers were more isolated, relied on landlords to a greater degree and were divided by race, geographic location and type of farm. While clearly the level of organization was important, also relevant was the degree to which movements could easily be co-opted into policies that favored the ruling class. The individualized nature of agriculture leaves it open to types of reforms that promise price increases that might help the individual farmers but hurt the class. Thus the policies developed reflected the co-option and industrialization approach.

The direction the capitalist state takes, and particularly the US state, rests on the balance of class forces as the state maintains its relative autonomy from particular class fractions but also must maintain legitimacy. If strong radical movements emerge the state in most instances will respond with reforms, although they are usually constructed in such a way as to not threaten elite control and often end up increasing it in the long term. The case of cotton sharecropper action tends to prove this point; absent policies to help out sharecroppers they developed more radical groups (Saloutos, 1973). The further development of the state institutional capacity is the reason many of the agrarian movements during the era did not take a more radical turn. But to fully appreciate this, we need to first get a proper handle on the nature of the New Deal state.

Theories of the New Deal Era State

In the interpretation of the New Deal, Skocpol and Finegold's work (1982; 1995) has become most prominent for its argument for the autonomous role of state agents and institutions. They placed particular importance on "policy legacies" and how they influence outcomes, arguing that "in neither the case of the Adjustment Act or Recovery Act can the demands, the organization, or the class economic power of social groups directly explain the results of the New Deal government interventions affecting the interests of either farmers or industrialists" (Skocpol and Finegold, 1982, p. 260; see also Finegold, 1981, pp. 20–21). Instead, they argued that state officials pursued an agenda that was distinct from that of the interest groups involved. Skocpol and Finegold also made the case that it was the entrenched nature of the AAA within an existing state agency – the USDA – that granted a greater degree of autonomy to the program and protected it from the class interests that would have doomed it. They compared the AAA to the National Recovery Act (NRA), which sought to use the government to restart the economy's industrial production. Both programs sought to remove the surplus of products, increase demand, and thereby increase employment in the two sectors. In contrasting the AAA with the NRA they held that the key difference in the more autonomous AAA to succeed was the pre-existence of the USDA. In doing so they went so far as to erroneously claim that the power of landlords in the south, banks and larger farmers in the Midwest, and capitalist farmers in California had little impact on the direction of the AAA program.

While Fred Block (1987) also asserted that during crises "the state managers can pay less attention to business opinion and can concentrate on responding to the popular pressure", this quickly gives way when the crisis has passed shifting to policies that work in the interest of capital accumulation and existing class relations (p. 66). Thus, policies born in crisis at the behest of lower class social movements – the "popular pressure" – worked to enhance the role of the state and in the long run this aided capitalist class interests (Block, 1987, p. 88). Block located the mechanism for state expansion in the drive of individual state institutions to maintain and expand the basis of their power, which once "normal" times reemerge result in increased pressure to transform themselves toward the interests of capital (Block, 1987). This he argues, is the source of the relative autonomy of the state: as the crisis subsided and pressure from the ruling class emerged to push the new state capacities in a particular, and perhaps narrow way, the state agents amended the implementation of policies and institutions working in the general interest of capital, thus reassuring their continued role against either being seen as noncapital oriented or as aiding a particular narrow capital interest. As Block (1987) argued, these state agents were "capable of intervening in the economy on the basis of a more general rationality" functioning through the self interest of institutional representatives (p. 62).

Skocpol and Finegold (1995) critiqued Block based on what they saw as his lack of inclusion of electoral politics. Indeed it would be hard to understand the changing nature of class relations in the postbellum era without an understanding of the role of electoral politics, and in particular how they played out through sectional concerns in the two parties and across different regions. However, Skocpol and Finegold (1995) analyzed the role of political power in a way that detached it from the influence of class relations. In the US, it is futile to attempt to analyze electoral politics without regard to the balance of class forces that exists. The integration of class forces into electoral politics has been so fully complete that often they are mistaken for being discrete social forces.

Skocpol and Finegold (1995) posited that the path dependency of state institutions influenced state policy formation during the New Deal in three ways: First, they were influential by giving rise to analogies affecting how public officials thought about policy issues; Second, the existing state policies and institutions created historical memories that suggested lessons as to how policies should be formed and implemented; And finally, they became compelling by imposing limitations that reduced the range of options (Skocpol and Finegold, 1995).

Clearly the past experience of state institutional involvement informed state policy options during the depression. Yet during the New Deal era the development of the AFBF through the class power of large farmers and the expanding agro-business sector led to a vested interest in the policies for not only those interests but others who became dependent on the organization due to the AAA programs facilitated through it. Thus, the institutional configuration built up through the connection of the AFBF and the state created both institutional pathways, or parameters for institutional development based on path dependency, as well as familiar actor pathways that were granted positive feedback – in this case government payments. This defies the notion of a complete autonomy of the state by highlighting the intersection of class, social movements and power in and through the state. The state did maintain the ability for autonomous action but it was relative to the balance of class forces, and was still limited by the capitalist nature of the state institutions that had developed. Moreover, the direction of change was conditioned by the development of new state institutional capacity built up in response to these movements.

Compared to labor, who sought more incremental gains during this era, farmers had sought a thorough remaking of the economy through mass political engagement. "They [farmers] might have been the most self-consciously political class in the nation...their goal was a thorough reconstruction of the national political economy, not the transformation of the sector into just one of what have become numerous interest groups within the federal and state policy system" (Bensel, 2000, p. 152). "Of the two, labor should have been more easily transformed, even tamed, into one of the meek constituencies of federal and state bureaus", instead, agriculture found an earlier and more comfortable accommodation within the state (Bensel, 2000, pp. 162–3). The state, in response to the prior agrarian militarism of the populist era and because of its prior work in agricultural institution building acting as a head start, moved quickly to incorporate agrarian demands into the New Deal proposals. Thus, neutralizing class based farm movements by incorporating them into the New

Deal Coalition (McMath, 1995; Eidlin, 2016). Farmers were thus better off in relation to their influence over government institutional policies than labor. This is due to the prior agrarian movements – the history of populism and its influence on state development – and the states increased role to combat these movements that left a much greater and more sophisticated state institutional apparatus in place for agriculture relative to industry. Through the New Deal the position of agricultural capitalists improved while that of industrial capitalists deteriorated Skocpol and Finegold (1995). This produced the outcome of fewer and fewer farms of larger and larger size who concentrated on less and less diversity of crops.

In contrast to Skocpol and Finegold (1995), Gilbert and Howe (1991) have sought to "examine the development of capacities both within agricultural state institutions and among farming classes – capacities that converged to shape the New Deal farm policy" (p. 1). To that point, we should recognize that it was also through state action that more class centered agrarian movements declined; with the FB, Grange and FFB all losing members, which by 1933 only one in ten farmers belonged to one of these three groups (Hamilton, 1999). However, it was through the state expansion of its role and its links with the AFBF that large farm interests and business interests were acting. So the relative autonomy of the state did not prevent it from acting in the interest of the ruling class to maintain a push toward industrial agriculture which undermined farm movements or consolidated them in an agri-business form.

These divergent theories of policy and institutional development produced competing views of the role of dominant and subordinate classes, state agents, institutions, and economics in the New Deal policy trajectory. From the perspective of state centered theorists, state autonomy emerged from the ability of the state to guide policy that was independent of the pressures of social classes. However, as has already and will be further shown, New Deal agricultural policies did, in fact, emerge out of the political pressure of various classes. Thus the level of the state's autonomy emanated from its position as the mediator of the class conflict in which both agrarian and labor movements as well as capitalist class interests were involved (Gilbert and Howe, 1991; Goldfield, 1989; Piven and Cloward, 1977). The mediation of class conflict by the state, as driven by various class interests, informed the development of state policies. The state's actions were not, as state centered theorists argue, independent from class interests (Evans, 1995; Hooks, 1990; Orloff and Skocpol, 1984; Skocpol, 1980). Instead they were the result of the state responding to various class and social actors. The state policies appeared as emanating from outside only to those who would hold a captured or hermetically sealed off understanding of the US state. In fact, it was due to the long history of US agrarian state capacity building that facilitated a response in the manner in which it did. Thus, it was neither captured nor completely autonomous but able to shift its policies in the context of the balance of class forces. And it did this while maintaining and enhancing the agro-industrial policies and state institutional capacities. In fact, it was due to the effectiveness of the prior agro-industrial changes to shift the focus towards higher prices and technological efficiency that enabled the particular AAA programs to become acceptable to both small and large farmers, along with agri-businesses.

Also important was the structure of state institutions that created a degree of greater or lesser openness to political influence by competing classes. The links of the AFBF with the County Extension Services revealed made the AFBF more malleable to the interests of large property owners than small farmers, and as one of the important agents of AAA payment programs that possessed a strong source of influence into policy directions, it was able to mold the outcome in specific ways. The porousness of the US state allowed it to remain open to many different policy positions reflecting a broad array of class forces. This could be seen in the USDA's openness to many farm groups alongside its clear favoring of the AFBF with its strong ties to larger farms and their business backers (Skowronek, 1982; Winders, 2002). The New Deal agricultural programs revealed how the scattered interests of farmers allowed for the relatively autonomous role of the state to mediate between the competing class interests by setting up programs that either favored large farms or increased the market dependence of smaller ones while appearing open to popular pressure.

The conflicts over the AAA can be seen as a reflection of contradictions between future and present benefits, with New Deal AAA programs acting to ensure the future accumulation needs of agri-businesses (McClellan, 1991). McClellan claims "at the origin of the AAA, agricultural capitalists were too disorganized to act in their own collective interests, more than industrial capitalists, they needed a relatively autonomous state" (1991, p. 183). However this claim that agricultural capitalists were disorganized is clearly false. Farmers' organizations had been around much longer and were more influential in the state than industry had thusly become. The Populists and the Farm Bloc had proved the power of collective farm action. Quite to the contrary of Skocpol and Feingold's claim that farm groups had diminished in power, and that New Deal policies had flowed from the state's land grant and extension services; it was the linkages between the state apparatuses, the agricultural organizations and the capitalist and large farmers that were determinant in the policy outcomes (Kolko, 1976). As Gilbert and Howe (1991) outlined, it was the class bias of the state programs and their connections to elite agriculture that led to outcomes that benefited larger agriculture. The scientific research of the USDA and land grant colleges had established close ties to and had benefited large farms and the extension services pushed to modernize smaller farms (Gilbert and Howe, 1991).

Skocpol and Finegold (1985) claimed that farmers' protests did little to alter federal policy as the agricultural groups acted "to insulate the national government from the effects of protests" (p. 185). Clearly in an earlier era agrarian protests did influence state policy and shifted the balance of class forces. At one point in their argument they claimed that agencies in agriculture had greater input than in other areas, that "agricultural economists exercised more policy influence than did economists studying other sectors" (Skocpol and Finegold, 1995, p. 187). However, far from showing an absence of class interests, this reveals the greater degree of organization by capitalist and large farmers and the heightened level of influence over the state they maintained. Class power manifests itself in the relative autonomy of capitalist state institutional capacity to work for the benefit of the class as a whole, against the more narrow interests of particular capital fractions. As Gilbert and Howe (1991) put it:

> While state institutions and class relations can be analytically separate, the former are part of the whole society and thus reflect, shape, and contain social relations...class relations are in part constituted by the state.... it is thus the convergence of the state factor – institutional capacity – and the society factor – class conflict – that must be examined to advance our empirical and theoretical understanding of the state...it is their mutually shaping relationship that determines the nature of these factors (p. 206).

Skocpol and Finegold in fact recognized this point of how New Deal agricultural policy had aided capitalists and hurt the agricultural underclasses through "state intervention under the AAA and successor programs worked to overcome the economic crisis of capitalist agriculture, leaving commercial farmers better off than they had been in 1933...[while] agricultural sharecroppers, tenants, and workers, unlike their landlords and employers, were devastated by the AAA" (1995, p. 192). It is important to maintain an understating of the goals of capital as worked out through the state, showing the "blurring of boundaries between state and society", as opposed to separate spheres of autonomous actors in the state and outside of the state (Quadagno, 1987, p. 119). The AFBF revealed the class power at work and its links with the AAA programs revealing how that class power was connected to the state institutional development. In fact, Skocpol and Finegold (1982) did state that the by-product of the AAA was that "commercial farmers, especially those in the South and Midwest, gained important political benefits" and "a major farm lobby organization, the American Farm Bureau Federation (AFBF), was able to expand its operations" (p. 258). No less important though, and overlooked by Skocpol and Finegold, was the history of the agro-industrial project by the US state that led to the formation of the AFBF and how this embedded class politics in the state. Once again this undermines their claim of state autonomy, instead pointing to the internally related movements of class actors and state institutional developments.

Class Influences on Institutional Development

One very important point to flag is how "the USDA/land-grant complex developed in a way that increased the capacity of the industrial or commercial farm class and structurally privileged them within the state" (Glibert and Howe, 1991, p. 1). As outlined in Chapter 5, these state agencies lacked complete state autonomy and developed in relation to class power, the state overcoming class fractions not in the absence of class influence, but in coordinating fractions. The role of class in influencing the early development of the extension services and land-grant colleges, as well as the AFBF, revealed how class power prefigured and directed the administration of the state during New Deal agricultural policy development. Furthermore, the very newness of these types of state interventions and institutions demonstrated the lack of state autonomy and institutional path dependency, while the class fraction of agribusinesses and large farms were coordinated through the drive of the programs.

Another point of criticism is outlined by Gilbert and Howe's (1991) review of the diverse class structures of the three major agricultural regions of the nation which Skocpol and Feingold (1995) reduced to commercial and underclass social forces (p. 207). As discussed at length in chapters one and two, the geographically distinct forms of agriculture developed in an uneven manner in the US, producing varying degrees of class consciousness and class power. Because of this, different political and institutional developments between and within the regions and the federal government developed to differing degrees and in different capacities. To reduce the influence of this unevenness would be to diminish one of the main impetuses of American institutional development itself. The federal government's ability to oscillate between national and particular sectional interests was a strong attribute that played a significant role in both agricultural and other policy areas. This institutional capability developed to the degree to which it did due to the uneven and distinct nature of US agriculture, in relation to political and class struggles that were also geographically distinct.

Gilbert and Howe (1991) also stressed the prior and ongoing social and political unrest that they claim was shifting the balance of class forces leading to the co-option policy of state institutions. The very fact that the USDA and land-grant system emerged during a period of intense class struggle prior to, during and immediately after the Civil War, created pressure for reform. The creation of these institutions represented a 'victory for small farmers' due to the progressive climate (Gilbert and Howe 1991, p. 3). However this 'victory' was small and short lived, if a real victory at all. It was, in fact, the development of these state institutions, in response to agrarian class pressure that led to the demise of the radical agrarian movements while simultaneously channeling farmers into market dependent forms and reformist movements seeking higher prices. As shown in Chapter 3, they represented the unique capacity of the state to deal with class struggle in a particular way that dissipated it while strengthening the state's capacity to intervene on behalf of the capitalist class by constructing market hegemony. By funneling agrarian class demands into policies that pushed agro-industrialization, the US state was able to assuage the demands of the agrarian movement by appearing to work in the interests of higher farm product prices, while the outcome was to favour particular development patterns that used the market to discipline farmers and concentrate them under capitalist social forms (Kolko, 1976).

The creation of the USDA represented a compromise between the interests and demands of agrarian social movements and the state, which was becoming increasingly commercial in its orientation (Gilbert and Howe, 1991; McConnell, 1953). The policies that emerged therefore represented state institutional attempts to deal with class or societal problems, and offered a more long term approach to the issue relative to immediate demands of specific class interests.

Much of this occurred through the 'USDA-research complex' – the land-grant university system and the State Agricultural Experiment Stations – which served a single purpose to develop and implement high-tech farming (Winders, 2002). Through its support of large-scale scientific agriculture, this complex fed into the emerging upstream and downstream agribusinesses that were popping up to supply the necessary tools, implements, inputs and processing tools for the raw commodity outputs, while simultaneously seeking to increase farm size and efficiency (Gilbert and Howe, 1991; Kloppenburg and Buttle, 1987). This was of course, also what was being pushed by the AFBF as the remedy to the farm crisis. With the acquiescence of the bulk of farmers to the idea that rising prices, as the solution to their problems, the state had just to advance policies that promised prosperity through the agro-industrial project.

The Experiment Stations benefited mostly larger commercial farmers (Rosenberg, 1978) as did most of the research done at the land grant colleges as the education leaders "strongly partook of the ideological suppositions of the existing order" (McConnell, 1953, p. 23). Gilbert and Howe affirmed this understanding, stating "From the outset, concerns about class conflict and the development of a particular form of agriculture shaped the mission of these state institutions" (1991, p. 208). The County Extension Service mission, goals, and funding were all geared towards scientism, private property, and capitalist markets. The American Bankers Association invested in early Extension Service funding because it thought that through farm modernization farmers would become "more successful producers, a better credit risk, and a more contented and prosperous people" (Gilbert and Howe, 1991, p. 208).

The AFBF itself was the outgrowth of a government and corporate program, with "a government bureaucracy – the extension service – that had suddenly created the largest and most powerful 'private' farm organization in the county, with many county extension agents becoming publicly-paid organizers for the Farm Bureau" (Gilbert and Howe, 1991, p. 48). It was because of these developments and the formation and power of the AFBF that the New Deal policies took the shape that they did. With the support of the state and corporate backers the AFBF actively sought to undermine radical farm groups such as the Nonpartisan League, the National Farmers Union and the Farmer-Labour Party (McConnell, 1969). The creation of the county Extension Service linked the state with the most prosperous farmers and actively promoted the methods they engaged in, which represented the large farming interests (Kolko, 1976). The FDR administration also sought to diminish the influence of the farmers groups who opposed the AAA. When the National Farmers Union (NFU) criticized the AAA for providing too little support for small farmers and too much support to large farms and landowners, the administration sought to discredit and undermine them. In fact, the Administration used the US Postal Service to investigate possible fraud, conducted congressional oversight investigations into the organizations, directed County Extension agents to oppose them, and used their influence to attack them in local newspapers (Choate, 2002). The actions against these groups showed the state's involvement in strengthening the class capacities of large farms and linking them with the state through the Extension Service and the Bureau, which sought to disorganize lower class organizations. This closed off any possibilities for the AAA to act in more small-farmer oriented ways (Gilbert and Howe, 1991).

Therefore, what appeared as a progressive victory for small farmers, in the end, turned out to be the basis for the development of state institutional capacities that ultimately re-solidified capitalist farmer power. FDR's main progressive advocate for New Deal Farm policies Rexford Tugwell himself outlined the connection of the Land Grant System with the "ruling caste of farmers, the most conservative Farm Bureau leaders, the cotton barons of the South, the emerging Associated Farmers of California, [and] the banker-farmers of the middle-west" (Lord, 1947, p. 381). The AFBF effectively redirected the bulk of farmers into an organizational form that would benefit large farms and push agro-industrialization of small farms.

The New Deal would work towards the goal of higher prices through production controls. "By emphasizing higher prices", this "reinforced the financial and property interests of family farmers, who benefited somewhat from the early programs" while in "the South the early New Deal harmed the subordinate class of tenants and sharecroppers, and they organized against it" (Gilbert and Howe, 1991, p. 210). Because of the struggles of the STFU and other farm groups across the south, along with, the importance of the Southern bloc to Democratic electoral success, the south played a prominent role in how the New Deal programs emerged. In the very short run, and absent any other hope, family farmers did benefit from and got behind the AAA production control policies. However, in the long run the outcome was an undermining of those very small farms as the policies clearly favored larger farmers and agribusiness.

Production in the major crops, measured as pounds or bushels per acre, witnessed massive increases under the policy regime of the AAA, "Between 1935 and 1970, yields of wheat, cotton, soybeans, and corn would more than double" (Kloppenburg, 1988, p. 88). This occurred both because of the economic policies that favored large producers and monocrop agro-industrial production models and also because of the technological advances, not least of all in seed development that also gave an advantage to agribusiness farming.

Kloppenburg argues "in the face of such yield vectors, reformist New Deal social programs would necessarily prove inadequate to the task of slowing differentiation among farmers...as the inadequacy of production controls... [make clear]... no amount of policy tinkering in the sphere of circulation can cope with a problem that originates not in the field but in the lab" (1988, p. 89). The problem with this understanding is twofold. First of all, it falls into a dichotomous understanding of production and state action. The understanding of the agro-industrial project of the state outlined in this study reveal the fallacy of this division, as agro-industrial development always meant both the state institutional development to favor technological agriculture while also easing the social dislocation and obfuscating the transition to it.

The development of the USDA as technocratic 'expert' of agricultural science, and importantly this seen as outside of politics and class connected farmers, produced the acceptance of agro-industrial development. Secondly, these technological developments also created further centrualfugal forces to pull farmers into agro-industrial production and markets, which was central to New Deal programs, not against them.

It would be nearly another decade and take World War II, with the growth and maturity of the labor movement, to get the state coordination in industry up to the level it had already achieved in agriculture by the mid-1930s or earlier. During the second "liberal" New Deal, agrarian capitalists in the South and the AFBF, through the prevention of the Wagner Act of 1935, the Social Security Act of 1935, and the Wages and Hours Act of 1938 from affecting agricultural workers, once again showed its true strength.

The Specific Case of California Agriculture

Despite the New Deal being a federal policy, it affected the various regionally distinct agricultural systems around the nation differently. As Gilbert and Howe (1991) stated it "These regional farming systems – California capitalism, southern plantations, and Midwestern family farming – provide the essential background to New Deal agricultural policy...The regional class conflicts directly affected policy-making" (p. 210). Therefore, another aspect of the agrarian movements' engagement in the 1930s was a group of labor strikes by employed farm hands and field workers. These represented the aspect of the labor movement that McWilliams (1966) called "factories in the field" which appear to exist outside of the common ideology of the American family farm.

Although agricultural strikes took place across the nation, the overwhelming majority of these agrarian labor strikes took place in California. Between 1933 and 1934 alone there were 99 strikes involving 87,365 agricultural workers. It was California that provided the staging area for over half of these strikes with 67,887 workers involved (Jamison, 1945). This geographic disparity in farm labor activity was due in part to California's containment of roughly 40% of the large-scale farms in the US with far more of them operated by hired hands than anywhere else (Bernstein, 1969). California agriculture at the time was summed up by Lloyd Fisher (1951) this way "that which is most distinctive about California agriculture were to be compressed into a single sentence, it could best be done by simply reversing a familiar phrase: Farming in California is a business and not a way of life" (p. 464). More than anywhere else in the US in the 1930s, California epitomized a full blown capitalist agricultural system.

It had geographically separated specialization and had moved into value added crops and agricultural products well before the rest of the nation (Henderson, 1991). California relied more heavily on capital intensive forms of production due to the scale of its development – with the state of California actively engaged in producing this larger scale through its land, banking, marketing and labor policies, it was reliant on finance capital to a larger degree that brought about distinct social relations (Henderson, 1991).[2] Thus, it already contained the specific aspects of agri-business that would come to dominate the bulk of US agriculture in the second half of the twentieth century. Yet most of the progressive labor laws of the nation and of California at the time did not apply to agriculture.

Across the nation it was the racialized poor who worked the labor intensive capitalist farm jobs: the Bravas, black Portuguese from Cape Verde in the Cape Cod cranberry bogs; blacks from the Southern US in the tobacco fields of the Connecticut Valley; Southern and West Indian blacks picked the citrus and the cane in Florida; Mexicans worked the pecan shelling sweatshops of San Antonio; and Mexicans worked the sugar-beet fields in Michigan as well (Bernstein, 1969).[3] In California this racialization of labor was even more unmistakable: the Chinese, Japanese, Hindustani, Armenian, the Filipino, and the Mexican are all noted examples of California's immigrant agricultural labor force (Berstein, 1969). And as the Depression gripped the east and the Dust Bowl spread across the plains a new group emerged looking for work in the fields of California: the Okies, Arkies, and Mizoos. As more and more previous farm owners, racialized farm workers, and displaced industrial workers flocked to the countryside the wages plummeted. In California the average daily rate for farm work had been $3.56 in 1929, falling to $1.91 by 1933 (Bernstein, 1969).

All this meant that the agricultural workers in California were ripe for organizing, if a union could look past the racial lines and diverse skill sets. It was mostly the Communist party that came and filled this gap (Bernstein, 1969; McWilliams, 1935). Fisher (1953) wrote how "agricultural labour in California

---

2   On the question of why California agriculture was more capital intensive Henderson (1991) asserted that it was because it could be "given the early concentration of finance capital in San Francisco and the regular migration of new capital and labour into the state" (p. 53). Also important was the particular history of land development and the timing of this development.

3   Increasingly the labor of California and other capitalist wage labor agricultural areas relied on migrant labor. Although the issue of migrant labor and immigration falls beyond the scope and space of this study, it should be acknowledged as a major force in both US agriculture and US social and political life.

during the 1930's was a very special object of Communist attention...no group ought to have been more susceptible of Communist persuasion that the landless, ragged, half-starved proletariat of the California harvest" (p. 138). It was the intense organizing by the Communist Party that really began the farm labor movement in California (McWilliams, 1935).

Bernstein (1969) asserted that "the New Deal triggered the farm revolt; [the] deeply rooted economic, social, and racial resentments were compounded by the discriminatory nature of the new legislation" (p. 150). He outlined numerous strikes and protests, some riots and even tarring and feathering, by farmers across the nation: from Cape Cod cranberry pickers to Florida citrus; from New Jersey blueberry harvesters to Texas nut shellers; From Montana and Wyoming sheep shearers to Washington state apple and hops pickers (Berstein, 1969). The farm labor unrest culminated in California though due to its more 'advanced' level of capitalist farm development.

And these more 'advanced' capitalist social relations in agriculture that had developed in California meant a distinctly capitalist manner of class conflict – the labor strike. There were ten major strikes that took place across the entire nation between 1930 and 1932 involving over 1,000 workers each, while the next year, after the New Deal began, have 37 of these large strikes in California alone (Gilbert and Howe, 1991). Clearly the agricultural laborers of California could see that the AAA was not going to help them.

Although the union maintained branch offices in most of the agricultural districts of the state, the most pressing labor activity centered on the Cannery and Agricultural Workers Union (C&AW) located in San Jose, California. The links to the Communist Party and the union were not kept a secret. In 1933 the union engaged in a number of strikes and work-stoppages across the state. Some were successful, while others failed (Bernstein, 1969).

The C&AW's main target was California's largest crop by value at the time – cotton. In the southern end of the Central Valley some 15,000 field hands converged yearly to harvest the crop. The picker's rate had fallen over the past few years from $1 a hundred weight to 40 cents (Bernstein, 1969, p. 153). Upon hearing of the organizational efforts by the union and the plan for a strike around the harvest, the growers assembled and agreed to raise the pay to 60 cents in the hope of undermining the union (Bernstein, 1969). The union set a rallying cry of "not a pound less than $1 a hundred" and managed to get 10,000–12,000 pickers to stop work (Bernstein, 1969). The entire strike had been coordinated by four communist party organizers who were able to get up to 12,000 pickers to strike across 114 miles of the valley (McWilliams, 1966). The strikers rented a farm and set up a makeshift compound for the striking workers and their families (McWilliams, 1966). Daniel (1981) called this strike the "greatest single strike in the history of agricultural labor relations in America" (p. 165). It led to violent conflicts and an eventual settlement at 80 cents per head. This was less than ideal for the union but the political hold of the growers on the legal system and law enforcement were too great at the time.

The California agricultural strikes of 1933 have been called "the most extensive strikes of their kind in the agricultural history of California, as well as of the US" (McWilliams, 1966, p. 228). All told, approximately 50,000 workers participated in the 37 recorded strikes that took place in 1933, covering 65 percent of the total crop value for California (McWilliams, 1966, p. 230).

In the end the strikes in California proved incapable of bringing about a substantial shift in the balance of class forces or to even bring about any real reform. Any connections between striking farm labor and striking industrial labor in California were destroyed through the reign of state terror brought down on labor organizers in the summer of 1934. This was timed to embarrass Upton Sinclair's campaign for Governor expressed by the San Jose News as part of an effort to "clean up a den of Communists and lead them boldly out of the country" (quote in McWilliams, 1966, p. 227).

The year following the great strikes witnessed a new level of coordination between the State of California and the farm owners of the state. In 1934 the Associated Farmers of California, Inc. was formed as an outgrowth of a AFBF and State Chamber of Commerce study on the farm-labor conditions in the state, producing a statewide push to have owners create organizations of reform (McWilliams, 1966). The Associated Farmers, as the umbrella group became known, claims to have been formed to "fight Communism" but as they explain in their 1937 annual report this included "opposing unionization of farm labour on any basis" (McWilliams, 1966, p. 262). In what McWilliams described as the "rise of farm fascism" the farm owners associations set to destroy the farm worker unions by almost any means, including maintaining an espionage department, using intimidation and violence, getting the press to attack and label all farmers engaged in union activity as communists, getting the federal government to ban "communists, reds and radicals" from the WPA payrolls, and even murder (McWilliams, 1966). The blowback would eventually leave leaders of the CAWIU imprisoned under the Criminal Syndicalism Law for two years before the law was overturned.

More to the point, the divisions across agriculture due to its uneven development across the nation meant that the strikes in California failed to connect with the STFU in the South or the Farmers Union and Non-partisan League in the Midwest. This inability to build broader agrarian connections between struggles produced isolated social movements that left the state able to divide, deal with individually, and conquer. The distinct developments in California, or the "telescopic" nature of its capitalist development as McWilliams (1966, p. 275) called it, highlighted the necessity to include in any analysis of US agriculture the uneven nature of agrarian development and its impact on the form of class struggle, the links to economic and political developments, and the abilities and strategies of state institutions to mediate the conflicts. Only in California where the hegemonic social form in agriculture represented a full blown capitalist, wage labor based system, and out of these we see strikes and workers seeking to increase the pay they received. This is not to even mention California's increased reliance on finance capital and how this infused the social relations (Henderson, 1998). In all other areas it was clear that the level of development produced different social demands – increased prices, parity, land, low interest rates, state subsidies – all of which were based on a distinct state involvement that appears as outside of the role of the capitalist state.

When it came to capitalist farming in California the state seemed involved in a distinct way that Produced the political as distinct from the economic that appeared more at ease with the capitalist state, while in the rest of the nation the AAA appeared as an over reach of the state into new territory. It was done, in the final analysis, to bring the rest of the nation into social relations that approached the capitalist ones in California that were more amenable to the capitalist state capacities.

The exact manner in which the New Deal programs worked toward the goal of agro-industrialization emerged in the way it was implemented. The idea that production controls would limit technological investment, increase farm size, and a move toward capitalist agriculture seems self-evident – by reducing acreage and raising prices it would appear that this approach would limit the influence and drive towards agro-industrialization. However, as Clarke (1994) has shown, by reducing market price instability the commodity programs stimulated farmer investment in machinery. By rewarding the most efficient farming techniques, creating conditions where credit for modernization could more easily be acquired, and creating stable and expanding markets for agricultural products, the AAA was fully engaged in the agro-industrial project.

Also important in this regard was the particular manner of the price supports, which because they were initially designed through the specific influence of large farms that favored and granted larger payments for more land set aside despite its quality. The act also raised prices and this created a drive towards efficiency because a farmer's ability to produce more on less land was rewarded. We know from the historical data that farm productivity continued to rise after these policies were in place, with multifactor productivity increasing at an average annual rate of 1.88 percent, or 400 percent overall, between 1949 and 1991 in agriculture (Craig and Pardey, 1996). Thus one of the lasting legacies of the New Deal era agricultural policies was the continued increase of farm productivity, concentration and modernization or agro-industrialization. The New Deal AAA was not really designed to reduce production, despite the so-called production control policies, but was more of the same state policies aimed at modernizing and growing farms and increasing productivity by rewarding the adoption of technological advancement and increased agricultural research (see figures 4 and 5).

Despite this, most agricultural product industries outside of direct production were opposed to the production controls of the AAA (Winders, 2003). It therefore is a testament to the political strength of farmers – including capitalist, petty commodity, and laborers – that they had the ability to influence state policy during the New Deal. The political strength of the food manufacturers would not fully surpass that of farmers until the 1950s, and a similar time horizon existed for industrial production (Constance, et al., 1990; Winders, 2003). In fact, it was the nature of the New Deal programs that would enlarge the political power of agri-business. So the success of farmers led to the strengthening of the food industry that would ultimately eclipse them politically (McConnell, 1969; MacLennan and Walker, 1980).

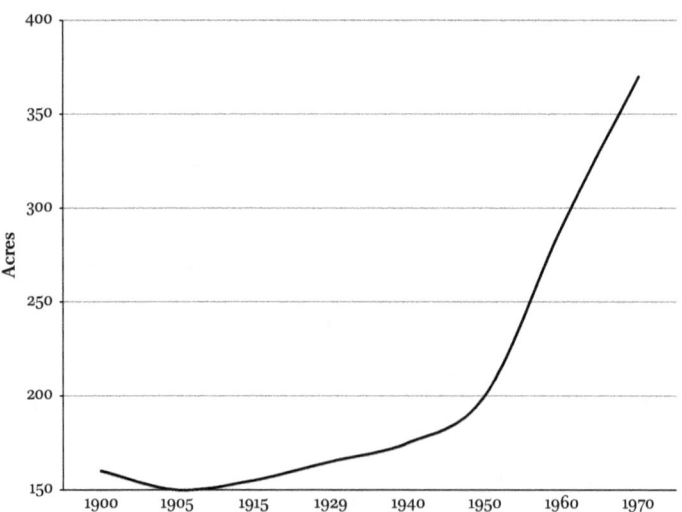

FIGURE 4 *Average farm size: 1900–1970*
SOURCE ERS/USDA

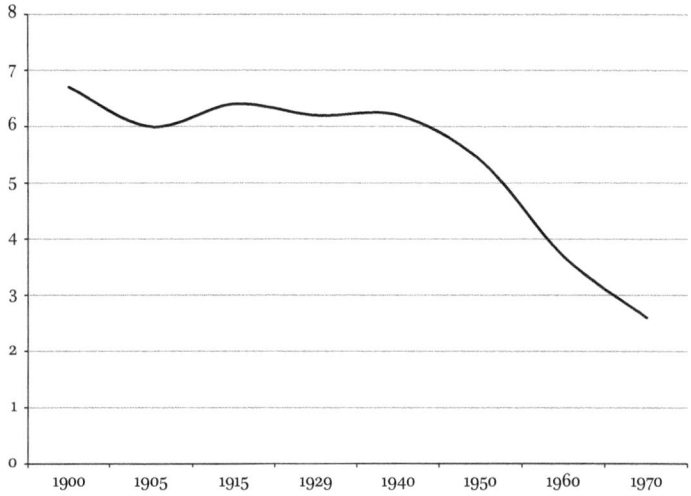

FIGURE 5   *Number of farms in the US (in Millions): 1900–1970*
SOURCE ERS/USDA

The Consistency of Trade Promotion

Despite the push for food aid during the middle of the 20th Century, and the appearance of it emerging out of good will, the US consistently maintained a focus on expanding agricultural trade. The history of agricultural trade promotion, in fact, has deep roots and long standing institutional capacities within the US state. The USDA posted its first employee abroad in 1882, with the assignment of Edmund J. Moffat to London. Moffat went out as a 'statistical agent' of the USDA's Division of Statistics but with the status of Deputy Counsel General on the roster of the Department of State at London. Early USDA work at promoting trade in foreign nations proved very successful. In early 1919 an agricultural trade commissioner was stationed in London to report on the post-War situation in Europe and to promote US agricultural products there (FAS, 1966). The successful work of the agricultural commissioner at London led to the establishment of additional posts. By 1922, the USDA would also have representatives in Argentina and the Balkans. The representative at Buenos Aires could be maintained for only part of 1923 due to lack of funds, but in 1924, the Department had agricultural commissioners in London, Berlin, Budapest, and Buenos Aires in addition to its representative with the International Institute of Agriculture at Rome (FAS, 1966, p. 9). In 1925, there were commissioners in London, Berlin, Vienna, and Mexico City; and in 1927, a commissioner was assigned to Shanghai to push agricultural trade in China and Japan (FAS, 1966, p. 10).

This process of institutional buildup of agricultural trade promotion through the USDA took a leap forward when the Foreign Agricultural Service (FAS) was created by the Foreign Agricultural Service Act of 1930 which President Herbert Hoover signed into law June 5, 1930. Its primary responsibility was to oversee the USDA's overseas programs – market development, international trade agreements and negotiations, and the collection of statistics and market information (FAS, 1966). In 1924, USDA officials Nils Olsen and Louis Guy Michael, working with Congressman John Ketcham, began drafting legislation to create an agricultural attaché service with diplomatic status. The act stated that the FAS should:

> Acquire information regarding world competition and demand for agricultural products and the production, marketing, and distribution of said products in foreign countries and disseminate the same through agricultural extension agencies and by such other means as may be deemed advisable.
> US House of Representatives, 1930, p. 1

Here we clearly see the coordination efforts of the US state regarding the world market for agricultural products in an effort to assert US dominance through the expanding productivity of an increasingly modernized agriculture system. It is important to note the early nature of this move to expand US agricultural trade. By 1930 the USDA was already expanding substantial resources to promote US trade and this would only expand. Even as the New Deal USDA programs appeared to be moving to reduce production through the AAA, it was simultaneously seeking to rebuild and expand the world market in agricultural products. As discussed in Chapter 6, Agricultural Secretary Wallace was openly discussing how production reductions were only a temporary measure and that expanding trade was the long-term goal of the USDA and the federal government.

At the time of its establishment, the early 1930s, FAS representatives discussed liberalization largely in terms of tariff concessions for US goods and financial or "dollar liberalization" that would allow other countries to increase dollar reserves and afford purchases of subsidized US agricultural goods (FAS, 1956; See Essex, 2005, p. 88 for discussion). Likewise, written into aid agreements were stipulations requiring all banking related to the aid and loans in the recipient country to be carried out through US bank foreign branches (Hudson, 2003, p. 234). A 1958 amendment required that 25 percent of all Title I local currency proceeds be set aside for loans to US businesses and foreign industrial development projects that required US products to be imported for purchase (Ahlberg, 1975, p. 22). This clearly reveals the marriage of food aid and trade promotion, PL 480 and the FAS, the disposal of US agricultural surpluses and globalization.

In 1934 with another move to place the USDA in the center of trade policy decisions, Congress passed the Reciprocal Trade Agreements Act, stipulating that the President must consult with the Secretary of Agriculture when negotiating tariff reductions for agricultural commodities. Secretary of Agriculture Wallace delegated this responsibility to the Foreign Agricultural Service Division, and thus began the FAS's role in formulation and implementation of international trade policy. The FAS led agricultural tariff negotiations, first concretizing new tariff agreements with first Cuba, followed by Belgium, Haiti, Sweden, Brazil and Colombia. By 1939, new agricultural tariff schedules were in place with 20 countries, including the United Kingdom, the United States' largest agricultural trading partner (FAS, 1966, p. 11).

In President Roosevelt's Looking Forward, a booklet made up of his campaign declarations, he outlines his goal of not only aiding farmers in the short term but also in promoting foreign trade of agricultural products:

> Instead of romantic adventuring in foreign markets we expect and hope to substitute realistic study and actual exchange of goods. We shall try to discover with each country in turn the things which can be exchanged with mutual benefit and shall seek to further this exchange to the best of our ability. This economic interchange is the most important item in our country's foreign policy.

Despite the usual rhetoric of mutual benefit from trade, this clearly shows the drive to rebuild the world market. Secretary Wallace also annunciated aspects of the agro-industrial project in his *America Must Choose* pamphlet written to sell the approach of the New Deal to reluctant farmers and businesses (Wallace, 1934). In it he marks the following points regarding the Government's approach to the crisis:

(1) New social controls over the market were here to stay
(2) It would be required to grow in order to facilitate a world market again
(3) Needed was a "planned and statesman like purpose" in new leadership
(4) The US would be required to import nearly a billion dollars' worth of goods
(5) That failure to do so meant continued economic hardship
(6) We need internationalist approaches

As Wallace toured around promoting his pamphlet he clearly articulated a new role for the state in not only propping up the market but in driving it onward in its capitalist development and market expansion. Particularly instructive is the goal to expand exports, Secretary Wallace signaled the US's intention to expand exports when he articulated how the export markets of the 1910s had closed, stating "we must reopen those markets, restore domestic markets, and bring about rising prices generally; or we must provide an orderly retreat for the surplus acreage, or both" (1933, p. 41).

Secretary Wallace also understood the affect the AAA would have on farm production, by favoring expanded production, and the expanded agricultural exports this required. After tossing around ideas about transforming the diets of Americans into something healthier and how that would meet the needs of both farmers and the poor, Wallace began to understand that expanding trade had to be the main goal of US agricultural policy. He had always "sharply opposed the idea of national self-sufficiency" knowing that the goal of opening up foreign markets for export was the key to once again creating a viable farm economy (Schlesinger, 1958; Wallace, 1933). Part of Wallace's perspective rose out of the idea that if the state moved too heavily into the regulation of agriculture it would crush the American spirit, lead to rebellion, or both (Schlesinger, 1958). Yet to open up markets for American agricultural exports to the tune of nearly a billion dollars according to Wallace, would require reduced tariffs and opening up many protected industries in the US to foreign competition (Schlesinger, 1958). Wallace knew even while he pushed for domestic farm aid, that short of social transformation, globalization would be the needed medicine. As early as 1934 the New Deal policies included provisions seeking to recapture the foreign markets for US agricultural products (Saloutos, 1982). This led to George Peek leaving the AAA to become the special advisor to the President on international trade. In addition, FDR created the Executive Committee on Commercial Policy and instructed the State Department to draft a trade policy statement charged to serve as "the regular channel of communication with all foreign governments on all policy matters affecting American export and import trade" (Saloutos, 1982, p. 139). At the same time Secretary Wallace was pushing hard for reciprocal trade agreements. At the AFBF meeting in 1934 he spoke of the need to restore foreign markets based on his understanding that the success of any New Deal farm program was based on how much it advanced the national interest (Saloutos, 1982). Clearly production control was set up to serve the agro-industrial projecct.

Harvard University awarded Secretary Wallace an honorary degree for his work on this new internationalist approach to domestic problems as his pamphlet sold out its first printing. He argued that reopening world markets were needed in order for the New Deal polices to be successful (USDA, 1935). In this he was departing from most of the New Dealers and the general public who thought mainly in terms of a national economy and a reduction of production to raise domestic prices and bring supply in line with domestic demand. When Wallace put forward a policy proposal to push for an expanded world trade in early 1934, it took many by surprise (Saloutos, 1982, p. 137). In this, it was Wallace who seemed to grasp the nature of the agro-industrial project of the state in its fullest. He clearly articulated how he understood that the New Deal AAA programs would not reduce production but would instead continue the productivity gains in agriculture and the commodification of farm products. It also showed that he understood the need for the state to intervene and coordinate not only the types of farms producing, but the way they produced and marketed to sell the products.

Much of the influence was coming from Secretary Wallace's own long-term understanding of the farming problems and also the work of the US Tariff Commission who, along with officials in the AAA were working on negotiating trade treaties in 1933 (Saloutos, 1982). Wallace's approach focused as much on expanding international markets as domestic ones and it quickly gained widespread acceptance, leading in 1934 to the Reciprocal Trade Agreements Act. The act marked a "pivotal turning point in international trading relations" by granting executive power over trade negotiations. Under the act the executive could enact reductions of up to 50 percent in US tariffs so long as other nations reciprocated (Cohen, Paul and Blecker, 1996). In 1934 a special committee was set up to coordinate all governmental activity on foreign trade and the Executive Committee on Commercial Policy was formed (Tasca, 1938, p. 29). Simultaneously, a series of bilateral negotiations commenced to reduce barriers to trade. Immediately, this shift in trade policy had little impact on the farm crisis as far as agriculture was concerned (Eisner, 2001).

However, in the long-term the changes in trade policy appear to have been significant, as bilateral trade agreements with twenty-five nations were in place by the early 1940s (Cohen, Paul and Blecker, 1996). More importantly, because of the most-favored-nations principle in effect the executive was rewriting the US tariff schedule, with the average ad valorem tariff rate falling from 50 percent in 1930 to 37 percent by the end of the decade (Mikesell, 1952). This was a major shift in trade relations, as "never before in world history had the direction of global trade relations moved so broadly and deeply toward reduced trade barriers" (Cohen, Paul and Blecker, 1996, p. 33). Here we see the enhanced role of the state in market relations beyond domestic concerns and clearly trade expansion did not represent the state moving in and replacing the market or reducing it. In fact, as I have shown in most other areas, the state's actions enlarged the market and enhanced market mediation of social relations. It is important to acknowledge that New Deal policies included this push for world trade. Secretary of Agriculture Wallace himself during this period was openly claiming that the expansion of international trade would stimulate production, boost national income, increase per capita spending, and boost farm revenue, all while also reassuring the business community that state initiated supply control was but a temporary measure until such time as trade could be expanded (USDA, 1936).

Clearly trade promotion was integral to agricultural modernization and industrialization. The state capacities required for this first emerge prior to but are greatly enhanced during the New Deal era. The agro-industrial project therefore wasn't restricted to agricultural modernization through state involvement; it also contained the requirement of state promotion of trade expansion.

Agriculture, the New Deal, and World War II

With the coming World War II the political landscape shifted rapidly and support for the agro-industrial farm programs increasingly took on a hegemonic form. First the Steagall Amendment was added to the farm bill, expanding the commodities that fell under supply management to include corn, wheat, cotton, rice, peanuts, and tobacco as the original bill did, and added hogs, eggs, chickens, turkeys, milk, butterfat, dry peas, dry beans, soybeans, flaxseed, and peanuts for oil (Winders, 2009). This along with the revised nationalism brought on by the war further undermined the efforts of radical farm movements around the nation.

Another example of the New Deal agricultural policies influencing the direction of agricultural change can be seen in the dissolving of the traditional plantation system in the South. Because AAA production controls paid farmers for acres retired while also raising prices on the crops from remaining acres by diminishing supply, southern landowners were able to use this capital to increase output through investments in modernization (Kirby, 1983). Because of these state produced 'market' incentives, tractor use expanded in the South: the number of tractors in the South rose from 36,500 in 1920 to more than 271,000 in 1940, and during the next two decades, they increased by a factor of five to reach more than 1.4 million (Musoke, 1981). The harvesting of cotton was most effected, as Fite (1980) described, "In 1950 only 5 percent of the American cotton crop was machine harvested; in 1960 it was 50...by 1963 some 72 percent of the crop was machine picked" (p. 204). These transitions emerged due to the expanded state institutional capacities built up through the New Deal programs.

The beginning of World War II would pull many of the recently displaced tenant and sharecroppers northward as jobs in industrial production of war machinery kicked into high gear (Mandel, 1978; Melman, 1949). In the first five years of US involvement in the war the South's farm population would decline by about 22 percent or three million people (Fite, 1984). This shift would, in turn, increase the rate of mechanization of southern agriculture and further push the South towards industrial agricultural production. However we shouldn't overlook the influence of the mechanical cotton picker, which would become widespread a decade later, and add further pressure towards industrial agriculture (Mann, 1990).

The state also pushed the South to diversify its crops during and immediately after the New Deal. The federal government achieved southern agricultural diversification through the war effort as it sought to source the food to feed the new military bases in the region by paying a premium for locally produced food. The result was that by 1949 the South produced 79 percent more wheat, 500 percent more soybeans, 34 percent more milk, 140 percent more peanuts, 79 percent more beef, and 49 percent more pork than it had in 1939 (Bloom, 1987). Thus the South would finally overcome the one crop evil that plagued it, finally and decisively throwing off the shackles of the plantation system all through heavy state institutional development.

Winders (2003) described these changes in southern agriculture as fundamental to understand the shifts in federal farm policy going forward, as the cotton plantation structure of Southern agricultural power was transformed to large commercial capitalist farms, policies also changed (2003). As the farm economy of the South changed so too did the economic interest and political power of cotton growers, shifting from rural landed elites to commercial farmers and eventually to agri-business corporations. The federal programs, originally designed to appease the landed elite of the South that were the most powerful aspects of the Democratic Party at the time, fueled material changes in southern agriculture and with it the South's support for the price supports and production controls also shifted (Winders, 2001).

The notion that a process of agro-industrialization continued to play a role in transforming American society, and particularly the agrarian economy after the New Deal was clearly witnessed in the transformations in agriculture that came with the second half of the twentieth century. The rural share of US population would fall under fifty percent for the first time in the 1950s just as the share of the labor force who worked on farms dipped to below 20 percent (USDA, 2005). This did not slow productivity gains however, as growth in agricultural productivity for the period of 1948–1999 was 1.9 percent annually, compared with just 1.3 percent for all industry (USDA, 2005).[4] In order to accomplish this growth in productivity with fewer farm workers, farms mechanized to a degree never witnessed before: growing from 246,000 tractors in 1920 to 920,000 tractors in use on US farms in 1935 and by 1945 there were 2.4 million, with the growth continuing until there were over 4.5 million by 1960 (USDA, 2005). A growing export base for agricultural goods was the main source fueling the changes as they grew on an index from zero to 65 between 1940 and 1960 (USDA, 2005).

As already discussed in previous chapters, this adoption of technology did not bring a renewed independence to farmers, in fact "they were increasingly tied to national and international affairs beyond their control…in order to afford these purchasers, farmers needed more income, which they often tried to achieve by purchasing more land and increasing productivity per acre" (Hurt, 2002, p. 50). This then made them further dependent on the land-grant colleges and state experiment stations, as well as the growing corporate research and food industry survival (Hurt, 2002). It also hitched them to the USDA support payments system that ultimately fueled increased modernization. The search for a technological fix to the contradictions inherent in a capitalist agricultural system created the need for more and more technology (technology treadmill).

Tracing the New Deal agricultural programs across the decade of the 1930s reveals the significance of the shift in the balance of class forces. The influence on the early New Deal agricultural programs of the class conscious and politically connected southern landlords through the AFBF held off radical social movements with the exception of the STFU and a few others that did manage to shift the balance of class forces and the response of the state. The push by FDR to strengthen the executive branch in the second half of the 1930s (Newstadt, 1964), is understood by the state-centric theorist view as a move to isolate the state and increase autonomy (Hooks, 1990). In reality this was simply the state response to the shift in the balance of class forces brought on by agrarian movements. In turn, as the war began to mobilize a nationalist ideology, the balance of class forces shifted again as this undermined politically left movements. Thus, the Roosevelt administration pivoted to a focus on military power, leaving New Deal strongholds open to a greater influence by capitalist class forces (Blum, 1976; Hooks, 1990; Polenberg, 1972). Anti-communism was also used as a means to undermine left leaning movements and the FBI aided

---

[4] Timmers (2009) shows the decline in farming as an occupation over time. His calculations of the historical trajectory lead toward the complete elimination of farming as an occupation. Clearly this is not a possibility but it reveals the rapid nature and degree of the decline.

through its intelligence support of the House Un-American Activities Committee (Young, 1956).

The entry into the war essentially ended the farm crisis, removing many farmers from their farms as they went off to war or off to the city to work in war related industries (Kolko, 1976). The war also diminished the farm surpluses as the need to feed the military and the military industrial workers increased demand. Farmers often are the first to benefit from a war economy, which also acts to undermine radical, often anti-war elements (Hurt, 2002). In fact, it was not long into the war that the government had completely reversed its depression policy and was asking farmers to increase production for the war effort. In 1942 farmers got Congress to pass the Emergency Price Control Act to ensure that with increased production farm prices would not fall below 110 percent of parity (Hurt, 2002). The war also brought the Bracero program to California fields, as the favoring of capitalist agriculture through state policy continued, moving forward with imported, temporary labor to further undercut farm labor militancy.

Although the war served as a major economic stimulus and aided in removing much of the agricultural surplus, this is connected to the increasing purchasing power of consumers which also helped to sop up the agricultural glut. It was also due to institutional shifts emerging from the greater importance of consumer-oriented policies (Maier, 1977; Cohen, 2003). This shift around the importance of consumer purchasing power was a major influence of the agrarian movements (Cohen, 2003; Prasad, 2012). These changes continued and the agricultural institutions and drive for a consumer based economy first witnessed in the agro-industrial project would spread to take on a hegemonic status in policy circles and the broader society.

The Federal Housing Administration (FHA), emerging in part out of agrarian demands for assistance with mortgages, came to inform the direction of US state policy going forward. It has been shown how the FHA lead to a mortgage backed consumer spending boom that undercut the development of welfare state provisions in the US while stimulating a relatively high home ownership rate (Schwarzt and Seabrooke, 2008; Prasad, 2012). These few examples reveal the influence of the success of the state led shifts, going back to the use of land policy to shift farmer spending through credit, acting as a model during the New Deal to inform the development of the welfare state going forward. By the time that Keynes publishes his defense of consumption-oriented economic policies, the US state institutions already had decades of experience using a politics of productivity in agriculture in response to the agrarian populists demands and real problems with agricultural 'overproduction' to use as a the basis of the construction of a private welfare state in the US based on credit, home ownership and consumption (Prasad, 2012). This state led agro-industrial model was replicated in industry and the growth of consumer society. Likewise, large government infrastructure projects that emerged in the New Deal era, exemplified by the Tennessee Valley Authority (Ekbladh, 2002; Cullather, 2010), were replications of the same state building approach to economic expansion and social movement neutralization as had been formulated in agriculture. The growth of the 'development project' is therefore directly traceable back to the class based agricultural resistance the US state had to learn to co-opt and direct into market based solutions through state institutional capacity building.

Conclusion

In conclusion, the onset of the Great Depression initiated speeding up in the process of state Institutional expansion in not only agricultural relations in the US but in the capacities created to deal with the crisis and changing economic relations of the nation. Many of these shifts were in response to and because of the memory and outcome of the populist unrest that proceeded. The state institutional response to farmer unrest came to act as a blueprint for the Fordist and consumer systems later to come, transforming industrial production during the 1950s and giving birth to the consumer society. During the boom period of the "golden age" farmer's good fortune meant a shift to moderate demands and the creation of state institutional linkages with farm groups, particularly the AFBF. This enabled the state to act in a manner conducive with agro-industrialization once the crisis hit agriculture in the 1920s–1930s.

As has been shown, the state's response to farm demands was based on the balance of class forces at the given moment while also resting on the institutional capacities available, all the while maintaining an agro-industrial bias. The acreage reduction policies of the New Deal represent an example of state institutional policy which both appeased and moderated agricultural movements while simultaneously moving farmers towards agro-industrialization through its focus on prices and productivity. It has also been shown how the shifts in the balance of class forces with, for example the STFU, affected state responses and institutional building – by appearing to reach out to the movements and deal with their problems while maintaining the agro-industrial project.

Major farm groups were allowed to be involved in the discussions over the way forward but where limited by the influence of representatives of other class interests, therefore their ability to alter the plan proposed by the agricultural economists behind the production control model was greatly diminished (Domhoff and Weber, 2012). As outlined in Chapter 4, the ability of the reform orientated farm groups to suppress all but discussion of prices as the root of the problem and focus of the solution to the plight of farmers represented the death knell of the populist movement. Coming into the New Deal agricultural policy discussions these groups were able to whip farmers into order behind the idea that the problems affecting agriculture were not the result of increasing industrial capitalist market domination or the increasing influence of large corporations, or the banking and finance industries but because prices were too low for farm commodities and too high for agricultural inputs (McConnell, 1953). The utter hegemony of this ideology within existing farm groups, or the few who had come to dominate above the others, already contained the limitation of the possible solutions to those that would continue to favor capital intensive agriculture over small farms. That is to say, it was based on the ready acceptance of more agro-industrialization as the means to solve the problems being caused by agro-industrialization. This along with the state institutional capacities which had developed over the past half century, namely the USDA and Extension Services/land-grant universities, were set up to push agricultural technology and modernization as the solution to rural problems. The very fact that many of the problems facing rural people had been caused by class domination coming through the increased modernization of agriculture – how the increased efficiency had led to overproduction and declining prices while requiring more land, more equipment, and more inputs, meaning more indebtedness requiring more output to pay back – seemed to be obfuscated behind a drive for higher prices.

As both the demands of the Farmers' Holiday Association and the drive for land by the STFU revealed, the balance of class forces pushed New Deal policy only until the movement's momentum subsided. In the process the relative degree of autonomy of the state was revealed to be based on the balance of class forces as the purge of the liberals revealed how government agents intent on maintaining lower class demands against the tide of upper class resurgence were washed away.

The state institutional development that unfolded rather rapidly during the few decades under discussion did involve a shift in the role of the federal government in the market place. Skowronek (1982) documented how the social stress of industrialization and economic disruptions moved the federal government from "state building as patchwork" into a role of "state building as reconstitution" (p. 286). The capitalist democratic state increased its role in building markets by recasting its relationship with farmers, businesses and banks.

However, this did not mean that the state came to replace the market. In fact, it was the state that moved to expand and prop up the market, moving it in a direction that gave the appearance of a separation was enhanced. The continued favoring of private ownership of the means of production by the state is the basis of this movement, as policies worked to enhance class power and control not through a captured state but through the creation of market imperatives that drove individuals to follow the dictates of the market and respond to its incentives. This represented the hegemonic capacities of the state, not only in its ability to produce legitimacy for the market but in its ability to create an internalization or reification of market imperatives. Agro-industrialization represents a cogent example of this internalization of market imperatives by farmers and agricultural workers. State institutional development during this era was of such a manner as to move radical agrarians into state responses that ultimately reproduced class dominance through the promotion and reification of market imperatives.

The previous two chapters, combined with this one clearly outline the manner in which US state institutions were developing the capacities to effectively deal with radical agrarian demands and social movements by shifting them to demands amendable with agro-industrial development. The development of these institutional capacities within the state represented one of the foundational strengths of the US going forward. The practical example this gives, as well as the actual institutional strength of the state it created, allowed the US to replicate the same processes first in industry and later around the world in the construction of a US empire. The farmer's resistance, and the strength of that resistance, created the requirement for a strong and sustained state institutional response that came to form the seed out of which grew the US state into a position of global power. In the Great Plains and fertile soils of the US came nourishment for its rising empire, not in a direct material manner but in the way this articulated itself in a vibrant farmers' movement that required a strong state institutional response, out of which the agro-industrial project was developed. We see here the dialectical movement of historical development from popular resistance to the drive of capitalism into the center of the very means of capitalism's domination through the state. This process presently continues and even has accelerated as the nation emerges from the conflict as the new hegemon of global capitalism.

CHAPTER 7

Sowing the Seeds of Globalization: Post-War Food Aid, Trade and the Agricultural Roots of US Hegemony

During the thirty years after World War II, US agricultural underwent a massive transition that brought about productivity increases to a larger degree than any other time in its history. This transition occurred largely because of the success of the agro-industrial project to modernize farms. The success of the agro-industrialization, in turn, was possible because of the desperate state of farmers during the depression (emerging in part due to advances in productivity) and also because of the success the state had at co-opting class based farm groups and steering famers into demands for higher prices and the acceptance of technology advances as the key means to achieve these advances. Important in this regard is the role of the USDA-research complex. Not only did this state institutional push to modernize agriculture through its education, outreach, and farm support systems, but it also worked to blunt radical farm movements. The effect of this was that the goal of raising prices and seeking efficiency gains became the accepted goals of farmers across the nation. Alongside this occurred the modernization of farms and the associated overproduction of US agricultural commodities. Through New Deal agricultural support programs and the USDA-research complex farmers became fully supportive of policies to increase farm size, specialization, mechanization and inputs as the means to attempt to achieve an increase their incomes. The work of the AFBF was central to this political acquiescence by farmers, as was the expansion of consumer markets that helped tie farm modernization with the purchasing of consumer goods.

 The decades after World War II marked the era of US ascendancy to international prominence in both military might and economic power. The role of agriculture as outlined by the food regimes approach (Friedman and McMichael, 1989; Friedman, 1987, 1993; McMichael, 1990, 1994) documents how the US used food aid to restructure nations around the world and align them with the growing world market, centered on US corporate dominance. The food regimes approach provides the basis of an understanding of the agro-industrial model expanded beyond the US borders.

 Recent scholarship has outlined some of the food regimes approaches shortcomings (Araghi, 2003; 2007; McMichael, 2009; Bernstein, 2010). This chapter seeks to augment the insights of the food regimes approach and transcend some of these shortcomings. It will outline how the agro-industrial model created the conditions for a surplus agriculture and how it also sought to expand US agricultural trade as the means to not only dispose of this surplus but to also spread this model internationally. Therefore it reveals how the drive towards surplus agricultural production is at the heart of globalization, internationalization and US Empire. Furthermore, it will elucidate how food aid was used to penetrate and transform receiving nations, not only opening them up for US agricultural imports but also creating a drive towards industrial development. In this we can see how the process of agro-industrial state institutional development became a model of capitalist development going forward.

Although building off of the food regimes literature this chapter will also offer a critical assessment of it by arguing that its dissection of history into discrete and stable eras, while initially offering many novel insights, rests on a number of assumptions that fail to stand historical scrutiny and confine our understanding. The various regimes identified all appear as neat packages of state policies despite the historical evidence to the contrary.

Related to the critical evaluation of the food regimes approach is another important insight of this chapter, to reveal the need to overcome the tendency in much International Political Economy and Agro-food studies to ontologize the distinction between states and markets (Panitch and Konings, 2006). The tendency is to discuss it as either markets embedded in liberal states or to describe the relationship as one of the disembedding of markets, or deregulation, meaning a reduction of the state in the market. Much of the approach in this regard is based on the Polyanian notion of a 'double movement' (Polanyi, 1944). To counter these socially bifurcated accounts, a historical analysis of the use of food aid to develop trade, transform societies, and construct the global market by the US will be outlined, one that connects class with political development allowing it to overcome this binary. This analysis will pay particular attention to the institutional and political shifts in the nature of the US state and how they are more accurately understood as shifts or reorientations within a continuous drive towards the construction of a world market, instead of one of greater or lesser state involvement in the economy. This view then shows how the 'post-war food regime' rather than failing, succeeded by actively pursuing and aiding in the development of capitalist globalization.

This chapter will explicate the general continuity of US agriculture's role in the post-war US reconstruction and expansion of a global capitalist market, or globalization. In doing so, it will elucidate the limits of the food regime approach and offer an alternative that places the US state, through expanded industrial agricultural production, as the author of globalization. This occurs through the active involvement of other states in the process of transforming and aligning social relations into a neoliberal globalized form. It will be shown how an expanding agro-industrial process of uneven development led by the US, often acting through other states, built a globalized capitalism. Therefore, rather than representing a specific set of policies as defining the discreet era, this period of the expansion of food aid was part of a process working towards a world market in agriculture that was continually responding to social forces, both domestic and global.

Food Aid as Globalization's Groundwork

In the immediate aftermath of World War II the US sought to stabilize and rebuild European capitalism. In this effort the Marshall Plan stands as the most obvious of US policies to aid in the reconstruction of Europe. Contained within the process of helping with the reconstruction also lay the goal of influencing the direction of development. Chief among this was the direction towards agro-industrial development. Friedmann notes that up to 40 percent of the overall Marshall Plan assistance came in the form of food aid (1982). Food aid was thought to quell the development of radical anti-capitalist beliefs and movements by offering a stimulus to industrial development, wages and capitalism and by keeping food prices low (Friedmann, 1993). This appears to have been what occurred though the US's food aid to Europe through the Marshall Plan. McMichael (2000) labels this 'green power'– using the US's strength in agriculture, through an agro-export strategy, in the form of aid to influence the balance of class forces and the developmental processes of nations around the world (On Green Power see also George, 1976; Revel and Ribound, 1986).

The use of US green power was not a policy that emerged suddenly in the 1970s but has its roots all the way back in the late 19th century USDA and other state institutions promoting of agricultural trade. It had been building strength through the New Deal as state institutional capacity was built up to deal with agrarian radicalism. As shown in the last chapter, the New Deal's supply management was always viewed as a temporary means to deal with overproduction until foreign markets for US agricultural products could be secured. The policy of agricultural food export promotion was always central to the US drive to modernize farms and can only be separated analytically not historically. The locating of this export promotion as outside and distinct from the project of agricultural modernization hinders our understanding.

Most of the US's food aid following the Marshall Plan was through the 1954 Agriculture Trade Development and Assistance Act, commonly known as Public Law 480 (PL 480). PL 480's stated intent was to "expand international trade, to encourage economic development, to purchase strategic materials, to pay United States obligations abroad, to promote collective strength, and to foster in other ways the foreign policy of the United States" (US Congress, 1954, p. 2). All told between 1954 and 1969 PL 480 accounted for an average of 23 percent of total US agricultural exports, with some years reaching higher than 30 percent (Hudson, 2003, p. 234).

The domestic political roots of PL 480 are often claimed to lay in the disposal of the massive farm surpluses accumulated through the Commodity Credit Corporation (CCC) (Friedmann, 1982; 1993; 2004; McMichael, 2000; 2003). The New Deal CCC bought up surplus crops with the stated goal of maintaining prices above the cost of production for farmers by sopping up excess production. The domestic effects of the New Deal agricultural programs were to aid the development of both highly productive large farms and to give this particular group of farmers a strong political constituency. Food aid, however was also always as much about trade promotion as domestic surplus disposal. Eisenhower said during the 1954 signing of PL 480 into law that the purpose of the legislation was to "lay the basis for a permanent expansion of our exports of agricultural products with lasting benefits to ourselves and peoples of other lands" (USAID, 2004, p. 18). Thus he lifted the veil of humanitarian aid to reveal the central goal of the program; "Food for Peace has its origins in American concerns over trade promotion, surplus disposal, and geopolitical advantage" (Barrett and Maxwell, 2005, p. 105). Additionally, as shown in the previous chapter and spoken of by none other than Secretary of Agriculture Wallace himself, many of the New Deal programs were constructed as temporary measures with aspects of trade promotion and trade expansion built into and eventually replacing 'supply management'.

Because US agriculture had developed in conjunction with expanding global capitalist trade, US farmers had historically done best when they had robust European and other foreign markets for their products. Two wars and the depression had interrupted what was a growing international market for US agricultural goods. As was well understood and even clearly articulated at times by US political leaders, the success or failure of US farmers rested on reconstructing these markets and expanding into new areas around the world (see Chapter 4–6). At the same time when the US emerged from WWII it took a more active role in managing global affairs. The goal was to apply a New Deal style social reordering of the world and a reconstruction of the world market (see Panitch and Gindin, 2004; 2012). To this end the US embarked on the Marshall Plan and later expanded this model outside of Europe through PL 480. These larger geopolitical and economic goals represent as much of the drive behind PL 480 as the desire to eliminate the surplus grain stockpiles that were the product of supply management. Elimination of the grain surpluses were the means to an end, not the end in itself of US policy in the post-war era.

The full array of agriculture regulations, programs, and agencies associated with the federal government enabled policy makers to adhere strictly to the principles of progressive farm modernization in the development and implementation of farm policies. These ideals emphasized industrialized, commercial farming by ever-larger farms they were set up in such a manner that many smaller farms did not receive the full benefit of federal farm aid. The resulting programs, by design, contributed significantly to the contraction of the farm population and the concentration of farm assets. The programs steered rural economic development into the channels of agribusiness as a strategy to manage the consequences of those policies.

Following World War II with higher, more stable incomes afforded by price supports and government loans, farmers increased capital expenditures on new technologies such as hybrid seeds, machinery and chemicals. Many of these technological developments were the products of USDA related research. Government regulations rewarded specialization and intensive farming practices that increased production. Ironically, the more farmers produced, the more the price they received decreased, and the more they needed to rely on support from the government. This treadmill of production only pushed them more into the market and increased their reliance on productivity advances through technological innovations. As a result of this cycle, yields quickly increased and industrial agribusiness became the dominant and organizing form in the sector (McConnell, 1969; MacLennan and Walker, 1980; McMichael, 2003).

Between 1930 and 1970 inputs of machinery increased more than 100 percent on US farms as farm size doubled and farm labor employment was decreased by 35% (USDA, 1973; 1975). Over the same time period, applications of agricultural chemicals increased five-fold, while yields continued to rise (USDA, 1975). As an example of this process, due to the development of hybrid seeds through the USDA-research complex, corn saw a tripling of yield per unit of land during the post-war era. This increased farmer reliance on the industrial treadmill and reproduced the reliance on government subsidies.

In the face of rising agricultural productivity and with the goal of stabilizing agricultural prices at a level that could maintain the farm economy, export market expansion was pursued and was pushed by farm organizations.

However, it wasn't just farmer political strength to push through a plan to deal with agricultural surpluses that accounts for the rapid growth of agricultural trade in the last quarter of the twentieth century. This was also due to the way the state institutions formed to deal with the political movements of farmers going back a century or more. The institutional capacity that developed because of US farmer strength created not only the means to steer farmers into agri-business but this institutional strength would also become the basis of US economic power around the world. By offering a blueprint for foreign affairs and by setting up political institutional strength in certain areas, this configuration proved useful in constructing the basis for empire. US state institutional capacity had developed the ability to assuage the demands of farmers while simultaneously reconstituting social relations in a manner more market dependent. In the US Midwest this is witnessed in the transition from farming to agriculture or agribusiness, through the long process of agro-industrialization pushed by the intervention of the state into agrarian relations (Bernstein, 2014). Led by the new institutional state capacities, developed in response to agrarian pressure, farmers were either continuing the long process of shifting to commodity agriculture or were disappearing as they were being gobbled up by other agribusinesses or having their farm foreclosed on.

The use of state policies and state institutional strength to guide domestic agriculture on a path that led to its increasing commodification is the key variable in grasping the economic development and the state-market relationship. The land policy, railroad support, banking rules and later USDA-research complex programs were all interventions by the state in an effort to transform agriculture away from subsistence and small scale farming into market dependent commercial agriculture and later industrial agri-business. The institutional capacities built out of this project structured the possible solutions within the confines outlined by the prior institutional development. The shift toward a global agricultural market is therefore the result of both to the success of this transformation of US agriculture into the most productive in the world, combined with, the US state response to strong farmers' movements. This explains why it was that the nation sought to reconstruct social forms and promote trade around the world. It was the early state institutional development around assuaging agrarian demands that led to the creation of the USDA, informed New Deal policies, the Marshall Plan and the subsequent US food aid foreign policy, and generally created both the state institutional forms capable of surplus disposal. This eventually led US agriculture into its current model, as Davis (2003) describes: "over the two decades following the creation of GATT, productivity gains and reformed national policies transformed US agriculture into an internationally competitive, export-oriented sector" (p. 7). Rather than an aberration from the New Deal era farm policies, trade expansion represents the coming to fruition of Secretary Wallace's goals as enunciated during the early New Deal interventions and put into practice through the USDA-Research complex.

Food Aid as Agro-Industrial Development Project

In this Section 1 will lay out the process of building US state institutional capacity in both food aid and agricultural trade promotion. These two goals, while often presented as distinct, are in fact, both within the same agro-industrial foundations and represent two parts of the same process. Food Aid emerges because of increased agricultural production through the changes initiated through the agricultural modernization drive of the state. Modernization of agricultural production led to overproduction and this became the means to penetrate and alter the social forces of other nations, thereby rendering them open to, and in most cases reliant on, US food imports. This occurs in a similar manner as it had previously across the US with agricultural productivity decreasing food prices that both released labor and fueled industrial development by reducing labor costs (Araghi, 2008; Moore, 2008). Thus, the surpluses that emerge, food aid, and trade promotion all stem from the same roots and occurred through the state institutional capacities emanating from the same project. This understanding counteracts the tendency to disarticulate AAA policies from trade expansion that results from ontologizing the state/market binary. Instead, it locates them as part of the same process of agro-industrial development.

Food aid became the major goal of the US agricultural policy in part because of the institutional capacities built up and used during the New Deal era to aid farmers. The institutional legacies influenced the possible approach going forward and the direction of future institutional development. These, along with the building up of commodity surpluses, were the main reasons for the turn toward food aid. However, as will be shown, this was done in a manner that used the food aid commodities as a tool for market construction and trade promotion. Postwar food aid policy was not simply aimed at reducing surpluses. Food aid served as a means to achieve the long term goal of agricultural trade expansion. Built into the industrial agricultural policies since their beginning, was the requirement for expanding markets for US products. Agricultural modernization had always rested on a need to expand markets and transform social relations.

Once the New Deal USDA policies had remade US agriculture, making it more efficient and market oriented, the surpluses had mounted. The second aspect of this approach emerged in the expansion of trade in agricultural goods. As discussed in Chapter 6, there was great effort in the 1940s and 1950s given to increase agricultural trade through the reduction of tariffs. There was also the work of the USDA's Foreign Agricultural Service (FAS) in pushing through an increase in agricultural trade. This along with the pro-trade policies of the PL-480 food aid program, acted to slowly but steadily rebuild the world market through agricultural goods. Building on the successes of these more limited programs at bringing agro-industrialization outside of the US by using food aid as a tool for reconstituting social relations in the receiving countries towards a global capitalist market, PL 480 allowed the US state to act as a foreign exchange broker to overseas markets through the sales of surplus commodities from the CCC in a much more expanded manner (see Table 7).

Title I of PL 480 – which constituted by far the largest percentage of the PL 480 programs – permitted the sales of surplus commodities with American agribusiness corporations negotiating the terms of sale with recipient governments and working out the transportation agreements. These corporations then received immediate payment from the US government to cover the costs while recipient countries had the ability to repay the US over a forty-year period with local currencies (Ahlberg, 2008). Thus the US state was acting as a lending house to facilitate the purchasing of large quantities of US agricultural commodities, generating very large corporate profits for agribusinesses and offering favorable terms along with the ability to repay the US with local currencies.

Section 104 of PL-480 specified the use of local currencies obtained in exchange for commodities, officially dubbed 'counterpart funds'. These funds were used by the US "to support agricultural development; trade development and promotion; loans for agribusiness; loans for agricultural facilities including cooperatives; private sector agricultural trade development; and agricultural research; and to make payments for US Government (USG) obligations" (USAID, 1993, p. 18). Title I programs "to help(ed) countries meet their long-term food security requirements. Priority was given to countries that (a) demonstrate the greatest need for food; (b) undertake economic reforms to promote food security, alleviate poverty, and promote development; and (c) have the demonstrated potential to become commercial markets for competitively priced US commodities in the future" (USAID, 1993, p. 27).

Building on the successes of Title I, Congress enacted the Title III "Food for Development" program (Sections 301–307 of P.L. 480) in 1977 to increase the developmental impact of P.L. 480 food aid. It did so to provide incentives

TABLE 7   *Overview of food for peace programs*

	Title I Economic assistance and food security	Title II Emergency and private assistance programs	Title III Food for development
Administered	– US Department of Agriculture (USDA)	– US Agency for International Development (USAID)	– US Agency for International Development (USAID)
Implemented	– Developing country governments	– Private voluntary organizations (e.g. not-for-profit, nongovernmental organizations) – Cooperatives – Intergovernmental organizations (primarily the United Nations World Food Program)	– Developing country governments
Provides	– Long-term loans to developing countries for the procurement of commodities	– Donations of commodities to address emergency needs – Developmental programs that reduce vulnerability to crises and improve the nutrition and food security of poor, malnourished populations	– Donations of commodities to developing countries to support food security programs

to developing countries to use P.L. 480 food aid as a development resource. The key incentive for the recipient country under Title III is that in return for carrying out agreed developmental activities the United States Government will offset all or part of the recipient government's Title I repayment obligations (USAID, 1993). The 1964 PL 480 Annual Report stated that "Public Law 480 generated foreign currencies, continued to be used to pay embassy operating costs and other overseas expenses of the Government, conserving dollars and strengthening the US balance of payments positions... [I]n the last two years, over $2.7 billion in such foreign currencies have been disbursed in place of dollar payments" (US Congress, 1964). Here we see the US use of food aid to strengthen the US dollar and to help maintain its global currency status, while simultaneously aiding the class of large agribusiness farmers it helped create through the New Deal and other policies. The role of the US dollar internationally in the construction of the emerging world market is one of the cornerstones of globalization (Seabrooke, 2001; Panitch and Konings, 2007). The use of food aid, therefore, was far more than just about the disposal of commodity surpluses to maintain domestic political acquiescence by the farm constituency. It was also part of the process of distributing US dollars around the world in an effort to construct a global market.

Food aid's ability to distribute dollars also aided in increasing US agricultural trade, as Hudson noted, "A further balance-of-payments contribution of the program is its stimulus to bona fide commercial farm exports" (2003, p. 230). This is confirmed in a PL 480 report to Congress, which states: "Expansion of dollar sales, owes much to the aggressive worldwide development efforts initiated under PL 480" (US Congress, 1969, p. 230). Meanwhile, local currency funds also boosted US exports more indirectly, by financing private sector agriculture and industry projects that rely on US exports and sometimes contain contractual obligations to purchase agricultural inputs only from US sources (Hudson, 2003, p. 231). The use of the collected 'counterpart funds' invested in the transformation of social relations in the host nation, often through purchases of US manufactured agricultural or industrial equipment or inputs and raw materials.

Another benefit of food aid was in its ability to overcome the 'Rhodes conundrum' (Patel, 2007) by effectively quelling hunger-driven political uprisings – many of them led by the left – in developing nations and former colonies. In the nations that accepted US aid with terms, it allowed for the rapid transformation of societies without a popular backlash. Food in the form of aid first stabilized the political situation by delivering bread to the masses, and then helped to bring down both the price of food, and therefore the cost of industrial produced goods (see also Araghi 2003; Moore 2008, 2010). In effect, food aid acted like a supplement to industrial production. The imported food also aided in the transformation of the division of labor as farmers were displaced by cheap imported food commodities, flooding urban industrial centers with cheap labor. The ability of cheap, industrial produced food to act as a social lubricant for the industrial transition that had ushered in the US industrial revolution were copied around the world through US food aid. Finally, when the aid was transitioned to trade, it integrated the nations into the emerging web of global capitalism through import dependency and debt. "Food for Peace is one instrument in a US policy which recognizes the need for economic development", said US Senator George McGovern (1964, p. 1), one major influence it has is that it "checks inflation of food prices that would otherwise result from development projects". Food for Peace was therefore in reality food for class peace during the jarring transitions to industrial society and the global marketplace.

All told, the cost of the food aid program appears to be minimal once the benefits are subtracted. Hudson calculates that the $8.1 billion of total balance-of-payments credits PL 480 generated just off set the amount the CCC would have had to pay to store the same amount of grain that was dumped abroad (2003, p. 234). Therefore the benefit in terms of expanded US corporate markets and the transformations of social relations was very cost effective. Food aid emerged out of the agro-industrial policies of the USDA – research complex; however, it was also based in a project to reconstitute the world market. That is to say, it was also about trade promotion and the penetrating and transformative powers of agricultural trade.

The Institutional Dimensions of Internationalization

Crucial to the transformations towards agricultural trade, stemming from the coming to fruition of agro-industrialization's push toward large scale agri-business, were the shifts in the role of institutions amid the further development of institutional capacity of the US state. Again, it is important to stress that these shifts emerged as the result of the success, rather than the failure, of the prior policy aims and their institutional basis. Furthermore, the overarching policy goals of the agro-industrial project remain intact throughout, however a new emphasis on internationalization is expressed in the development of institutional capacities along these lines.

The Kennedy administration initiated many policies that reveal the federal government's drive to expand exports and continue the agro-industrial trends both domestically and internationally. Domestically the focus on marketing controls over production controls produced the very real outcome of increasing the productivity of US farms and with it, the expansion of Food for Peace (PL-480). This along with the implementation of an export subsidy on cotton represents one example of the consistency of the drive, aligned with the political reality of Southern Democrats, to integrate US farm products into a world market (Hurt, 2002, pp. 127–129).

During this period the various independent institutional parts of the US state pulled agricultural policy in different directions, and this institutional autonomy shouldn't be overlooked (Winders, 2009). Importantly, this autonomy of state agencies aids in state legitimacy, particularly during this period when corporate interest took greater hold of the reins of agricultural policy, and yet, there emerged little farmer discontent. However, there does emerge a concerted plan undergirding US state policy along the lines of least resistance. This approach would fulfill the twin goals of appeasing domestic agrarian demands and projecting US power around the world.

The two most important state agencies shaping US agricultural policy around the world have historically been the Departments of State and Agriculture. The tensions between these two arise out of the domestic pressure of farmers who look to the Department of Agriculture as their spokesperson and the international goals put forward by the State Department. A source of much of this tension lays in the Department of Agriculture being heavily staffed with specialists- in what was the Health, Education and Welfare Branches of that department- while the State Department contained many generalists- such as what were in the Office of Management and Budget and the Council of Economic Advisors (Hopkins, 1980, p. 111). Based on both outcomes and stated policy goals it appears that the states policy orientation never conflicted to the point of contradiction with the base of legitimacy, as sometimes claimed by the food regimes approach (Friedmann and McMichael, 1989).

Although there is a large degree of continuity around the goal of trade expansion the state institutions did witness significant reorganization in order to improve the balancing of interests and policy coordination (Hopkins, 1980, p. 110; Winders, 2009). The interests that require balancing include domestic objectives to macroeconomic growth, low unemployment and inflation concerns, international objectives of balancing and expanding international trade, and the goals of transforming (developing) countries of the global south to create political stability and enhanced economic opportunities. Exactly how policies emerged to achieve the long-term goal of reconstructing and expanding the global market can be explicated by focusing on the shifts in state institutions that, though often acting contradictory, form the strength of the US form of subjugating the class struggle to the requirements of US Empire.

Building off the trade policy moves of the late 1930s and 1940s discussed in Chapter 6, the launching of the FAS in 1953 to "market development and commodity programs", led to a shift in USDA personnel from what was mostly the culture of "farm boy with a PhD" to one of "commodity specialists" and economists who were more knowledgeable of products and markets (Mustard, 2003, p. 38). These latter analysts formed partnerships with the private-sector in what were called cooperative agreements to develop overseas markets for US agricultural products (Mustard, 2003). In 1961, Kennedy, under the advice of Secretary of Agriculture Orville Freeman and FAS administrator Ray Ioanes, instructed FAS authority to enter into closer agreements with industry cooperator groups and shifted authority making capacity over surplus disposal from the more domestically oriented Commodity Stabilization Service to the FAS (Mustard, 2003). As Essex convincingly showed, the FAS unlike its predecessors, would allow for a "much greater role of agro-food capital in shaping the agency's strategic selectivity...[making it] a more attractive and open site and a more effective strategy for US based agro-food capital in its efforts to open foreign markets and internationalize" (2005, p. 130). Thus the move to the FAS allowed for greater corporate input over trade promotion and also created new institutional capacities to push for trade. The success of the FAS was real, as Agricultural trade in dollars would triple during the first 30 years of the FAS's work (USDA, 2011).

Instead of being separate and contradictory programs, supply management, food aid, trade promotion, and farm modernization all stem from the same approach of federal farm management, which is the outgrowth of the twin projects of capitalist development and US state building. They are all the product of a drive to take the strength in US agriculture, augment it with federal government research and policies to make it stronger, and then use this 'green power' as a means to project US policies around the world and to penetrate international social formations to guide institutional development and political systems to construct a US interests in the service of Empire construction As outlined above, the strength of US agriculture grew out of the state institutional capacity built up to quell many agrarian demands. The USDA-research complex sought to increase the efficiency and productivity of US agriculture, while also seeking agricultural trade promotion at the same time. Its desire to use US surpluses to build up trading partners comes from its institutional strength which was able to remake US agriculture and promote the disposal of US surpluses first through aid and later through trade.

The result of the agro-industrial project at this time was to create a highly productive, mechanized agriculture that was producing far beyond the dietary needs of American's and the efforts to reduce the downward pressure on markets through the CCC program was failing to sop up enough of the surplus.[1] Concurrently, while the work of the FAS and others to increase international trade in agricultural goods and more specifically to expand US agricultural exports, were seeing success, the productivity gains of the increasingly

---

[1] This expansion of agricultural exports was necessary despite the rise of US consumer caloric intake and massive increases in the industrial food products produced during post-war era due mostly significantly to the agri-industrial USDA- research complex developments (Pollan, 2008).

mechanized and large-scale US farms were outpacing the expansion of markets. It is for this reason that the US state turned to use food aid as a means to expand trade. As outlined in FAS (1966) documents themselves:

> Through 1953 and early 1954, House and Senate committees considered various ways to dispose of the growing farm surpluses without disrupting world markets. The result was Public Law 480, sponsored by Senator Andrew Schoeppel of Kansas and Representative Robert Harrison of Nebraska, which authorized the sale of US farm surpluses to friendly foreign countries for their currencies and also provided for barter and donation programs. As the 1950's progressed, market development work became an increasingly important aspect of the agricultural attaché's responsibilities (pp. 11–12).

PL 480 was therefore, both a means to dispose of agricultural surpluses and to construct markets and promote trade. The enactment of PL-480 would be the mechanism to penetrate other nations and alter their policies from the inside.

One of the major shifts in food aid came with the addition of Title IV to PL 480 in 1959. When first added it was only a minor aspect of the overall PL 480 program, but one that required the food aid to be paid for in US dollars or in convertible currency over the period of up to twenty years with interest (George, 1976, p. 196). Over time, the number of local currency sales were cut back: the percent of total PL-480 payments in local currencies floated just under 20 percent in the first half of the 1960s but decreased to about 3 percent for the early 1970s (Hopkins, 1980, p. 75). This process was furthered along in 1966 when PL 480 was amended to instigate a transfer of all Title I (local currency or counterpart funds) to US dollar sales, a process not completed until 1971 (George, 1976, p. 196).[2] This shift was one aspect of a move to shore up the US's increasing balance of trade deficits and to maintain the dollar's place as global currency. Overall the value and quantity of food aid had peaked in the 1960s- value in dollars peaked in 1965 and volume peaked in 1962 (Wallerstein, 1980, p. 52).

One of the initial drives toward increasing the agricultural production of LDC's, and thereby shifting them toward a global reorientation and an international capitalism, was an aspect of the changes initiated by President Johnson in 1966, and even before him through Kennedy's Alliance for Progress in 1961 (Wallerstein, 1980, p. 45). In March 1961, President Kennedy proposed a ten-year plan for Latin America:

---

2 There was an exception made for South Vietnam to continue to pay into a counterpart fund used for political purposes there.

...we propose to complete the revolution of the Americas, to build a hemisphere where all men can hope for a suitable standard of living and all can live out their lives in dignity and in freedom. To achieve this goal political freedom must accompany material progress...Let us once again transform the American Continent into a vast crucible of revolutionary ideas and efforts, a tribute to the power of the creative energies of free men and women, an example to all the world that liberty and progress walk hand in hand. Let us once again awaken our American revolution until it guides the struggles of people everywhere-not with an imperialism of force or fear but the rule of courage and freedom and hope for the future of man.
>   Presidential Papers, 1961

McMichael states that the Alliance sought to reform agrarian relations across Latin America by seeking to "quell peasant militancy and...as a method of reducing tenancy and promoting owner occupancy on a smallholding basis" (2004, pp. 66–67; See also Araghi, 1995). The Alliance for Progress appears to be another attempt to impose agro-industrialization as a US foreign policy goal. This direct imposition turned out to be no more effective than the more delicate penetration of the social forces that food aid allowed. As McMichael summarized "food aid subsidized wages, encouraging selective Third World industrialization, and secured loyalty against communism and to imperial markets, leading to a process where "...'development states' internalized the model of national agro-industrialization, adopting Green Revolution technologies, and instituting land reform to dampen peasant unrest and extend market relations into the countryside" (2009, p. 141). This reveals the process that altered the destination of US FDI and loans toward the south and how it occurred much earlier than the 1970s, predating the transition away from the second food regime (Panitch and Gindin, 2012, p. 123).

During the decade of the 1960s the shift from food aid to agricultural trade was the main goal of the use of agriculture to maintain the US's position in the global economy and instigate the move to internationalize economies. This, alongside the long-standing institutional push to expand US agricultural trade, created the drive towards globalization that occurred through food.

The late 1950s and 1960s witnessed an "explosion of US FDI" as US corporations learned that the Marshall Plan in Europe had been successful at rebuilding the economies and creating the conditions for profitable investment (Panitch and Gindin, 2012, p. 113). To facilitate FDI in developing nations the US sought to use existing institutional capacities of the US state alongside the building up of US and international organizations to push through necessary changes to both allow capital to invest and ensure its safety from expropriation. While the US Federal Reserve sought to deal with the emerging US Dollar crisis, financial institutions were developing the means to break the Bretton Woods structure (Panitch and Gindin, 2012). Congress also passed the US Foreign Assistance Act in 1962, designed to forestall any radical land or tax reform aimed at US corporations abroad; "According to Section 620 (e) of the Foreign Assistance Act of 1962, the President is instructed to cut off all foreign aid to any country which either nationalizes or places excessive tax burdens upon corporations operating on its territory" (Horrowitz, 198, p. 139).

An example of this is what became known as the US/EC chicken war. In 1962 the European Economic Community raised tariffs on imported chicken, effectively shutting US producers out of a growing and lucrative European poultry market (Talbot, 1978). One year later, the United States retaliated by boosting tariffs on four products important to European exporters: potato starch, dextrin, brandy, and light trucks. The Chicken War represents not a failure of US policy to prevent challenges to its agricultural export strength but the success of its program to restructure Europe and integrate its domestic production with the world market. While it is true that the US then had to create new institutional structures to insure its markets, this process was less about a drive for control than it was about building up markets. It is less about US versus Europe and more about the growing global capitalist power facilitated through the US state. The main form of US power rests in this ability to restructure the social forces of other nations through this type of economic penetration; thus realigning the social order with one that fits within a US Empire based on an integrated global capitalist market.

Again, if we compare the first half of the 1960s with the 1970s, we see a decrease from just fewer than 30 percent of all agricultural exports being under PL 480 to around 10 percent and decreasing (Hopkins, 1980, p. 75). This shift is even more striking when we remember that the overall volume of US agricultural exports and overall production expanded greatly during this time: production increasing from an average of 168.3 million metric tons a year in the first half of the 1960s to 264.5 million metric tons by the second half of the 70s and the percent of this export increasing from 32.5 to 86.1 percent for the same periods (see figure 6) (Hopkins, 1980, p. 38–39). These changes trace back to the creation of import dependency through food aid in the 1950s and 60s, changed with the policy changes and institutional shifts in the mid-1960s, finally culminating in the fruition of a large US agro-export market in the early 1970s and into the latter part of the decade. PL-480 exports peaked between 1961 and 1964 before falling off and then rising again after 1973 (USDA, 1974). However the percent of total US agricultural exports that fell under the

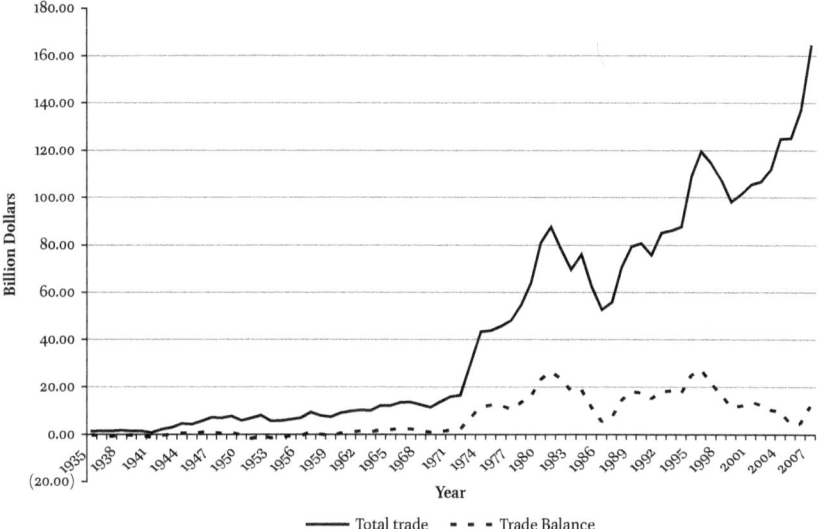

FIGURE 6   *Agricultural trade and trade balance: 1930–2010*
SOURCE USDA ERS 2011

program continued to decline after its peak of 29 percent in 1962 and remained in the single digits for most of the 1970s (USDA, 1974). This shows the continued expansion of non-PL 480 agricultural exports through the 60s, which registers the success, not failure, of PL 480.

The Crisis of the 1970s

In the 1970s the US economy entered the largest downturn since the Great Depression. During the post war era, in both Japan and Europe, industrial manufacturing had advanced rapidly, with these nations exports cutting into what had been US markets (Brenner, 2000). Meanwhile, workers in the 1960s and 1970s had been very active and had achieved some significant gains (Armstrong, Glyn and Harrison, 1991). Globally the early 1970s also witnessed the energy price crisis that set off a chain of economic problems. Despite this, US agricultural production remained strong and there emerged a concerted effort to use this strength to aid the US economy overall. In late 1969 the Nixon administration set up a number of presidential task forces to analyze the US's shifting position in the global economy. One of these commissions, the Williams Commission – named after its chair Albert L. Williams, the CEO of

IBM – as tasked with analyzing the US's position on international trade and investment policy. The commission's summary report pinpointed two areas where the US still maintained a competitive advantage in world production and trade: high technology manufactured goods (capital equipment, armaments and computers topped the list) and agriculture (notably grains and oil seeds) (Williams Report, 1971). The productivity growth of agriculture was still outpacing all other non-farm industries, with a 6 percent annual productivity growth rate between 1960 and 1970 compared to a 2.6 percent rate for all other industries (Burbach and Flynn, 1980, p. 45). In response to this and other reports the policy to aggressively promote exports of agriculture as America's "ace in the hole" emerged (Burbach and Flynn, 1980, p. 61). A Forbes article in March 1973 entitled "Can Agriculture Save the Dollar?" revealed the plan. Meanwhile, in that same year farm product exports doubled over the previous year to reach $17.6 billion, giving the US an agricultural trade surplus of over $10 billion (George, 1976, p. 198). So despite the overall slipping of US economic standing, agricultural production and export growth remained robust.

The Williams report cited "the long-term prospects of expanding agricultural export markets overseas to be excellent" shows the importance of increasing agricultural trade and the transformative impact this would have (Williams Report, 1971). The claim that US agriculture would single handedly save the dollar and US capitalism by acting as the lone export necessary to offset the balance of trade, is of course, an overstatement. There is some truth though to the claim that US agriculture would play a continuing and increasing role in expanding the US Empire though the 1970s. However the true strength of US agriculture lay not just in its size and productivity but in its capacity to penetrate and transform other nation's economies, as well as in the model of political development it offers through the history of US agro-industrialization. It is through this process of economic penetration of other nations, alongside the corollary building of institutional linkages, that the US constituted the building of its emerging 'informal empire' (Panitch and Gindin, 2004, p. 48). Thus the US Empire, as outlined by Panitch and Gindin (2003; 2014), was developed to rest on a much different set of relationships than the colonial system of the prior British Empire. It relied much more heavily on the internal transformations of economic and political systems than on direct territorial control (Panitch and Gindin, 2002). This does not mean a reduction in the role of the state, on the contrary, it was through states and the shifts in orientation toward the global economy they entail that the new imperialist structure relied (Panitch and Gindin, 2012).

The US entered into a trade deficit, which in 1971 was the first such deficit since 1871, as imports grew about 25 percent faster than exports during the decade of the 1960s (Burbach and Flynn, 1980). At this point there was no idea how far this imbalance could be extended and the US officials were almost unanimously seeking to stem its further growth (Panitch and Gindin, 2004). Agricultural trade was not declining and would in fact continue to expand through the 1970s. Manufacturing exports, on the contrary, were declining as the policies of the US led to restructuring of the global division of labor, in part through cheap food exports.

One of the consequences of the US's success in Europe through the Marshall Plan and other early success at reconstructing the global market, such as Japan and Korea, was that these nations now presented an increasing level of competition (Brenner, 2000). A USDA study that was ordered by the Nixon administration to study the European agricultural markets raised two major concerns. First, it flagged the protective trade barriers of the European countries set up to keep overly competitive US exports out, which had caused a 15 percent reduction in US agricultural exports to Europe between 1966 and 1969 (Burbach and Flynn, 1980, p. 53). These were part of the 1957 Common Agricultural Policy (CAP), which the US had supported under the logic of a desire to unite Europe and breakdown the barriers to trade and capital flows around the continent. Second, it noted the impact of Western European governments subsidized their grain exports to offset the prices of the US. Together the USDA report estimated that the relaxation of the European and Japanese trade barriers could net an $8 Billion dollar increase in US trade balance by the end of the 1970s (Burbach and Flynn, 1980, p. 53).

The shift that did occur was in the nature of US agricultural exports, as the amount of governmental funding for food aid programs declined from a 1971 high of $1.1 billion of the total $7.6 billion in agricultural exports to only $863 million of the $17.6 billion in agricultural exports in 1973 (Morgan, 1979, p. 214). During the 1960s the US accounted for more than 90 percent of total world food aid and this figure dropped to 76.1 percent in 1970 and down to 58.0 percent in 1973 (Friedmann, 1982, p. 276). Aid as a percentage of US agricultural exports fell from more than 35 percent in the early 1960s to between 5 and 6 percent by 1970 (Friedmann, 1992, p. 276). As stated, the shift from aid to trade was one of the original stated goals of the PL-480 legislation: "to increase the consumption of US agricultural commodities in foreign countries, to improve the foreign relations of the US and for other proposes" (US Congress, 1964).

In a second Nixon era report, ordered by Kissinger and undertaken by the CIA, entitled *Potential Implications of Trends in World Population, Food Production and Climate,* it was outlined how the increasing reliance on US food, created in part through food aid and cheap grain surpluses, "portends an increase in US power and influence, especially vis-à-vis the poor, food-deficit countries"

(CIA, 1974; for a discussion of this report see Morgan, 1979, p. 344; Burbach and Flynn, 1980, p. 68). The report specifically mentions how

> [A]dequate incentives and inputs for farmers imply a major shift in the rural – urban terms of trade in most LDCs. If food prices paid to farmers go up, the urban poor cannot afford the increase. Either they get subsidized [imported] food, or starve...and the world's dependence on North American agriculture will continue to increase.
>
> CIA 1974, p. 24

This reveals the conscious effort to use the US's agriculture surpluses to grow the power base of the US, using its "levers of influence" (CIA, 1974, p. 34), through the penetrative and transformative capacities that industrial agriculture contained.

The US state had ample evidence to this transformative ability and how it could be used to aid US power. One example of this is evident in the way Cooley Loans, facilitated by USAID, operated and what their goals were. Cooley Loans were loans of local currencies generated by PL-480 food aid that were loaned to US businesses to use in the recipient nation. During the 1960s these loans amounted to $481.8 million, with all of it ending up in the hands of US firms. In India this was the tool used by US corporate interests to gain entry into the fertilizer and other agriculture sectors and break the barrier that had been in place to foreign investment (Wallerstein, 1980). Over one-third of Cooley loans in the Near East and South Asia were made to US fertilizer companies (Gaud, US Senate Testimony, 1965). These loans dropped off as these local currency sales were phased out in the 1970s, however the evidence clearly exhibits how agricultural commodities were used to penetrate, open up and transform developing nations.

Because PL 480 was jointly administered by the Departments of State and Agriculture, the developments in the early 1970s – the rise in prices, the increase in export sales, and the rapid reduction of grain surpluses – left the USDA much less interested in the program relative to the State Department. Also in the wake of Vietnam, there was emerging a domestic resistance to US 'imperialist' wars and programs. Into this void stepped the National Security Council and Henry Kissinger who according to USDA officials, increasingly became directly involved in the decision-making process regarding food aid (NACLA, 1975). In total $2.2 billion would be funneled into military and internal police projects during the 1970s through PL 480 counterpart funds (George, 1976, p. 206).

There was also a heightened use of food aid as a direct political tool – prime examples being in India and Chile.[3] However this directly political use of food aid was part of the overall project of transformation and a focus on it alone tends to lead to a diminished view of the market based social transformative effort of food aid, which represents the other main thrust of PL 480. Thwarting economic nationalism became one of the main goals guiding US foreign policy in an effort to construct a new form of imperialism through the construction of a global market (Panitch and Gindin, 2004, p. 17). Direct use of food as a tool in diplomatic affairs was far from new. The use of food to transform and alter the balance of class forces of other nations appears to go back to 1946 when US Assistant Secretary of State William Clayton withdrew US support for the US Relief and Reconstruction Administration due to its overly multilateral assignment of aid by economic need, instead of US strategic aims (Hudson, 2003).[4] Special Advisor to the President on Food Aid George McGovern wrote in 1961 that "Food for Peace is one instrument in a US policy which recognizes the need for economic development...[it] checks inflation of food prices that would otherwise result from development projects" (1964, p. 1). It is worth noting that the Argentine government of the time felt the same way and sought assurances that the US would do more to aid in development rather than simply dump food commodities (McGovern, 1964, p. 2). This penetration and transformation of domestic policy goals of other nations in-line with US interests became an important source of US power during this era.

In the 1970s this strategy of directly using food to force social transformation continued. Burbach and Flynn cited the growing discontent over the Vietnam War, and Congress's attempts to wind down the war, as reasons for a shift away from channels "vulnerable to the congressional scalpel" and toward executive level programs such as food aid as a diplomatic tool (1979, pp. 68–69).[5] Food

---

[3] Other examples include in 1967 when Egypt went to war with Israel all food aid and sales stopped and in 1972–73, a full 70 percent of PL 480 dollars purchased food for South Vietnam and Cambodia (Morgan, 1979, p. 338).

[4] The use of control over food supply could also be argued to be one of the bases of the entire history of the US dating to the elimination of American Bison to displace native populations.

[5] This pressure would eventually lead to the indirect funding of US foreign policy aims through multilateral institutions- UN, World Bank, IMF and WTO- to further offer political cover and autonomy from purely domestic politics and as these have come under scrutiny this has been giving way to a new form of financial control through complex and global financial market development. These transformations are given precise detail in Panitch and Gindin (2012) and together represent the move to delink political accountability from the process of imperial formation and maintenance.

aid was seen as a means to keep consumer prices down in Vietnam and thereby allow more government resources to go into the war effort, as well as the fact that food aid would help polish the damaged image the US was getting from the Vietnam War (Ahlburg, 2008, p. 116, 124). By offering flexible funding, the use of food aid under PL 480 became a powerful weapon for the executive to counterbalance policy shifts emerging out of domestic concerns. The president was authorized in the early 1970s to spend up to $1.9 billion under Title I and $660 million under Title II by borrowing from the CCC, just as Congress, responding to growing domestic opposition to the Vietnam War, was looking to reign in the aggressive US foreign policy (Burbach and Flynn, 1979, p. 69).

In India and Pakistan, food aid was also used as a carrot to pressure governments toward change in an industrial developmental direction (Ahlburg, 2008; Burbach and Flynn, 1979; Morgan, 1979). This increase in pressure applied by the US and the policy changes that underlie them were more accurately understood as shifts in orientation rather than complete changes s due to an alleged crisis of the hegemonic order. They clearly continue and extend the same stated goals that initially launched PL-480 and possibly go back to the early USDA foreign trade promotion of the 19th Century. These were added to and expanded through counter-part funds and the Alliance for Progress. However the roots of the approach a traceable back to Agricultural Secretary Wallace, as well as the open door policy.

Another example of food aid used as a blunt weapon was in Chile in the 1970s. US food aid almost immediately stopped after the election of Allende in 1970. Chile had been one of the countries whose reliance on food importation had been growing as it sought to develop its industrial capacities. Prior to Allende's election Chile had been importing almost a third of its wheat requirements- between 380,000 and 600,000 tons per year (Morgan, 1979, p. 339). After his election, the US's share of that importation dropped to 8,000 tons in 1971–2, then just two years later when the military junta of Pinochet took control of the country the US would send over 600,000 tons of wheat to Chile after working to secure a credit line from the CCC for the new dictatorship (Morgan, 1979, p. 341). Public outcry over the US's role in the coup led to a congressional ceiling on economic assistance to Chile of $25 million and the cutting of military aid altogether. The administration circumvented this by using PL 480 to get food to Chile, generating counterpart funds to aid the Chilean military in the purchasing of US weapons (Burbach and Flynn, 1979, pp. 70–1).

Similarly, the US used food aid to prop up Egypt's Sadat by reopening PL 480 assistance to Egypt in exchange for Sadat's participation in Kissinger's Middle

East peace plan in 1974. This produced counterpart funds that were used to aid regional stability by financing covert and overt operations. In South Korea we also see this same use of food aid to prop up dictatorships that then use the state to reorganize the domestic balance of class forces. South Korea not only received large amounts of food aid to maintain the US aligned Park dictatorship but it also saw one of the first uses of food aid to limit the exports of textiles to the US. The food aid "allowed the government to maintain low grain prices to hold down industrial wages", which allowed important textile exports fueled by labor transfers from the countryside allowing integration into US markets (McMichael, 2004, pp. 55–6). All of These more overtly political uses of food aid, however, should be understood as part and parcel of US goals of promoting expanded global capitalism.

The blackmail politics should be properly understood as serving the same goals as the seemingly more benign and seemingly separate economic means. In fact, these two aspects of development elucidate the connections between the state and the market in American global leadership. Food is no more or no less a weapon when it is used as a lever to force other nations to respond than when food aid is used to alter the balance of class forces by transforming the social relations and aligning the goals of development and industrialization of this nation with the US construction of a global market. Once the connections between states and markets are recognizable, the unity of these often bifurcated forces of food as a blunt weapon and as development policy tool. Political uses of aid augment rather than replace the market transformative influence.

This connection between these two approachs was confirmed in a longitudinal study of the policy drives behind food aid revealed "[w]hile humanitarian concerns are central to food aid donations for disaster relief, a significant portion of bilateral program food aid and project food aid were motivated by both political and economic interests of the donors" (Awokuse, 2011, p. 2). The goal as it emerged the projection of US 'green power'; "from the Marshall plan through the Third World Green Revolution, the US state encouraged international agribusiness with export credits and counterpart funds designed to universalize the American farming and dietary models" (McMichael, 2009, pp. 145–6). Universalization of the agro-industrial project as a strategy runs through the entire period.

An investigation of the uses of food aid reveals how it portends the reorientation towards a new informal US imperial rule "characterized by the penetration of borders, not their dissolution...[and] the reconstitution of states as integral elements of an informal American empire" (Panitch and Gindin, 2004, p. 17). US agricultural strength and its use as a significant tool in the construction of a global empire mostly took an *economic* form, thus it is depoliticized as part and parcel of the very process of imperial expansion.[6]

In 1973, National Security Adviser Henry Kissinger ordered a study led by the Council on International Economic Policy (CIEP) along with OMB, who were responsible for the budget aspects (Gelb and Lake, 1975). This study involved a high-level Food Policy Committee under Kenneth Rush; Deputy Secretary of State and later economic counselor to Nixon; an Assistant Secretary-level food aid group under Dolph Bridgewater of OMB, with representatives of Agriculture, State, Treasury, and NSC on staff; and the US Coordinator for the upcoming World Food Conference, Ambassador Edwin M. Martian. There was division among this group over their main concerns, as well as, on the immediate and long-term goals of food policy. Treasury Secretary Schultz was concerned about the balance-of-payments problems and "saw food exports for cash as a major way to build up the credit side of the ledger" (Gelb and Lake, 1975, p. 179). Schultz and Kissinger agreed that rising food costs in LDC's could be used as a lever on OPEC. Part of this latter goal required the opposition to the IMF plan to recycle OPEC petrodollars back to LDC's through long-term low-interest loans, instead hoping to squeeze LDC's into putting pressure on OPEC and thereby rolling back oil prices for the long run. This policy emerged after there occurred a shift in Kissinger's orientation – which Gelb and Lake referred to as the "conversion of Henry Kissinger" – after a meeting with Hubert Humphrey, Robert MacNamara and Peter Peterson (1975, pp. 179–81). From here out he put forward a new perspective based on the inclusion of food in the overall discussion of a general raw materials shortage, which required the US to step up food aid, the IFI's to increase loans and aid the LDC's to increase resource extraction and international exchange, and OPEC to expand output.

Opposition to Kissinger's new proposals came from the Treasury, which was worried about the inflationary effects of food aid exports. Alan Greenspan, then head of CEA, along with the Director of OMB Roy Ash, was concerned about the budgetary increase that the plan would require. The compromise worked out included both Kissinger's goals to create a hegemonic position for the US overcoming the resource shortage by leading the way through an increase in food production, aid, and trade, which would also increase world

---

6 This is used and put in italics to highlight the manner by which economic forces are discussed and promoted as outside of the political realm in neo-classical ideology. This is a formal and not substantial distinction and the point of a neo-marxist political economic analysis is to highlight the fiction of this separation and how the ideology of this separation is produced and what it does to the social formation and the class structure.

economic interdependence. It would also achieve Agricultural Secretary Butz's desire to use private sources for US grain overproduction storage and dispersal as well as his goal to get the poorer countries to do some "belt-tightening" (Gelb and Lake, 1975, p. 182).

In this we see the policy debates and institutional struggles occurring as agencies sought a means to deal with the economic crisis through the projection of US power to restructure the world market. In turn, it elucidates the relative autonomy between the different branches of government involved and how this relative autonomy prevented policy decisions that were too short sighted and narrowly focused. The overall structure that emerged sought to aid as many divergent interests as possible without harming the overall goal of economic integration behind US leadership. This structure would serve as one of the backbones for the transformations that would come to be known as neoliberal globalization.

The congressional side also witnessed some slight shifts in agricultural policy orientation in the 1970s, emerging from the coming to fruition of larger international policy goals. With food and agriculture increasing in importance as an international issue, there was a move away from the usually dominant Senate Agriculture Committee and Agricultural Appropriations Subcommittee toward the inclusion of the House Committee on International Relations and the Senate Committee on Foreign Relations into agricultural policy debates (Frankel et al., 1979, p. 124). The marriage of the farm bloc with the trade and military institutions would produce the development project, debt crisis, and globalization in the coming decades.

The growth of US agricultural exports was further facilitated by the 1973 Farm Bill, which removed the production constraints that had been put in place during the New Deal and also encouraged commercial exports. The acres placed under conservation contracts declined from 28.6 million in 1960 steadily downward, until the last land left the reserve in 1972 (USDA, 1984, p. 29). The decline of land set-asides came out of shifts in farm policy in the 1970 Agricultural Act. These shifts represent the coming to fruition of Secretary Wallace's goals during the New Deal era to seek to construct foreign markets to eventually relieve the need for production controls (see Chapter 6). Congress was responded to the rise in exports, seen as finally able to offset the tendency to overproduce. To accomplish this Congress was relaxing planting restrictions by replacing acreage diversions on specific crops with a general set aside. In this way, farmers could decrease their acreage of those crops that tended to be overproduced and increase the acreage of those that could be exported. This reorientation was furthered through the 1973 Food and Agriculture Act that set up a dual system of target prices, replacing price supports and only kicking in when market prices fell below target levels, further encouraging international trade (USDA, 1984, pp. 29–32).

When the Commodity Futures Trading Committee in 1974 was created, through an amendment to the 1936 Commodity Exchange Act, this also set in motion the process of financial liberalization and innovation facilitating the increases in global agricultural trade (Panitch and Gindin, 2012). This was closely related to what Seabrooke cogently called the "diffusion of power through the dollar" after the breakup of the Bretton Woods exchange rate system but very much part and parcel of the dollar based credit expansion that succeeded it. (2001, p. 68). The Chicago Mercantile Exchange was central to the development of financial derivative markets and importantly for globalization, a futures market in currencies, beginning in 1971 (Panitch and Gindin, 2012, pp. 149–51; FN 16, p. 349). In the early 1970s market innovation, based on already existing links between Chicago Mercantile agricultural commodities traders and foreign currency traders was in facilitating new ways for the global expansion of financial capital with the state actively aiding in the creation of these new forms of finance to enable an expanded global market. The ramifications of these changes on agriculture going forward were significant and dramatic.

The very successful project of agro-industrialization in the US had transformed food production by bringing labor input in agriculture down by 70 points by the early 1970s relative to 1948, while output increased from a scale of 100 in 1948 to 200 by 1979 (USDA, 1984, pp. 6–9). Agricultural output even continued to show compound annual growth right through the supposed crisis periods of the 1970s and 1980s – with growth rates doubling in the 1970s over the decade of the 1960s and increasing through the first half of the 1980s (USDA, 1984, p. 5). Concurrently, right through the period of the crisis, the US continued to increase its percent of total world exports in food crops. For example, US cereal exports as a percentage of total exports in the last few years of the 1960s and early years of the 1970s was around 35 percent but in the decade that followed US percent of cereal exports increased to 47 percent (USDA, 1984).

These productivity and export gains occurred during a period of falling direct payments by the government, with payments declining sharply after 1972 and not rising back up until the mid-1980s (USDA, 1984, p. 49, Table 3–9). Rather than a crisis of US agricultural hegemony, there was a nearly unprecedented expansion of productivity gains and exports all while US agricultural trade expanded from under 20 billion dollars in the late 1960s and early 1970s to over $80 billion by the end of the decade (Figure 7 USDA, 2011).

The US took an offensive on lowering agricultural trade barriers in 1973 at the third round of GATT negotiations. Agriculture was the key issue on the

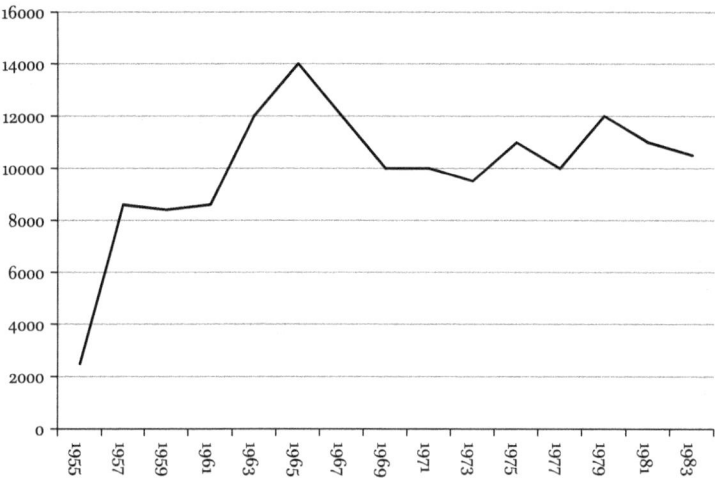

FIGURE 7   *Value of commodity exports under USDA: 1960–1985*
SOURCE USDA 1990

agenda for US negotiators, one of whom put it succinctly, "some sort of breakthrough on agriculture is a 'sin qua non' for the agreement" (quoted in Burbach and Flynn, 1980: 54). The basis of the US's position was that the Europeans were subsidizing their less efficient agriculture and that the best route for all was to let the market regulate through comparative advantage and 'free trade'.

The Trade Act of 1974 introduced key changes in the escape clause provision, the antidumping and countervailing duty laws, and the reauthorization of presidential fast-track authority. These changes shifted power from Congress to the executive branch of government; "the result was that authority over protectionist measures was delegated to the administration" (Chorev, 2007, p. 668). As Chorev (2007, p. 673) argued:

> In the 1970s and 1980s heightened protectionist sentiments did not lead to a parallel increase in traditional protectionist action. Instead, the government offered a restrained kind of intervention. This was possible because the new institutional arrangements introduced in 1974, which shifted decision-making authority from Congress to the Administration, changed the 'weight' of competing factors ... Congress, the main conveyer of domestic factors, was no longer the central site of decision-making. In the Administration, in turn, the position of the Department of State, STR, CIEP, and Treasury, the official carriers of international factors, prevailed over the position of the Departments of Commerce and Labor.

The engagement of the US state to prevent a return to protectionist policies reveals its commitment to the goal of world market construction.

This drive to reconstruct the global market through the push to transfer authority onto the executive actually goes back to the 1962 Trade Expansion Act (Cohen, Paul and Blecker, 1996, p. 142). This act created the position of the president's Special Representative for Trade negotiations (STR) and the Trade act of 1974 made the STR a statutory position, after Nixon's efforts to weaken it (Destler, 1995, p. 105).[7] The 1979 Trade Act added to this process of increasing the executive ability to both reduce domestic trade barriers and to push export barriers. In addition, Section 201 of the Act placed domestic relief authority in the hands of the President upon recommendation by the International Trade Commission, which was consistent with the GATT's escape clause (Cohen et al., 1996, p. 143). Under Section 201 agricultural producers were granted greater access to relief due to the ability of the Secretary of Agriculture to recommend ITC investigation (Cohen et al., 1996, p. 145). Section 301 of the 1974 Trade Act also increased the capacity of the USTR to retaliate against foreign trade policies that hurt US imports. The Export Administration Act of 1979 (EAA) also increased the executive's authority to control exports. President Carter used this act to prohibit grain exports to the Soviets in 1979. Thus, Cohen, Paul and Blecker (1996) summarize US trade policy as a two-fold approach that is occasionally contradictory:

> On the one hand, the economist's faith in the benefits of free trade has led to laws liberalizing the flow of imports to the United States. On the other hand, the political need to respond to domestic producers and workers injured by imports has led to laws restricting the flow of imports…these laws provide relief to uncompetitive industries as a way of buying off their opposition to free trade policies generally (p. 146).

Out of these contradictory purposes Congress acted throughout the 1970s to transfer authority to the executive, thereby granting themselves some political cover from the fallout over the shifts in the social relations as international concerns began to trump domestic ones and the Tokyo Round of GATT talks

---

7 Nixon's secretary of Commerce, Maurice H. Stans, made a strong push in 1969 to take over trade coordination, which was blocked by congress due particularly to agricultural interest group pressure. Again in 1971 Nixon's newly created Council for International Economic Policy head, Peter M. Flanigan moved to have the STR incorporated into the CIEP. And again, Congress blocked this move out of fear of the STR losing its perceived non-partisan status (Destler, 1995: 108).

faltered and made little gains for US interests. Destler claimed, "Congress continued to respond to new trade policy demands by shifting the basic pressure and responsibility onto the president" (1995, p. 17). The executive, with its enhanced trade policy strength through the STR, also acted to prop up those industries harmed by liberalization: "the office showed greater sensitivity to protection-seeking forces than did, say, the State Department or the Council of Economic Advisers" (Destler, 1995, p. 106).[8]

As the complexity of issues surrounding agricultural policy began to converge with export policy and domestic supply concerns, in the late 1960's- early 1970's reinvigorated push towards international trade and a shift towards interagency agricultural policy emerged around long-term polices of economic integration. This increased the influence of some agencies that once played only marginal roles in agricultural policy: the State Department's Bureau of Economic and Commercial Affairs expanded the size of its food policy division and the Treasury hired Hal Worthington,[9] a specialist in foreign agricultural affairs, who built up a team in the Treasury to study how the increasing global interconnections of food impacted prices and currencies (Hopkins, 1980, p. 112). Similar expansions in the size and involvement in agricultural policy occurred in the Office of Management and Budget, National Security Council, and the Council of Economic Advisors (Hopkins, 1980, p. 112). All told the shift in institutional strength is quite telling of the overall goal of US agricultural policy going forward as focusing less on the appeasement of domestic forces, especially any residual farming concerns, and more about the overall way to use agriculture to restructure other economies in an effort to rebuild a world market and integrate economies. However there isn't sufficient evidence to claim that this was a major policy shift or turning point, in fact there is evidence to the contrary. Instead it was part of the evolution of institutional development toward capitalist expansion through internationalization.

---

8   Section 241 of the Trade Expansion Act of 1962 established two roles for this new trade official: 'chief representative' of the United States in trade negotiations and as chairman of the 'interagency trade organization' which managed these negotiations for the president. The act did not specify the location of staff of this position; however, Kennedy insisted that he have the leeway to define this himself and did so through Executive Order 11075 on January 15 1963, which placed the new unit within the Executive Office (Destler, 1995, p. 107).

9   As Hopkins outlined, "Worthington was a former official in both the Agriculture and State Departments and had just completed the 'Flannigan' report for the Nixon administration, the major background analysis of possible benefits from lower trade barriers written as a prelude to negotiations on agricultural tariffs and non-tariff barriers in the trade talks of the MTN" (p. 199).

The Flannigan Report, published in 1973, was one major government study of trade policy options going forward. Its conclusions presented several different trade liberalization paths forward and was import in that it was "offering direction for US negotiators in the upcoming trade talks that centered on pushing for full liberalization of the grain-feed-livestock sector, commodity-by-commodity agreements for other agricultural products to ensure American access to foreign markets, and linked negotiations on monetary, industrial, and agricultural issues" (FAS, 1973, p. 30). The Flannigan Report outlined benefits from such an approach as "threefold: a substantial improvement in the balance of payments; an important reduction in government expenditure; and a significant increase in farm income" (FAS, 1973, p. 10). However, rather than the more traditional approach, the report recommended a commodities agreement. Again though, not the usual commodities agreement, not one "limited to a single commodity which seeks to rig international prices at artificially high levels....[instead] the agreement we foresee could cover a family of commodities (FAS, 1973, p. 33).

Out of this report emerged the goal to use GATT to move toward complete market orientation on a range of interconnected commodities which the US held an advantage. The leverage the FAS recommended the US use to achieve its goals was to threaten to move for "the withdrawal of the United States from GATT and the return of its import duties to much more protective levels" (FAS, 1973, p. 33). The FAS was also well aware of the fiscal burden and placed the reduction of farm support payments at the center of its strategy. Although it was cautious not to do so to the extent it would undermine the US competitive advantage in agricultural exports (FAS, 1973, p. 141). The report suggested product by product agreements "for other politically or economically sensitive commodities should be entered into for whatever specific concessions would be meaningful for the commodities involved... [as this would keep producers of such goods]...in the ranks of supporters of trade liberalization" and it would be done without the economically destabilizing removal of domestic commodity supports (FAS, 1973, p. 28).

At this point the US policies of trade liberalization and its support for protectionist policies in both Japan and Europe began to collide, therefore "the political advantages of European and Japanese protection in the agro-food sector had become an economic liability for profitability in the US agro-food sector" (Essex, 2005, p. 92). What emerged would be a strengthening of the former as "the earliest stirrings of proto-neoliberalism could be seen in relevant state institutions and policies" (Essex, 2005, p. 92). Yet the shift was based on years of groundwork laying out the precursors and pushing for agro-trade liberalization. Neoliberal policies would become dominant in US state institutional orientation to a degree not seen before, as the shift towards the institutions and aspects of institutions that could facilitate these goals grew relative to others, all emerging out of agricultural policy and the institutional work that had been previously done. As Essex (2005, pp. 110–111) accurately summarized:

> The US Department of Agriculture, along with USTR and the broader US executive, has thoroughly adopted the neoliberal ideology of free trade and made it an institutional pillar within long-term policy strategies. This has been achieved through the use of USDA as a strategy in a state project of neoliberalization, and as a site for neoliberal rollout through department restructuring, research and development initiatives, and even personnel turnover, through US farm policy, written by legislators often beholden to narrow local interests, has not always been on board. It has encountered resistance in the form of environmental and labor movement opposition, and the recalcitrance of certain factions of agro-food capital (such as the sugar and processed sweetener industry), all of which have shaped the character, implementation, and transformation of neoliberalism within and through the US state, which shapes processes of neoliberalization in the international state system, which in turn depends largely on the success of efforts to institutionalize and legitimate free trade.

The new trade program would need to rely on an increase in executive authority to thwart domestic input. These shifts in state policy focus, away from domestic stability towards an international orientation, gradually restricted the political influence of protectionist industries through this concomitant shift from Congress to the Executive, and then to expanding trade regimes. Therefore, this process not only changed the relative political influence of various competing groups, but transformed the very nature of politics (Chorev, 2007, p. 12). Thus, "the institutional project of globalization entails a process of depoliticization, where bureaucratic orientation and structural constraints dominate the process of decision making, at the expense of public debates and political deliberations" (Chorev, 2007, p. 12). This weakening of political influence of various constituencies while strengthening the power of the executive and the institutional capacities to act toward liberalization and integration results from these very processes of institutional realignment.[10]

Increasingly it was the rules set up by the GATT and agreed upon by the President, passed on an up or down vote due to the Fast-Track authority, that

---

10   This process was presciently and cogently outlined by Poulantzas (1978).

came to serve as the new policy direction of the state. Cut out of the discussion were domestic agricultural groups whose concerns were bought off by the contracts large agro-businesses received and who now were dominant in "farmers' organizations". As Chorev stated, "the legalization of the decision-making process would render the political influence of protectionists less determinant of the final outcome" (2007, p. 12). Thus, the domestic protectionist agricultural interests were being defeated not through loss of political pull but through the establishment of new rules and new ways to codify the rules.

This is part of the process of the "New Constitutionalism" (Gill, 1998) which involved an end-run around the democratic processes that once served at the very least as a legitimation check on policies. This comes through the long-term trend of increasing market mediation of social processes witnessed in specific policy shifts. The shifts in policy and the increase in the use of rules reveal the manner in which the state depoliticized the economy. However rather than seeing these as abrupt changes forced by a hegemonic crisis, this in fact was the outcome of the long-term projects of agro-industrialization and the rebuilding of the world market through neoliberal globalization.

Harvesting Free Trade

As the rate of manufactured imports in the US rose in value – from less than 14 percent in 1969 to 38 percent in 1979 – there emerged a dramatic rise in the trade deficit (Ferguson and Rogers, 1981, p. 10). This caused America's growing balance of payments deficiencies. The increasing trade deficit was somewhat offset by Japan and Europe increasing their agricultural import dependence between 1970 and 1999 from 21 to 42 percent for Japan and 18 to 33 percent for Europe, the US was able to use its agricultural strength to impact the balance of class forces in Europe and Japan by increasing imports into these regions, forcing them to shift policy to influence the direction of development (USDA, 1999). Europe eventually transformed much of its agricultural sector in an effort to challenge the US in some international markets and to stabilize their domestic politics that were set asunder by the social dislocation of increasing industrial development.

The increase in US agricultural export produced a shift towards the food importation dependency in much of the third world. The third world's percentage of total wheat imports rose from 10 percent in the 1950s to 57 percent in the 1980s (McMichael, 2000: 132). The developing countries' total food imports "rose from being practically non-existent...to taking almost half of the world imports in 1971- and at their peak in 1978, they bought 78 per cent of American wheat exports" (Friedmann, 1990: 20). Altogether, US agricultural exports to developing countries increased from $2 billion in 1970 to over $8 billion by 1975, or over a fourfold increase (Hopkins, 1980: 13). These shifts caused transformations in the source and consumption patterns of the developing world and by the early 1970's 26 percent of all cereal consumption in the developing world was from imported wheat; a shift of 69 percent in a decade (Friedmann, 1990: 21). Furthermore, total world cereal importation would triple between 1960 and 1980 (FAO, 2000). In Mexico the number of landless increased from 1.5 to 14 million between 1950 and 1979, while in El Salvador the proportion of the population without land grew from 12 percent to 41 percent between 1961 and 1975 (Burbach and Flynn, 1980:147). "The international division of labor had been remade if not reversed" by 1980, as "the third world's exports included more manufactured goods than raw materials and the first world was exporting 36% more primary commodities ...[while] the Third world share of agricultural exports fell from 53 to 31 percent between 1950 and 1980" (McMichael, 2003, p. 51). Furthermore, in the global south TNCs and international banks began a major push into the region with investment in the south growing at a rate of 13.8% per year in the 1970s as firms from the global north increased their investments from $3.7 billion in 1970 to $13.5 billion by 1979 (Sussman, 1987:304). The increase in bank lending from OECD based firms between 1970 and 1978 increased from 15.4% to 27.7% of all net financial flows to 62 developing countries and these investments ended up mainly stimulating industrial production (Sussman, 1987:305). The investment in agriculture in the global south also grew, representing the US and other northern firm's investments that overwhelmingly went to just three crops – tea, coffee, and cocoa – all for export (Sussman, 1987:305). There was also a rapid expansion of foreign agribusiness investment in food processing industries in Latin America; the number of TNCs food processing subsidiaries in the region more than tripled between 1960 and 1975 (Burbach and Flynn, 1980, p. 108). Thus the flow of funds went to investment in industrial production or export crops facilitated by the increase in US food imports supplanting domestic food sources. This reorientation toward export orientation occurred not out of a crisis during the conjuncture but out of the long process of US agro-industrial development made possible through food aid.

The general drive towards a global economic reorientation of agriculture began to clash with the domestic remnants of the process of agricultural change- namely the states support for some farms and other aspects of the economy (manufacturing), that had not kept pace with the productivity gains of the most advanced sectors. The shifts in state policy came to reflect the increased favoring of the global reorientation and the resulting disruptions in the economy should not be seen as the failure of the US or the loss of its hegemony but as a rescaling of its influence.

Through this process and during the entire post-World War II era the US exported its agricultural production model more widely, using its agricultural surpluses and higher levels of agricultural productivity growth to alter the social relations in the developing world (Araghi, 1995, p. 354). There was also an increased effort to stimulate the agro-industrial development project around the world. The export of fertilizer and agricultural production and food processing techniques as part of what became known as the *green revolution* to parts of the developing world transformed subsistence agriculture into an export oriented, technological, and FDI dependent agri-business model. As a result, world fertilizer consumption doubled and Latin America fertilizer consumption more than tripled between 1965 and 1975, while the number of tractors used in agriculture increased globally by 80 percent and in Latin American by 75 percent (UNFAO, 2000; Burbach and Flynn, 1980, p. 84). In 1975 this became more overt as the International Development and Food Assistance Act sought to connect food aid with domestic agricultural development assistance (Wallerstein, 980, p. 49; Panitch and Gindin, 2005).

These changes in the developing world brought about an increase in US agro-capital penetration. In Brazil, Chase Manhattan invested over $100 million into soybean production; with Brazilian soybean production increasing by 8–12 percent per year in the 1970s (Burbach and Flynn, 1980, p. 133). The increase in capital investment was gigantic, with commercial bank lending to the global south increasing by 4,400 percent between 1972 and 1981 (Araghi, 2003, p. 150). These purchases were also made possible by USAID assistance and guidance towards types of contract farming and technology transfers more suited to export orientated growth models (Watts, 1996, p. 151). As Wood documents, the Euromarket banks facing domestic stagflation looked increasingly to the developing nations to loan out capital in an effort to maintain high interest rates (Wood, 1980). As a Development Assistance Committee report in 1980 claimed it was "the only way to expand business in the face of slackening domestic credit demand and increased competition among banks" (DAC Review, 1980, p. 161). It wasn't just European banks that saw an opportunity and took it, from the mid-1970s US banks made more profits overseas than on their domestic operations, with many making twice as much outside the US as with in it (Wood, 1980, p. 81). It was also innovations in financial services and state regulations that facilitated this move toward the south by banks in the 1970s (Wood, 1986, p. 80; Panitch and Gindin, 2012).

An important aspect of the export of the 'green revolution' is the role of individual states. The rise of what Araghi called *agrarian welfare states* during the export substitution development era of the post-Second World War global south- to thwart socialist/nationalist peasant movements- was dismantled during the 1970's (2003, p. 150). Coming to replace it was an export-oriented model based on the importation of cheap agro-industrially produced food commodities and 'green technology' agriculture as developing nations *"replicated and modernized* the US model of state organized agrofood production model" (Friedmann, 2004, p. 46, emphasis in original). One of the countries to fully implement this agricultural development path is Brazil. Over the course of the 15 years between 1964 and 1979 Brazilian agriculture received between one-fourth and one-third of total state credit, and in 1979 alone it benefited from $18 billion in credit and loans from the state, with the state-owned Banco do Brasil as the largest agricultural lender in the world (Burbach and Flynn, 1980, p. 97). The transformative capacities of this capital lies in its misdistribution: only 28 percent of all producers received rural credit and "three of Brazil's major staple crops (black beans, manioc and maize) received only 13 percent of government-subsidized credit from 1970 to 1977, while huge amounts of credit were channeled to export production" (Burbach and Flynn, 1980, p. 104). The shift in the developing world away from primary commodities toward manufacturing – being a much slower process beginning in the 1960's but would only completely take hold in the 1990s with the aid of the multilateral trade organizations- was directly facilitated by the cheap food imports coming out of the US, which were predicated on the aid of the 1950s and 1960s, which were possible because of the state intervention into agriculture in the US during the early part of the century (Friedmann, 1990; Araghi, 1995; McMichael, 2004).

Across the Global South the ratio of food imports to food exports increased from 50 percent in 1955–1960 to 80 percent by 1980 (Araghi, 2003, p. 148). The above data seems to call into question the notion that the US's shift toward a global capitalist orientation came about in the 1970's with a new 'food order' due to the failures and general crisis of the US economic model or of a decline in its hegemonic leadership role. Instead, it confirms that it was the process of intensive capitalist development, first domestically and later internationally, through the intervention of the US state in partner with the governments of other nations outside the US, initiating institutional growth and reconfiguration that reorientated agriculture and by extension the whole of the economy towards highly productive and market mediated systems altering the once distinct social relations across the globe. By the end of the decade, a dramatically larger portion of the world's population was eating at the same globally connected and capitalist market mediated trough. Moreover, it is out of these changes and the interconnections they imbued that the whole process of globalization can be traced. Even the USDA recognized the changes in the 1970's as coming out of the 1960's, as they state it was "more of a shift in emphasis than a major departure from the policies of the 1960's" (USDA, 1984, p. 27).

In the US the drive toward corporate concentration and financialization were increasingly informing the development of the agricultural sector of the economy. The inelasticity of food renders value-added product differentiation as a key site of market expansion. These means of market expansion opened themselves up to financial penetration to an increasing degree through the 1970s and into the 1980s (Marsden and Whatmore, 1994). These changes "enabled industrial capital to overcome many of the rigidities associated with exploiting farm-based activity and established revised economic and social parameters for the regulation and flow of capital and technology" (Marsden and Whatmore, 1994, p. 109). These changes altered the influence of finance over agriculture because "this structure ties the 'business-oriented' farmer more directly to the financial/technological fix" (Marsden and Whatmore, 1994, p. 123).

From the role of the extension services and agricultural research universities in the application of scientific and industrial rationality to agriculture, to the role of the Volker Shock (the rapid rise of interest rates in the late 1970s under Treasury Secretary Volker) in applying added pressure to farmers to either streamline with the needs of industrial agri-capital or perish, we witness the institutional development that facilitated and pushed the transition. As demonstrated in the previous chapters, the New Deal AAA programs were aimed not only at helping struggling farmers or even at simply trying to stabilize agricultural markets, but also to remake the sector into one more malleable to the needs of investment capital. The state though, it must be noted, did this while also needing to maintain legitimate authority which was accomplished by masking the transitionary advance and pressure in the form of popular struggles between competing interests. Thus, it subordinates agrarian resistance to the needs of capital by first appearing to bend to the demands of this resistance before using state power to create outcomes more aligned with the needs of capital in the form of commodification and export orientation.[11]

In the developing world the 1980s brought the debt crisis as the loans taken out to facilitate industrial development saw their interest rates rise precipitously. Developing Nations then turned to IFIs for bailouts and loans to maintain payments to private banks, which meant structural adjustments or a reduction of state support and a turn toward the international market. Having already laid the groundwork for globalization, the next step was for the full integration into a capitalist world market under the guise of a continued US Imperial regime through the WTO.

---

11   On social movement co-optation along these lines see Piven and Cloward (1977).

The Food Regimes Approach

The food regime approach registers the rising European and NIC challenge to US agricultural dominance as a failure of not only the US agricultural policy but of the US's hegemonic position. This fails to properly grasp what exactly US hegemony rests on, which is the construction of a global capitalist market whose centrifugal force further transforms and constructs the market and with it economies around the globe. The institutional configuration of legitimation for liberalization shifted away from its initial support of protectionist agricultural policies; similar to how the New Deal policies planted the seed of its own destruction, which was a central part of the original policy (see Chapter 6). The growth of agricultural export centers in the EC and the NICs occurred not through the failure of the US project but its success at transforming those nations. By first reconstructing and reorienting these countries toward the international market, and second, acting through them to extend the imperial reach and reconstruct the rest of the world with their active assistance, the US was able to build the global market (Panitch and Gindin, 2004).

Investigating what the approach deems the 'post-war food regime',[12] we see that they do highlight the US's use of food aid to remake the global landscape and to promote the growth of the world market. In this the approach uncovered the connections between expanding capitalist markets, transformations into market mediated social forms, and the role of state policies to these ends (Friedmann, 1993). It was a major breakthrough in understanding agriculture's role in constructing the global market, the US' leadership role through the use of food aid, and the project of transforming developing nations through state led agro-developmental processes. Pritchard (2009) summarized the second food regime, running roughly from the end of World War II through to the mid-1970s, thusly:

> The post-1945 food regime was established around the ability of the US to subsidize and export large agricultural surpluses, thereby maintaining harmony within domestic farm constituencies and furthering diplomatic aims abroad. The Marshall Plan and subsequent food aid legislation created sizeable external markets for US agriculture, and in the process, entrenched food import dependency among many newly decolonized nations (p. 299).

---

12 Subsequent iterations of the approach have labeled the same era the 'the surplus regime, 1947–72' (Friedmann, 1993), 'the mercantile-industrial food regime' (Friedmann, 2004), and the 'US-centered intensive food regime' (McMichael, 2013).

This understanding offers many novel insights, most fundamentally the notion that food aid was part of the process of constructing markets by harmonizing social relations. The approach outlined the role of US state policies in the "transformation of self-sufficient agrarian populations into mass consumers of commercial food" (Friedmann, 1982, p. S267).

However, there are a few problems and misconceptions that both limit the effectiveness of the regime approach and prevent further developments. One such limitation comes from the focusing on stable and discrete forms of agrarian relationships that inform the overall global economy. The approach contains shortcomings with regards to transitions between 'regimes' which lead to the overlooking of consistent goals, policies and institutional arrangements that overlap multiple 'regimes'. McMichael made the claim that the approach was in part based in "conceptualizing key historical contradictions in particular food regimes that produce crisis, transformation and transition" (2009, p. 140). However, it is unclear as to whether the crises identified are a result of the real world contradictions of socio-economic forces or are merely identifiable through the lens of looking for "stable set[s] of relationships through which the food regime articulated with periods of capital accumulation" (McMichael, 2009, pp. 134–4). This is most evident in the problems related to the approach's understanding of the 1970s crisis and the claim that it brought about the end of one 'food regime', which was claimed to be based in "neo-mercantilist state policies of protecting agriculture from the global market" (Friedmann, 2004).

In the food regimes literature the crisis of the 1970s is understood as having resulted from the contradictions of the system, which led to government intervention in a form that undermined the legitimating narrative of the order (Friedmann, 1987, 1989, 1993, 2004, 2005; McMichael, 1994). The *post-war food regime* is characterized as one based on state support for the development of agricultural production leading to over-production, with the US taking a lead role in these developments. Friedmann and McMichael (1989) describe the regime:

> The second food regime is a rather more complex and contradictory set of relations of production and consumption rooted in unusually strong state protection and the organization of the world economy under US hegemony. As US hegemony has declined, the basic tension between nationally organized economies and transnational capital has been amplified. The only real drive identified towards an internationally linked agricultural market is in US food aid (p. 103).

Friedmann went so far as to re-label the regime the 'mercantile-industrial food regime' in an effort to emphasize its foundations in "state-protectionist policies" (2004, p. 240). She argued that "the defining features of the regime – government-held surplus agricultural commodities – were like a lake whose elevated level depended on the dam between the rival political blocs" (Friedmann, 2005, p. 132). McMichael has characterized the regime as one based on Ruggie's notion of "embedded liberalism", "where the national model of economic growth...was diffused across the expanding state system in the context of decolonization, informing development strategies of import-substitution in both industry and agriculture" (1994, p. 2). The defining feature of the regime is said to be centered in the disposal of US surplus commodities created by the New Deal interventions, so that food aid is seen as a system based on domestic concerns with overproduction (Friedmann, 1993; 2005). However, as shown above, liberalism was hardly ever embedded. From the very moment of the inter-war crisis in the global economy an effort was being put forward, most noticeable from the US, to rebuild that global economy. The embedding was part of the process of stabilizing the ruling order through temporary political reforms.

Within the regimes approach an issue arises around the claim of contradictory goals of building international trading partners and a general reorientation of economies towards the world market versus the claim of an 'embedded liberalism' based on state protection of domestic production from those same international markets. The regime is said to have ended due to a shift towards the type of international trade that emerges with the changes to the GATT, which is seen as undermining the regime. It is argued that the regime came to an end out of a crisis that emerged due to an end of US surpluses and a shift to trade instead of aid, as the state support and involvement retreated. Thus the end of the post-war food regime is claimed to be an abrupt change from state regulated agricultural production to enhanced market control as the "combination of the freedom of capital and the restrictions of trade" formed the axis of a contradiction (Friedmann, 1993, p. 36; see also Friedmann, 2004).

The food regimes approach posits that the post-war food regime collapsed in the 1970s as the US entered a crisis of its hegemonic role. This crisis resulted from the European and the New Agricultural Countries' successful reproduction of the US model of farming, which destabilized and ultimately undermined the US aid centered post-war food regime (Friedmann, 1982, 1990; Friedmann and McMichael, 1989; McMichael, 1990, 1994). As the 1970s rolled on it quickly became apparent that the political economy of the second food regime was in disarray, due to the rising costs of US farm subsidies and the emergence of new competition from the EU and some nations of the Global South. Complicating the situation was the emergence of the US-Soviet Détente, which allowed as one of its measures the sale of US wheat to the Soviet Union.

In 1972–3, the Soviet Union imported 18 million tons of US grain (Burbach and Flynn, 1980, p. 51; Friedmann, 1993; 2004).[13] Because of this sale and the decline in the US dollar, grain exports nearly doubled between 1972 and 1973 and total agricultural exports increased by 25 percent (see Figure 6) (USDA, 1984). This nearly wiped out US grain reserves and triggered a rapid rise in the global price of grain (USDA, 1984). Due to these factors, during the 1970s US agriculture entered what could be called its second golden age, as:

> Export demand continued to grow and prices for wheat, feed grains, rice, and cotton reached new highs between 1973–75. Net farm income soared to a record $34.4 billion in 1973 and remained at historically high levels for the next 2 to 3 years. Government payments to farmers fell to just $530 million in 1974, the lowest level (in current dollars) since 1955.
> USDA, 1984, p. 31

The destabilizing impact of the US-Soviet grain sales, Friedmann argued, "[w]ere so large that they precipitated a prolonged crisis of the post-war food regime" (1994, p. 258). Thus it is argued that the end of excess US food surpluses resulted in a major reduction of food aid which undermined the very basis of the existing food regime.

Due to these changes, Friedmann claimed, there was a "dramatic shift" in the early 1970s and that this shift "indicated a crisis in the strict sense" or a "turning point in the international order" emerging from the end of the "constantly reproduced American wheat surpluses, maintained on behalf of American farmers and disposed of through various subsidies centered on food aid" (Friedmann, 1982, p. S271). She goes on to claim that the success of the food aid programs in changing the nature of the receiving countries- how they had first been made food import dependent on the surpluses created by the US's continued increases in agricultural productivity- had made the programs redundant, and thus, had created a crisis of the entire prevailing order or food regime (1982, p. S271).

McMichael was clear that subsidies for crops appeared in the immediate post-war era, but "they did not seriously affect trade volumes until the 1970s",

---

[13] This 1972–1973 during the Nixon years was not the first to export grain to the Soviets; in 1963 Kennedy had authorized the sale of 4 million tons of wheat and flour. This was, in part made possible by changes to the Export Control Act in 1962 (See Morgan, 1979, pp. 161–3). The USSR grain sales were booms to private companies who made the actual grain sales to the USSR, which they kept secret in order to get federal subsidies tied to market prices, which remained low as long as the sales were secret.

as the subsidized US crops, in this view, were propped up in an effort to aid farmers and because of the political necessity created by agrarian movements (1997, p. 637). Friedmann argued, in "the 1980s agro-food corporations joined efforts, led by governments which could not compete in the mercantile game, to end government management of agricultural commodities" as "industry and technology quickly outgrew the mercantile framework" (2005, p. 130). She also claimed that this development signaled the end of the *post-war food regime* and created a political crisis of hegemony for the US as it "quickly lost its dominance" (2005, p. 132). To summarize the argument: the decline of US surpluses and the emergence of rivals led food corporations and foreign governments to call for an end to government management of agricultural commodities. Friedmann and McMichael contend that as "US hegemony has declined the basic tension between nationally organized economies and transnational capital has been amplified... [leading to the] integration in the agro-food sector [that has] undercut *national policies* not only in the peripheral economies, but also in the centre countries" (1989, pp. 108–10, emphasis in original).

Here we see perhaps most clearly how, within the food regimes literature, the transition from one regime to the next is predicated on a crisis of hegemony which initiates a reconfiguration of the 'regime' governing the global food order. This crisis, it is argued emerges out of the failure of the hegemon to forestall the sharpening of the contradictions of its own model, leading to the undermining of the national agricultural policies of supply management. The outcome is said to be a general undercutting of national government intervention in the market. However, the larger question of a crisis for whom is left unaddressed by this approach; clearly the state was as interventionist in agriculture in the post 1970s era as it had been in the previous. Likewise, why did agricultural exports continue to rise through the supposed crisis of the US in the 1970s if the surplus producing productive US agriculture has faltered? While the institutional configuration that provides hegemonic legitimacy for continued accumulation did face sharpening contradictions and some sort of legitimation crisis in the 1970s, it was far from a crisis of the US's goal of creating a world market through agriculture or even of US power to do so. How then is it that the food regimes approach understands the success of the agro-industrial project as a crisis and what does this understanding obfuscate?

The view that "the proposals to deregulate agriculture posit a form of post-hegemonic global regulation, via multilateral institutions, of a world market organized by the transnationals" (McMichael, 1994; see also McMichael and Myhre, 1991; Watkins, 1991) doesn't address the continuity in the role of internationalizing agro-food capitals in the development and implementation of US policy which clearly goes back at least to the 1950s and came to play a much greater role in the 1970s. The growth of multilateral governance is built out of US leadership and part of the project of construction of the global market. The shift to multilateral forms of governance should be viewed as the concretization of the common rules and operations into a form of neoliberal constitution (Gill, 1992). This emerges from "a growing fear on the part of both domestic and transnational capitalists that *ideology cannot continue to substitute for legal obligation* in the internationalization of the state" as "the continuing absence of the ideological consensus or capacity to bring about a transnational regulation of capital markets, of formal interstate treaties designed to enforce legally upon future governments general adherence to the discipline of the capital market" (Panitch, 1994, p. 74; Emphasis in original).

To theorize the development of the GATT, and later the WTO, as arising out of a crisis of internationalization of the state is to overlook the long historical roots of this process within and through states prior to this moment of constitutionalization of neoliberalism. It is to artificially split the internationalization of the state from the processes of globalization through economic integration. The farm payments and food aid state interventions are therefore correctly understood as transitional and part of the ongoing remaking of the social order.

Clearly the use of US Green Power – using the US's strength in agriculture, through an agro-export strategy, to recast the world in to a form more favorable to the US – was not a policy that emerged suddenly in the 1970s but stretches back much further. In fact, in some form it had been used by the US state all the way back in the late 19th century and had been building strength and use as a policy through the New Deal, just as it was also the very basis of the food aid program. Additionally, the state management of agriculture hardly ended in the 1970s as farm support programs continue to this day. Finally, there was an increase in state involvement in export promotion and trade policies going forward from the 1970s that hardly portends a decrease in state intervention. While US agricultural policy would focus less and less on food aid the notion that aid was more than just a legitimizing veil to hide trade promotion and imperial penetration appears to be strengthened by the food regimes notion of discrete regimes. In the process the consistency of trade promotion to reconstruct a global market are lost to discrete and stable eras (regimes) of accumulation.

As it happens much of the food regime's notions of hegemonic crisis rest on Realist International Relations theorists' assumptions of hegemonic collapse in the 1970s. The Realist idea that absent a hegemonic power the global system would slip into interstate competition and war, took on new vigor as the claims piled on that the US was losing its edge in the early 1970s (Krasner, 1976; Gilpin, 1975, 1981; Lake, 1984). Liberal IPE theorists too claimed the decline of the US as immanent, although disagreeing with Realists that this would automatically give way to international chaos and war (Ruggie, 1982; Keohane, 1984). This idea, that the US was in decline, and that this was the source of the economic problems of the 1970s, spread even into critical analysis (Cox, 1981; Arrighi, 1982). It isn't surprising then given the ubiquity of the idea of US decline and crisis in the 1970s and 80s that scholars of agro-food systems would pick up on the notion (McMichael and Friedman, 1989; Friedmann, 1982; 1993; McMichael, 1992; McMichael and Myhre, 1991).

For many of the International Relations scholars to the absence of an actual US decline in the decades that followed the 1970s was of a renewed hegemony through restructuring. Likewise, the food regimes approach reconfigured analysis rests on the notion that the crisis of hegemony of the 1970s led not to decline and challenge to US power but that it was a turning point, during which the US was able to reestablish its hegemonic control through a shift in institutional forms and sources of power. The story is of a falling hegemony that is reestablished.

Much as with the realist and liberal IPE schools, it is important to recognize exactly how the food regime theorists notion of crisis and regimes hides the complex and consistent forces of US and capitalist power and the institutional and political form this power takes. This is particularly important because the crises of the 1970s did little to stop the movement toward a global capitalist market. In fact, it sped up the process toward capitalist globalization under a US empire, while furthering agro-industrialization at home and abroad. The third world debt crisis of the 1980s and globalization in the 1990s are both the result of the consistent US policy stretching back to the mid-19th Century of constructing a world market for their agricultural products. Conversely the domestic farm support programs and disposal through food aid of the 1940–70 era represent a small exception to this overarching globally oriented goal of world capitalist market integration, not the rule. Additionally, it was through the very food aid that global trade in food was built up, which would make the food aid redundant. Meaning there is more similarity than difference between the eras and to posit discrete regimes misses the continuity of the global agro-industrial project.

In its analysis of the development of international relations, the food-regimes paradigm correctly locates the role of food and agriculture state policy in both aid/surplus disposal and in the promotion of property rights and international trade. As McMichael cogently put it "arguably, the ultimate goal was extending the 'reach of the state' by incorporating peasantries into market relations... [As it] introduced the agro-industrial dynamic into Third World food production" (1997, p. 639). However, by dissecting the historic developments of the second half of the twentieth century into two ideal-typical food regimes, this approach tends to gloss over the continuity of the two eras, overwhelming and hiding important insights into the nature of state action. The approach tends to artificially break political-economic development into distinct eras, understood by one aspect of that structure, containing competing powers which are driven by distinct political forces; one force in government intervention and the other one being more market mediated. McMichael (2014) states "capitalism was periodized in geopolitical terms and its periodization coincided with two different moments in the life of the nation-state" (p. 1). Thus by breaking the historical development of the state apparatuses of market formation into discrete and opposing eras, artificially opposing states and markets, this approach obfuscates the state's consistent role in an increasing market mediated social order. This bifurcation of states and markets leads to locating the deciding factors of the regime's policies post-hoc, claiming one regime ending and a new regime has emerged, while the same processes of global capitalist market creation and state policies that push them are at work during both eras. Within the food regimes approach the two eras are only understood as being connected by a crisis of one regime leading to the construction of the next.

Murdoch (1995) argues that regulationist accounts of economic change lapse too easily into structuralism because institutional relations and practices are only explained through their structural 'coupling' to the prevalent modes of production and regulation. Therefore these approaches tend to apply a post-hoc functionalism. It is only after the fall of the post-war food order that the food regimes approach is able to establish the principal mechanisms of that order as resting in the structural capacities which are said to have emerged out of state goals. In doing so it actually masks the central and systemic dynamics at work. With the true nature of the aims and goals of the system being misconceived by the regime and then projected backward to form discrete eras. Furthermore, this leads to an understanding of the outcome of the order as undesirable and as contradictory, rather than as part of the trajectory of the project of the construction of a world market of agricultural goods. It also views one form of state intervention into the market as such, and the others as not. To view two main agricultural policy goals – firstly, surplus disposal/international aid, and secondly foreign and domestic agricultural transition, commodification, and global market integration – as not part of a coexisting and even coproducing program but instead as the second suppressed by the first under one regime and the positions reversed in the next reveals a major limitation of the approach.

Most fundamentally the approach fails to properly locate the role of the state – in its multiple, varied and often competing aspects – in fostering both policies not as contradictory but as the path to mediate various political and class pressures alongside the dynamics of the world market in a given epoch. While some of these aspects have been recognized in later regimes approach writings, the desire to hold tight to the regimes approach has been maintained despite the mounting evidence against it. If the initial forming of the different regimes is based on some false assumptions and these assumptions are later amended, does the regime hold and how useful are the regimes going forward.

Important and competing aspects of the US state are downplayed by the notion of a unitary guiding policy under a given food regime. What Friedmann and McMichael located as the source of the "transitory character of this food regime derived from the contradictory national and international movements around which it was constructed" are in fact the continuous policy goals of a relatively autonomous US state aimed at constructing a world market (McMichael, 1997, p. 641). They are a reflection of shifts in the balance of class forces, international power changes and economic developments. Surplus disposal, for example, was never more about appeasing domestic political demands than it was about expanding the agro-industrial processes beyond the narrow scope of domestic agriculture into all aspects of society through the world market. The history of the building up of institutional capacities, in fact, reveals the congruence and interconnections between these goals. Likewise, the end of food aid that distributed the farm surpluses occurred not because the regime had failed, but ultimately because of its success at penetrating and transforming receiving nations in concert with what this expanded trade did to relieve the agrarian pressure on the state.

Although McMichael has said in some of his work that the food regime approach is largely heuristic, pointing to primary tendencies and trends, and not meant to be strictly indicative of abrupt changes, failures and crises, at other times he uses the regime structure to lay out a historically specific understanding of how we got to where we are. He has elsewhere called for a 'historicization of theory' to replace a tendency to 'theorize history' (McMichael, 1990). The combination of this heuristic device and a functionalism that seeks to explain history based on the outcomes could produce the effect that the food regimes approach appears to be letting one aspect used to construct a heuristic device define an entire era. For example, the notion that the post-war food regime, and by implication US agricultural policy, was guided by surplus disposal misses many aspects, most importantly the long term and long central goal of agro-industrial growth. Surplus disposal, growing out of the agrarian unrest caused by the depression, is merely one example of the state's maintenance function, while the later move to shift to a globalized agriculture represents another, with the two seemingly contradictory policies aligning in their use of the state to push agro-industrialization. To posit overarching regimes to describe even the main thrust of US state agricultural policy goals is to confuse this maintenance function of the state for its role in the economy. While the state sought to reproduce legitimacy through a highlighting of specific policies, this does not eliminate its actions in other areas to produce different outcomes, nor the ways the policies shifted the balance of class forces, altered social relations, and ultimately changed the impact of the policies going forward.

The neatness of positing regimes of accumulation – periods of stable patterns of accumulation (McMichael 2014, p. 2) – comes only in post hoc forms, as descriptions of the processes of the past based on appeals to functionalist explanations of social change. It is a "tool of hindsight" used to "help order and organize the messy reality" (Pritchard, 2007, p. 8). However, in the process the stable patterns actually only exist in the mind of the researcher and are in fact just part of the process of continual change.

For example, the "Post-war Mercantile food regime" describes the era as one of US surpluses dumped on the world, through a large degree of state involvement in the market. The approach claims that the drive to rid the US of agricultural surpluses explains US food aid orientation during this era. However, a deeper analysis, included in some food regime writings, reveals how it was also done to build up import dependence around the world and create export markets for US agricultural products.[14] Thus the use of food aid was part of an effort to alter the social relations of receiving nations in a drive to increase industrial production and reliance on capitalist markets, rather than simply to strengthen the US domestic price of farm goods and remove government held surpluses. Once the policy objectives are widened the discrete nature of the era collapses. As McMichael and Myhre (1990) recognized while discussing regime theory "Regulation theory cannot adequately explain this erosion of national regulation" (87). Despite their claim that what was occurring was an inability of the nation-state to deal with global market demands on it, the critique of the general regime approach holds: it lacks the ability to deal with the change endemic to capitalist society.

The entire food regimes school could be broken down into early and late food regimes approaches based on the very different characteristics of the same regimes. Earlier analysis relied more heavily on a domestically orientated agricultural state policy, more recently, McMichael (2003) has highlighted the

---

14   Some of the authors within the food regimes approach acknowledge as much (e.g.: McMichael, 2009), which only begs the question as to why explain the regime in terms of one aspect amongst many.

shift to liberalization through agriculture within the post-war food regime, in what he labels "green power". However he focuses on the crisis of US power and legitimacy and locates the strengths this system contained, the "green power", as a byproduct, outside of rather than central to, a coherent US policy (McMichael, 2003). We can overcome this bifurcation of state policies by highlighting how they led to the penetration and transformation of societies by shifting the balance of class forces in favor of larger, more market dependent farms and transnational big food processing and farm input corporations, leading to state institutional development of a specific capacity and the resulting social economic changes which then engendered a different but no less active state response (Panitch and Gindin, 2004). To put it briefly, the era circumscribed as the 'Mercantile-Industrial food regime' always contained an effort to transform receiving nations into market mediated social formations and was never a stable means to use mercantile relationships to maintain US dominance. It was the extension of the policy to use the state to transform domestic agriculture and social relations beyond national boundaries. It was the agro-industrial project applied globally.

The historically grounded argument presented in this chapter elucidates how the post-war food aid was the springboard and foundation of the following globalization of agriculture and trade. Furthermore, it reveals how the social transformative nature of food aid was by design part of a long term policy to expand agricultural trade and eventually the social relations of other nations, all while reconstituting a world capitalist market. Far from a crisis of US hegemony or the nation-state, the transition in orientation of food policy in the 1970s, was the result of the coming to fruition of the long term policy goals of the US. By highlighting state institutional shifts, it is shown how the changes of the 1970s were due less to a crisis of the US led international order and more to the coming to fruition of the project to construct a global capitalist market based on the projection of US strength, in part, through agriculture export facilitated by increases in agricultural productivity. The events of the 1970s are located in the contradictions that the US model produced as it moved further down the road toward its goal, a goal that included the global reordering of the division of labor. These contradictions emerge in US institutional configurations between the need to appease agricultural class interests by propping up domestic production at home and abroad and the drive to liberalize agriculture and the entire economy. The drive towards internationalization, in which US agricultural policy was so central, required continual shifts and expansion of the institutions and apparatuses, necessitating constant institutional change and engagement with class forces tied to globalization and agro-industrialization.

The breaking of US policy orientation into discrete eras or regimes, while offering valuable insights into how institutional configurations crystalize around the needs of capital, can become too rigid in their distinctions between market forces and political actors. The notion that market forces created a contradiction with institutional and political forces reifies the separation of markets and states. For example Friedmann and McMichael claimed that the crisis of the 1970s ushered a change in food regimes as "the overriding shift is from state to capital as the dominant structuring force" (1989, p. 112). This juxtaposing of states and capital results from the periodization of capitalist development and overlooks the ongoing management of the contradiction created by capitalist development through the state. Clearly to see both the pre-1970s era as absent capital control and the post-1970s as absent state control are both incorrect overgeneralizations. Overcoming this ontologizing of the binary separation between states and markets can be done by drawing out the politics behind these economic forces, or better yet, locating the connections between the political and economic aspects by tracing the state institutional shifts as they respond to the balance of class forces.

Conclusion

The post-war era for US agriculture is marked by the complete hegemony of the USDA-research complex, which created very productive, modern, agro-business oriented farms while almost eliminating agrarian movements. Along with this came massive commodity surpluses. These surpluses came to form the basis of the US projection of power and the penetration and alteration of social formations around the globe. These occurred because of the institutional capacities of the US state to engage in the agro-industrial project, including both pushing agricultural modernization and trade expansion leading towards the construction of a world market.

During the 1970s we see a shift not in the position of the US internationally or a movement away from state involvement toward greater market control, but in the focus of domestic and foreign policy due to the emerging and strengthening of a globally orientated, intensively expanding capitalist development. The role of food in this development was first, to use the US's strength in food production as a form of geopolitical power. The second key development in the 1970s was the use of this power to restructure the internal social relations and by extension reshaping the global division of labor in favor of neoliberal capitalism. In a global repeat of domestic processes, the state was used to mediate and direct the development towards forms which were more productive of surplus-value by consolidating class power and using it against political opposition. In turn, this enhanced the disciplinary power through heightened international market reliance. This was, in part, accomplished through the limiting of farmer influence by increasing executive authority in trade, alongside a diminished and weakened farm movement through its reliance on the state and its focus on prices (Chorev, 2007). By first imbricating agriculture into the market using state aid and programs, the transformation of US agricultural orientation toward the global market was constructed through the very programs conceived as a buffer to the global market. Then through a second step of creating multilateral trade institutions and the reduction of governmental supports that brought agriculture completely under market mediation.

Many, including the food regimes approach, locate a declining US in the shift to a more global orientation and retraction of state involvement. However, it is only by taking your eye off of class and the processes of class restructuring engendered in these developments and how this aids the US, that one can come to the erroneous conclusion that US power ebbed during the 1970s. On the contrary, what occurred was not a break with, but the coming to fruition of the US led construction of global capitalism. The slight shift of state institutional focus from domestic to international orientation was in no way a decrease in the role of the state or US global power. In fact, it signals the opposite occurring on both accounts.

In all of the ways outlined above, the US was able to export its own economic problems of the 1970s through its dominant position in agriculture to construct a highly integrated world market based on its structurally superior position regarding the strength of agriculture and the state institutional configurations. The capacities and unique ability, at both the political and state levels, arise out of the US's long history of state formation that navigated the unique relationship with agriculture and required a particular type of state with distinct forms of autonomy and intervention (Post, 1984; Page and Walker, 1991; Kulikoff, 1992; and Headlee, 1991). Thus, in a similar manner as the process of domestic economic penetration of agriculture using state aid to realign the social relations and balance of class forces toward more market-orientated relationships, the US advanced on a global scale. Concordantly, the very capacities the US had just developed or was developing during the New Deal to use consumer goods to integrate workers more fully into capitalism (Lacher, 1999) became the basis of a policy to use food to integrate workers in the developing countries, which represents a break from the form of incorporation which had and was occurring through *harder* forms of primitive accumulation and direct colonialism. This represents the novel form and strength of US Empire. US agrarian changes, the political responses and state policy changes, led to a foreign policy goal of using food aid to both transform the social relations of receiver countries and to lay the basis for the reconstitution of a globally integrated capitalism.

Food aid itself should be seen as both a response to domestic political pressure resulting from food surpluses and as the foreground of international orientation. From the outset PL 480 was saddled in this divide, on the one had taking direction from the USDA with its domestic orientation, while on the other, the PL 480 act gave the agency the unique power to sign agreements with foreign countries without the advice and consent of the US Senate. The other player in PL 480, the Department of State while mostly orientated toward international strategy, during the politically heady years of the Vietnam War, was also on a shortened domestic leash. The changes represented not the breakdown of the old order or a declining hegemony, but the increasingly global orientation of the US arising out of its domestic production growth and the attainment of the goals of PL 480 to transition the aid recipient countries into capitalist food importation. This meant that food aid, or even granting access to cheap imports of the highly efficiently produced and subsidized US grains, was the means to prioritize industrialization during the decade of development of countries of the global south (Bernstein, 2010). Therefore, the seemingly at odds goals of PL-480 were never as contradictory as some argue. Instead, both goals emerged from the same processes: the agro-industrial project.

While McMichael and other food regime theorists correctly identify the role of the development project and later neoliberalism in reproducing the structures of power, their insistence on a discord in the states actions during different regimes seems highly overstated. Far from it being the case of a failure of the development and aid projects leading to a complete shift in US policy, instead what occurred was an application of the same overarching project under the guise of an ideological shift. What appear as discrete regimes are simply two different ideological representations of the same agro-industrial goals. The same goals guided US policy toward agriculture and domestic development for over a century: the use of the state to transform agriculture and privilege industrial capital while claiming to be looking out for farmers and offering them slight benefits in return for their acquiescence and the ability to use them as part of the drive to imbricate them in capitalist development.

When the state expanded its focus on international concerns, it was still within the long-term goals and project that did not represent a distinct era. Thus, a focus on the process of change, rather than moments or discrete eras of punctuated differences, reveals the manner in which the long term continuity was masked, depoliticizing the goals and means, and how this obscures the state institutional policy drive of creating an integrated world market that favors capital. It is this very depoliticization that lies at the heart of the processes of agro-industrialization and neoliberalism. The lessons learned from the domestic depoliticization of farmers in the US over the course of the 19th and early 20th Century was applied first to other areas of the US and later to the rest of the world.

The changes in agricultural markets during this era were always closely related to the changing role of the US state. Over the course of the decade the strength of US agriculture was put to the test and became the bases of a resurgent US capitalism on a newly enlarged global scale. The US used its advance position in the development of a highly productive and efficient agricultural system as a structural advantage to integrate and alter the social relations of other states and pull them into global market dependence. This strength lies in the ability to force others to privilege inter-market relations over democratic ones. Using agriculture to alter the balance of class forces in favor of a global market discipline the US was able to reconstitute a global capitalism.

The US's ability to shift the balance of power back and forth between Congress and the executive offers the necessary political flexibility that is the bases of part of its relative autonomy. The shifts from congress to the executive represent the overall transition to a more global orientation that requires less domestic input. The changes that would emerge out of the 1970s should, therefore, be located within the constant, yet shifting, relationship between the state and capital. Not as a decisive rupture of one organizing principle, or regime of accumulation, and shift to another. Neoliberalism understood not as "merely a deregulatory political mindset or kind of ideological software, [but] increasingly concerned with the roll-out of new forms of institutional hardware" (Peck and Tickell, 2002, p. 389). In fact, it is this depoliticization that lies at the heart of the processes of agro-industrialization and neoliberalism – viewed here as merely an expansion to agro-industrialization outside of agriculture as well as outside the domestic sphere and onto the world market – that is at the heart of American Empire and global capitalism. The US's global restructuring came to be heavily reliant on the food price crisis of the 1970s and the grain surpluses the US had and continued to produce. The surplus grain disposal and crisis of US farms was initiated by their success. This then put pressure on, and came to serve as, the basis through which the US used commodities as food aid and later trade which created a centrifugal force pulling political leaders and state social relations out of a spatially concealed, politically mediated and managed industrial development process and into a global market competitive system. All this occurred while the US empire expanded through globalization and the sources of power that underwrote this move were obfuscated and depoliticized as being not part of the state or as a crisis of the hegemonic state.

CHAPTER 8

Conclusion

This study has outlined the US institutional capacity formation through the influence of farmer strength in the economy and state building. This has revealed the specific way farmer interest groups informed US institutional efforts and state building. It has shown how the state institutional development path created capacities that had important implications for US economic development and international relations going forward. In demonstrating the specific and important influence of agriculture and agricultural social movements on US state institutional formation, it showed that the two forces of state intervention and social movement pressure converged in a symbiotic relationship to produce agro-industrialization. This confluence resulted in both the dynamic form of the US state and a form of agriculture capable of producing massive surpluses and with it a form of 'green power' that was used to project US power and influence around the world. It is out of agro-industrialization and its influence on the state capacity building that served as the source of the US' position at the apex of global power in the last half of the twentieth century. It is this combined influence of agrarian social movements, capitalist market development and state institutional capacity building that was entailed in the agro-industrial project.

As laid out through this work, the development of the state institutional capacity in the United States that facilitated the rise of the US to a position of global leadership occurred under the particular pressure produced by the relatively strong influence of agrarian demands. The nature of the new nation and its novel form of settler colonial agriculture combined to form a type of government open to the demands of farmers. This produced the unique and particular developmental path that emerged. The need to legitimize the actions of the state because of constitutional and democratic requirements caused the development of unique institutional capacities as the demands of agrarian movements combined with prior state institutions within the existing balance of class forces. What emerged was a form of state development that sought a means to appease social movements while simultaneously pushing agricultural modernization and capitalist market expansion. The drive to use a democratic ideology as the basis for the rebellion against the crown required the inclusion of the settler yeoman class. Securing the land and claiming to offer the opportunity of self-rule built the political basis necessary to stave off counter revolutionary tendencies as well as to secure and unite the polity.

CONCLUSION 267

However, the turn toward an extensive geographic expansion in the late 19th century was both tepid and based solidly in the growth of a dynamic intensive market. That is to say, America's territorial expansion, and the eventual American empire, was due not to the limitations of a home market leading to expansion for trading partners but grew instead, out of and because of a uniquely dynamic and robust agro-industrial based intensive capitalist development that spawned a political response from the strong agrarian class. The turn toward expansion to ameliorate the social dislocation produced by the shift towards greater commodification of social life became political expediant. While this external expansion did occur, the story of the nineteenth, and to a greater degree the twentieth century, is really one of a continued internal expansion of capitalist social relations and increased market dependence of agricultural producers. The growth of the machinery, farm input and food processing, along with a consumer goods market were the key developments in the US during this era. This relentless growth of an increasingly market mediated social form, required an equally burgeoning state institutional counterpart as the basis for an expanding power base for the US. It was out of the particular state responses to agrarian pressure that productivity advances through emerged, leading to the seeking of external markets.

The objective of this inquiry was to outline, through historic detail, the co-development of the US state institutional capacity and the construction of an industrial capitalist based agriculture under the specific conditions that existed in the US. It did this while tracing state capacity building through the dialectical and socially contingent process involved in state formation and social development. Appling the agro-industrialization thesis aided in elucidating the specific details that made the US case significant.

This thesis posits that the industrial development in the United States was the result of indigenous developments in the Midwest, and not a function of the expansion of industry from the east. It was a function of the state induced agro-industrial development built out of an effort to quell agrarian movements that emerged as farmers were forced into market mediated social relations and continued commodification of their lives. US agriculture was effectively subsumed under the capitalist law of value through increased specialization towards marketable cash crops, decreased farmer self-sufficiency, the reliance on the purchasing of the elements of subsistence, created or increased agricultural inputs, and through the imbrication of agricultural production into global circuits of capital through mortgages and other loans (Post, 1995). That is to say, its development was structured by capitalism and agro-industrial development going forward despite the lack of wage-labor in most US agriculture during the 19th Century. The birth of the agro-industrial revolution was fed by and fed into its own force of inertia; as cash crop specialization resulted in increased revenue that was returned to manufacturing to produce the means of further productivity increases; and as specialization and mechanization reduced production costs and decreased prices, requiring the planting of more acreage and increased mechanization to maintain farm incomes. This "propulsive nature of commercialization", as Page and Walker (1991, p. 11) stated it, compelled farmers to become improvers by the logic of the market to increase productivity and total output, leading to declining prices and propelling farmers further into commercialization that in turn, spurred and impacted overall industrialization. "This advance in the social division of labor, the transition from rural to specialized industrial producers, was the product of the subordination of agrarian production to the law of value" (Post, 2011, p. 31). The fundamental point is that this indigenous industrial development was in relation to existing forms of agricultural production in the Midwest. As farmers adjusted to the encroaching capitalist pressures of the market this stimulated and amplified further pressure on others.

Agro-industrial understandings emphasized the relationship between the forms and changes of agriculture at the time, at first part of the process of transitioning from independent production to petty commodity production and the development of industrial production systems, and later the continued commodification pressure to transition to agra-businesses. These agricultural transitions were both fueling the changes as well as being spurred on by them. That is to say, as a form of agriculture emerged that relied increasingly on specialization, mechanical production, transportation across vast distances, the storing and sorting or commodification of the product, and complex systems of finance and banking, the society was innovating in these directions through the increasing role of industrialization. As some farmers began to adopt petty commodity production, initially as a defensive maneuver against full-on market involvement and out of the debt incurred through land policies and pressures, this began to first produce and then expand agricultural markets in a competitive manner. This competitive pressure emanating from the expanding market was fed by the increasing productivity of mechanized agriculture, as well as producing the growth of the industrial production technologies. This theory of the co-development of commodity forms of agricultural and industrial production is an important contribution to our understanding of US economic development.

Advancing on these insights I traced how farming commodified and Midwestern agriculture industrialized going forward based on the continuation and expansion of this process. It was shown that the main force in this process of change was the active involvement of the US state, which was often done in response to farmer resistance to commodification. These state responses, combined with the process of agro-industrial development, I have labelled the agro-industrial project – the state institutional developments that encouraged an increase in the market mediation of agriculture, state policies that advanced the reliance on markets by farmers and furthered the push towards market dependence, which emerged due to the desire to ameliorate the demands of agrarian movements. Therefore, this investigation highlights the state institutional developments that sought to nudge resistant farmers into forms of production and relations of market reliance that imbricated them in market forms. State action to quell farmer social movements by pushing development of methods, technologies, relations of trade, delivery and payment were part of this process. As outlined, these state actions continued to influence the development of agriculture and associated agribusinesses for decades, running all the way through today. Concordantly, this increase in market dependence led to increased resistance by farmers as these changes rolled out altered social relations. In response, the state sought to appease these agrarians and this led to a renewed agro-industrial push by state institutions and new state capacities through further institutional development. This dialectically informed developmental path, with industrial development, agribusiness growth, state institutional capacity building, and forms of political resistance concentrically building off each other, led to a highly productive form of agriculture which was fully enmeshed in capitalist social relations.

These changes also led to the development of very effective forms of state institutional capacities that were both built out of the necessities of the time which rested on many of the contingent and unique factors of the social formation, political structure, and material resources of the location – and led to further social, political and economic changes, requiring a renewed round of state institutional development and agro-industrial project.

The historical mechanisms of the agro-industrial project have been outlined in the above chapters. During the early- to mid- 19th Century the main forces were the US state's role in land policy. Through the expansion of the frontier and the manner in which the federal government distributed this land, it was able to effectively create a significant force towards agrarian commodification. It has been shown how land offerings going back to at least 1800 were set up to favor speculative activity and turn agricultural land into a commodity. Only during times of acute farmer agitation for a change in land policy the state did respond. However even these changes – most notably the Preemption act of 1841 and the Homestead Act of 1862 – did not go very far in shifting the effects of the land disposal policy away from greatly favoring merchant capital and producing a debt ridden farming class.

So, despite the rhetoric of freedom and independence emerging from the vast expanses of land, the actual result, due to state policies and institutional development that led to the particular manner the land was distributed, increasing dependence of farmers on market forces. As was shown, state land policy explicitly sought to increase farmer reliance on markets through the debt they incurred to purchase or maintain land. The mortgages taken out to purchase land created a debt that required the sale of farm products in a market; it required they become petty commodity producers. Overall as more and more farmers entered into these market relationships due to their land debt and taxes, these markets from agricultural products grew and prices declined. This then meant farmers incurred further pressure to engage in market mediated relationships to purchase either more land or mechanize to produce more to make enough to service their debt.

This inquiry reveals how the US state, as a capitalist state, neutralized agrarian social movements and resistance by turning them into forms amenable with the representative democracy and economic systems. The pedagogical role of social movements on state building therefore can partially explain the growth and strength of the US through the 20th Century as well as its ability to rapidly expand capitalist social relations and deal with the movements formed from its social dislocation.

As shown through multiple historical cases, agrarian responses to increased market mediation of their lives often resulted in farmer resistance and sometimes agrarian social movements. These social movements, furthermore, were time and again assuaged through state institutional interventions. One specific and important state institutional responses, and a central part of the agro-industrial project, is the USDA-research complex. As shown, the push by the USDA to 'modernize' farms was key to the continued productivity increases in agricultural production. Importantly, the USDA was also viewed as offering the solution to the declining prices that emerged due to the USDA pushing technological innovation and the ensuing production increases. Thus, the US state was capable of not only turning farming first into capitalist farming and later into agriculture and agribusiness, but also able to deal with the responses and resistance to these changes in a manner that further pushed the process along.

The central concern of this study was to show how the development of this capacity to use state institutional building to both push agro-industrialization and to overcome the resistance it creates. Importantly, this institutional capacity building of the US state came to overall strengthen the state's ability to not only respond to class based challenges but to spread its capitalist model and imbricate other nations into a global American empire. By advancing the understanding of the agro-industrial project, this study has offered a way

CONCLUSION 271

to overcome many of the problems in analyses that are premised on a state-market dichotomy. Furthermore, by including the role of class struggle, as economic and non-economic force, in the analyzing of societal development, the historical sociological account offered here identified the source of much of the strength and institutional capacity of the US informal empire by the mid-twentieth century, oriented as it was in good part to building of the global market through agriculture. Indeed, the continuity of capitalist market expansion that marks the entire era under study here – running from the mid-19th Century right up to the late 20th century – reveals how US state institutional development pursued agricultural production into a form that both undermined radical movements and enhanced market dependence while aiding in US industrial development and the building of a global capitalist market under the leadership of a US empire.

It is this insight into the nature of US state building that, at once, emerges from social movements and interest groups, while also, preventing them from shifting the balance of class forces away from capitalist economic development, which fundamentally grants new understanding to the nature of the US Empire. The development of the state institutions comes to tame the agrarian class and in the processes the state gains the capacity to act as both protector of capitalism and the force through which its expansion emerges as this process is replicated across society and the world.

APPENDIX A

Historical Timeline: Farm Organizations & Movements

18th century
Civic and intellectual leaders in colonial and revolutionary America copy the aristocratic and fashionable Europe interest in agriculture, science, and commerce, and form societies to promote these interests

1785
The Philadelphia Society for the Promotion of Agriculture and other rural concerns are organized

1794
Whiskey Rebellion, a farmers' revolt against taxes on grain in whiskey

1802
George Washington Parke Custis institutes an agricultural fair in Arlington, VA

1811
Berkshire Agricultural Society organized under Elkanah Watson's leadership

1817–25
Agricultural societies and fairs flourish under State aid

1838
Proposals made to use James Smithson's grant to establish a National Agricultural College

1840–60
Interest in agricultural societies revived

1850s
Farmers begin cooperative to make cheese and to market wool and tobacco

1850s
Farmers' clubs proliferate in Midwest

1852
United States Agricultural Society organized

1860
941 agricultural societies in the United States

1867
National Grange organized

1871
National Grange sanctions cooperative enterprise

1873–76
Granger movement at its height

1874–80
Farmers' Alliance movement begins

1880–96
Agricultural pressure groups gather strength

1882
Agricultural Wheel formed

1891
Populist Party launched on national scale

1896
Height of populist movement

1902
Farmers' Union started; American Society of Equity formed

1905
California Fruit Growers Exchange formed

1906
Appointment of first county agricultural agent

1909–17
Boys' and girls' club work underway

HISTORICAL TIMELINE – FARM ORGANIZATIONS & MOVEMENTS

1910
Farmers' Equity Union organized

1911
First Farm Bureau formed in Broome County, NY

1915
Non-Partisan League formed

1915–17
International Workers of the World ("Wobblies") organize thousands of wheat harvest workers

1919
American Farm Bureau Federation formally organized in Chicago, Illinois

1920s
Farm organization set up strong lobbies in Washington

1920–32
Cooperative movement spreads

1922
Capper-Volstead Act gives cooperatives legal standing

1925
Beginning of the Master Farmer movement

1929
National Council of Farmers Cooperatives organized

1930
11,950 cooperative with 3 million members

1932–23
Farmers' Holiday movement stages strikes and blocks farm sales

1934
Southern Tenant Farmers Union formed to cope with sharecroppers displaced during the New Deal

1947
National Farm Labor Union (formerly Southern Tenant Farmers Union) organizes strike among California farmworkers

1950s
10,051 cooperatives with 7 million members

1955
National Farmers Organization formed

1960s
United Farm Workers Organizing Committee begins unionizing California farmworkers

1960s
Commodity groups move to forefront of influence with Congress

1962
Silent Spring, by US biologist Rachel Carson, warns of dangers to wildlife from indiscriminate use of persistent pesticides, such as DDT. The book becomes a best-seller

1966
Fair Labor Standards Act extended to include agricultural labor; Federal minimum wage extended to some farmworkers

1970
7,994 cooperatives with 6.2 million members

1970
Earth Day is celebrated for the first time

1971
The Maine Organic Farmers & Gardeners Association is organized

1973
Fifty farmers organize California Certified Organic Farmers

1977
The American Livestock Breeds Conservancy is formed to protect endangered breeds of livestock

1979
The American Agriculture Movement organizes a "tractorcade" demonstration in Washington, DC

1986–88
Country singer Willie Nelson organizes first of the Farm Aid concerts to benefit indebted farmers

APPENDIX B

Major US Agricultural Laws 1860–1929

Law	Year	Details of the Act
Morrill Act	1862 & 1890	Granted states federal land whose sale proceeds went toward the establishment of agricultural universities. Expanded in 1890 to the former confederate states with special allocations for black colleges.
Hatch Act	1887	Created an office of Experiment Stations within the USDA. Allocated $15,000 per state to set up education and research facilities.
Agriculture Appropriation Act	1906	The act acquired farm and architectural functions of the Rural Engineering Investigations Division of the Office of Farm Management. Many programs fall under this act such as the Food and Nutrition Program, and Conservation Program.
Underwood Tariff Act	1913	Reduced tariff rates on manufactured goods to pre-Civil War levels, with agricultural machinery placed on the free list.
Smith-Lever Act	1914	Establish and fund country agriculture extension agents to demonstrate farming techniques through land-grant universities.
Cotton Futures Act	1914 (16)	Authorized the USDA to establish physical standards as a means of determining color grade, staple length and strength, and other qualities and properties for cotton. Intended to minimize speculative manipulation of the cotton market.
Grain Standards Act	1916	Set standards for the grading certain commodities, also restricting some speculation and market manipulation.
Warehouse Act	1916	Permitted Federal Reserve member banks to give loans to farmers on the security of their staple crops which were kept in Federal storage units as collateral
Federal Farm Loan Bill	1916	Established twelve Federal Land Banks modeled after the Federal Reserve System

MAJOR US AGRICULTURAL LAWS 1860–1929

Law	Year	Details of the Act
Smith-Hughes Act	1917	Established the vocational education schools to educate farmers.
Food Protection Act	1917	Placed USDA demonstration agents in every agricultural county to promote food protection standards.
Food Control Act	1917	Established the US Food Administration run by Herbert Hoover, set a minimal price for wheat and encouraged maximum production.
Packers and Stockyards Act	1921	To Regulate interstate and foreign commerce in livestock, livestock produce, dairy products, poultry, poultry products, and eggs.
Future Trading Act	1921	To institute regulation of grain futures contracts and, particularly, the exchanges on which they were traded.
Capper – Volstead/ Co-opMarketing Act	1922	It gave "associations" of persons producing agricultural products certain exemptions from antitrust laws.
Agricultural Marketing Act	1929	Established federal support to cooperatives to relieve farmers from seasonal and yearly ups and downs in market prices. It also allotted $500 million in federal loans to cooperatives, and created the Federal Farm Board.

Bibliography

Primary Sources

Chicago Daily Press 1857. Annual Review for 1857, Chicago Ill.

Commission on Country Life 1918. *Report to the President from the Commission on Country Life 1918.* Washington DC.

Dimitri, Carolyn, Anne Effland, and Neilson Conklin. 2005. "The 20th Century Transformation of US Agriculture and Farm Policy." ERS/USDA. Washington DC: USGPO.

Farmers' Alliance Newspaper 1890, August 23 1890.

Foreign Agricultural Services [FAS]. 1973. *Agricultural Trade and the proposed Round of Multilateral Negotiations: Report Prepared at the Request of Peter Flanigan, Assistant to the President for International Economic Affairs, for the Council on International Economic Policy.* Washington, D.C.: Government Printing Office.

Gray, Carrol 1934. "Objectives in the Land Use Planning Programs of the United States Government." Proceedings of the Western Farm Economics Association, 7th Annual Meeting. Berkeley, CA.

Huntington, A.T. and Mawinney, Robert 1910. *Laws of the US concerning Money, Banking and laws 1910.* National Monetary Commission Publication Washington Government Printing office Lincoln, Abraham 1962. *Proclamation upon the signing of the Act to establish a Department of Agriculture.* Messages and Papers of the Presidents, VI, 133.

Lindert, David 1988. *Long-Run Trends in American Farmland Values* Working Paper Series No. 45. Agricultural History Center University of California, Davis CA.

McGovern, George 1961, Memorandum for the President on PL-480 Program Attachment on Argentina. Presidential Corrispondence. Washington DC.

Populist Party 1896. *Statement of the Populist Party 1896.* Archive.org.

Rasmussen, Wayne D., Gladys L. Baker, and James S. Ward, 1976. "A Short History of Agricultural Adjustment, 1933–75." Economic Research Service, United States Department of Agriculture, Agriculture Information Bulletin No. 391.

Trolley, H.R. Assistant Administrator, AAA 1934. *Agricultural Planning in a Democracy",* Association of Land Grant Colleges and Universities, Convention Proceedings, p. 64.

True, Alfred 1937. *History of Agricultural Experimentation and Research in the United States, 1607–1925: Including a History of the United States Department of Agriculture,* USDA Publication no. 251.

Udall, Morris 1961. "The Foreign Assistance Act of 1961: A Special Report by Congressman Morris K. Udall." Accessed September 23, 2013.http://www.library.arizona.edu/exhibits/udall/special/foreign.html.

United Nations Conference on Trade and Development (UNCTAD), 1997. *The Least Developed Countries 1997 Report*. United Nations, New York, NY.
USAID *Food for Peace (P.L. 480, Titles II and III)* [Formerly U.S.AID Handbook 9].
USAID 2004, Food For Peace Celebrating 50, PD-ABZ-818.
US Agricultural Society 1850. *Journal of the United States Agricultural Society*.
———. 1856. *Journal of the United States Agricultural Society* 4:66–68 (June).
———. 1860. 8:57 (April).
United States Department of Agriculture (USDA) 1883 *Tenth Census, Agriculture* Washington DC.
———. 1888. *Report of the Commissioner of Agriculture, 1887*. Washington DC:USGPO.
———. 1895. *Report of the Secretary of Agriculture, 1894*. Washington DC:USGPO.
———. 1915. *Report of the Secretary of Agriculture*. Washington DC:USGPO.
———. 1930. *United States Census 1930*. Washington DC:USGPO.
———. 1933 *Yearbook of Agriculture 1933*. Washington DC: USGPO.
———. 1935 *Yearbook of Agriculture 1936 1935* . Washington DC.:USGPO.
———. 1935 *Yearbook of Agriculture 1935*. Washington DC: USGPO.
———. 1936 *Yearbook of Agriculture 1936*. Washington DC: USGPO.
———. 1936. *Agricultural Statistic, 1936*. Washington DC.:USGPO.
———. 1940. *Technology on the Farm*. Special report by an interbureau committee and the Bureau of Agricltural Economics. Washington DC. USGPO.
———. 1942. *Agricultural Statistic, 1942*. Washington DC.: USGPO.
———. 1942. *Farm Market Program,* Washington DC.
———. 1957. *Agricultural Statistics, 1957*. Washington DC: USGPO.
———. 1974. *Foreign Agricultural Trade of US* May 17. Washington DC: USGPO.
———. 1978. "Changes in farm production and efficiency, 1977." Statistical Bulletin no.612, Economics, Statistics and Cooperatives Services. Washington DC. USDA.
———. 1984. USDA Report, *History of Agricultural Price-Support and Adjustment Programs, 1933–84*. Washington DC. USGPO.
———. 1984. *Foreign Agriculture Services Testimony By Deputy Secretary Of Agriculture:Richard E.Lyng Before The House Select Committee On Hunger*. June 26. 1984.
———. 1989. *Agricultural Progress in the Third World and its Effects on US Farm Exports*. Washington, DC. Congressional Budget Office.
———. 2005. *Agricultural Statistics 2005* (?).
United States Department of Commece 1890, *US Census 1890*. Washington DC.
———. 1900. *US Census 1900*. Washington DC.
———. 1910. *US Census 1910*. Washington DC.
———.1933. US Census 1933. Bureau of Labor Statistics, Washington DC.

United States Department of Labor 1964. *US Census 1964*. Bureau of Labor Statistics, Washington DC.

US Senate 1965, "William Gaud 1965 testimony before the Committee on Foreign Relations US Senate", 89th Congress, 1st Session pp. 543–544".

US Treasury Department (1958) "Grain Trade of the US" Department of the Treasury, Washington DC.

Wallace, Henry 1933. *The Farm Crisis*. Accessed from http://newdeal.feri.org/wallace/haw04.htm#8.

Wallace, Henry 1934. *American Must Choose*. Accessed from http://newdeal.feri.org/wallace/haw08.htm.

Williams Report, 1971. *United States International Economic Policy in an Interdependent World. Report To the President submitted by the Commission on International Trade and Investment Policy*.

Books and Journals

Aglietta, Michael, 1979. A *Theory of Capitalist Regulation: the US Experience*. New York, NY. Verso.

Ahlberg, Kristin L. 1975. *Transplanting the Great Society: Lyndon Johnson and Food for Peace*. Columbia, Missouri University of Missouri Press.

Ahuja, Jaspreet K.C., Moshfegh, Alanna J., Holden, Joanne M., and Harris, Ellen 2013. "USDA Food and Nutrient Databases Provide the Infrastructure for Food and Nutrition Research, Policy, and Practice" *Journal of Nutrition*. 143(2): 241S–249S.

Ames, Glenn, 1990. "US-EU Agricultural Policies and GATT Negotiations". *Agribusiness*, 6(4): 283–295.

Araghi, Farshad, 1995. "Global Depeasantization, *1945–1990*". *The Sociological Quarterly*, 36(2): 337–368.

———. 2003. "Food Regimes and the Production of Value: Some Methodological Issues". *The Journal of Peasant Studies*, 20(2): 41–70.

———. 2008. "The invisible hand and the visible foot: peasants, dispossession and globalisation." In: A.H. Akram-Lodhi and C. Kay, eds. *Peasants and globalisation. Political economy, rural transformation and the agrarian question*. London and New York: Routledge, pp. 111–47.

Armstrong, Philip, Glyn, Andrew and Harrison, John 1991. *Capitalism Since 1945*. Cambridge, MA: Basil Blackwell.

Arrighi, Giovanni 1982. "A Crisis of Hegemony." in Amin, S, Arrighi, G. and Wallerstien, I, Eds,. *Dynamics of Global Crisis*. New York, NY: Monthly Review Press.

Ashworth, John 1995. *Slavery, Capitalism, and Politics in the Antebellum Republic, Volume I: Commerce and Compromise,* Cambridge, Cambridge University Press.

——— 2007. *Slavery, Capitalism, and Politics in the Antebellum Republic, Volume II: The Coming of the Civil War, 1850–1861,* Cambridge, Cambridge University Press.

———. 2013. "The American Civil War: A Reply to Critics", *Historical Materialism* 21.3 (87–101).

———. 2014. "Book Review of American Road to Capitalism", *Journal of Agrarian Change*, Vol. 14 (2): 305–321.

Attack, Jeremy 1989a. "The Evolution of Regional Economic Differences within Illinois, 1818–1950," in Peter Nardulli (ed.), *Diversity, Conflict, and State Politics: Regionalism in Illinois*. Urbana, IL: University of Illinois Press.

———. 1989b. "The Agricultural Ladder Revisited: A New Look at an Old Question with Some Data for 1860." *Agricultural History*, 63(1): 1–25.

Attack, Jeremy and Fred Bateman 1987. *To Their Own Soil: Agriculture in the Antebellum North*, Aimes, University of Iowa Press.

Awokuse, Titus 2011. "Food Aid Impacts on Recipient Developing Countries: A Review of Empirical Methods and Evidence." *Journal of International Development*, 24(4):493–514.

Badger, Anthony. 1989. *The New Deal: The Depression Years, 1933–1940*. New York, NY: Hill and Wang.

Bailey, Liberty Hyde 1918. *What is Democracy*. Ithaca NY, Comstock Publishing.

Baker, Gladys 1939. *The County Agent*. University of Chicago Press.

Banaji, Jairus 2010. *Theory as History: Essays on Modes of Production and Exploitation*. Leiden, England: Brill.

Baptist, Edward 2014. *The Half Has Never Been Told: Slavery and the Making of American Capitalism*. NY:Basic Books.

Barnes, John K. 1922. "The Man Who Runs the Farm Bloc" *World's Work*, November 1922.

Barrett, CB and Maxwell, DG 2005. *Food Aid after Fifty Years*. Routledge: London.

Barry, Peter J. 1995. *The Effects of Credit Polices on US Agriculture*. Washington, DC. The American Enterprise Institute (AEI) Press.

Bartley, Numan 1987. "The Southern Enclosure Movement," *Georgia Historical Review*, 71(3): 438–50.

Bateman, Fred and Thomas Weiss 1981. *A Deplorable Scarcity: The Failure of Industrialization in the Slave Economy*, Chapel Hill, University of North Carolina Press.

Beard, Charles 1936. *An Economic Interpretation of the Constitution of the United States* NY: Macmillan.

Beard, Charles and Mary Beard 1927. *The Rise of American Civilization*. NY: MacMillion.

———. 1930. *History of the United States*. Norwood MA: Norwood Press.

Beckert, Sven 2001, *The Monied Metropolis: New York City and the Consolidation of the American Bourgeoisie, 1850–1896*, Cambridge: Cambridge University Press.

Benedict, Murry B. 1953. *Farm Policies of the United States, 1790–1950*. NY: Twentieth Century Fund.

Bennett, Jon, 1987. *The Hunger Machine: The Politics of Food*. Toronto, CA: CBC Enterprises.

Bensel, Richard 1984. *Sectionalism and American Political Development, 1880–1980*, Madison WI: University of Wisconsin Press.

———. 1990. *Yankee Leviathan: The Origins of Central State Authority in America, 1859–1877*. Cambridge: Cambridge University Press.

———. 2000. *The Political Economy of American Industrialization, 1877–1900*. NY, NY: Cambridge University Press.

Bernstein, Irving. 1969. *The Turbulent Years: A History of the American Worker, 1933–1940*. Chicago, Ill: Haymarket Books.

———. 2010. *Class Dynamics of Agrarian Change*, Sternling, VA. Fern.

Black, John and Allan, R.H. 1937. "The Growth of Farm Tenancy in the United States," *Quarterly Journal of Economics* 51(3): 393–425.

Blackburn, Robin 2011. *The American Crucible: Slavery, Emancipation and Human Rights*. Brooklyn, NY: Verso.

Blackmon, Douglas 2008. *Slavery by Another Name: The Re-Enslavement of Black Americans from the Civil War to World War II*. NY: Random House.

Blandford, David, Carter, Colin A. and Piggott, Roley, 1993. *North–south Grain Markets and Trade Policies*. Boulder, CO: Westview Press.

Block, Fred 1987. *Revising State Theory: Essays in Politics and Postindustrialism*. Philadelphia, PA: Temple University Press.

Bloom, Jack M. 1987. *Class, Race, and the Civil Rights Movement*. Bloomington: Indiana University Press.

Blum, John V. 1976. *V Was for Victory: Politics and American Culture during World War II*. New York: Harcourt Brace Jovanovich.

Bogue, Margaret B. 1959, *Patterns from the Sod: Land Use and Tenure in the Grand Prairie, 1850–1900*. Springfield Ill: University of Illinois Press.

Bogue, Allan G. 1968. *From Prairie to Cornbelt*. Chicago, Ill.: Quadrangle Paperback.

———. 1972. "'Profits' and the Frontier Land Speculator". In Nash, Gerald D. *Issues in American Economic History*. Lexington, MA.: D.C. Heath and Company.

Bowers, William 1974. *The Country Life Movement in America, 1900–1920*, Port Washington, NY: Kennikat Press.

Boyle, James 1922. *Chicago Wheat Prices for Eighty-one Years*. New York NY: Macmillan.

Brake, E.K. 2013. *Uncle Sam on the family farm: Farm policy and the business of southern agriculture, 1933–1965*. (Order No. 3568777, Duke University). ProQuest Dissertations and Theses, 379.

Brenner, Robert 1985 (1976) "Agrarian Class Structure and Economic Development in Pre-Industrial Europe" In Aston, T.H. and Philipin, C.H.E. *The Brenner Debate: Agrarian Class Structure and Economic Development in Pre-Industiral Europe*. NY: Cambridge.

———. 1977. "The Origins of Capitalist Development: A Critique of Neo-Smithian Marxism," *New Left Review*, 104: 25–92.

———. 1986. "The Social Basis of Economic Development" in Roemer, John *Analytical Marxism*. NY: Cambridge.

Brooks, Robert 1914. *The Agrarian Revolution in Georgia, 1865–1912*. Madison WI: University of Wisconsin Press.

Bruce, Philip Alexander 1905. *Rise of the New South*, Lansing: University of Michigan.

Buck, Solon 1920, "The Agrarian Crusade" 18–19. NY: United States Publishers Association.

Buckland, Jerry, 2004. *Ploughing up the Farm: Neoliberalism, Modern Technology and the State of the World's Farmers*. Winnipeg, CA: Fernwood Press.

Burbach, Roger and Flynn, Patricia, 1980. *Agribusiness in the Americas*. NY: Monthly Review Press/ NACLA.

Burnstein, Henry 2008. "Agrarian questions from transition to globalisation." In: A.H. Akram-Lodhi and C. Kay, eds. *Peasants and globalisation. Political economy, rural transformation and the agrarian question*. London: Routledge, pp. 214–38.

Buttel, F. 1996. "Theoretical issues in global agri-food restructuring". In *Globalisation and agri-food restructuring: Perspectives from the Australasia region*, ed. D. Burch, R. Rickson, and G. Lawrence. Avebury: Aldershot.

Buttel, F., and H. Newby (eds.). 1980. *The rural sociology of the advanced societies: Critical perspectives*. Montclair: Allanheld,Osmun.

Buttel, F., O. Larsen, and G. Gillespie. 1990. *The sociology of agriculture*. NY: Greenwood Press.

Cammack, Paul 1989. "Review Article: Bringing the State Back In?" *British Journal of Political Science* 19(2): 275–76.

Campbell, Christina. 1962. *The Farm Bureau and the New Deal*. Urbana: University of Illinois Press.

Carpenter, Daniel 2001. *The Forging of Bureaucratic Autonomy: Reputations, Networks, and Policy Innovation in Executive Agencies, 1862–1928*. Princeton NJ: Princeton University Press.

Carrier, Lyman 1937. "The United States Agricultural Society, 1852–1860: Its Relation to the Origin of the United States Department of Agriculture and the Land Grant Colleges", *Agricultural History*, 11(4): 278–288.

Carville, Earle and Hoffman, Ronald (1980) "The Foundation of the Modern Economy: Agriculture and the Costs of Labor in the United States and England, 1800–60" *American Historical Review* 85: 1055–94.

Chandler, Alfred 1968. *The Changing Economic Order: Readings in American Economic and Business History*. New York, NY: Harcourt, Brace and World.

———. 1977. *The Visible Hand: The Managerial Revolution in American Business*. Cambridge, MA: Belknap Press.

Chorev, Nitsan, 2007. *Remaking US Trade Policy: Form Protectionism to Globalization*. Ithaca, NY: Cornell University Press.

Chote, Jean. 2002. *Disputed Ground: Farm Groups that Opposed the New Deal Agricultural Program*. Jefferson: McFarland.

———. 2008. "A Fluid Divide: Domestic and International Factors in US Trade Policy Formation." *Review of International Political Economy*, 14(4): 653–689.

Chernow, Ron 1990. *The House of Morgan: An American Banking Dynasty and the Rise of Modern Finance*. New York, NY: Atlantic Monthly.

Clark, Christopher 1979. *The Roots of Rural Capitalism: Western Massachusetts, 1780–1860*. Ithaca, NY: Cornell University Press.

———. 1990. *The Roots of Rural Capitalism: Western Massachusetts, 1780–1860*. Ithaca, NY: Cornell.

———. 2006. *Social Change in America: From the Revolution Through the Civil War*. Chicago Ill.: Ivan R. Dee.

Clark, John 1966. *The Grain Trade in the Old North-West*. Urbana Ill: University of Illinois Press.

Clarke, Sally H. 1994. *Regulation and Revolution in United States Farm Productivity*. Cambridge: Cambridge press.

Cohen, Lizbeth. 2003. *A Consumer's Republic: The Politics of Mass Consumption in Postwar America*. New York: Knopf.

Cohen, Stephen D., Paul, Joel R. and Blecker, Robert A. 1996. *Fundamentals of US Foreign Trade Policy*. Boulder CO: Westview Press.

Conrad, Alfred and John Meyer 1955. "The Economics of Slavery in the Ante Bellum South", *Journal of Political Economy*, 66, 2:95–130.

Constance, Douglas H., Jere L. Gilles, and William D. Heffernan. 1990. "Agrarian Policies and Agricultural Systems in the United States." In Alessandro Bonanno ed., *Agrarian Policies and Agricultural Systems*. Boulder, CO: Westview Press.

Countryman, Edward 1974. "'Out of Bound of the Law': Northern Land Rioters in the Eighteenth Century." In Young, Alfred *The American Revolution*, DeKalb, Ill.: Northern Illinois University Press.

Cox, Robert, 1981. "Social Forces, States and World Orders: Beyond International Relations Theory." *Millennium: Journal of International Studies*, 10(1): 126–155.

———. 1987. *Production, Power, and World Order: Social Forces in the Making of History*. NY: Columbia University Press.

Craig, Barbara J. and Pardey, Philip G. 1996. "Productivity Measurement in the Presence of Quality Change," *American Journal of Agricultural Economics* 78:1349–54.

Crapol, Edward and Schonberger, Howard 1972. *The Shift to Global Expansion, 1865–1900*, NY: Penguin.

Cronon, William, 1983. *Changes in the Land: Indians, Colonists, and the Ecology of New England*, Hill & Wang.

———. 1991. *Nature's Metropolis: Chicago and the Great West.* NY: W.W. Norton and CO.

Cullather, Nick 2010. *The Hungry World: America's Cold War Battle Against Poverty in Asia.* Cambridge, MA: Harvard Press.

Curti, Merle 1959. *The Making of An American Community: A Case Study of Democracy in a Frontier County.* Stanford CA: Stanford University Press.

Danbom, David 1979. *The Resisted Revolution: Urban America and the Industrialization of Agriculture 1900–1930.* Ames, IA: Iowa State University Press.

Danhof, C. 1962. "Farm-Making Costs and the Safety Valve, 1850–1860," in Carstensen ed., *Public Lands Studies the History of the Public Domain.* Madison, WI: University of Wisconsin Press.

Daniel, Cletus E. 1981. *Bitter Harvest: A History of California Farmworkers, 1870–1941.* Berkeley: University of California.

Das, Dilip K. 2007. *The Evolving Global Trade Architecture.* Northampton, MA: Edward Elgar.

David, Paul 1967. "The Growth of Real Product in the United States Before 1840: New Evidence, Controlled Conjecutres" *Journal of Economic History*, 27, 2: 151–97.

———. 1971. "The Mechanization of Reaping in the Antebellum Midwest" in *The Reinterpretation of American Economic history*, edited by Robert Fogel and Stanley Engerman, NY: Harper Collins.

Davis, Ronald 1982. *Good and Faithful Labor: From Slavery to Sharecropping in the Natchez District, 1860–1890.* Westport, Conn: Greenwood Press.

Destler, I.M. 1978. "United States Food Policy 1972–1976: Reconciling Domestic and International Objectives." *International Organization.* 32 (Summer).

———. 1986. *American Trade Politics.* Washington, DC. Institute for International Economics.

Dubois, W.E.B. 1935. *Black Reconstruction in America: An Essay Toward a History of the Part Which Black Flolk Played in the Attempt to Reconstruct Democracy in America, 1860–1880* NY: Russel and Russel.

Domhoff, William and Weber, Michael 2011. *Class and Power in the New Deal: Corporate Moderates, Southern Democrats, and the Liberal-Labor Coalition.* Stanford, CA: Standford University Press.

Dowd, Douglas 1974. *The Twisted Dream: Capitalist Development in the United States Since 1776.* Cambridge, MA: Winthrop Publishers.

Eidlin, Barry 2016. "Why Is There No Labor Party in the United States? Political Articulation and the Canadian Comparison, 1932 to 1948" in *American Sociological Review.* May 2016.

Eisner, Marc Allen 2001. *The American Political Economy: Institutional Evolution of Market and State.* NY: Routledge.

Ekbladh, David 2002. "'Mr. TVA'": Grass-Roots Development, David Lilienthal, and the Rise and Fall of the Tennessee Valley Authority as a Symbol for US Overseas Development, 1933–1973." *Diplomatic History* 26(3).

Ellsworth, Clayton 1960. "Theodore Roosevelt's Country Life Commission." *Agricultural History* 34: 155–172.

Ely, Richard T. and Wehrwein, George S. 1940 *Land Economics*. New York: Macmillan.

Emery, Henry Crosby (1896) *Speculation on the Stock and Produce Exchanges of the United State*. NY: Columbia University Press

Essex, Jamey. 2005. *The State As Site and Strategy: Neoliberalization,Internationalization, and the Foreign Agricultural Service*. Dissertation, Syracuse University.

———. 2007. "Getting what you pay for: Authoritarian statism and the geographies of US trade liberalization strategies." *Studies in Political Economy*, 80: 75–103.

———. 2013. *Development, Security, and Aid: Geopolitics and Geoeconomics at the US Agency for International Development*. Athens, GA: University of Georgia Press.

Evans, Peter. 1995. *Embedded Autonomy: States and industrial Transformation*. Princton; Princeton University Press.

Farmer, Hallie 1972. "The Economic Background of Frontier Populism" In Nash, Gerald D. *Issues in American Economic History*. Lexington, MA: D.C. Heath and Company.

Ferleger, Herbert Ronald 1942. *David A. Wells and the American Revenue System, 1865–1870*. NY, NY: Private Printing; Reprinted by Porcupine Press, 1977.

Ferguson, Thomas and Rodgers, Joel 1981. "The Reagan Victory: Corporate Coalitions in the 1980 Campaign." In Ferguson, Thomas and Rodgers, Joel eds., *The Hidden Election: Politics and Economics in the 1980 Presidential Campaign*, NY: Partheon Books.

Finegold, Kenneth.1981. "From Agrarianism to Adjustment: the Political Origins of New Deal Agricultural Policy." *Politics and Society* 11:1–27.

Fisher, Llyod. 1953. *The Harvest Labor Market in California*. Cambridge MA: Harvard University Press.

Fishlow, Albert (1964) "Antebellum Interregional Trade Reconsidered" American Economic Reviews, 54(352–64).

———. 1965. *American Railroads and the Transformation of the Ante-Bellum Economy*, Cambridge MA: Harvard University Press.

Fite, Gilbert C. 1954. *George N. Peek and the Fight for Farm Parity*. Norman, OK: University of Oklahoma Press.

———. 1980. "Mechanization of Cotton Production Since World War II." *Agricultural History*. 50:190–207.

———. 1984. *Cotton Fields No More: Southern Agriculture, 1865–1980*. Lexington, KY: University Press of Kentucky.

Fornari, Harry (1973) *Bread Upon the Waters: A History of United States Grain Exports*. Nashvill Tenn: Aurora Press.

Foner, Eric 1970. *Free Soil, Free Labor, Free Men: The Ideology of the Republican Party before the Civil War*. Oxford: Oxford University Press.

———. 1984. *Nothing but Freedom: Emancipation and Its Legacy*. Baton Rouge: Louisiana State University Press.

———. 1988. *Reconstruction: America's Unfinished Revolution, 1863–1877*. NY:Harper and Row.

———. 1990. *House Divided: America in the Age of Lincoln*. with Olivia Mahoney. Chicago: Chicago Historical Society.

———. 2013. "The Civil War and Slavery: A Response", Historical Materialism 19.4(92–98).

Frankel, Richard, Hadwiner, Don and Browne, William eds. 1979. *The Role of Agriculture in American Foreign Policy*. New York, NY: Praeger.

Friedmann, Harriet, 1978. "Simple Commodity Productin and Wage Labour in the American Plains". *Journal of Peasant Studies*, 6:71–100.

———. 1980. "Household Production and the Natrional Economy: Concepts for the Analysis of Agrarian Formations." *Journal of Peasant Studies*, 7:158–184.

———. 1982. "The Political Economy of Food: The rise and Fall of the Postwar International Food Order". *In Marxist Inquiries*, ed. Michael Burawoy and Theda Skocpol. American Journal of Sociology 88: S248–82.

———. 1990. "Origins of Third World Dependancy". In *The Food Question*, ed. Henry Bernstein, Ben Crow, Maureen Mackintosh, and Charlotte Martian. London. Earthscan.

———. 1993. "The Political Economy of Food: A Global Crisis". *New Left Review* 196:29–57.

———. 2004. "Feeding the Empire: The Pathologies of Globalized Agriculture". In *Socialist Register 2005: The Empire Reloaded*. Panitch, Leo and Leys, Colin eds. NY: Monthly Review Press.

———. 2005. "From Colonialism to Green Capitalism: Social Movements and Emergence of Food Regimes," in Frederick H. Buttel, Philip McMichael (ed.) *New Directions in the Sociology of Global Development*, Emerald Group Publishing Limited.

———. 2005. "From colonialism to green capitalism: Social movements and emergence of food regimes." *In New directions in the sociology of global development*, ed. F. Buttel, and P. McMichael, 227–264. Oxford: Elsevier.

———. 2009. "Discussion: moving food regimes forward: reflections on symposium essays." *Agriculture and Human Values*, 26:335–344.

Friedmann, Harriet and McMichael, Philip 1989. "Agriculture and The State System: The Rise and Fall of National Agricultures, 1870 to the Present". *Sociologia Ruralis* 29 (2): 93–117.

Gates, Paul 1934. *The Illinois Central Railroad and Its Colonization Work* Cambridge MA: Harvard Press.

———. 1960. *The Farmer's Age: Agriculture, 1815–1860*. NY: Harper Torchbooks.

———. 1968. *The History of Public Land Law Development*. Washington, DC:US Government Printing Office.

———. 1972. "The Role of the Land Speculator In Western Development". In Nash, Gerald D. *Issues in American Economic History*. Lexington, MA: D.C. Heath and Company.

———. 1973. *Landlords and Tennents on the Prairie Frontier*. Ithaca NY: Cornell University Press.

Gelb, Leslie and Lake, Anthony 1974. "Less Food, More Politics." *Foreign Policy* 17: 176–198.

———. 1975. "Congress: Politics and Bad Policy." *Foreign Policy* 20: 232.

Genovese, Eugene 1967. *The Political Economy of Slavery: Studies in the Economy and Society of the Slave South*. NY: Vintage Books.

George, Henry 1904. *The Complete Works of Henry George: Our Land and Land Policy:Speeches, Lecutres and Miscellaneous Writings*. NY: Doubleday Page and Company.

George, Susan, 1976. *How the Other Half Dies: The Real Reason for World Hunger*. NY: Penguin Books.

Gilbert, Jess and Howe, Carolyn. 1991. "Beyond 'State VS. Society': Theories of the State and New Deal Agricultural Policies". *American Sociological Review*. 56:204–220.

Gill, Stephen 1992. "The Emerging World Order and European Change." In Milliband, Ralph and Panitch, Leo eds., *Socialist Register 1992: New World Order?* Halifax, NS: Fernwood.

Gilpin, Robert. 1975. *US Power and the Mulitnational Corporation: The Political Economy of Foreign Direct Investment*. NY. Basic Books.

———. 1981. *War and Change in World Politics*. NY: Cambridge University Press.

Glick, M. and Brenner, Robert 1991. "The Regulation Approach: Theory and History," *New Left Review*, 186:45–160.

Goldfield, Michael 1997. *The Color of Politics: Race and the Mainspring of American Politics*. NY: The New Press.

Goodman, David and Redclift, Michael, 1985. "Capitalism, Petty Commodity Production and the Farm Enterprise". *Sociologia Ruralis*, 25(3/4): 231–247.

Goodman, D., and M. Watts. 1997. *Globalising food: Agrarian questions and global restructuring*. NY: Routledge.

Goodwyn, Lawrence 1978. *The Populist Movement: A Short History of the Agrarian Revolt in America*. NY: Oxford.

Gray, Lewis 1933. *History of Agriculture in the Southern United States to 1860*. 2nd Volumne, Washington D.C.: The Carnegie Institution.

Greely, Horace 1860. *An Overland Journey*. NY: C.M. Saxton, Barker and Company.

Hacker, Louis, 1940. *The Triumph of American Capitalism*. NY. McGraw-Hill.

Hadwiger, Don F. 1982. *The Politics of Agricultural Research*. Lincoln, NB: University of Nebraska Press.

Hahn, Steven 1971. "The Freeman Administration and the Poor." *Agricultural History* 45.

———. 1983. *The Roots of Southern Populism: Yeoman Farmer and the Transformation of the Georgia Upcountry, 1850–1890*. NY: Oxford.

Hahn, Steven and Prude, Jonathan 1985. *The Country Side in the Age of Transformation*. Chappel Hill, NC: University of North Carolina Press.

Hammond, Matthew 1897. *The Cotton Industry*. NY: Mac Millan Company.

———. 1911. "Railway Rate Theories of Interstate Commerce" *Quarterly Journal Of Economics*, I V–VI: 200–222.

Hammond, Bray 1957. *Banks and Politics in America: From the Revolution to the Civil War*. Princeton, NJ: Princeton University Press.

Hamilton, David E. 1991. *From New Day to New Deal: American Farm Policy From Hoover to Roosevelt, 1928–1933*. Chapel Hill: University of North Carolina.

Hanson, Mark. 1991. *Gaining Access: Congress and the Farm Lobby, 1919–1981*. Chicago: The University of Chicago Press.

Harding, Thomas Swan 1947. *Two Blades of Grass: A History of Scientific Development in the US Department of Agriculture*. University of Oklahoma Press.

Harding, Charles 1955. *Freedom in Agricultural Research*. Minneapolis: University of Minnesota Press.

Harris, Carl V. 1976. Journal of Southern History 42 "Right Fork or Left Fork: The Sectional Party Alignment of Southern Democrats in Congress, 1873–1897."

Harvey, David 2006. *Limits to Capital*. NY: Verso.

Hawk, Emory 1934. *Economic History of the New South*. NY: Pretence-Hall.

Headlee, Sue 1991. *The Political Economy of the Family Farm: The Agrarian Roots of American Capitalism*. NY. Praeger.

Hedges, Joseph 1935. *Commercial Banking and the Stock Market before 1863*. Baltimore, MD: The John Hopkins University Press.

Helleiner, Eric 1994. *States and the Emergence of Global Finance: From Bretton Woods to the 1990s*. Ithaca, NY: Cornell University Press.

Henderson, George. 1998. *California and the Fictions of Capital*. Philadelphia: Temple.

Henretta, James A. 1991. "The Transition to Capitalism in America", in *The Origins of American Capitalism: Collected Essays*. Boston, MA: North-Eastern University.

Hicks, John D. 1955. *Populist Revolt: A History of The Farmers' Alliance and the Peoples Party*. Minneapolis, MN: University of Minnesota Press.

Hightower, Jim 1973. *Hard Tomatoes, Hard Times: The Failure of the Land Grant College Complex*. Washington, DC: Agribusiness Accountability Project.

Hirst, Paul and Hindess, B. 1975. *Pre-Capitalist Modes of Production*. London: Routledge & Kegan Paul.

Hofstadter, Richard 1955. *The Age of Reform: From Bryan to FDR.* NY:Vintage.

Holloway, John and Picciotto, Sol 1977. "Capital, Crisis and the State." *Capital & Class.* 1(2): 76–101.

Hooks, Gregory 1990. "From an Autonomous to a Captured State Agency: the Decline of the New Deal in Agriculture" *American Sociological Review* Vol.55:29–43.

Hopkins, Raymond 1980. *The Global Political Economy of Food.* Madison, WI: University of Wisconsin Press.

Hopkins, Raymond and Puchala, Donald 1980. *Global Food Interdependence: Challenges to American Foreign Policy.* New York, NY: Columbia University Press.

Horwitz, Morton J. (1977) *The Transformation of American Law, 1789–1860.* Cambridge MA.

Hudson, Michael 2003. *Super Imperialism – New Edition: The Origin and Fundamentals of US World Dominance.* London: Pluto Press.

Hurt, Douglas 2002. *Problems of Plenty: The American Farmer in the Twentieth Century.* Chicago: Ivan R. Dee.

Jaffee, David 1991. "Peddlers of Progress and theTransformation of the Rural North, 1760–1860." *Journal of Agricultural History* 78:511–535.

James, E.J. 1910. *The Origin of the Land Grant Act of 1862 ... and Some Account of Its Author, Jonathan B. Turner.* Urbana-Champaign: University of Illinois Press.

Jamison, Stewart.1945. *Labor Unionism in American Agriculture,* BLS Bull. No. 836.

Jessop, Robert 2008. *State Power.* Cambridge, MA: Polity Press.

Kautsky, Karl, 1988. *The Agrarian Question, Two Vol.* London: Zwan.

Keohane, Robert 1984. *After Hegemony: Cooperation and Discord in the World Political Economy.* Princeton, NJ: Princeton University Press.

Kirby, Jack Temple. 1987. "The Transformation of Southern Plantations. C. 1920–1960." *Agricultural History.* 57(3):257–267.

Klien, Joseph 1911. "The Development of Mercantile Instruments of Credit in the United States." *Journal of Accountancy* 12.

Kloppenburg, Jack 1988. *First the seed. The political economy of plant biotechnology, 1492–2000.* Cambridge: Cambridge University Press.

Kloppenburg, Jack and Frederick H. Buttel. 1987. "Two Blades of Grass: The Contradictions of Agricultural Research as State Interventions." *Research in Political Sociology.* 3:111–115.

Kodas, Janet, 1993. "Shifting Global Strategies of US Foreign Aid, 1955–90". *Political Geography,* 12(3): 232–246.

Kolko, Gabriel 1963. *The Triumph of Conservatism: A Reinterpretation of American History, 1900–1916.* NY: The Free Press of Gencoe.

———. 1965. *Railroads and Regulation, 1877–1916.* Princeton NJ: Princeton University Press.

———. 1984. *Main Currents in Modern American History.* NY: Pantheon Books.

Konings, Martijn 2015. *The Emotional Logic of Capitalism: What Progressives Have Missed*. Stanford CA: Stanford University Press.

Krasner, Steven 1976. "State Power and the Structure of International Trade." *World Politics* 28(3): 317–347.

———. 1985. *Structural Conflict: The Third World Against Global Liberalism*. Las Angeles, CA: University of California Press.

Kulikoff, Allan, 1992. *The Agrarian Origins of American Capitalism*. Charlottesville VI: University Press of Virginia.

Lacher, Hannes, 1999. "Embedded Liberalism, Disembedded Markets: Re-Conceptualizing the *Pax Americana*." *New Political Economy*, 4(3):343–60.

———. 2006. *Beyond Globalization: Capitalism, Territoriality and the International Relations of Modernity*. NY: Routledge.

Lake, David 1984. "Beneath the Commerce of Nations: A theory of International Economic Structures." *International Studies Quarterly*, 28: 143–270.

Lebowitz, Michael 1992. *Beyond Capital: Marx's Political Economy of the Working Class*. NY: Palgrave McMillan.

LeDuc, Thomas 1950. "The Disposal of the Public Domain on the Trans-Mississippi Plains: Some Opportunities for Investigation," *Agricultural History* 244: 199–204.

Le Heron, Richard, 1993. *Globalized Agriculture: Political Choice*. NY:Pergamon Press.

Lenin, Vladimir 1974. "New Data on the Laws Governing the Development of Capitalism in Agriculture". In *Collected Works*, Vol. 22:17–102. Moscow: Progress.

Lewontin, R.C., 2000. "The Maturing of Capitalist Agriculture: Farmer As Proletarian". In Magdoff, Fred; Foster, John Bellamy; and Buttel, Fredrick H. ed. *Hungry For Profit: The Agribusiness Threat to Farmers, and the Environment*. NY: Monthly Review Press.

Livesay, Harold and Porter, Glen 1971. *Murchants and Manufacturers*. Baltimore, MD: The John Hopkins Universtity Press.

Livingston, James 1986. *Origins of the Federal Reserve System: Money, Class and Corporate Capitalism, 1890–1913*. Ithaca, N.Y.: Cornell University Press.

Lord, Russell. 1947. *The Wallaces of Iowa*. Boston: Houghton Mifflin.

Madison, James Federalist No 10, Dawson Edition.

Maier, Charles 1987. *The Search for Stability: Explorations in Historical Political Economy*. NY: Cambridge.

Mandel, Ernest 1978. *The Second Slump. a Marxist Analysis of Recession in the Seventies*. London: New Left Book.s.

Mann, Susan 1990. *Agrarian Capitalism in Theory and Practice*. Chapel Hill: University of North Carolina Press.

Mann, Susan and Dickenson, Henry 1978. "Obstacles to the Development of a Capitalist Agriculture." *Journal of Peasant Studies* 5(4):466–81.

Marsden, Terry and Whatmore, Sarah 1994. "Finance Capital and Food System Resturcturing: National Incorporation of Global Dynamics." In McMichael, Philip *The Global Restructuring of Agro-Food Systems.* Ithaca, NY: Cornell University Press.

Marx, Karl 1861. *The American Question in England.* New-York Daily Tribune, October 11, 1861.

———. 1973. *Grundrisse.* Hammondsworth: Penguin.

McConnell, Grant. 1953. *The Decline of Agrarian Democracy.* NY: Atheneum.

———. 1966. *Private Power in American Democracy.* NY: Alfred A. Knopf.

McGovern, George 1964. *War Against Want: America's Food for Peace Program.* NY: Walker.

McMath, Robert C. 1992. *American Populism: A Social History, 1877–1898.* NY:Hill and Wang.

McMichael, Philip 1984. *Settlers and the agrarian question: Foundations of capitalism in colonial Australia.* Cambridge: CambridgeUniversity Press.

———. 1992. "Tensions between National and International Control of the World Food Order: Contours of a New Food Regime". *Sociological Perspectives* 35(2): 343–65.

———. 1994. "World Food System Restructuring Under a GATT Regime". *Political Geography* 12(3): 198–214.

———. ed. 1995. *Food and agrarian orders in the world economy.* Westport, CT: Praeger.

———. 2000. "Global Food Politics". In Magdoff, Fred, Foster, John Bellamy, and Buttel, Fredrick H. ed. *Hungry For Profit: The Agribusiness Threat to Farmers, and the Envrionment.* NY: Monthly Review Press.

——— 2004. *Development and Social Change: A Global Perspective.* Thousand Oaks CA: Pine Forge.

———. 2005. "Global development and the corporate food regime." In *New directions in the sociology of global development,* ed. F. Buttel, and P. McMichael, Oxford: Elsevier.

———. 2007. "Feeding the World: Agriculture, Development and Ecology". In Panitch, Leo and Leys, Colin eds. *Socialist Register 2007: Coming to Terms With Nature.* NY. Monthly Review Press.

———. 2009. "A food regime genealogy". Journal of Peasant Studies 36(1): 139–169.

McWilliams, Carey. 1966. *Factories in the Field: The Story of Migratory Farm Labor in California.* Berkeley: University of California Press.

Merrill, Micheal 1976. "Cash is Good To Eat: Self-Suficency in the Rural Economy of the United States", *Radical History Review.* 3(4):42–72.

Meyer, David 1980. "A Dynamic Model of the Integration of Frontier Places into the United States System of Cities," *Economic Geography,* 56:120–140.

———. 1989. "Midwestern Industrialization and The American Manufacturing Belt in the Nineteenth Century." *The Journal of Economic History,* 49:921–37.

Mikesell, Raymond 1952. *United States Economic Policy and International Relations*. NY: McGraw-Hill.

Minot, G.R. (1788, repr. 1971). *History of the Insurrections in Massachusetts in 1786*. Massachusetts Historical Society.

Moore, Barrington 1966. *Social Origins of Dictatorship and Democracy: Lord and Peasant in the Making of the Modern World*, Boston MA: Beacon Press.

Moore, Jason 2008. "Ecological Crises and the Agrarian Question in World-Historical Perspective", *Monthly Review* 60(6): 54–63.

———. 2010. "The End of the Road? Agricultural Revolutions in the Capitalist World-Ecology, 1450–2010" *Journal of Agrarian Change*, 10(3), 389–413.

Mooney, Patrick 1983 Towards a Class Analysis of Midwestern Agriculture. Rural Sociology 48(4): 563–84.

Morgan, Dan, 1979. *Merchants of Grain*. NY: Viking.

Morton, William 1951. "The Significance of Site in the Settlement of the American and Canadian Wests" *Agriculturarl History* 25: 97–104.

Moyer, Wayne and Josling, Tim 2002. *Agricultural Policy Reform: Politics and Process in the EU and US in the 1990s*. Burlington, VT: Ashgate.

Mundlak, Yair, 2005. "Economic Growth: Lessons from Two Centuries of American Agriculture". *Journal Of Economic Literature*, XLII, 989–1024.

Musoke, Moses E. 1981. "Mechanizing Cotton Production in the American South: The Tractor, 1915–1960." *Explorations in Economic History*. 18(4):347–375.

Mustard, Allan 2003. "An Unauthorized History of FAS." *Foreign Service Journal* 80:36–43.

Nash, Gerald D. 1972. *Issues in American Economic History*. Lexington, MA: D.C.Heath and Company.

Nemi, Albert 1970 "A Further Look At Interregional Canals and Economic Specialization: 1820–1840" Explorations in Economic History, 7:4.

———. 1987 (1974). *State and Regional Patterns in American Manufacturing 1860–1900*. Westport, CT: Greenwood Press.

Neustadt, Richard E. 1964. *Presidential Power: the Politics of Leadership*. NY: John Wiley.

Nimtz, August 2003. *Marx, Tocqueville, and Race in America: the "Absolute Democracy" or "Defiled Republic"*. NY: Lexington Books.

North, Douglas C. 1961. *The Economic Growth of the United States: 1790–1860*. NY: W.W. Norton and Company.

———. 1966 *Growth and Welfare in the American Past* Englewood Cliffs, NJ.

OÇonnor, James 1975. "The Twisted Dream". In *Monthly Review* 26(10): 41–54.

———. 1976 *A Note on Independent Commodity Production and Petty Capitalism* Monthly Review 28 (1) : 60–63.

Offer, Avner. 1989. *The First World War: An Agrarian Interpretation*. NY: Oxford.

Orden, Paarlberg and Roe 1999, *Policy Reform in American Agriculture: Analysis and Prognosis.* Chicago, IL.: University of Chicago Press.

Orloff, Ann Shola and Skocpol, Theda 1985. "Why Not Equal Protection? Explaining the Politics Of Public Social Spending in Britain, 1900–1911, and the United States, 1880s–1920." *American Sociological Review.* 49 (6):726–750.

Olmstead, Alan and Rhode, Paul 2002. "The Red Queen and the Hard Reds." *Jouranl of Economic History* 62:929–966.

Opie, John 1994. *The Law of the Land: Two Hundred Years of American Agricultural Policy.* Lincoln, NB: University of Nebraska Press.

Paarlberg, Robert, 1979. "The Failure of Food Power". In Fraenkel, Richard M., Hadwiger, Don F., and Brone, William P. eds. *The Role of US Agriculture in Foreign Policy.* NY: Praeger Publishers.

Paarlberg, Robert and Paarlberg, Don. 2000. "Agricultural Policy in the Twentieth Century". *Agricultural History.* 74:2 136–161.

Pabst, Margaret 1940 "Agricultural Trends in the Connecticut Valley Region of Massachusetts, 1800–1900," *Smith College Studies in History,* Vol XXVI.

Page, Brian and Walker, Richard 1991. "From Settlement to Fordism: The Agro-Industrial Revolution in the American Midwest." *Economic Geography* 67: 281–315.

Panitch, Leo 2004. "Globalization and the State" in *The Globalization Decade*, Panitch, Leo, Leys, Colin, Zuege, Alan, and Konings, Martain (eds). Nova Scotia, BC: Fernwood.

Panitch, Leo and Gindin, Sam, 2004. "Global Capitalism and American Empire". In Panitch, Leo and Leys, Colin eds. *Socialist Register 2004.* NY: Monthly Review Press.

———. 2005. "Finance and American Empire." In Panitch, Leo and Leys, Colin eds. *Socialist Register 2006: The Empire Reloaded.* NY: Monthly Review Press.

———. 2012. *The Making of Global Capitalism: The Political Economy of American Empire.* NY: Verso Press.

Panitch, Leo and Konings, 2009. "The Myth of Neoliberal Deregulation" *New Left Review* (57).

Parenti, Michael 1974. *Democracy for the Few.* Boston MA: Cengage Learning.

Patel, Raj 2007. *Stuffed And Starved: The Hidden Battle for the World Food System.* Brooklyn, NY: Melville House Publishing.

Paxon (1914) "The Railroads of the Old Northwest Before the Civil War" Transactions of the Wisconsin Academy of Sciences, Arts, and Letters, 17, Part 1: 243–74.

Peck and Tickell 2002. "Neoliberalizing Space", *Antipode* 34(3).

Philips, Kevin 2002. Wealth and Democracy: A Political History of the American Rich. NY: Broadway.

Piven, Frances Fox and Cloward, Richard 1977. *Poor People's Movements: Why they Succeed, How they Fail.* NY: Random House.

Polanyi, Karl 1944. *The Great Transformation.* NY: Farrar and Rinehart.

Polenberg, Richard. 1972. *War and Society: The United States, 1941–1945*. Philadelphia: J.B. Lippincott.

Post, Charlie 1982. "The American Road to Capitalism." *New Left Review*, I(133): 30–51.

———. 1995. The Agrarian Origins of US Capitalism: The Transformation of the Northern Countryside Before the Civil War. The Journal of Peasant Studies, 22(3): 389–445.

——— 1995. "The Agrarian Origins of US Capitalism". *Journal of Peasant Studies* 2(3).

———. 2011. *The American Road to Capitalism: Studies in Class-Structure, Economic Development and Political Conflict, 1620–1877*. Boston MA: Brill.

Potter, David 1972. *The South and the Concurrent Majority*. Baton Rouge. Louisiana State University Press.

Poulantzas, Nicos 1973. *Political Power and Social Classes*. London, England: New Left Books.

———. 1978. *State, Power, Socialism*. London, England: New Left Books.

Prasad, Monica 2012. *The Land of Too Much: American Abundance and the Paradox of Poverty*. Cambridge MA: Harvard University Press.

Pred, Allan 1966. *The Spatial Dynamics of US Urban Industrial Growth, 1800–1914: Interpretive and theoretical Essays*. Cambridge: MIT Press.

———. 1980. *Urban Growth and City-Systems in the United States, 1840–1860*. Cambridge MA: Harvard Press.

Pritchard, Bill 1996. "Shifts in food regimes, regulation and producer cooperatives: insights from the Australian and US dairy industries." *Environment and Planning*, 28(5), 857–75.

———. 1998. "The emergent contours of the third food regime: evidence from Australian dairy and wheat sectors." *Economic Geography*, 74(1), 64–74.

———. 2007. Food regimes. In: R. Kitchin and N. Thrift, eds. *The international encyclopedia of human geography*. Amsterdam: Elsevier.

———.2009. "The long hangover from the second food regime: a world-historical interpretation of the collapse of the WTO Doha Round" *Agriculture and Human Values* 26:297–307.

Pritchard, B. and D. Burch. 2003. *Agro-food globalisation in perspective. International restructuring in the processing tomato industry*. Aldershot: Ashgate.

Prude, Jonathan 1983. *The Coming of Industrial Order: Town and Factory Life in Rural Massachusetts, 1810–1860*. Cambridge MA: Harvard Press.

Pudup, Mary Beth 1987 "From Farm to Factory: Structuring and Location of the US Farm Machinery Industry" Economic geography, 63 (203–22).

Quadagno, jill. 1987. "Theories of the Welfare State." *Annual Review of sociology* 13:109–28.

Ragin, Charles 1987. The Comparative Method: Moving Beyond Qualitative and Quantitative Strategies. Berkeley CA. University of California Press.

Ransom, Edward and Sutch, Richard 1972. "Debt Peonage in the Cotton South After the Civil War. *Journal of Economic History* 32(3):643–667.

Rasmussen, Wayne 1969. "The American Revolution and American Agriculture: A Comment", *Agricultural History*, 43(4):125–8.

———. Ed. 1975. *Agriculture in the United States: A Documentary History.* 4 vols. New York: Random House.

Rasmussen, Wayne and Baker, Gladys 1979. "Price Supports and Adjustment Programs from 1933 through 1979: A Short History." *United StatesDepartment of Agriculture, Agricultural Information Bulletin* No. 424.

Raynolds, Laura 1994. "The restructuring of Third World agro-exports: changing production relations in the Dominican Republic." In: P. McMichael, ed. *The global restructuring of agrofood systems.* Ithaca, NY: Cornell University Press, pp. 214–37.

Raynolds, Laura, et al. 1993. "The 'new' internationalization of agriculture: a reformulation." World Development, 21(7), 1101–21.

Reardon, Thomas and Barrett, Chistopher 2000. "Agroindustrialization, Globalization, and International Development: An Overview of Issues, Patterns, and Determinants." *Agricultural Economics*, 23(3):195–205.

Revel, Alain and Ribound, Christophe 1986. *American Green Power.* Baltimore, MD: John Hopkins.

Rochester, Anna 1940. *Why Are Farmers Poor: The Agricultural Crisis in the United States.* NY: International.

Rodgers, George and Neu, Irene D. 1956 *The American Railroad Network, 1861–1890.* Cambridge MA.

Rosenberg, Emily S. 1985. "Foundations of United States International Financial Power: Gold Standard Diplomacy, 1900–1905." *Business History Review* 59.

Rothenberg, Winifred 1981. "The Market and the Massachusetts Farmers, 1750–1855", *Journal of Economic History*, 41(2):283–314.

———. 1985. "The Emergence of a Capital Market in Rural Massachusetts, 1730–1838", *Journal of Economic History*, 45(4):780–807.

———. 1988. "The Emergence of Farm Labor Markets and the Transformation of the Rural Economy: Massachusetts, 1750–1855", *Journal of Economic History*, 48(3):537–66.

Royce, Edward 1985. "The Origin of Southern Sharecropping: Explaining Social Change". *Current Perspectives in Social Theory* 6:279–299.

Rubenson, Richard and Sokolovsky, Joan. 1988. "Patterns of Industrial Regulation: Railroads in the World-economy." In *Rethinking the Nineteenth-Century World-Economy*, edited by Francisco Ramirez. NY: Greenwood Press.

Rueschmeyer, Dietrich and Evans, Peter 1985. "The State and Economic Transformation: Toward an Analysis of the Conditions Underlying Effective Intervention" in Peter Evans, Dietrich Rueschemeyer and Theda Skocpol, eds., *Bringing the State Back In.* Cambridge: Cambridge University Press.

Ruggie, John 1982. "International Regimes, Transactions, and Change: Embedded Liberalism in the Postwar Economic Order." *International Organization*, 36(2):379–415.

Saloutos, Theodore 1960. *Farmers Movements in the South 1865–1933*. Lincoln, NB: University Of Nebraska Press.

———. 1962. "Land Policy and its Relation to Agricultural Production and Distribution, 1862 to 1933," *Journal of Economic History* 22 4: 445–60.

———. 1982. *The American Farmer and the New Deal*. Ames: The Iowa State University Press.

Sanders, Elizabeth 1989. *Roots of Reform: Farmers, Workers and the American State, 1877–1917*. Chicago, Ill: University of Chicago Press.

Schlesinger, Aurthur M. 1958. *The Coming of the New Deal: the Age of Roosevelt*. Boston: Houghton Mifflin.

Schmidt, L.B. 1920. "Origin of the Land Grant College Act of 1862," *Iowa Homestead*, 65 (11):1, 27, 28, 53.

Schwartz, Herman and Seabrooke, Leonard 2008. "Varieties of Residential Capitalism in the International Political Economy: Old Welfare States and the New Politics of Housing." *Comparative European Politics* 6(3): 237–261.

Scott, R.V. 1962. "Railroads and farmers: educational trais in Missouri 1902–1914." *Agricultural History* 36(I): 3–15.

Seabrooke, Leonard 2001. *US Power in International Finance: The Victory of Dividends*, NY: Palgrave.

Shaikh, Anwar 1978. Political Economy and Capitalism: Notes on Dobb's Theory of Crisis Cambridge Journal of Economics, No.2.

Shannon, Fred A. 1972. "A Post Mortem on the Labor-Safety-Valve Theory" In Nash, Gerald D. *Issues in American Economic History*. Lexington, MA. D.C. Heath and Company.

———. 1977. *The Farmer's Last Frontier: Agriculture, 1860–1897*. White Plains, NY: M.E. Sharpe.

Sheldon, A.E. 1904. "Chapter 7: Nebraska Territory," *Semi-Centennial History of Nebraska*. Lincoln, NE: Lemon Publishing.

Shepherd, James. 1980. "The Development of New Wheat Varieties in the Pacific Northwest." Agricultural History 54: 52–63.

Shugg, Rodger 1939. *Origins of Class Struggle in Louisiana*. Baton Rouge, LA: Louisiana State University Press.

Sklar, Martin 1988. *The Corporate Reconstruction of American Capitalism, 1890–1916: The Market, the Law, and Politics*. London: Cambridge University Press.

Skocpol, Theda. 1980. "Political Responses to Capitalist Crises: Neo-Marxist Theories of the State and the Case of the New Deal." *Politics and Society*. 10:155–201.

———. 1984. Vision and Method in Historical Sociology. NY: Cambridge University Press.

Skocpol, Theda and Finegold, Kenneth. 1982. "State Capacity and Economic Intervention in the Early New Deal" in *Political Science Quarterly*, Vol. 97 No 1: 255–278.

———. 1995. *State and Party in America's New Deal*. Madison: University of Wisconsin Press.

Skowronek, Stephen. 1982. *Building a New American State: The Expansion of National Administrative Capacities 1877–1920*. NY: Cambridge University Press.

Sloan, Thomas J. 1979. "The Political Role of US Grain Exports in a "Hungry World"". In Fraenkel, Richard M., Hadwiger, Don F., and Brone, William P. eds. *The Role Of US Agriculture in Foreign Policy*. NY: Praeger Publishers.

Sokoloff, Kenneth L. (1986) "Productivity Growth in Manufacturing During Early Industrialization: Evidence from the American Northeast, 1820–1860" in Engerman, Stanley and Gallman, Robert (Eds.) Long-term Factors in American Economic Growth, Chicago: University of Illinois.

Sorj, Bernardo, Goodman, David and Wilkinson, Richard 1987. *From Farming to Biotechnology: A Theory of Agro-Industrial Development*. NY: Blackwell.

Stephenson, George Malcolm (1917) *The Political History of the Public Lands, from 1840 to 1862: From Pre-Emption to Homestead*. Public Domain originally published in Boston by Richard G. Badger.

Stewart, Charles 1987. "Does Structure Matter? The Effects of Structural Change on Spending Decisions in the House, 1871–1922" *American Journal of Political Science* Vol. 31, No. 3: 584–605.

Stinchcombe, Arthur 1978. Theoretical Methods in Social History. NY: Academic Press.

Stock, Catherine McNicol (1996) *Rural Radicals: From Bacon's Rebellion to the Oklahoma City Bombing* NY: Penguin.

Summerhill, Thomas 2005. *Harvest of Dissent: Agrarianism in Nineteenth-Century New York*. Chicago Ill: University of Illinois Press.

Sussman, Paul, 1989. "Exporting the Crisis: US Agriculture and the Third World". *Economic Geography* 65(4): 293–313.

Swanson, Merwin 1977. "The Country Life Movement and the American Churches". *Church Hisotry* 46(3): 358–359.

Sylla, Richard 1967. "Finance and Capital in the United States, 1850–1900," *Journal of Economic History*, (December 1967), 621–24.

Talbot, Ross 1978. *The Chicken War: An International Trade Conflict Between US and the European Economic Commission, 1961–1964*. Ames, IA: Iowa State.

Taska, Henry J. 1938. *The Reciprocal Trade Policy of the United States: A Study in Trade Policy*, Dissertation, Philadelphia PA: University of Pennsylvania.

Taylor, Charles (1917) *History of the Board of Trade of The City of Chicago*. Chicago Ill: Robert O. Law.

Teschke, Benno 2003. *The Myth of 1648: Class, Geopolitics, and the Making of Modern International Relations*. NY: Verso.

Therborn, Goran 1983. "Why Some Classes are More Successful than Others." *New Left Review*, I/138.
Tilly, Charles 1990. *Coercion, Capital, and European States, AD 990–1990*. Cambridge, MA: Basil Blackwell.
Timberlake, Richard 1978. *The Origins of Central Banking in the United States*. Cambridge, MA: Harvard University Press.
Timmers, Peter 2009. *A World Without Agriculture: Structural Transformation in Historical Perspective*, Washington D.C.: AEI Press.
Toma, Peter, 1967. *The Politics of Food for Peace*. Tucson, AZ.: University of Arizona Press.
True, Alfred 1900. "Agricultural Education in the United States." *Yearbook of Agriculture, 1899*. Washington DC.
———. 1929. History of Agricultural Education in the United States, 1785–1925.
Turner, Fredrick Jackson 1893. *The Frontier Thesis in American History*. NY: Henry Holt and Company.
Vogeler, Ingolf, 1981. *The Myth of the Family Farm: Agribusiness Dominance of US Agriculture*. Boulder, CO: Westview Press.
Wallace, Henry A. 1934. "American Agriculture and World Markets" *Foreign Affairs* 12:216–30.
———. 1934. *American Must Choose*. New York.
———. edited by Russell Lord 1944. *Democracy Reborn*. NY: Reynal & Hitchcock.
Wallerstein, Michael, 1980. *Food for War, Food for Peace: United States Food Aid in Global Context*. Cambridgem MA: MIT Press.
Walsh, Margaret. 1982. "From Pork Merchant to Meat Packer: The Midwestern Meat Industry in the Mid Nineteenth Century." *Agricultural History*. 56:127–37, 167–71.
Watkins, Kevin, 1991. "Agriculture and Food Security in the GATT Uruguay Round". *Review of African Political Economy*, 50: 38–50.
———. 1996. "Free Trade and Farm Fallacies: From the Uruguay Round to the World Food Summit". *The Ecologist*, 26(6), 244–255.
Watts, Michael, 1996. "Development III: the Global Agrofood System and Late Twentieth-century Development (or Kautsky Redux)". *Progress in Human Geography* 20(2): 230245.
Webb, David 1977. "The Thomas Amendment: A Rural Oklahoma Response to the Great Depression." in *Rural Oklahoma*, ed. Donald E. Green. Oklahoma City: Oklahoma Historical Society.
Weiman, David 1983 "Petty Production in the Cotton South: A Study of Upcountry Georgia, 1840–1850" PhD Dissertation, Stanford University 1983.
Weiss, T. 2007. *The global food economy. The battle for the future of farming*. London: Zed Books.
Wiebe, Robert. 1967. *The Search for Order: 1877–1920*. NY: Hill and Wang.

Wiener, Jonathan 1978. *Social Origins of the New South: Alabama, 1860–1880*, Baton Rouge: Louisiana State University Press.

Williams, W.M. 1961."Changing Functions of the Community" *Sociologia Ruralis* Vol. 4:299–314.

Winders, Bill. 2001. *Welcome to the Free Market: Class Bases of US Agricultural Policy, 1938–1996*. Dissertation Emory University.

———. 2009. *The Politics of Food Supply: US Agricultural Policy in the World Economy*. New Haven: Yale.

Winters, Donald L. 1978. "The Agricultural Ladder in Southern Agriculture: Tennessee, 1850–1870". *Agricultural History*. Vol. 61, 3: 36–52.

Wolf, Eric 1982. *Europe and the People Without History*. Las Angelis, CA: University of California Press.

Wood, Ellen Maeiksins 1995. *Democracy Against Capitalism: Renewing Historical Materialism*. Cambridge, UK: Cambridge University Press.

———. 2002. *The Origin of Capitalism: A Longer View*. NY: Verso.

———. 2010. "Peasants and the Market Imperative: The Origins of Capitalism" in *Peasants and Globalization: Political Economy, Rural Transformation and The Agrarian Question by* Akram-Lodhi, A. Haroon and Key, Cristobal (eds) NY: Routledge.

Wood, Robert, 1986. *From Marshall Plan to Debt Crisis: Foreign Aid and Development Choices in the World Economy*. Berkley CA: University of California Press.

Woodman, Harold 1979. "The Old South: Global and Local Perspectives on Power, Politics, and Ideology." *Civil War History* Vol. 25, No. 4.

Young, Roland. 1956. *Congressional Politics in the Second World War*. NY: Columbia University Press.

Zeichner, Oscar (1939), "The Transition from Slave to Free Agricultural Labor in the Southern States" *Agricultural History* XIII, No. 1.Bernstein, Henry 2010. *Class Dynamics of Agrarian Change*, Sternling, VA: Fern.

Index

abolition 14, 33
abolitionists 78, 118
accumulate 5, 12, 149
accumulation 8, 13, 21–22, 25, 161, 188, 191, 252, 255–256, 260, 263, 265
American Farm Bureau Federation (AFBF) xi, 27, 135–136, 139, 151, 155, 165, 168, 170–171, 173–174, 176, 179–186, 189–197, 200, 206, 210, 212, 215
agitation 47, 52, 78, 114, 117, 138, 269
Aglietta, Michael 3, 10, 22, 282
Agrarianism 126, 129, 169, 288, 300
agrarians 43, 59, 98, 119, 127, 135, 158, 172, 214, 269
agribusiness 13, 26–27, 121, 140, 155, 180, 185, 193–194, 196, 219–220, 222, 224, 237, 247, 269–270, 282, 285, 291, 293–294, 301
Agricultural Adjustment Act (AAA) viii, xi, 28, 174–182, 184–186, 188–189, 191–192, 195–196, 199, 201–202, 204, 206–208, 221, 250, 280 *see also* production controls, domestic allotment, Federal Farm Board
Agrofood 249, 298, 301
Ahlberg, Kristin 204, 222, 236, 282
Alabama 1, 83, 87, 95, 126, 132, 302
Alaska 1
antagonism 2, 41, 75, 80, 112, 114
antebellum 6, 16, 64, 73, 75, 94, 282–283, 287–288
antidumping 241
antitrust 131, 279
appropriation 52–53, 142, 146, 152–153, 239
Araghi, Fershad 215, 221, 224, 229, 248–249, 282
Argentina 203, 235, 280
aristocratic 33, 79–80, 273
Arizona ii, 301
Arkansas 55, 83, 179
Arrighi, Giovanni 257, 282
Attack, Jeremy 91, 132, 283
Australia 294
Awokuse, Titus 237, 283

balance of class forces 3, 9, 26, 29, 31, 35–37, 59, 72–73, 75, 83, 88, 99, 101, 105, 111, 116, 121, 123, 125, 129, 138–140, 145, 161, 165, 170, 174, 180–181, 184–185, 187, 189, 191–192, 194, 200, 210, 212–213, 217, 235, 237, 246, 259–263, 265–266, 271
Banaji, Jairus 13, 85, 283
Bankhead-Jones Act 184
Beard, Charles 33, 76, 105, 283
Bensel, Richard 79–81, 101, 106, 156, 189, 284
Bernstein, Irving 13, 42, 53, 157, 184, 197–199, 215, 220, 264, 284, 285, 289
black codes x, 86, 89–90, 97, 102 *see also* reconstruction
Block, Fred 19, 188, 284
Bogue, Margaret 91, 132, 284
Brenner, Robert 4, 16, 19, 98, 231, 233, 284, 290 *see also* political marxism
Bryan, William Jennings 123, 126, 128, 130–131, 292 *See also* fusionism,
Buck, Solon 107–109, 113–116, 119–120, 134, 285
Burbach, Roger and Flynn, Patricia 232–236, 241, 247–249, 254, 285
Buttel, Frederick 26, 194, 285, 289, 292–294
Butz, Earl 239

California ii, viii, 121, 132, 141, 174, 180, 188, 196–201, 211, 274, 276, 280, 287–288, 291, 293–294, 297, 302
Carville, Earl and Hoffman, Ronald 10, 77, 285
Chicago Mercantile Exchange (CME) 240
Chorev, Nitsan 26, 241, 245–246, 263, 286
Clark, Christopher 5, 8, 12, 34, 39–40, 70, 78–80, 96, 286
Commodity Futures 240 *see also* Chicago Mercantile Exchange (CME)
Confederacy 88, 90, 96
Connecticut 39, 60, 113, 198, 296
cooperative 112–113, 115, 119, 121, 130, 157, 167, 173, 226, 273–275
cooperatives 112, 119–122, 130, 168, 171–172, 175, 222, 223, 275–276, 279, 281, 297
Countryman, Edward 2, 41–42, 286
Cronon, William 48, 60–61, 63–65, 67–68, 71, 164–165, 287

cropper 73, 84, 84, 86–87, 92–93, 96, 97, 99–100, 103, 132 *see also* Share Cropping, Tennancy
Cuba 127, 205
currency 38, 65–66, 91, 101, 108–109, 114–116, 124, 131, 156–158, 183, 204, 224, 228, 234, 240
Curti, Merle 91, 132, 287

Danbom, David 54, 165, 287
Daniel, Cletus 39, 54, 144, 150, 186, 199, 285, 287
Davis, Ronald 89, 220, 280, 287
Daws, S.O. 120, 122 *see also* Populists, populist movement, Farmer's Alliance
deflationary 101, 108, 109, 110
Delaware 113
Democratic 122, 124–128, 130, 174, 178, 196, 209
Democrats 113, 119, 124–126, 131, 163, 169, 178–179, 225, 287, 291
demonstration 61, 93, 162, 165–166, 277, 279
Domestic allotment 174, 176–178, 182, 183 *see also* production controls, Agricultural Adjustment Act
Domhoff, William and Weber, Michael 135–136, 176, 178–181, 183, 213, 287
Donnelly, Ignatius 115–116 *see also* Populist, populist movement, Farmer's Alliance
drought 92, 111
Dubois, W.E.B. 87, 287 *see also* Reconstruction

Eichengreen, Barry 110
Eisenhower, Dwight D. 218
Ellsworth, Clayton 52–53, 142–143, 288
empire i, iii, 3, 22, 214, 216, 220, 230, 232, 237–238, 257, 263, 265, 267, 270–271, 289, 296
England 3–5, 39, 59, 76–77, 283, 285, 287, 294, 297
enterprises 6, 36, 50, 51, 86, 111, 274, 284
entomology 52, 148, 150
entrepreneurial 68, 71
Essex, Jamey ix, 204, 227, 244–245, 288
European Union (EU) 253, 282, 295
Euromarket 248
Europe 36, 64, 106, 134, 145, 203, 217, 219, 229–231, 233, 244, 246, 273, 284, 302

European xi, 13, 30, 183, 217–218, 230, 233, 244, 248, 251, 253, 290, 299–301
Executive authority 133, 163, 165, 206–207, 210, 235–236, 241–243, 245, 263, 265, 285
Experiment Station 26, 278
Development of 148, 152–153, 155, 160–161
Populist influences 160–161
during the New Deal 194–195, 210
export 31, 48, 60, 69, 109, 116, 147, 171, 173, 206, 210, 217, 219, 221, 225, 230, 232, 234, 237, 240, 242–243, 246–251, 254, 256, 260–261, 263
exported 68, 106, 239, 248
exports x, 53, 66, 79, 107, 127, 134, 136, 143, 147, 149, 298
promotion of 172, 206, 218, 224–225, 227, 230–233, 237–242, 244, 247, 249, 254–255,

Farm Bureau (FB) vii, xi, 134–135, 159, 165, 177, 180–182, 185, 193, 195–196, 275, 285
Farmer's Alliance (FA) 122–123
Federal Farm Board (FFB) 171–173, 279
Federalist 33, 293
finance 36, 51, 81, 101, 117, 158, 198, 201, 213, 240, 250, 268, 286, 291, 294, 296, 299–300
financial 3, 9, 43, 51, 81–82, 92, 97, 100–101, 106, 112, 116–117, 120, 156–157, 183–184, 196, 204, 230, 235, 240, 247–248, 250, 298
Finegold, Kenneth 28, 185, 187–190, 192–193, 288, 300
Fishlow, Lawrence 50, 63, 288
Fite, Gilbert 169, 171, 185–186, 208–209, 288
Flannigan Report 242–243, 280
Florida 83, 147, 198–199
flour 6, 52, 57, 63, 68–69, 71, 107, 167, 254
Foner, Eric 86, 88–90, 93–94, 100, 118, 124, 289
Food Regimes Approach viii, 1, 20–22, 31, 143, 215–216, 226, 251–253, 255–260, 262–263, 282, 289, 297 *see also* Friedmann, Harriet and McMichael, Philip
foreclosures 39, 43, 83, 111, 121, 170, 220
Foreign Agricultural Service (FAS) xi, 203–205, 222, 226–228, 244, 280, 288, 295
France 124
Franklin Delano Roosevelt (FDR) 163, 171, 176–178, 195–196, 206, 210, 292

INDEX

305

Freedman's Bureau   88–90, 92–93, 99, 103–102
Frie's Rebellion   41, 44
Friedmann, Harriet   1, 4, 20–22, 85, 143, 217–218, 226, 233, 247, 249, 251–255, 257, 259, 262, 289
Frontier   5, 29, 45, 63, 107, 154, 269, 284, 287–288, 290, 294, 299, 301
fusionists   125, 126, 130 *see also* populists movement, Bryan, William Jennings

Gates, Paul W.   4–5, 35–37, 45–47, 50–51, 53–54, 58, 60–61, 64, 68, 91, 95, 107, 132, 146–147, 154, 289
GATT (General Agreement on Trade and Tariffs)   xi, 220, 240, 242, 244–245, 253, 256, 282, 294, 301 *see also* WTO, trade
Georgia   42, 55, 95–96, 99, 283, 285, 288, 291, 301
Gilbert, Jess and Howe, Carolyn   26, 169–170, 185–186, 190–197, 199, 288, 290
Gill, Stephen   246, 256, 290
Gindin, Sam   15, 158, 218, 229–230, 232–233, 235, 237, 240, 248, 251, 261, 296 *see also* Panitch, Leo
Goodman, David   20, 94, 166, 290, 300
Goodwyn, Lawrence   91, 108–109, 112, 115–120, 122, 126, 290
grain elevator   60, 65, 67 *see also* Chicago, Cronon, William
grain   10, 12, 48, 60, 64–69, 91, 98, 106, 114, 147, 149, 164–166, 169, 171, 219, 225, 232–234, 237, 239, 242, 244, 254, 264–265, 273, 278–279, 282, 284, 286, 288, 295, 300
Grange   25, 112–117, 119, 121, 124, 130, 158–159, 177, 190, 274 *see also* Patrons of Husbandry, populist movement
Granger Laws   114–115 *see also* Grange
Greenback   101, 108–109, 115–116, 119, 123–124, 156, 183

Hahn, Steven   96, 107, 112–113, 119, 291
Hamilton, Alexander   138, 171–172, 177–178, 181, 183, 190, 291
Hammond, Bray   36, 79, 83, 156, 291
Harding, Thomas   52–53, 142–143, 150, 153–154, 166, 171, 291
Harvey, David   16, 23–24, 148, 291

Headlee, Sue   4–5, 12, 60–61, 66, 68, 70–71, 76, 156–157, 263, 291
hegemonic   9, 21, 101–102, 133, 180, 201, 208, 211, 214, 236, 238, 246, 249, 251, 253, 255–257, 265
hegemony   viii, 3, 18, 81, 108, 133, 140, 173, 179, 194, 213, 215, 240, 248, 251–252, 255, 257, 261–262, 264, 282, 292
Helleiner, Eric   291
Henderson, Susan   24, 61, 198, 201, 291
Henretta, James   5, 96, 291
Hicks, John D.   91, 99–100, 110–111, 117, 291
Hofstadter, Richard   111–112, 122, 127–129, 292
Homestead Act   38, 46, 50, 77–78, 82, 145, 156, 269, 299–300
Hoover, Herbert   166, 169, 171, 204, 279, 291
Hurt, Douglas   130–131, 133–134, 136, 138, 145, 157–158, 161, 164, 166–169, 171–172, 182, 210–211, 225, 292

Illinois   48–51, 57–58, 68, 113–114, 149, 159, 275, 283–286, 289, 292, 300
implements   10, 26, 49, 57, 59–60, 62, 67–68, 71–72, 113, 120, 194
independent commodity production   39, 295
India   234–236
Indiana   48, 55, 58, 284
industrial   vii–viii, x, 3–4, 6–14, 19–21, 23–27, 29–35, 37, 39, 41–43, 45, 47, 49–51, 53–57, 59–67, 69–74, 76–77, 80–82, 86, 92–93, 103–105, 107–109, 112–113, 116–118, 129–130, 136–138, 140–159, 161–166, 168–173, 175–178, 180, 182, 184, 187–188, 190–191, 193, 195–198, 200–202, 204–209, 211–217, 219–221, 224–225, 227, 231, 234, 236–237, 244, 246–248, 250–252, 257, 259–262, 264–271, 284, 288
industrialists   59, 76, 95, 165, 187
industrialization   viii, 6–9, 11–15, 20, 28, 30, 49, 53, 59–60, 62–63, 66, 68–69, 71–73, 75, 77, 127, 133, 136, 148, 152–153, 156, 158, 160, 162, 169–170, 176–177, 179, 185, 187, 194, 196, 201–202, 208–209, 212–215, 220, 222, 225, 229, 232, 237, 240, 246, 257, 260–261, 264–268, 270, 283–284, 287, 294, 300
industrialized   146, 150, 219, 268
industrializing   92, 116, 127, 156

industrially   10, 12, 55–56, 76, 150, 152, 154, 249
industries   6, 10, 24, 30, 49, 51, 57, 60, 62, 65, 71, 100, 107, 160–161, 168, 202, 206, 211, 213, 232, 242–243, 245, 247, 297
industry   4, 12, 21, 36, 51–52, 55–57, 59, 63, 66–68, 71–73, 80, 89, 93–94, 99, 106, 110, 127, 141, 145–146, 151, 153–154, 156–157, 162, 164–165, 168–169, 171, 177, 181, 183, 190–191, 197, 202, 210, 212, 214, 224, 227, 245, 253, 255, 267, 291, 297, 301
Iowa   58, 69, 115, 132, 160, 283, 287, 293, 299–300

Jeffersonian   79, 122, 133

Kansas   58, 110–111, 125–126, 132, 155, 160, 228
Kennedy, John F.   225–226, 228, 243, 254
Kentucky   52, 55, 288
Kissinger, Henry   233–234, 236, 238
Kloppenburg, Jack   26, 54, 56, 145, 148, 153–154, 161, 165, 194, 196, 292
Kolko, Gabriel   130, 135, 170–172, 177, 180, 184–185, 191, 194–195, 211, 292
Konings, Martijin   28, 36, 216, 224, 293, 296
Korea   233, 237
Krasner, Steven   15, 256, 293
Kulikoff, Alan   4, 35, 42, 263, 293
KY, see Kentucky

LA, see Louisiana
Lacher, Hannes   15, 263, 293
Land Grant   47, 50–51, 64, 82, 86, 137, 144–145, 155, 160, 166, 179, 191–192, 194–196, 280, 285, 291–292, 299
landlord   43, 84, 86, 96–97, 99, 184–188, 192, 210, 290
Lexington   284, 288, 290, 295, 299
lien   93, 97, 99–100, 116–117, 119, 121 see also crop lien system, tenancy, share cropping
Lincoln, Abraham   79, 145, 159, 280, 289, 291, 296, 299
Livesay, Harold   51, 81–82, 293
livestock   77, 106, 148, 174, 244, 276, 279
llinois   286
London   ii, 4, 183, 203, 282–283, 285, 289, 291–293, 297, 299, 301

Louisiana   52, 83, 90, 95, 178, 289, 297, 299, 302

MA, see Massachusetts
machinery   6, 8, 10, 55–57, 60, 65, 68–69, 71, 93, 98, 107, 109, 158, 201, 209, 219, 267, 278, 297
MacNamara, Robert   238
Madison, James   33, 38, 48, 284–285, 287, 292–293, 300
Maier, Charles   165, 211, 293
Maine   41–42, 44, 51, 55, 127, 276
Mann, Susan   24, 61, 84, 86, 88–89, 92–95, 102, 184, 186, 209, 293
Marshall Plan   31, 217–220, 229, 233, 237, 251, 302
Marx, Karl   16, 19, 24, 88, 98, 102, 293–295
Marxist   12, 15–16, 23, 75, 238, 285, 289, 293, 299
Massachusetts   39–41, 51–52, 60, 62, 282–284, 286–292, 295–298 295–299, 301
McConnell, Grant   123, 129, 131, 135–137, 162, 164, 166, 170, 176–177, 179–182, 185, 194–195, 202, 213, 219, 294
McKinley, William   127, 129
McMath, Robert   84, 91, 94–98, 100, 113, 121–122, 124–125, 190, 294
McMichael, Philip   1, 20–22, 26, 143, 215, 217–219, 226, 229, 237, 246–247, 249, 251–255, 257–262, 264, 289, 294, 298
McNary-Haugen   xi, 169–170, 176–177
McWilliams, Carey   197–201, 294
meat   6, 52, 153, 155, 169, 301
meatpacking   71
mercantile   xi, 21, 31, 164, 240, 251–252, 255, 260–261, 292
mercantilist   252
Mexico   203, 247
Meyer, David   48, 57, 59, 62, 69, 286, 294
Michigan   48, 58, 198, 285
Midwest   5, 7, 9, 11, 13–14, 25, 45, 48–50, 56–57, 59–64, 66, 68–70, 72, 74, 77–78, 82, 93, 110–111, 114, 120, 171, 180, 188, 193, 200, 220, 267–268, 273, 287, 296
Midwestern   x, 5, 7, 10–11, 48–49, 51, 56–57, 59–63, 66, 69, 71, 73, 82, 96, 109, 117–118, 124, 153, 158, 170, 197, 268, 294–295, 301
Minnesota   58, 111, 113–115, 291

INDEX

Mississippi 45, 61, 83, 90, 95, 179, 293
Missouri 50, 55, 58, 134, 282, 299
modernization 2, 9, 21, 26–27, 30, 50, 54, 82, 103, 145, 147, 157, 159–160, 180, 195, 201–202, 208, 210, 213, 215, 217, 219, 221, 227, 262, 266
modernize 3, 30, 34, 53, 56, 140, 143, 145, 147, 158, 170, 178, 185, 192, 202–204, 215, 217, 221, 249, 270
monetary 101, 109, 127, 183, 244, 280
monocrop 196
monoculture 98
Montana 134, 199
Moore, Barrington 80, 221, 224, 295
Morrill Act 82, 137, 145, 148, 159, 278
mortgage 24, 39, 47, 72, 93, 99–100, 110–111, 117, 170, 180, 183, 211
mortgages 4, 7, 42, 117, 141, 172, 183, 211, 267, 270
multilateral 235, 249, 255–256, 263, 280

National Farmers Union (FU) 135, 195
NC, see North Carolina
NE, see Nebraska
Nebraska 58, 110–111, 117, 126, 130, 228, 291, 296, 299
Nemi, Albert 49, 55, 57, 59–60, 69, 76, 295
neoliberal 31, 217, 239, 244–246, 256, 262, 296
neoliberalism 244–245, 256, 264–265, 285
neoliberalization 245, 288, 296
Nevada 113
New Deal viii, 28, 30–31, 53, 136, 174–181, 183–187, 189–193, 195–197, 199, 201–213, 215, 217–218, 220–222, 224, 239, 250–251, 253, 256, 263, 275, 283, 285–288, 290–292, 299–300 see also Agricultural Adjustment Act
New Jersey 2, 41, 285, 291–292, 295
New York iv, 1, 2, 32, 41, 73, 105, 140, 174, 215, 266, 273, 275, 278, 281–296, 298–302
Nimtz, August 88, 295
Nixon, Richard 233, 238, 242–243, 254
Non-partisan League 134, 200, 242, 275
North Carolina 2, 40–42, 97, 132, 283, 291, 293
North Dakota 134, 165
Northeast 8–9, 60, 300

Northeastern 2, 5, 41, 92, 106
Northern 6, 28, 55, 73–74, 76, 78–79, 81, 87, 95, 101–102, 106, 118, 127, 122, 174, 179, 247, 286, 297
Northwest 36, 120, 122, 296, 299
nutrient 152, 282
nutrition 152, 167, 223, 278, 282
Nutritional 151–152, 167
NY, see New York

Ohio 38, 48–49, 58, 132
OK, see Oklahoma
Oklahoma 95, 130, 183, 288, 291, 300–301
one crop evil 91, 209
Oregon iv, 156
overproduction 26, 109, 137, 151, 154, 173, 175, 211, 213, 215, 217, 221, 239, 253
overseas 153, 204, 222–223, 226, 232, 248, 288
oversupply 108 see also overproduction

PA, see Pennsylvania
Paarlberg 134–136, 168–169, 181, 296
Page, Brian and Walker, Richard 4, 8, 59, 62, 71, 263, 268
Panitch, Leo ix, 10, 15, 23, 28, 158, 216, 218, 224, 229–230, 232–233, 235, 237, 240, 248, 251, 256, 261, 289–290, 294, 296
Patent Office 52–56, 142–146, 149, 159
patriarchal 44, 93
Patrons of Husbandry 112, 159 see also Grange
peasant 8, 42, 229, 249, 257, 282, 285, 289, 293–295, 297, 302
Pennsylvania 41–42, 55, 60, 100, 145, 284, 300
pesticides 71, 148, 276
petty commodity production: development of 2, 4–9, 11–12, 14, 16, 24, 32, 34–36, 39–40, 44, 60–62, 69–71, 73–74
persistence of 79, 82, 84–86, 92, 95, 98
role in populism 107, 109, 137, 268, 290
Philadelphia 273, 284, 291, 297, 300
Piven, Frances Fox 25, 123, 190, 250, 296
plains 11, 98, 124, 198, 214, 289, 293, 299
planter 52, 73, 77, 79–80, 83–84, 86, 90–95, 94, 97, 99–100, 102–103, 116, 137, 146, 179, 184, 187
planters 75, 82, 86–88, 103, 146
Pleuropneumonia 52

Polanyi, Karl   216, 296
Polanyian   22, 216
Political Marxism, *see* Political Marxist
Political Marxist   12, 15–16 *see also* Brenner, Robert, Wood, Ellen Meiksins
populism   111–112, 115, 118, 120–121, 123, 126, 162, 190
Populism   vii, 83, 105, 111–112, 126, 288, 291, 294
populist   2, 16, 25, 29, 88, 103, 105, 112, 115–117, 119, 123, 125–130, 137–138, 140, 155–157, 159, 161–164, 183, 187, 189, 212–213, 274
Populist   vii, 25, 73, 104, 118, 123, 126, 128, 130, 160, 274, 280, 290–291
populists   112, 118–120, 122, 124–129, 133, 136–137, 139, 164, 191, 211
Post, Charles   iv, viii–ix, 4–9, 12, 16, 39–40, 45, 61–62, 70, 73, 76, 83–84, 99, 215, 260, 263, 267–268, 297, 299
postbellum   vii, 83, 96, 100–101, 103, 105, 118, 188
potato   230
potatoes   91, 178
Poulantzas   19, 26, 245, 297
prairie   64, 111, 284, 290
prairies   61, 63, 95, 114
Prasad, Monica   108, 110, 117–118, 132, 165, 211–212, 297
Production Controls   172, 176–179, 196, 201–202, 208–209, 225, 239
Progressive   129, 133, 138, 157, 162–164
progressive   3, 118, 130, 136, 162, 194, 196, 198, 219
progressives   138, 185
Progressives   151, 293
progressivism   162

race   73, 88, 91, 125, 187, 284, 290, 295
racial   97, 104, 119, 124–125, 128, 179, 198–199
racialization   198
racially   88, 103, 178
racism   102
railroad   vii, 14, 37, 43, 45, 47, 48, 50–51, 57, 61, 63–64, 68–69, 72, 82, 96, 109, 113–115, 118–119, 120, 121, 123, 133–134, 156, 165–166, 220, 289, 298
railroads   49–51, 63–64, 97, 100, 113–115, 117, 120, 155–157, 161, 288, 292, 296, 298–299
railway   51, 82, 114, 137, 145, 156, 291

rebellion   25, 33, 39–41, 44, 59, 206, 266, 273, 300
reconstruct   31, 220, 242, 251, 256, 287
reconstructing   31, 185, 218, 226, 233, 251
reconstruction   31, 86, 101–102, 133, 147, 189, 216–218
Reconstruction   vii, 31, 86–87, 91, 94, 99, 101–102, 118, 133, 147, 189, 216–218, 235, 287, 289, 299
refinance   117, 183
regime   21–22, 31, 108, 196, 216, 229, 250–261, 264–265, 294, 297
regimes   viii, 1, 15, 20–22, 31, 143, 215–216, 226, 245, 251–253, 255–260, 262–264, 282, 289, 297, 299
Relative Autonomy   181, 187–188, 190, 192, 239, 265
Republican   76, 78–81, 100–102, 107, 118, 124, 127, 144, 163, 171, 289
resistance   vii, 1, 3, 5, 9–10, 15, 17, 20, 23–26, 29–30, 33, 39, 42, 45–46, 59, 67, 72, 79, 88, 105, 138, 153, 168, 171, 177, 212, 214, 226, 234, 245, 250, 269–270
revenue   8, 36, 43, 47, 70, 106, 208, 268, 288
revolt   10, 41, 73, 104, 112, 133, 152, 199, 273, 290–291
revolution   x, 4, 6, 8, 10–11, 14, 32, 36, 59, 62, 64, 70, 76, 137, 171, 224, 229, 237, 248, 267, 285–287, 289, 291, 296, 298
revolutionary   2, 6, 13, 39, 41, 127, 180, 229, 266, 273
rhetoric   27, 47, 76, 78, 80, 149, 161, 176–177, 183, 205, 270
Rhode Island   60, 113, 137, 296
riots   2, 41, 199, 286
Rockefeller   136, 162, 179
Ruggie, John   15, 253, 257, 299
rural   4–5, 10, 12, 43, 59, 70, 77, 80, 94–95, 113, 120–121, 124, 128, 137, 157, 161, 163, 167, 171, 209, 213, 219, 234, 249, 268, 273, 278, 282, 286–285, 292, 294–295, 297–298, 300–302

Saloutos, Theodore   34, 87, 89, 91, 105, 107–108, 132, 177, 179–182, 184–185, 187, 206–207, 299
Sanders, Elizabeth   36, 59, 76, 109, 116, 130, 299
scarcity   89, 110, 283

INDEX 309

Schlesinger, Arthur   170–171, 177, 181, 184–185, 206, 299
science   ii, 142–143, 145, 147, 149, 151, 155, 159, 161, 164, 197, 273, 285, 296, 300
scientific   13, 26, 54, 56, 142–143, 148–149, 154–155, 159–160, 165, 191, 194, 250
seasonal   10, 171, 279
Secretary of Agriculture   135, 161, 167, 171, 175–177, 205, 208, 218, 226, 242, 281
Secretary of State   235, 238
sectional   48, 54–55, 78, 80, 102, 113, 116, 118–119, 125, 188, 193, 291
sectionalism   80, 119, 284
sector   6, 13, 31, 49, 70–71, 101, 137, 145, 189, 219, 221–222, 224, 226, 244, 246, 250, 255
seeds   i, iii, viii, 52, 54–56, 72, 83, 98, 107–108, 129, 142, 145–147, 150, 215, 217, 219, 232, 233, 235, 237, 239, 241, 243, 245, 247, 249, 251, 253, 255, 257, 259, 261, 263, 265
segregated   103
segregation   102
selfsufficiency   13, 91, 95, 97 see also independent commodity production, yeoman
Senate   39, 112, 114–115, 118, 133, 165, 171, 228, 234, 239, 264, 282
Senator   39, 79, 114, 135, 159, 165, 183, 225, 228
settlement   8, 34, 51, 59, 80, 200, 295–296
settler   3, 5, 10, 13–14, 33, 35–36, 39, 45–47, 266
Shannon, Fred   14, 51–53, 83–84, 87–90, 94–97, 99–100, 107–108, 110, 120–121, 128–129, 148, 151, 299
sharecroppers   84, 86, 91, 97, 113, 174, 182, 185–187, 192, 196, 209, 275
sharecropping   83–87, 89, 91–95, 99–100, 103, 112, 116–117, 184, 186, 287, 298
Shays' Rebellion   25, 33, 39–42, 44, 59
shipment   65, 69, 147, 153, 171
shipping   49, 63–68, 153
Skocpol, Theda   28, 185, 187–193, 289, 296, 298–300
Skowronek, Stephen   14, 114–115, 162–163, 191, 213, 300
slave   29, 53, 73–76, 79, 86–89, 94, 96, 98, 102, 142, 283, 290, 302
slavery   vii, 14, 19, 29, 74–76, 78–81, 81, 83–89, 91, 93, 95, 97, 99, 101, 103, 105, 137, 283–284, 286–287, 289–290

slaves   75–77, 79–80, 83–84, 87–90, 94, 96, 100
Smith-Lever Act   135, 165–167, 179, 278
Socialist   130, 162, 249, 289–290, 294, 296
South Carolina   89–90, 95
South Dakota   45, 95
Southern Tenant Farmers Union (STFU)   xi, 184–185, 196, 200, 212–213
soybeans   153, 196, 208–209, 248
species   38, 52, 101, 116, 142
speculation   vii, 5, 35–36, 38, 43, 45–47, 54, 107, 110–111, 164, 278, 288
speculative   5, 35, 37, 45–47, 66, 68, 74, 96, 269, 278
speculator   35–36, 38–39, 44–48, 66, 107, 284, 290
squatters   38, 45
squatting   14, 33, 38, 45
Stephenson, George   47–48, 77–78, 300
stimulus   49, 60, 211, 217, 224
storage   52, 66–67, 114, 124, 239, 278
strike   121–122, 177, 180, 184, 197, 199–200, 230, 275–276
strikebreakers   122
structural   75, 88, 126, 128, 178, 245, 250, 258, 265, 293, 300–301
subsidies   28, 174, 178, 180, 184–185, 201, 219, 253–254
subsidize   148, 157, 204, 229, 233–234, 241, 249, 251, 255, 264
subsidy   36, 52, 225
subsistence   4–5, 13, 17–18, 29, 40, 42, 61, 96, 220, 248, 267
Sub-Treasury Plan   123–124 see also Farmer's Alliance, Peoples Party, populists, Macune
sugar   52–53, 55, 79, 127, 142, 146–147, 198, 245
Summerhill, Thomas   40, 42–44, 300
survey   35–36, 38, 52, 64, 151, 167

tariff   xi, 52, 76, 83, 100–101, 109, 114, 127, 133, 146, 156, 158, 168–169, 204–207, 222, 230, 243, 278
tax   2, 5, 7, 34, 39, 41, 43, 47, 49, 70, 90, 101, 117–118, 120, 125, 156, 158, 178, 182, 230
taxes   5, 9, 39, 42–43, 45, 47, 90, 109, 117–118, 157, 176, 270, 273
Taylor, Charles   48, 65, 69, 300

technologies   4, 26, 98, 137, 141–142, 150, 153, 155, 219, 229, 268–269
tenancy   vii, 29, 44, 83–84, 86–87, 89, 91, 95, 99, 103, 105, 112, 116–117, 121, 133, 174, 179, 184, 229, 284
tenant   xi, 2, 41, 43, 73, 84–85, 87, 95, 103, 132, 184–186, 209, 275–276
tenants   viii, 41, 43, 84, 87, 95, 97, 100, 103, 113, 132, 137, 182, 184–186, 192, 196
Tennessee   212, 288, 302
Territory   9, 33, 35, 109, 156, 201, 230, 299
Texas   90, 116, 119–120, 122, 156, 179, 199
Tilly, Charles   19, 81, 301
tobacco   52, 79, 85, 94–95, 97–98, 146, 150, 178, 181, 198, 208, 273
tractor   208, 210, 248, 295
transcontinental   50, 156
transport   48–49, 61, 66, 153
transportation   48–49, 57, 61–62, 66, 71, 107, 120, 150, 222, 268
Treadmill of production   82, 106, 210, 219
Treasury   65, 101, 123–124, 145, 147, 152, 156, 164, 183, 238, 241, 243, 250, 282

uneven development   vii, 29, 54, 72, 77, 83, 92, 95, 102–103, 105, 111, 137, 141, 200, 217
Union   xi, 33, 68, 106, 120, 122, 130, 135, 144, 184, 195, 199–200, 253–254, 274–276
United States Agency for International Development (USAID)   xi, 218, 222–223, 234, 248, 281
United States Department of Agriculture   viii, xi, 23, 26, 27, 30, 31, 46, 51, 53, 55, 58, 67, 69, 82, 94, 131, 134–135, 281, 282
   development of and early research   139–173
   New Deal role   174–214
   food aid program (PL 480)   215–270
upcountry   95–97, 107, 113, 291, 301
urban   43, 59, 70, 77, 90, 106, 151, 161, 171, 181, 224, 234, 287, 297
USDA-Research Complex   viii, 23, 30, 140, 142, 144, 150, 172, 215, 219–221, 227, 262, 270 *see also* Winders, USDA

Vermont   2, 41, 295
Vietnam   228, 234–236, 264
Virginia   55, 90, 97, 293
VT, *see* Vermont

Wallace, Henry   161, 171, 181, 185, 204–208, 218, 221, 236, 239, 282, 301
Washington   40, 159–160, 168, 199, 273, 275, 277, 280–284, 287, 290–291, 301
West   9, 38, 42, 45, 47, 49–50, 64, 70, 74, 76, 78, 82, 95, 107, 109–111, 116, 120, 122, 133, 147, 196, 198, 286–287
Western   9, 10, 14, 39, 41, 43, 47–48, 56, 59, 63, 74, 76, 80, 82, 96, 100, 107, 110–111, 118, 120, 124, 134, 158, 233, 280, 286, 290
westward   5, 11, 32–34, 46, 70, 74, 77, 107–109
Whiskey Rebellion   33, 41, 44, 59, 273
WI, *see* Wisconsin
Wilson, Woodrow   127, 133, 157, 178
Winders, Bill   26, 70, 134, 158, 164, 166, 169–170, 172, 178, 191, 194, 202, 208–209, 225–226, 302
Winters, Donald   91, 132, 302
Wisconsin   45, 58, 87, 114, 132, 284–285, 287, 292, 296, 300
Wobblies   275
Wolf, Eric   85, 302
Wood, Ellen Meiksins   16–18, 31, 33, 248, 302
Woodman, Harold   89, 91, 302
WTO   xi, 235, 250, 256, 297
WWII   137, 147, 218
Wyoming   199

Yearbook   151, 281, 301
yeoman   25, 32, 35, 43, 80, 96, 98–99, 101, 113, 132, 266, 291
yeomen   79, 90, 94, 96
Young, Roland   2, 40, 211, 286, 302
Zeichner, Oscar   89, 94, 302

www.ingramcontent.com/pod-product-compliance
Lightning Source LLC
Chambersburg PA
CBHW070909030426
42336CB00014BA/2342